SECOND EDITION

UNDERSTANDING POLICE CULTURE

JOHN P. CRANK
Florida Atlantic University

Routledge
Taylor & Francis Group

LONDON AND NEW YORK

Understanding Police Culture, Second Edition

First published 2004 by Anderson Publishing

Published 2016 by Routledge
2 Park Square, Milton Park, Abingdon, Oxon OX14 4RN

and by Routledge
711 Third Avenue, New York, NY 10017, USA

First issued in hardback 2015

Routledge is an imprint of the Taylor & Francis Group, an informa business

Copyright © 1998, 2004 Taylor & Francis.

All rights reserved. No part of this book may be reprinted or reproduced or utilised in any form or by any electronic, mechanical, or other
means, now known or hereafter invented, including photocopying
and recording, or in any information storage or retrieval system,
without permission in writing from the publishers.

Notices
Practitioners and researchers must always rely on their own experience and
knowledge in evaluating and using any information, methods, compounds, or
experiments described herein. In using such information or methods they should
be mindful of their own safety and the safety of others, including parties for whom
they have a professional responsibility.

Product or corporate names may be trademarks or registered trademarks, and are
used only for identification and explanation without intent to infringe.

Crank, John P.
    Understanding police culture / John P. Crank. -- 2nd ed.
        p. cm.
        Includes index.

ISBN-13: 978-1-58360-545-5 (pbk)
ISBN-13: 978-1-13816-959-3 (hbk)

Cover design by Tin Box Studio, Inc.

EDITOR Janice Gail Eccleston
ACQUISITIONS EDITOR Michael C. Braswell

Preface

This book stems from my long-term interest in the behavior of the police and my curiosity about people, what makes us what we are, and what it means to be human. Understanding the behavior of the police, I believe, requires an approach that locates them as participants in a creative cultural process, a process that is alternately celebratory and tragic, self-fulfilling in its values, densely moral, and profoundly meaningful. Yet, if it is their culture that uniquely marks them, and I think it is, it is also their culture that makes them so like the rest of us. Culture marks humans: we seem compelled to commit our energies to the creation and sustenance of culture. The capacity of the police to reproduce culture is a mark of their humanity, their similarity to us, not their difference. Critics of police culture, who hold that the so-called "police subculture" is the primary impediment to change and reform and must be expunged, are unwittingly advocating that we strip cops of their humanity.

I have been troubled by the tendency of existing literature to oversimplify the police. Police are typically described in either unquestioningly supportive platitudes, or in sharply negative critiques. The penchant to judge cops in simplistic terms of good and evil obscures our ability to understand cops as actors on a human stage, complex individuals who struggle daily to determine where good and evil lie. In this book, I have looked for meaning not only from what I have read and observed about the police, but from my personal reflections and understandings about what it means to be human. The book, though aimed at developing middle-range theory, is written in the spirit of discovery and self-reflection.

If there is a predisposing bias in my writing (and of course there are many), it is my two years of solicited experience as a grunt in the U.S. army, an experience that has left me with a profound understanding of rank structure, sympathy for the sad sack on the bottom of the chain-of-command, and a flat-out distrust of superior officers. This experience also left me with a visceral appreciation for the unpredictability of life, a perception that I think helps me comprehend a great deal of what the police are about. Ten years of post-military experience as a hard-drinking construction worker, living frequently on the edge of the law and often outside respectability, left me with an instinctive edginess in the presence of the police that I still carry today into my criminal justice classrooms. If this seems to set me too far apart from the police to write about them, consider the following observation:

> People don't like cops. People don't like us. I get a reaction when I see a cop—and I'm a cop. I'll be driving down the street in a police car. I look up, and there's a squad car in my rear view mirror. I think, what does this asshole want? What's he doing following me? (Fletcher, 1990:1)

Today, as a veteran of university affairs, I have developed particular skills appropriate for survival in the dog-eat-dog world of academic politics. I understand bureaucracy, and am good at it, though I care for it no more than when I was decades younger. I have also learned how bureaucracies—of necessity—focus on issues irrelevant to the work of the employees for whom they exist. If 20 years ago my distrust of bureaucracy was instinctual and unfocused, today it is reasonable and lucid. Readers of this book will find meager the charitable offerings toward police bureaucracies, not because I hold animosity to the police, but because I know bureaucracy too well.

The second edition varies from the first primarily in Part I. I have watched research and writing continue to spread on police culture, and much of it is quite interesting. Yet little of it begins with a notion of culture that drives a conception of culture among the police. This edition accordingly primarily differs from the first by putting forth a notion of police culture grounded in a notion of culture generally. It is hoped that this integrative step will spur others to think about the interdisciplinary potential available on the theory and methods of cultural analysis from the fields of anthropology, sociology, and political science. In view of what appear to be increasing militaristic tendencies among the police, I have also added a new theme, called militarism.

I have received a great deal of assistance and support from many people. Dr. Betsy McNulty read an early draft, and gave the manuscript a powerful kick in the you-know-what, forcing me to re-think the concept of the book itself. The book is much improved for the sharp critique. Her loss is a painful reminder of the brevity of life. Dr. Victor Kappeler provided a detailed review for which the book has benefitted greatly. And I have always been able to faithfully count on Dr. Robert Langworthy to critique my work and *get to the point*, a skill too often lacking in the nervous lairs of academe. To the many fine scholars I cite in the book (and I hope they don't hide their faces for it) thank you for letting me peer through your vision.

Special thanks are given to two. To Patti, mi corazón amante y compañera, from whom I've learned that still waters run deep. To my mother, who died while this manuscript was being written, thank you for the gift.

John P. Crank

Table of Contents

Preface   iii

Introduction   1

Part I
Understanding Police Culture   9

Prologue   11

Chapter 1
Culture and Knowledge   13

Chapter 2
Issues in the Study of Police Culture   29

Chapter 3
Culture and Cultural Themes   53

Chapter 4
Articulating Police Culture and Its Environments:
Patterns of Line-Officer Interactions   63

Part II
Themes of Police Culture

Section I: Coercive Territorial Control   77

Chapter 5
The Moral Transformation of Territory   81
Theme: Dominion

Chapter 6
Force Is Righteous   97
Theme: Force

Chapter 7
Crime Is War, Metaphor   113
Theme: Militarization

Chapter 8
Stopping Power   127
Theme: Guns

Section II: Themes of the Unknown   *141*

Chapter 9
The Twilight World   143
Theme: Suspicion

Chapter 10
Danger Through the Lens of Culture   155
Theme: Danger and Its Anticipation

Chapter 11
Anything Can Happen on the Street   163
Theme: Unpredictability and Situational Uncertainty

Chapter 12
No Animal Out There Is Going to Beat Me   173
Theme: Turbulence and Edge Control

Chapter 13
Seductions of the Edge   185
Theme: Seduction

Section III: Cultural Themes of Solidarity   *197*

Chapter 14
Angels and Assholes: The Construction of Police Morality   201
Theme: Police Morality

Chapter 15
Common Sense and the Ironic Deconstruction of the Obvious   213
Theme: Common Sense

Chapter 16
No Place for Sissies   229
Theme: Masculinity

Chapter 17
Mask of a Thousand Faces   237
Theme: Solidarity

Chapter 18
America's Great Guilty Crime Secret   **255**
Theme: Racism

Section IV: Loosely Coupling Cultural Themes   *269*

Chapter 19
On Becoming Invisible   273
Theme: Outsiders

Chapter 20
Individualism and the Paradox of Personal Accountability   279
Theme: Individualism

Chapter 21
The Truth Game   289
Theme: Deception

Chapter 22
Cop Deterrence and the Soft Legal System   305
Theme: Deterrence

Chapter 23
The Petty Injustice and Everlasting Grudges   311
Theme: Bullshit

Section V: Death and Police Culture   *329*

Chapter 24
Thinking About Ritual   331

Chapter 25
The Culture Eater   339
Theme: Death

Chapter 26
Good-bye in a Sea of Blue   353
Theme: Police Funerals

Postscript   **365**

References   **367**

Index   **385**

Introduction

The past 30 years have witnessed an explosion of interest into the habits and customs of American municipal police. There have been a number of thoughtful investigations into police culture, and the quality of this work has been consistently creative. Connoisseurs of police culture are versed in concepts like Skolnick's symbolic assailant, Manning's impossible mandate, Niederhoffer's cynicism, Wilson's craftsmen, Reuss-Ianni's two cultures of policing, and Van Maanen's kinsman and "asshole." Yet this work has remained largely unintegrated. The field of police studies is generally bereft of efforts to creatively organize cultural works into more general syntheses of the police.

The current lack of integration of police culture research is not an altogether troubling circumstance. Scholars, students, and interested readers must read original works, and are consequently exposed to the full force and potency of authentic thought. Summaries tend to provide easy overviews of literature, sterilized of troubling inconsistencies and complex ideas that mark real-world processes. In this book, I try to retain the intellectual vigor of original writers by casting their ideas—as much as possible—in their original intent, with full conceptual baggage appended, for all the mess and confusion the baggage sometimes entails.

What I seek to accomplish in this book is to bring together and to creatively organize the thoughts of others that have written on police culture. Observers of the police, I believe, have been looking at a phenomenon that is culturally similar across police departments, despite the geographical diversity of police agencies. The current work is motivated by the notion that culture tends to reproduce itself in similar ways in different organizations, and hence that writings on police culture can be systematically organized.

1

The present effort is a work of creative integration, not of mind-numbing summarization. As such, I bring my own ideas to bear on existing research. Police work, like writing, is a craft, and excellence at either is not science but artistry. I seek moods and perspectives, slants and twists, different ways of thinking about what has already been thought about. I link themes and associate ideas in order to provide a roughly systematic way of thinking about culture that celebrates research that has gone before. It is a Mertonian effort to build middle-range theory, creatively organizing and presenting in a cohesive way existing literature on the topic of police culture.

Police Work Through the Lens of Culture

In this book I try to lay out the celebratory and exciting aspects of police work without becoming blindingly high-minded. At the same time, the darker aspects of police work are seen in context, like shadows that mix and blend, rather than the brooding darkness that infuses much academic fare. The product, I believe, is cultural.

Central to the ideas presented here is that the behavior of the police only makes sense when viewed through the lens of culture. But what is the lens of culture? My idea is one of metaphorical reduction—from the blinder, to the eye, to the mind. Let me explain.

Sometimes culture is presented as a set of blinders, such as worn by a horse so that it will not be distracted. The work of the police, according to this metaphor, presents them with a jaded image of life and contributes to a contempt for the public. If officers could be involved in other aspects of work, it is thought, police culture would lose its grip on officers. Culture, according to this notion, is a set of fixed prescriptions for behavior that permit no variance from culturally prescribed rules.

Culture-as-blinders is also the essence of reformer logic in the age of community policing. Consider walking patrol, a common tactic advocated by contemporary police reformers. By changing what officers see, for example, by having officers do walking patrol and mix with citizens that actually like them, it is hoped that officers will change their attitudes toward citizens. However, I believe that this idea of culture change is limited. Police do not have ideological or cognitive "blinders" that force them to look at the world from a particular point of view. This "horse and blinder" analogy does not capture the way in which powerful human emotions are harnessed to cultural values, to enable behaviors and ways of thinking as well as to constrain them. Put another way, as a cognitive process, culture is not simply limiting, but also creative and adaptive.

Nor is culture, to regress the analogy one step, the eyes that see. The eyes are a mechanical device that organize and frame our vision, and we manipulate them so that we can look at particular themes. Eyes don't think, they process information. Pursuing this analogy, we think that if police have better information or intelligence, or if they have more sophisticated record-keeping, they can do their work better. On the reformer side, it is thought that if police acquire more education, particularly about minority and ethnic groups, they will be more sensitive to the plight of urban minorities.

Culture-as-eyes, however, is too mechanical an image of police work. It fails to capture the values that mobilize police work. Cultures are more than information processors for some rational (or irrational) mind. Cultures are dense in values and beliefs, rituals, habits, full of historical prescriptions and common sense that guide action. Culture processes information, but in value-laden ways and in moral predispositions that are self-affirming.

The regression, I believe, must be complete. Culture is the mind that thinks, that takes in information from the world around it and acts on that information in predispositive, though not wholly predictable, ways. Culture is how we act out our moral and social identities—it carries the values we bring to bear on what we see, our behaviors, and is present in the categories through which we organize the world seen and imagined. It is in the implicit assumptions we make, and it is in the hidden edges and implicit meanings of the metaphors we use and take for granted. Culture is carried within us, not a thing set apart and reified from social action. Culture made plain is our common sense about things, what every fool sees (as Geertz so cogently observed), our traditions cast as knowledge, our metaphors taken as the thing in itself. It is a self-affirming blend of our traditions—the world past—and the world of today that we see around us and on which we act. We share our thoughts, therefore culture exists. We act out shared thoughts in self-fulfilling behaviors, and culture is confirmed.

Culture covers a lot of intellectual and emotional territory. Police organizational structures, policies, behaviors, arrest patterns, corruption, education, training practices, attitudes toward suspects and citizens, forms of patrol, and all other areas of police work—the whole ball of wax—are witnessed and practiced through the lens of culture. All areas of police work have meaning of some kind to cops, and as every reformer and chief who has sought to change any organization knows, these meanings tend to bind together in sentiments and values impossible to analytically separate and individually change.

Carried in the minds of street cops who work together, culture enables a wide variety of police activities to link together in ways that are, though not systematic, sensible enough to give meanings to different kinds of situations in which cops find themselves. Organizational traditions are customary ways of doing things, and they take on common-sense value that cannot be changed easily or frivolously. This is why many insiders say that efforts to change the police, whether the change concerns traditional ideas of patrol, getting officers to talk about corrupt fellow officers, even changing the type of weapons they carry, must first win the hearts and the minds of its officers. Until advocates of police change recognize the importance of culture, they will continue to be as surprised as they have been for the past 100 years at the profound limitations of reform efforts to yield real and enduring changes (Crank, 1997).

General Plan of the Book

The book is organized into two parts. Part I reviews theory of police culture and describes the conceptual underpinnings of the book. Part I has been extensively rewritten and expanded for this book so that I can address a central concern in the widening body of literature on police culture. Concepts of police culture are rarely informed by a concept of culture. Writings on police culture tend to take the notion of culture as a given, whose meaning is already known, and all that remains is to identify the unique dimensions of police culture. Because of this, the concept of culture in police studies is poorly developed and has become little more than a gloss for reformist critiques of police practices.

Part I has three interrelated purposes. Chapter 1 lays out a definition of culture that is consistent with literature on culture generally. It emphasizes central issues in culture analysis, such as the role of conflict, agency versus structure, the diverse elements that constitute culture, and the issue of standpoint, which is the relationship between the observer and the observed. Chapter 2 reviews different perspectives on police culture. Three frames are assessed: institutional perspectives, interactionist perspectives that locate culture more or less coterminously with local agencies, and a group of contemporary views of police culture that consider the presence of multiple cultures within individual organizations. Recent works carried out by Chan (1996; 1997; 2001), Paoline (2001) and Paoline, Myers, and Worden (2000) have invigorated important debates about culture and the police. Both argue for the presence of multiple cultures and the works of both are considered. Chapter 3 develops the perspective used in this paper—culture is assessed in terms of themes, identifiable in the context of daily police work, which are areas of cultural activity that unite elements of predisposition, action, and social structure.

What, then, is daily police work? Police culture is made possible because police officers interact with other groups in routine, observable, identifiable ways. These groups, citizens and street people, the courts, police administration, and the media are principal drivers of police culture. The work of the police is embedded in these groups—what I have called elsewhere their "institutional environment" (Crank & Langworthy, 1992) and police culture is in large part a reciprocal understanding of police reactions to and influences on these groups. Whether they are criminals, the administration, or citizens, these groups interact with line-officers in concrete encounters, providing the cultural foundations for the social identity of the police. Part I concludes with a discussion of the various groups with which police officers routinely interact, and how they contribute to the formation and sustenance of culture.

Part II of the book presents the themes that characterize police culture. It is divided into five sections. The first section is called coercive territorial control. Simply put, this is the idea that the police view much of their work in terms of the use of coercion to control, individually or en masse, a particular assigned territory, metaphorically described as the "beat" or more romantically, "the street." Coercion, one of the themes, is not only the simple use of physical violence, but the employment of threats, lies, cajolery, and arrest to control or to direct the behavior of individuals with whom they come into contact during their work. Coercive territorial control is not a single theme, but a concatenation of inter-related themes emerging in the everyday process of police work. Together, these themes provide insight into elements of police culture thought to be foundational by many observers of the police.

As a form of police knowledge, coercive territorial control is a con-geries of stories, common-sense anecdotes, metaphors, and training strategies that provide police with a practical store of common-sense knowledge for problem-solving on the beat. It forms elements central to what Swidler (1986) called a cultural tool kit: a set of skills that officers use to control their territories. Ways of using command voice in routine encounters, abrading a citizen's personal space, a sense of authority and righteousness regarding one's beat, all are aspects of the tool kit that officers carry into their daily work routines.

The second section focuses on themes of the unknown. I use the word "unknown" as a noun, even though it is more correctly used an adjective. For cops, the unknown is a palpable, real presence: Police activity routinely puts officers in circumstances that are unpredictable and that are sometimes beyond their control. The unknown is at the center of much police work: routine activity involves dealing with crimes, maintaining the public order, coordinating the flow of traffic, and other encounters where citizen interests often lie in withholding or not admitting information. Events unfold in unpredictable ways: trivial encounters may take on humorous overtones, or unexpectedly escalate into uncontrollable danger. A paradox is thus at the center of police culture: ideas of common sense emerge around what's not known rather than what is known.

Officers develop a wide variety of strategies, gambits, and common lore for dealing with the unknown. The unknown becomes the basis for shared knowledge, a way of thinking integral to police culture. Four themes—(1) suspicion, (2) danger and its anticipation, (3) unpredictability and situational uncertainty, and (4) interaction turbulence and edge control, each reveal different facets of the way the unpredictable elements of their work shape cop culture.

The third section of the book looks at solidarity themes. These themes separate the police from other groups and provide them with a sense of occupational uniqueness. The central characteristic of these themes is the emotional bonding and intense loyalty associated with solidarity. The sense of morality officers carry into police-citizen encounters, their unusual sense of common sense, a practical, work-driven sense of hostility toward particular ethnic groups, the excitement of their work, and their solitary individualism—reinforced by the shift in the modern era to one-person patrol cars—all are themes that invigorate a strong sense of solidarity among officers.

In this section I draw from the work of Coser (1956) to describe the way in which relations with other groups reinforce solidarity within cop culture. In his writings on the functions of social conflict, Coser argued that solidarity emerges from external-group conflict. Extending this idea to the police, I contend that a great deal of police solidarity emerges from the conflicts with other groups with whom they regularly interact. Every threat to the cop culture or to officers individually serves to strengthen culture and bind officers closer together. Contemporary and past reform efforts are received as threats to officers' authority to do their work, reinforcing rather than diminishing the influence of police culture over line officers.

The fourth section focuses on loosely coupling themes. Loose coupling is a term taken from institutional theory (Meyer & Rowan, 1977) to describe organizations whose goals and objectives are not closely linked to the daily activity of organizational members. Loose coupling permits managers to deal with influential people and groups, while lower-level personnel focus on the crime control business of the organization. Police administrators, for example, may put into place what are, in principle, harsh internal review mechanisms to placate community groups fearful of police abuse of authority. Street officers, in response, develop informal ways to nullify the effects of internal review when abuse takes place during routine police encounters (Christopher, 1991). Loose coupling thus allows police to do their work unhampered by external inspection.

Put another way, loose coupling themes serve to de-couple line activity from organizational goals and policies when they are perceived by officers to obstruct or undermine the ability of the police to do their work.[1] Like the solidarity themes stemming from out-group conflict, loose coupling themes are characterized by their strength in the face of resistance—the more the organizational administration seeks to control line behavior, or the greater the effort of a community to impose outside control over the behavior of individual officers, the more important these themes become to organizational members. Thus, themes in both the solidarity and loose coupling sections of this book strengthen and protect culture in times of adversity—indeed, adversity is the stimulus that gives rise and sustenance to these themes. It is through these cultural devices that reform efforts engender police cultural backlashes that ultimately deflect or nullify sought changes.

The final section focuses on death in the police culture. Of all aspects of police culture, none has such a profound impact, nor is as little understood, as the death of a police officer. This section provides an exploration of this emotionally moving topic.

I approach death and funerals not simply as cultural themes, though they are both heavily imbued with the most powerful themes of police culture, but in terms of powerful police rituals. The anthropological literature, particularly Clifford Geertz (1973, 1983) and Victor Turner (1969, 1974) has much to offer on thoughts about ritual activity. This body of literature allows us to reclaim a feature that has been lost in most writings on police culture—the way in which culture channels the emotions of its members, and what it means when an officer is killed.

Chapter 25, titled "The Culture Eater," looks at the impact of death on police culture. Death repudiates many of the myths that sustain culture. Important tenets of police culture—that officers are safe when their training is finished and their focus is true, that they can develop knowledge about the unknown, control the unpredictable, rule the dangerous country of human relations, that their common sense will protect them—are utterly defeated when an officer is killed. The final chapter looks at how funerals, steeped in symbolic imagery and departmental tradition, pull together a department after an officer has been killed. Building on its own symbols and drawing from other institutions, funerals reawaken the significance of what it means to be a cop.

One theme is not separately discussed in the book. When I have my academic pointy-hat on, I call it a meta-theme. This theme is that the police have become what we the people want them to be. They enact our desire to be protected against life's unfairness. Their actions profoundly reflect our expectations. Their morality mirrors our own, as Black (1973) wisely noted, and their behavior, alternatively professional and brutish, flows from our solicitations.

This meta-theme is a drumbeat, a constant presence in all of the diverse themes laid out in this book. In some of the themes, the drumbeat is as loud as a thunderclap. In others you will have to listen very carefully to hear it. Yet it is always present. You should listen very closely.

John P. Crank

Understanding Police Culture

Part I

Prologue

"Its a Cop Thing.
You Wouldn't Understand."

The quote above, displayed in large black letters, was on the front of a T-shirt worn by a heavily muscled off-duty police officer. I watched him as he casually walked to the back of the convenience store, a smile on his face. It was late June in Las Vegas, and the summer winds were already hot. Reaching into a cooler, he grabbed a quart of Gatorade.

A thick coat of sweat covered my brow. My thoughts rumbled over the implied question—What is a cop thing?

John P. Crank

1

Culture and Knowledge

Culture is an extraordinarily broad topic. At its heart, the study of culture is the study of what it means to be human. Culture enables a great many of those things that mark us as quintessentially human. Our capacity for moral and ethical development, the way we describe and act out fundamental institutions of marriage, church, government, and economy, the labeling of others as friend or foe, our ability to act in ways that display justice and fair play, our identity as citizens, all of these are expressions of culture.

This book is about police culture. It breaks from public presentations of police culture as a hostile influence in efforts to instill organizational reform. Consider a news story from CNN (2000) that reported the following response to a Board of Inquiry report on corruption in the Los Angeles Police Department:

> The culture of the Los Angeles Police Department is to blame for its corruption scandal, a study commissioned by the police officer's union found. . . . "The Board of Inquiry report fails to recognize that the central problem in the Los Angeles Police Department is the culture," said the report's author . . . "There will not be meaningful reform in the Los Angeles Police Department until the culture is changed."

The perception that a police "culture" is a source of hidden, unpleasant police characteristics is not only a media construction. It is also widely present in academic literature. Police culture has been described in terms such as a "culture of violence," "suspicion," machismo," racial prejudice," "distrust," and "siege mentality" (Shanahan, 2002). As Chan (1996) has noted, culture is an umbrella term for a range of negative values and practices among the police. Waddington (1999:293) noted the limitations of this view of culture:

> Its (the term "culture") 'convenience' lies in its condemnatory potential: the police are to blame for the injustices perpetuated in the name of the criminal justice system.

The purpose of much of this research, Waddington (1999) reminds us, was not to understand what police do or think, but to change them. It is about reform. Citing Reiner (1985:85), Waddington noted that the impulse for change "was a civil libertarian concern for the extent and sources of police deviation from due process of law." The literature on police culture, Waddington concluded, ends up telling us what is wrong with police culture from the perspective of the observer of the culture. It does not tell us anything about culture from the perspective of its participants. Consequently, and consequentially, we learn a great deal about the perspective of the observer, not the observed. The interaction of the observer and observed is a central and unsolvable dilemma in all research on culture, and particularly haunts narratives on police culture popular in both the popular and academic media.

Literature on police culture is rarely embedded in any sort of definition or notion of culture. Police culture emerges uniquely from the organizational setting, yet the broader notion of culture is unaddressed or taken for granted. What is needed is a definition of culture that provides a bridge to literature on culture generally, and from which descriptions of police culture make sense.

Central to ideas of culture is the recognition that culture is neither bad nor good, but rather is a central organizing principle of social life. Human culture brings out a central feature of our humanity—our capacity to find meaning in our lives. So it is for the police as well. It is culture that makes police like the rest of us, not different from us.

This chapter and Chapter 2 are framing chapters. I will review central issues on culture and on police culture, providing contexts or "frames" for thinking about these issues. Framing is not intended to provide answers, but aims at providing a basis for conversation on culture. I review current research both in and out of the fields of policing and criminal justice to develop ways of thinking about each of the issues framed in this chapter. The chapters are somewhat theoretical, and are intended to review the notion of culture generally and to think about current research on police culture.

I address the following frames. Chapter 1 asks, What is culture and what constitutes cultural knowledge? Chapter 2 asks, What should be the focus of cultural studies? Examined are institutional perspectives, interactionist standpoints that focus on emergent properties of local cultures, and theories that argue for multiple cultures within the organization. Chapter 3 presents thematic analysis as a way to sketch out the interplay of many elements of police culture. This book identifies 20 themes that, considered together, provide a sensibility to think about what it means to participate in the culture of the police.

The second purpose, and the substance of Part II, is the elaboration of themes of police culture. The central purpose of Part II of this book is to show how culture is a powerful and multifaceted dynamic that infuses police work with meaning. Through the presentation of the cultural themes in Part II, I hope to show how police work is meaningful to its participants. Some of the themes may appear to be negative, and others positive. However, negative and positive views of cultural themes are ethical judgments, and the reader is reminded that such judgments are reflective of their own cultural predispositions, not those of police officers. Cultural knowledge is acquired through recognition and understanding of differences, not through exclusionary ethics that label some cultural characteristics wrong and others right.

What Is Culture?

A working definition. In this section, I will lay out a working definition of culture. This will be followed by a discussion of many aspects of culture encompassed by this definition. This discussion is somewhat theoretical, and I hope the reader will bear with me while I present it. The aspects of culture discussed here provide the theoretical frame for police cultural themes developed in Part II of this book.

Below I present a working definition of culture, adapted from Hall and Neitz, (1993:4-5), and Sackmann (1993) with a "behavioral element" added and tool and social elements of culture distinguished:

> Culture is collective sense-making. Sense-making has ideational, behavioral, material, social structural, and emergent elements, as follows:
>
> > (1) ideas, knowledge (correct, wrong, or unverifiable belief) and recipes for doing things, (2) behaviors, signs, and rituals, (3) humanly fabricated tools including media, (4) social and organizational structures, and (5) the products of social action, including conflicts, that may emerge in concrete interpersonal and inter- social encounters and that may be drawn upon in the further construction of the first four elements of collective sense-making.

This definition is useful for several reasons.

1. It recognizes that ways of thinking about issues are an element of police cultural study. This is the *ideational component* of culture, that is, the part of culture related to thinking about problems and organizing information to create coherence in occupational life. This element is described by Manning (1989:360) in terms of the organization's history, its traditions, and "what is taken for granted by its members, things that are invisible but powerful constraints . . ."

   This element of culture also includes ethical prescriptions. For example, the practice of public order maintenance is fundamentally different from law enforcement—it requires a normative judgment by officers as to what constitutes local order (Wilson, 1968). This judgment is often linked to secondary judgments about the likelihood of conviction and attitude of the complainant (Black, 1980). In making such judgments, officers are tied to local community dynamics and shared notions of public order. In this example, a powerful ideational component—notions of public order—tie officers to communities and provide a basis for enforcement/non-enforcement decisions.

2. It recognizes that culture has a *behavioral component*. This part of culture is recognized in Manning's (1989:360) definition of culture as "accepted practices, rules, and principles of conduct that are situationally applied." Van Maanen (1973), for example, discussed the practices associated with pre-service training. A boot-camp training environment, with emphases on group punishments for minor infractions and stress training contributed to a perception by recruits that they could only trust each other, not superior officers. A training practice, in this example, resulted in a distrust of superior officers that infused professional work long after training was completed.

   Behaviors are not causal or consequential to ideas, but exist in a reciprocal and occasionally independent relationship to them. A person acts in a certain way because it is a culturally appropriate way to act, and a person thinks about that action in particular ways because that way of thinking is also appropriate. Culture is in this sense a conglomeration of thought and behavior. A handshake is a behavior, and it carries with it a certain way of thinking; that we express introduction and friendliness through a handshake.

   Manning noted that "culture links seeing, doing, and believing." These elements are not necessarily linked harmoniously. Behavioral components should be recognized and analytically distinguished, because each might have fundamentally different implications for the study of police culture. Waddington (1999), for example, suggested that police attitudes about their work are frequently at odds with their actual behaviors. Attitudes, carried by what he called "canteen culture"—how police talk about their work—are often expressed as overtly racist sentiments, and research into police attitudes concluded that police were racist. On the other hand, studies of police occupational behavior rarely revealed racism.

Waddington concluded that canteen culture exists, in part, to justify police beliefs about the world in the face of social and legal constraints over their actual behavior. A further implication of Waddington's research is that research conducted only on attitudes (attitudinal surveys) or of occupational behaviors (ride-alongs with police officers that assess police-citizen encounters) would be limited and carried enormous potential to be misleading.

3. It recognizes that culture has a *material component*, in which culture is expressed as tool-making and information-processing structures. According to this element of culture, sense-making emerges in response to "brute facts" about the world. In turn, the tools may take on a social vitality of their own, independent of their practical tool-making properties. Guns are an example of this element of culture. Guns have a "brute fact" practicality—they may enable a person to protect him or herself against another dangerous human or to put food on the table. However, they have accumulated cultural value and are dense with cultural meaning. In many quarters in American political life guns are infused with values of patriotism and protection against a threatening central government.

    Print media also has this quality. The print media and the machinery that enable it are daily fare for many people for gaining information about the world around them. As many have observed, the print media has a profound effect on the social dynamics it talks about. The phrase "the medium is the message" popularized by Marshall McLuhan in the 1970s is another way of saying that material and social culture are highly interpenetrated. In the same way, cops shows, though highly edited and polished versions of observed police activity, provide public notions of what police work is like. The public is exposed to the "huff and puff of the chase" even though observers of the police have repeatedly commented that most police work has little to do with such activity and is generally routine.

4. It recognizes that culture has a *social structural* component. This means that it is expressed in physical and organizational "things" (see Fine & Kleinman, 1979:7). It encompasses the physical structure of a police department, the physical geography of beat boundaries, and organizational features of the police such as operational strategies and goals, training practices, and patterns of occupational differentiation. As Hall and Neitz (1993:11) observed, "structure" does not always exist independently of 'culture.' Indeed, insofar as culture delimits a patterned basis for a group's structure, we may speak of those patterns as 'cultural structures'." Police occupational practices like random preventive patrol are examples of such cultural structures, as are police uniforms. This element is in recogni-

tion of Chan's (1997) critique of existing theories of police culture to recognize the importance of the social structural setting in which the police carry out their work.

5. It recognizes that there is an *emergent component* of culture. Four aspects of the emergent component are important here.

    First, products of social action—that is, the behavior that flows from the decisions we make about things—can give rise to new ideational and physical components of culture. The arrest practices of a department are a product of social action, that can have a substantial impact on the lives of those arrested. Released felons in turn may seek revenge on police officers, broadening the way officers perceive, train for, and tell stories about "officer safety." This element is consistent with Chan's (1997) admonition that police are not passive recipients of culture but are actively involved in its creation.

    Second, "emergence" recognizes that culture construction is a creative activity. Culture is highly duplicative—there are many kinds of blue jeans, for example—and people are constantly selecting among existing cultural elements, recombining them in stylistic ways (Willis, 1993). This view is consistent with a symbolic interactionist view of culture which emphasizes "the importance of face-to-face interaction in the generation and activation of cultural elements" (Fine & Kleinman, 1979:8). Muir's (1978) discussion of officers' styles, for example, revealed artistic adaptation to common police dilemmas associated with the use of force.

    Third, emergence is also a product of new relations among social groups. Civil service, a late 1880s federal program, was incorporated into police organizations at the beginning of the twentieth century. It has had a pervasive influence on police personnel systems, locking in local personnel and sharply limiting the ability of managers to develop innovative practices by hiring creative or knowledgeable people into the middle or senior ranks (Guyot, 1986). In the 1970s the increasing interpenetration of academics, police, and federal grants organizations led to a revolution in police research, and has fundamentally changed the way police do their business (Crank & Langworthy, 1993).

    Fourth, the emergence of cultural elements may be a product of conflict with other groups. Participation in the life of a particular group—the finding of one's identity and meaning—is often tied to the separation or rejection of identity with other groups. Douglas (1986:1) reminds us that "Writing about cooperation and solidarity means writing at the same time about rejection and mistrust." Widely recognized in political science is the formation of ethnic identity as a consequence of cultural contacts (see, e.g., Eller, 1999). The idea that conflict is central to the formation of cultural identity is in sharp contrast to traditional notions of cultural isolation and solidarity. This definition rejects the notion that culture emerges in stable social circumstances. The historical existence of a truly isolated and solidary community, a doubtful precept, simply is irrelevant to today's highly interactive and mobile world. This element recognizes that culture is an ongoing, contemporary, emergent process and that conflict is one if its integral elements.

Culture and the Nature of Knowledge

Culture is an idea of extraordinary breadth. In its origins, culture was conceived broadly, that there are bounded, isolated, and stable social entities called cultures, and these cultures provide the measure of a whole way of life of a people. Redfield (1939), for example, described culture as people who shared common understandings and who produce and consume their own goods. Kluckhohn (in Geertz, 1973:4-5) provided 11 definitions for culture, including "the total way of life of a people," "a way of thinking, feeling, and believing," and "a set of techniques for adjusting both to the external environment and to other men." Culture occupied such a large intellectual space in the early days of anthropology that it has been described as the "root metaphor" of the field (Geertz, 1973).

The study of culture emerged in ethnographies of "primitive"or non-Western societies (Hall & Neitz, 1993). Early conceptions of culture, carried out by ethnographic observers of indigenous peoples in far-away places such as Africa, developed a conception of culture as a bounded way of ethnic or tribal life. Cultural theory in turn contrasted such "folk" or "traditional" cultures with modern or Western societies (Levi-Strauss, 1966).

Many of the founding ideas of culture have been reconsidered. The notion that human cultures should be thought of as isolated and autonomous social entities has been largely abandoned in the current age. Appadurai (1988) suggested that the idea of culture may have been a product of the way colonialists encountered African villages. Culture emerged as synonymous for the local villages they encountered—villages were taken for cultures—and the notion that local villagers were uniquely characterized by tradition or local autonomy only extended to their lack of previous contact with Europeans.

Wolfe (1982) noted that many non-European cultures studied by anthropologists were not isolated, but were involved in complex interrelations with other (non-European) groups. Cultural identity, he suggested, might emerge from the efforts of groups to construct identity that set them apart from other groups with whom they interacted. Identity, in a word, emerged around differences, not similarities. Similar process of ethnic identity formation have been noted by Eller (1999) in his research on international ethnic conflict, suggesting that the formation of cultural identity in response to contact with other groups is a contemporary process quite active in the world today.

Early observers of culture were concerned with "going native," becoming so involved in local cultures that the observer or ethnographer began to take on the trappings of local identity and lost their independent viewpoint. However, the independence of the "Western" viewpoint has itself been sharply challenged in recent years. These challenges have two elements. On the one hand, many observers contend that there are particular aspects of the Western worldview that carry predisposing biases— for example, that British patterns of colonialization in Africa placed boundaries over autonomous and local groupings of people. On the other hand is the notion that there is no such thing as an independent viewpoint. The notion that somehow we can stand outside culture and study it from a noncultural standpoint is today considered by many to be a particular kind of viewpoint associated with "enlightenment" ideas of objective social science.

Cultural Observation: A Thought Experiment

I am going to carry out a thought experiment to illuminate three issues central to cultural studies: cultural autonomy, observer objectivity, and the location of culture. Imagine that a young ethnographer is walking through a deep forest in some unknown country and suddenly she comes upon a village. She finds that people are dressed in unusual ways, and some have odd make-up on their faces. Sometimes they dance. They talk. They behave in ways that seem to be communicatory, but she has no idea what is being communicated. They act as if they have never seen a person like her before. Her interest is piqued. She wants to know about them, what they are saying and thinking, why they do and act as they do. Why, she could write a dissertation about this group! Our young ethnographer might think that, because they seem to find her pale skin strange, they are an isolated or autonomous group. Relatedly, she might suspect that their identity as members of the village—their "cultural" identity, is what is called local or traditional, produced by their lack of contact with civilization. She moves in and lives with the villagers for one year. Over time, she records their patterns of collective sense-making. She witnesses interactions with other groups. She observes their use of material culture, their social hierarchies, the significance of some of their facial markings and their rituals. She develops rudimentary language skills. At the end of the year she writes a narrative of the encounter.

Cultural autonomy. First consider the issue of cultural autonomy. This is the idea that a group is a stable and independent social entity, as she learned about them, she noted inter-village behavior. It might have involved trade, religion, warfare, family contacts, or even slavery. The inter-village behavior might be seen as shaped by the different cultures of the villages. That is, the intergroup behavior is, to a degree, an outcome of the cultures of the different groups. However, today, ethnographers are considering how intergroup behavior can serve as a *cause* of cultural identity. Villager identity might not have emerged because of their separation from "civilization," but have resulted from being embedded in civilization.

Importantly, it might be that some aspects of culture, what Eller (1999) called "ethnic identity," helped them protect their group identity. Seen this way, local or so-called "traditional" culture may not be a precursor of modern mass society—it may be a consequence of it. This is important for the consideration of culture in the United States today. Perhaps we should think about group cultures, not in terms of their emergence from some traditional ethnic "cultures," but in terms of their interactions and conflicts with other groups in mass society. Local culture, in this sense, is produced by modern society.

By the same notion, we can see that her interest is forged in the crucible of difference. She is interested in precisely those things about them that violate her sense of cultural propriety. It might be structures, such as the way they construct their dwellings, or it might be their manner of face painting. Her professional identity is framed in terms of her difference from them. Indeed, her villagers may be wearing face paint and acting in an odd way precisely because she is there. It might be their way of dressing up to respectfully greet an uninvited guest.

Objectivity and observer dependency. This leads to the second issue, framed by a question: Can an observer be objective? Our anthropologist concluded her year by writing a narrative that described the villagers, their patterns of interaction, family life, structures, customs, symbols, rituals, and other notions associated with their cultural identity. Her narrative—and a central concern in all efforts to witness and describe culture generally—is that it occurred within her way of ordering the universe. This is quite important, because a reader can never be sure whether she is reading the actual account of a group as it understands itself, or an account of the ethnographer interacting with the group. That is, the content of the narrative is "observer dependent."

To explore the notion of observer dependence, we need to begin with another idea—institutional facts. *Institutional facts* are statements about human relationships: As Searle (1998) noted, "Humans . . . talk together, own property, get married, form governments, and so on." Institutional facts are always observer dependent. This means that, without someone to consider them, they would simply cease to exist. They are not like rocks, that would go on and on until their molecular structure decays at the end of time no matter who watched them. If humans ceased to exist tomorrow, institutional facts such as property, marriage, or justice would also vanish.

Institutional facts, Searle (1998) noted, can be recognized because they are always in a functional form, such that "this behavior (two people in a church in front of minister) functions for that purpose (marriage), or this colored material (flag) functions as (country)." Stated differently, the functions assigned to behaviors create institutional facts. These functions can be variously called meanings, values, or messages, and they are how we assign social identity to institutional facts.

An example will help clarify the idea of institutional facts. In policing, we might say that this behavior (driving around in marked police vehicles) serves the function (random preventive patrol). Hence, we have an institutional fact called random preventive patrol. In turn, we can say that this institutional fact (random preventive patrol) serves the function (deterrence). Hence, the behavior of driving around police vehicles described above has an extended meaning. First, it means *random preventive patrol*, and second, it means *deterring potential criminals*. In this way, institutional facts can be used to create another institutional fact. This is the "iterative function" of institutional facts, and enables humans to build quite complex normative and ethical systems from quite simple building blocks.

It is the observer-dependent element of institutional facts that makes them tricky to deal with for observers of human culture. The functions—that is, the meanings we assign to behaviors—are located wholly in the view of the observer. So when I see behavior occurring, the meanings I give the behavior are wholly dependent on my point of view, or my *standpoint* in the popular vernacular.

Searle reminds us that the most fundamental institutional fact is language.[1] Searle suggests that language *constitutes* the world of institutional facts. When we witness anything associated with an institutional fact, we are not simply using language to describe. We use language to create meanings for what they see. Language does not "represent" the outside world. In the area of institutional facts, it creates the outside world.

For example, I cannot think about a flag if I have no word for flag. It would have no meaning. And if I saw someone burning a flag, my attention would likely be drawn to the brute fact of fire. If the fire were close I would probably run from it. That it was a flag that was burning would have no meaning to me without a vocabulary to make it meaningful. However, once I have a vocabulary that contains the word "flag" I can assign a function to it such as "patriotic." Additionally, I can call flag-burning "unpatriotic" or an "exercise in free speech." In this example, language creates the possibility for my way of thinking about the flag. I have located it in the realm of institutional fact, it has meaning, and it can mobilize my sentiments. Language does not mediate between me and the institutional fact, it creates the institutional fact I observe. This means that, when our ethnographer is observing the culture in which she is interested, she is not simply "recording" activity. Her cultural predispositions are creating the meanings that she observes. The "culture" exists because she is witnessing it.

Let me explain this in another way that is sometimes uncomfortable for readers. When I view the flag-burning as an "exercise in free speech," I have assigned value or function to the flag-burning. And that value exists because I have a language that can provide it. Language precedes and constitutes value. That is, value is relative to language.

Many people do not like to think of their values as relative. They like to think of their set of values as something more important than the words they use, perhaps even timeless. Many people locate their values in moral tradition or religious scripture. When I state values are relative, that does not mean that they are relative to infinity. They are relative to the cultural history of the human population, which is broad but certainly not infinite. Lakoff and Johnson (1999) note that our conceptual systems tend to be widespread across languages and cultures. Humans share similar neural systems, derived from neural adaptive processes attuned to and, to a large extent, embodied by the social and physical environments in which we find ourselves (though highly malleable to historical contingency). This limits the capacity for pure, uncontrolled relativity in human adaptive processes. Wilson (1993) has similarly noted that some moral and ethical traditions seem to have a remarkable tendency to repeat themselves cross-culturally. Nevertheless, our values are located within a cultural framework—they are a standpoint—and they find their meaning from cultural prescriptions, not timeless truths.

The upshot of this is that when our young ethnographer begins her investigation of the village, the way in which she finds meanings in their behaviors is wholly constituted by her language. Her social cosmology—the whole ball of fluid social wax—is pre-structured by her language. The meanings or functions she witnesses—the institutional facts—are meanings created by her culture. It is important to understand this—there is not something more fundamental than the language and its way of assigning function, meaning, and value. She cannot wholly comprehend their cultural standpoint until, within her mind, their language organizes her thoughts before her native language does. This is the central point of observer-dependency. There is no exterior, value-neutral, or independent point of view that we can take to comprehend the meanings of another culture. It does not work that way. Some underlying neural-adaptive similarities enable the capacity for learning, but cultural knowledge is not immediately unavailable or pregiven.

When she finishes with her ethnography, she writes a narrative account of her experience. The narrative authenticates the culture. This means that there is no culture without a written description of their activity as a culture. Culture is itself a word for the amalgam of behaviors, a product of Western social science. Culture is, in a word, an institutional fact. Characteristics of the culture exist because she has written them down. We see in this that, regarding institutional facts, the social identity of the observer and the observed are completely entangled.

A narrative is simply a story of "events germane to the inquiry" (Hall, 1999). The narrative account is a document that provides running dialogue of what she saw, the principal features of the social and physical environments, the people in it, what it all meant from their point of view, and perhaps broader implications of the findings. Put simply, a narrative is a written story of the ethnography. But the narrative will not fully capture the "difference" between the ethnographer's world and the world studied. It is an entity in itself, a standpoint whose meanings engage the reader with the ethnographer's meanings about the world.[2]

The location of culture. Our ethnographer has developed an image of the culture that she is observing. She writes it up, and presents it as a prospectus for a doctoral dissertation. She meets with her committee to defend the proposal. One of the professors, a stale old bone, asks her "So you saw interaction between your group and other groups. Well, where did it all come from? How did they know how to act? Did the culture spring up from the group itself, or from other groups? Can you point to something and say, This is the source of culture?"

It is a good question. She realizes it is a trapping question. She mulls over it for a minute. Then, pulling out her wallet, takes out her driver's license, puts her finger on her photograph, and says "Here's culture."

She was pointing to herself. The culture was in her. That is source enough. The lesson was that culture is in our heads. There is no culture separate from the humans who carry it. It is not something different, not some great thing that exists outside us. When we are dealing with culture we are dealing with humans. So it must be in our heads. There is no other place to find it.

Recognizing that culture is in our heads helps put into focus the abstract argument that humans are not "cultural dopes." Culture is not something imposed, it is something that we carry with us and that helps us interpret our social setting, including its social structural and material elements. We interpret and act. To talk of culture is to always talk about humans acting and finding meaning in their actions, interpretations, and creations.

Chan (1977) recognizes the centrality of human action in the production of culture in her (1977) description of police practice. Figure 1.1 is reproduced from her discussion of culture.

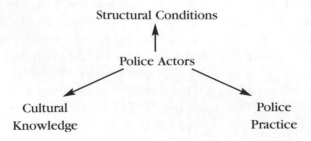

Figure 1.1
An interactive model of the production of police practice. From Chan (1997:74) *Policing in a Multicultural Society*.

The model above locates police actors as "active participants in the construction and reproduction of cultural knowledge and institutional practice" (Chan, 1997:73). In it, Chan rejects the notion that broad structural conditions lead to cultural knowledge that humans learn and act upon. Instead, structural conditions, cultural knowledge, and practice are all mediated through individuals. The central feature of this model is that individuals are in the center and culture exists through their expression of it. That they are aware of their conscious role in the creation of their social environment is noted by Barker:

> Police officers are consciously aware of their role as active participants in the creation and interpretation of this social world. They are aware of the perceived necessity for adherence to their construction of reality in order to perform their job. They believe that the ordering of reality is essential for social survival and also for literal survival. Adherence to the police version of the world confers actual, literal, survival in the performance of a job that has extraordinary risks and deals with high levels of uncertainty and danger (Barker, 1999:21).

Culture and police culture. This thought-experiment and discussion has several implications for the study of police culture.

Culture and observer-dependency. There is no such thing as police culture in the objective "out there" (see DiCristina, 1995). It does not exist independently of the observer. When academicians write about police culture, their values and predispositions are completely intertwined with the standpoints of the membership of whatever police group they are studying. In writing about police culture, academicians authenticate it. The values of the observer are not separable from the object of the research, and are fully in place from the moment the researcher uses the word "culture" to describe a group of police officers. In a real sense, the researcher is always investigating her interaction with the people being studied. It is not and never can be objective.

Language. Language is critical to understanding the life of any group. By the study of language we "engage the text," that is, we learn about what is different and what is similar about the people studied. Consequently, students of police culture should recognize the preeminent role played by language. Van Maanen (1978) recognized the centrality of language in his article called "The Asshole," in which he explored the meanings the word "asshole" carried for police officers.

Culture, intergroup interactions, and conflict. To speak of police culture is not to suggest that the police sub-populations of interest are somehow autonomous, by which I mean that members' identities are determined only by their "traditional" group affiliation or that they are independent of the influence of other groups. Cultural identity may be stimulated by the interaction with other groups. Cultures are not "homogenous, static, and closed" to borrow a phrase from Fine and Kleinman (1979).[3] Recognizing this, patterns of interaction and are integral to the formation of police culture.

Cultural identity is closely tied to conflict. This notion carries a rejection of the idea of static and closed societies. When we deal with culture, we are dealing with notions of solidarity and identity. Central to this book is the thesis, developed by Coser (1968), that conflict is central to the formation of group identity, group boundaries, and group solidarity. Consequently, the specification of culture requires that we recognize groups with which the group of interest is in conflict.

Conflicts range from resentment to violence. Among the police, we see such conflicts with regard to the courts, with management, and with criminals and troublemakers. Each of these groups has particular implications for police culture. The conflicts between the police and these groups are the basis for the formation of a great deal of cultural identity.

Culture is in our heads. This clement reminds us that the study of culture is always the study of people. When we talk about understanding organizational culture, we are talking about, in some fashion, understanding the people in it.

The recognition that culture is in our heads bears on the debate on the socialization/predisposition argument concerning sources of police "personality." Socialization proponents argue that police are heavily influenced by police departments in their first few years of service. In his classic article on police socialization, Van Maanen (1973) argues that the early socialization process is characterized by four periods: pre-entry, admittance, encounter, and metamorphosis. These periods collectively last about four years. They represent that period during which a recruit is most vulnerable to organizational influences.

Predisposition proponents argue that a recruit's views are largely in place by the time they are hired. Crank and Caldero (1999) contend that a recruits views are largely in place upon hiring. Subsequent changes in their outlook are minor and largely unaffected by organizational experiences. Because departments screen recruits for particular moral types, efforts to change organizations by hiring more minorities and women does not result in significant change in the organizational culture.

The idea that culture is in our heads means that, when someone is hired, they bring with them a complete complement of cultural behaviors, values, and predispositions. The organization may have a socialization effect, but its effect will be, like our ethnographer interpreting the village culture she witnessed and participated in, interpreted through recruits' already fully-in-place worldview.

Culture reproduces itself. Managers in the police organization tend to hire people like themselves, who see the world like they do. The organization consequently has little effect: its members, through the organizational experiences, reproduce their already existing cultural worldview. For socialization to have a large experience, it would have to be contrary to the way recruits previously looked at the world. Yet the screening process is designed to assure the opposite effect—that recruits are fit for police work.

Understanding: Engaging the text on its own terms. Understanding emerges from the ability to understand the culture in its own terms. The ability of our ethnographer to engage and learn from the villagers, to "share a conversation with them" as it is sometimes put, is tied to her experience and knowledge. In Gadamer's terminology, our ethnographer sought to "engage the text on its own terms." In this case the culture is the text. This way of thinking recognizes that police cultures are products of time and place, and understanding them requires an effort to understand the interior and externalized meanings carried by the police themselves. It also requires the reader to put herself in the place of the writer—that is, to try to capture the meanings as the writer experienced them.

In our thought experiment, as our ethnographer spent more time in the village, she learned more about the people, she expanded her sense of cultural understanding, that is, her knowledge of the human stock of institutional facts. She became both more worldly and more wise in the ways of humans.[4] She may have developed insights to help her better understand her own people. Her sense of language may have expanded, either by the addition of their language, or by her ability to broaden the use of her language to understand the people she studied.

This suggests that researchers interested in the culture of the police should engage the police on their own terms. This is accomplished through participation and the study of elements of their written, spoken, symbolic, social, and physical culture. The study of the police, like the study of any group a researcher wants to label a "culture," will be personally broadening to the extent that the researcher views her task as "engaging the text in its own terms."

The capacity to learn from studies of police culture are tied to our ability to engage them on their own terms. As did our young ethnographer, we will never be "objectively" studying the police culture, as it were, but subjectively studying our interactions with the police. Kraska (1996) incorporated this insight into his narrative inquiry into police militarization practices among a small number of off-duty officers. When we study police culture, to a surprising degree we are studying ourselves.

Endnotes

[1] "I believe that language is the fundamental institution in the sense that other institutions such as money, government, private property, marriage, and games, require language, or at least language-like forms of symbolism, in a way that language does not require the other institutions for its existence" (Searle, 1998:153).

[2] A text has its life in language as well, and so engages the reader in an interpretive process. The task of interpretation is to find "the right language to understand the text" (Johnson, 2000).

[3] Cited in Hall and Neitz, 1993:231. Fine and Kleinman were describing the concept of subculture; however the idea is apt for understanding culture as well.

[4] This does not mean that she became either more trustful and kind, or distrustful, or cynical. The development of cultural knowledge here is not meant to be interpreted as a "hand-holding" experience, but a harsh, sometimes gut-wrenching cultural shock that tends to accompany sharp expansions of practical knowledge. In terms of being human, it simply means that she became "more."

2 Issues in the Study of Police Culture

How do we frame a "police culture?" By frame, I mean identify the source of the values, social structures, and other elements that make up some organizational "culture." There are three frames commonly used in literature on police culture. The first frame is interactionist, and locates culture and cultural emergence in the face to face interactions of officers in local settings. The idea that the police are a "local culture" suggests that the outlooks and predispositions of police officers emerge from their work setting and occupational environment. The second frame looks at police organizations in terms of subcultures, that is, whose values and cultural predispositions are imported from outside, and uses an institutional perspective to identify common subcultural elements. According to the institutional perspective I look at broad institutional or national patterns and their effects on local structures and the values carried by local actors. The third frame draws from a variety of contemporary writings to argue that multiple cultures co-exist in police organizations. This literature defies easy categorization and individual authors will be considered.

Limitations On a Common Distinction Between "Culture" and "Subculture"

The terms "culture" and "subculture" are commonly used interchangeably to describe particular police subgroups and the way they do and think about their work. However, the choice of terms we make carries important implication for how we think about police work and the values and ethics police have. Most generally, culture can be described as "the occupational beliefs and values that are shared by officers across the country" (Roberg, Crank & Kuykendall, 2000:265). Subculture, on the other hand, is the "values imported from the broader society in which officers live" (Roberg, Crank & Kuykendall, 2000:265).

This distinction between culture and subculture above is practical for reform-minded professionals, because it permits us to both view how values are adopted from broader society (police as a subculture) and how police recruits are socialized into a prevailing way of thinking about police work (hence culture). If problems are cultural, they can be addressed by changing the organization or its formal and informal socialization processes. If problems are subcultural, they can be addressed by changing recruitment practices.

This way of distinguishing between of culture and subculture, however, is limited. First, it does not recognize complexity in the relationship between culture and subculture. Municipal police departments across the United States, for example, are characterized by similar patterns of rank-structure, occupational differentiation, and patrol practices (Crank & Langworthy, 1991), suggesting that all subgroups in these organizations can be described by a similar material culture. Similarly, research on the police as a culture, particularly research focusing on cultural themes or attitudes often fail to notice subtle patterns of subcultural differentiation (see Fine & Kleinman, 1979:7). Christensen and Crank (2001), for example, noted that police tended to display a general pattern of themes similar to those proposed in this book. However, on close inspection, subtle differences were noted. They concluded that:

> An outsider visiting police organizations in two jurisdictions may encounter the same theme concepts . . . However, our research also suggests that the conclusion of equivalence is too facile and overlooks nuanced but important differences in the way officers think about their work (Christensen & Crank, 2001:94).

In other words, the presence of similar police "themes" may hide important differences in local meanings appending to those themes.

Second, when we examine only ideational components—values, beliefs, and ethics—associated with municipal police organizations, we might observe that some elements seem to be present in all departments, suggesting the presence of a general "culture" of policing, while others appear to be local, suggesting subcultural variation. For example, it has been suggested that a conservative, order-oriented attitude is widely shared among police officers. However, attitudes toward minority hiring practices may vary substantially among different groups within a police department. In other words, depending on which elements we look at, ideational elements can be both cultural and subcultural at the same time.

Third, all of this is complicated by the predispositions of the observers. One observer might look at a pattern of similarity or divergence in some practice, value, or organizational element, and conclude that they are quite similar, while another might conclude that they, in fact, reveal startling differences! Recall that there is no objective way to study culture and that researchers are, to a degree, always studying themselves in interaction with the "culture" studied. For example, one observer might look at police shift work and conclude that police are amazingly similar everywhere—they tend to have three shifts; these shifts are aligned around late morning to early afternoon, early afternoon to evening, and evening through to morning again. Variations on this theme are typically minor and adaptive to local dynamics. Another observer might look at the same shifts and note incredible diversity: Shifts are not all on the same hour, some places do a split shift, some do an overlapping shift, a few departments run on 12-hour shifts. Indeed, the second observer states, each shift tells us something different about each department and how it has adapted to its public constituencies. In other words, the presence of common cultural elements is in the eye of the beholder as much as it is a product of the organization itself.

Fourth, to identify a subculture begs the question: What is the larger culture of which the police are a subculture? Should we define culture geographically, using nation-states or political units as boundaries? Some themes seem to have international scope (Waddington, 1999). Perhaps language is the key to common cultural identity: language was presented as the key to common understanding. This suggests that culture, in the broadest sense, is made up of people who share a common language. Can we then say that the languages that share Latin as a root share some cultural elements? Can the French and Spanish be thought of as subcultures of their Latin progenitors?

At this point, the reader might want to throw up her hands and ask, Is culture simply a mass gadgetry of colorful wheels, gewgaws, cams, rolling pins and levers, bells, quacks, buzzers and whistles, all running in different directions at the same time, all powered by some unknown source, all producing a great deal of motion and excitement, but resulting in very little clarity?

The image of culture carried by this author is that culture exists in varying degrees at all levels (it IS a gewgaw of rumbling and squeaking parts!) and flows in all directions—from individual to society and back again. We are embedded in culture—as Geertz (1973:5) put it in an oft-cited quote, "Believing, with Max Weber, that man is an animal suspended in webs of significance he himself has spun, I take culture to be those webs . . ." We think about national issues. We share mass thoughts about the morning's coffee while we call up the *New York Times* on the Internet. We wonder who is going to be at war and what the editorials will say. We set about cleaning the house before guests arrive—tonight is bridge

night. All of these things reveal our embeddedness in social constructions, from housework behavior to polity concerns over the adroitness or
stupidity of congressional leaders. They operate within each of the cultural frames—they respond to institutional concerns, they actively create
an ongoing cultural life together, and they interact on various levels with
different friends who may embed them in different cultural milieus.

Their lives are embedded in each of the cultural frames simultaneously. Yet the frames are not separate from them—culture is carried in
people, and their creativity, aesthetic interests, or misunderstandings can
create new cultural knowledge. Their participation in the different
frames reveals the complexity of cultural life in mass society. Each of
these frames is discussed below.

The Police as Local Culture

According to the interactionist perspective, culture emerges locally in
concrete social interactions and radiates out to other groups in patterns
determined by the social interactions of the groups members with other
groups. We do not simply and blindly take culture as it is handed down
to us. Interactionists focus on *emergent properties* of culture.

Humans are constantly engaged in a process of interacting with other
people, and the meanings these interactions hold for us emerge in a practical, common-sense way from these interactions. According to this idea,
we create meaning daily as an ongoing process of acting and reacting to
other people and events in simple everyday life. Meaning emerges in the
form of common sense, or what works as individuals together seek to
solve routine problems (Geertz, 1973). These meanings tend to provide
a sensibility out of which future action is conditioned.

Observers of culture have developed a diverse and colorful terminology to describe the interactive process: as shared typifications (Berger &
Luckmann, 1966), as common-sense knowledge (Geertz, 1973), as figurative action (Shearing & Ericson, 1991), as documentary interpretation
(Garfinkle, 1967), as a tool-kit (Swidler, 1986), and as a humanistic coef-
ficient (Znaniecki, 1936). These descriptions share a common theme.
Culture is a body of knowledge that emerges through the shared application of practical skills to concrete problems encountered in daily routines
and the normal course of activities. This body of knowledge contains
both information, values, and behaviors that tend to interact in ways that
are self-confirming, reproducing culture through confirmation.

Knowledge about how to act and how to think about work derives
directly from real-world experiences shared by its members. Viewed
through the lens of culture, the content of day-to-day activity becomes
meaningful, collects value, and is understood in a vocabulary of common

sense (Shearing & Ericson, 1991; Geertz, 1973). The constructed world is an everyday one, and cultural vocabularies that describe it are pragmatic (Willis, 1990).

Problem-solving is not a solitary exercise, but occurs in the sharing of problems concretely experienced (Berger & Luckmann, 1966). Many problems are similar, and come to be recognized, discussed, and shared as a common type of problem; to use the language of phenomenology, they are a typification. These pragmatic typifications or areas of similarly perceived experience are the building blocks of culture. When added together they become a store of "common knowledge" about how things work (Wuthnow et al., 1984:47).

Skolnick, for example, discusses the "symbolic assailant," a person whose clothes and mannerisms suggest that the person will cause trouble and is a likely candidate for a stop and frisk. Training officers teach recruits what to look for in terms of potential danger, and officers tell each other stories about things they have seen that mark individuals as dangerous—a type of tattoo, piece of clothing marking a gang member, or the like. Thus, typifications indicating the potential for trouble and danger arise from the concrete doing of police work, are shared by cops (and hence the phrase "shared typification") and become a part of the lore of a local police culture.

In time such typifications are regarded as common knowledge that carries common-sense value. Put sensibly, common knowledge is part of a cultural tool-kit for carrying out everyday activities (Swidler, 1986:275). This tool-kit is described by, she observes, "action and values" . . . "organized to take advantage of cultural competences." Common knowledge, with its roots in shared everyday experience, is a way of thinking about the world, of organizing information into typifications that enable an actor to do their work with the competency to know how events will unfold. In the case of police culture, culturally shared meanings represent how cops think about their working environment, and with the passage of time they indicate how cops think about their lives.

Consider the following example of problem-solving and the way it reproduces culture. A house in a small rural community is widely believed to be a source of drugs, and many residents are upset. They meet with the recently assigned local county sheriff's deputy, and together they develop an informal organization to consider how to deal with the problem. One day a person who is carrying a package approaches the house that, to a citizen watching the house, looks as if it might contain drugs. Two citizens confront him, and the deputy quickly arrives. A fight breaks out among the citizens, the deputy, and the residents of the house. The residents are ultimately arrested. The incident becomes part of the local lore of the sheriff's department and the community as well. The fight eventually attains the status of institutional fact: a "function" or a "value" is given the fight, it is "doing something about bad guys."

Are there other cultural interpretations of the same incident? There are many. For example, a citizen might wonder why the deputy and some of her friends are physically assaulting a person at their home. Or they might think that drugs are personal behavior and question the right of the government to intervene in citizens' lives on such a moral basis. Or they might think that, if the drugs are dangerous, only family members of the person to whom they are a danger have the right to intervene. Or they might think that only local residents have the right to intervene, that it is none of the government's business. A family member of the person that the deputy fought with might believe that there is no higher purpose than to protect members of the family, and that her responsibility is to kill the attacking police officer. An ethnographer might think that the entire spectacle is ritual behavior whose purpose is the confirmation of power of community leaders and the degradation of peripheral group members.

With changing times, the police begin to adopt elements of community policing. The fight receives a new institutional fact designation: it is seen as an example of (a function of) community policing in action, sometimes called "aggressive order maintenance." And rural police propagate the idea that they have always been doing community policing. What we have in this example is an institutional fact emerging within a setting already dense with institutional facts (such as deputy, merchandise, robbery, house, and the like), then being redesignated with changing circumstances in the occupational setting.

An element of the incident was that it was somewhat unpredictable. The deputy might have been killed. Or the deputy might not have decided to fight, but instead to bring in more sheriff's deputies. Stated differently, the deputy and the community members, informed by a variety of institutional facts, made decisions about how to act. The circumstances and outcome of the incident in turn became added to local cultural lore. Unpredictability, in its many forms, are a central ingredient in police culture (Manning, 1997).

This incident also has implications for studies of local police cultures. Because a particular culture is always undergoing change, any study of it will of necessity be incomplete. It can never be wholly understood, because there is not this "finished" or complete entity to understand. Cultural understanding, for both its participants and its observers, is a continual process of interpretation, never complete, always changing and adapting to new historical circumstances.

The incident reaffirms and reproduces culture. Drugs are still bad, bad guys deal with drugs and police justifiably treat them roughly. All this must be done to protect the community. In this way, the cultural dispositions and behaviors that justified the original encounter lead to further acts that confirm the views. Culture is reproduced in a concrete setting. Central tenets of culture are established—in this real-world example, culture is a self-fulfilling circle.

The aesthetics of local culture. At this point, I am going to review a way of thinking about cultural process that I think is particularly useful to understanding the practical nature of police culture. This way of thinking about culture was developed by Willis (1990) to describe common culture among British youth. Youth culture was organized around what Willis called "grounded aesthetics." Grounded aesthetics resemble typifications in that they both describe how meaning and common sense arises from everyday experience. Like Swidler's (1986) "tool-kit," Willis' idea of grounded aesthetics suggested that individual artistry was present in the production of culture. The importance of Willis' notion of grounded aesthetics is that it shows how culture is grounded in everyday activity, yet also how powerful media and commercial influences transmit cultural elements across otherwise unconnected groups. This perspective thus allows us to see how police culture, though based locally in individual agencies, also is transmitted nationally through media influences that contribute to a general "culture of policing."

Willis observed that common culture could be seen in the way young people copied popular modes of dress, ways of speaking, and other forms of concrete behavior. He described the way youth selected various cultural goods as "the creative process whereby meanings are attributed to symbols and practices and where symbols and practices are selected, reselected, highlighted, and recomposed . . ." (Willis, 1990:24). The attire, behavior, vocabulary, and goods an individual used to express him or herself, and the meanings that those elements held for young people, became that person's "grounded aesthetic." A young person who dressed in the popular attire of the day, who talked using the appropriate slang, and who styled their hair in popular ways, he held, was selecting a way of expressing themselves from among common cultural goods available to youth. In Swidler's terms, they were developing stylistic "competencies" that combined available cultural goods and values into a distinctive cultural phenomena. The term "grounded" indicated that symbols and practices used by youth to celebrate their identity arose from concrete, ordinary life events. The term "aesthetic" was selected to emphasize the creative process by which particular practices came to be valued by young people—that youth creatively selected from among common cultural goods to construct an identity that they found personally compelling and comfortable.

Willis described what was meaningful to British youth, and the image he captured was the excitement and the enjoyment of shared elements of popular culture. Popular musical groups commonly seen on British television or heard through various media, for example, were more likely to be copied in the culture, as were styles of dress, haircuts, and argot. Popular culture was carried across tabloid, television, and radio media, which served to diffuse common cultural goods to young people. Cultural goods were thus at the same time widespread and uniquely and intensely celebrated as sources of identity construction for British youth. Culture was thus at once artistic, personally experienced, and grounded in widely shared experience.

Youth culture emerged from the way in which individuals shared their aesthetics, made available through media transmission of common cultural goods. Aesthetics could be and frequently were manipulated by mass media. The recordings of particular artists were sold, or performers would wear a special brand of shoe; thus, cultural elements were also advertising booty. Commercial media thus served to expand opportunities for the transmission of culture, extending it to people that were not in personal contact with each other. Because aesthetics are transmitted by media, Willis's idea of culture have a post-modern vigor (which he himself strongly denied in his book) where interaction among individuals plays a lesser role in the transmission of culture, and cultural forms take similar (media-sponsored) forms among geographically unconnected groups. Thus, individual "grounded aesthetics" were global in scale, transcending particular communities or neighborhoods that gave rise to them.

The idea of grounded aesthetics has much to offer to our understanding of the culture of policing. By thinking of the police in terms of grounded aesthetics, we can focus on concrete events, style of dress, forms of patrol, ways of talking, styles of weaponry, and rituals of celebration and of grieving; in short, the styles of behavior they choose to adapt to their various audiences. We can also think about stories that cops tell, those that are retold and become part of the cultural lore of an agency, both for the meanings they carry about the process of police work and for the artistry that goes into their construction.

We can also think about police discretion as an artful response to practical exigencies of police work, in which officers select among different cultural "competencies" when deciding how and when to act. By cultural "competency" I mean behaviors or communications that are believed to have known or desired results. Seen in this way, discretion is the art of selecting, from among various alternative courses of action, one's personal and preferred competencies.

The artistry inherent in the idea of a grounded aesthetic suggests that members of the police culture are not simple dopes (Garfinkle, 1967) mindlessly responding to powerful environmental forces—the institution of crime control, the courts, or their own organization. Cops are selecting modes of adaptation that they prefer, that they sometimes, to use a term uncommon to scholarly studies, simply like. The term aesthetics suggests an emotive element to how officers adapt to their audiences: they make choices—that is, they select competencies—that are pleasing to them, that make them feel good, or that at appropriate times make them angry.

The transmission of local culture. If culture is a product of local interactions, then how can so many police departments have elements that are so similar to one another? To explain this, mechanisms by which local cultural elements reach a wider audience must be identified. Fine and Kleinman (1979) identify four ways that cultural elements are transmitted to other groups:

Multiple group membership is a primary mode for the transmission of information. Many police officers, for example, are also members of clubs such as the Elks and may give occasional presentations at the meetings.

Weak ties, which are the friendship or informal contacts in a person's regular routine, assist in the dissemination of information. A university professor might invite a police commander for a barbecue and discuss students who are also police officers or recruits.

Structural roles may place people into different groups. Police middle managers, for example, frequently are expected also to attend voluntary associations and community functions. Line officers may be in regional police labor organizations.

Media diffusion can spread information to a large audience rapidly. Graphic footage of officers killed in action has helped spread to the public generally police concerns about officer safety.

Van Maanen and Barley use the metaphor of Venn diagrams to display an image of overlapping subcultures. The more groups share common cultural features, the greater is their overlap. "Organizational culture is therefore understood as a shadow-like entity carried by subcultures and defined as the intersection of subcultural interpretive systems."[1] By assessing the overlap of values across different organizational personnel, one can measure the extent to which organizations share or diverge from a common culture.

Processes of media transmission also provide for a common core of cultural symbols across organizations. Training films that discuss danger and show cops killed in action contribute to a shared, and particularly intense way of thinking about danger among the police. Magazines selling various products describe particular types of weapons available to the police and enable the selection of defenses—lead-lined gloves, baton, hand-weapons, shotguns, knives, and the like—according to personal taste and skills of the officer. Television shows such as "Cops," where media ride along with officers in the hopes of gleaning a moment of excitement in the hum-drum of routine patrol, are talked about and provide a forum for thinking about good (and "stupid," as one cop described "Cops" to me) police behavior. In short, many elements of cop culture are available through print and TV media that give local agencies a national audience and provide an easily and widely accessible pool of cultural goods that cops select to enhance their self-image as tough enforcers (Kappeler, Blumberg & Potter, 1993).

The Police as Subculture in an Institutionalized Environment

Some elements of police culture—ideational, behavioral, material, and social structural—exist at a level that transcends individual police departments. These characteristics have an inter-organizational reach. Many are at the level of inter-organizational sector—they seem to characterize all police agencies. By inter-organizational sector is meant a "domain identified by similarity of service, product, or function (Scott & Meyer, 1992:137). The boundaries of a sector are functional, not geographical. Other elements—the stern belief by many police officers in individual responsibility, for example—appear to be adapted from broader society, the boundary of which may be nation-state based and intensified within particular political predispositions. These levels are institutional levels, and institutional theory of organizations is about how local organizations adapt to the expectations and values carried in their institutional settings. This section looks at individual police organizations as members of exist within institutional environments, and these environments carry cultural elements shared by organizations or incorporated into organizational structure and behavior.

Elements of cultural similarity. That the police display similarities in some cultural elements has been noted by Waddington:

> I maintain that there is indeed a police subculture whose core elements are to be found across a remarkably broad spectrum of police talk in a wide variety of jurisdictions. Throughout the United States, which contains many significant elements of internal divisions between jurisdictions and law enforcement agencies, the core elements of police subculture recognizably the same. Those elements are shared throughout the various jurisdictions that constitute the United Kingdom, including Scotland and even Northern Ireland . . ." (Waddington, 1999:295-296).

Citing a wide literature,[2] Waddington noted that similarities in police culture are recognizable in Canada, Australia, and India. Some common elements are trans-nationally recognized: "When Punch (1979) describes the policing of inner-city Amsterdam, he might be just as easily describing a British, American, or Australian city" (Waddington, 1999:296).Waddington attributes these similarities to the authoritarian and coercive nature of police work, located within the due-process constraints placed on the use of their authority in democratic societies. And anyone who has read Chan's (1997) analysis of culture and reform in New South Wales can only be astonished at their similarities to issues in the United States even though the countries are on opposite sides of the planet.

Certain features of police social structure are also widely present. Manning (1989:362) noted that the police have "characteristic organizational features and careers: broad recruitment, a pyramid shaped organization, a flat hierarchy, little inter-organizational mobility, limited vertical and extensive horizontal mobility, characteristic formal and informal specialization, and bases of job attachment/commitment." This organizational structure is pervasive to policing, and cannot be explained simply in terms of individual-to-society processes of cultural transmission.

The presence of some elements of police culture across national and international settings suggests that they have become institutionalized: they are elements of culture that have a broad acceptance, and we do them because we share a belief that they are the right things to do. Consider, for example, the institution of marriage. Marriage is the most common institutionalized form for propagating families between consenting adults in the United States—many people strongly believe in the formality of marriage and frown upon couples that are not heterosexual, that live together without formal marriage vows, and that have children out of wedlock. There are powerful, harsh terms for violations of these values: children out of wedlock are "bastards," unmarried couples are "living in sin," and homosexual couples are "queers." This example, simple though it is, reveals the power with which values attach to and legitimize or stigmatize particular forms of behavior. It is very hard to act against the moral grain.

Social control is also an institution. It is acted out informally through everyday routines that discourage particular kinds of behaviors. It is acted out formally through the enactment of legal sanctions that punish particular behaviors and sometime require others. Police are the part of the institution of social control responsible for identifying and seizing violators of legal sanctions. They also act informally, using the law as a threat to gain proper behavior rather than automatically invoking formal sanctions of the law. That the police tend to under-enforce the law has been widely cited (see, e.g., Wilson, 1968). As an element of the institution of social control, the police carry a variety of values, predispositions, and behaviors that collectively override the influence of any particular police organization.

An example of how police organizations act out widely held values can be seen with regard to the value called "personal responsibility." Our society carries a deep-seated belief in the free will of individuals, and it is widely thought that people will use a pleasure-pain calculus before they do something—they will do things that bring them pleasure, and avoid things that bring them pain. The criminal justice system in the United States embodies this powerful belief in the form of what is called deterrence, a way of thinking about people that includes policies and punitive strategies that seek to increase some sort of pain associated with wrongdoing. It is a widely held belief that increases in pain, in whatever symbolic form, will decrease the likelihood that particular types of behavior will not occur. The organization of police work is similarly structured around deterrent strategies intended to increase the likelihood of pain. Through the presence of police officers in patrol cars on the streets of neighborhoods, the police seek to deter possible wrongdoing.

Random preventive patrol and 911 rapid response to citizen calls are highly institutionalized forms of crime control practice. The founder of contemporary police patrol, August Vollmer, believed that random preventive patrol would end crime in the United States. The form of patrol that he proposed and developed in the 1920s, random preventive patrol, is the dominant form used in police organizations across the United States today. Rapid-response emergency 911 police systems also seek to deter by providing a quick response to particular types of calls for assistance from the public. Police seek to prioritize calls for service, and give top priority to "in progress" calls, in the hope that the actual crime may be prevented if perpetrators are stopped in time.

Both 911 systems and random preventive patrol also reflect beliefs about how our society views human nature, rather than rational ideas about effective police work. Both are based on the notion of deterrence, seeking to up the ante of potential pain of wrongdoing by increasing the likelihood of being caught. That their ineffectiveness hints at the wrongfulness of commonly held ideas of human nature is beyond the scope of this book. The point here is that organizations, particularly police organizations, are powerful carriers of cultural elements, including behaviors, ways of thinking, and other predispositive strategies for organizing the work environment.

How is it that local police departments receive broad institutional elements of culture into their organizations? The "new institutional" research has tended to focus on the relationship between institutional environments and organizations (DiMaggio, 1991). One of the themes in this literature is a study of the processes by which institutional information is transmitted to individual organizations. Scott (1991) provides an overview of different ways institutions are tied to local organizations. He specifically focused on the transmission of elements of organizational structure to local settings, what I have defined previously as physical culture. We can straightforwardly extend his ideas to other elements of culture, as follows.

Imposition of organizational structure and behavior. Scott (1991) noted that some environments are so powerful that they can impose their notion of appropriate ways of doing things. Imposition, in this case, carries the idea of force: cultural elements can be forced on particular organizations, even in the face of organizational resistance. In justice systems, we see the imposition of structure through court order, for example, requiring the employment of minority members and women. Police departments with a history of corruption have sometimes been placed under consent decrees—documents from a federal court requiring changes in procedure. This imposition is accompanied by value orientations, for example, that employee representation in the police organization should mirror local community demographics, or should display a lower level of human rights abuses.

The authorization of organizational structure and behavior. This is the process by which broader social or sector-wide norms are defined and enforced. The development and formalization of ethics statements by police organizations represents such recognition of such norms. The values associated with the adoption of such ethics are spelled out in the statements themselves. Accreditation is another form of norm recognition across the sector of police organizations.

The inducement of organizational structure and behavior. Inducement occurs when the broader environmental sector cannot force change, but carries sufficient resources to induce structure. Crank and Langworthy (1996) discuss how the National Institute of Justice, through its granting programs, can "seduce" organizational structure by offering large grants to police departments on the condition that they experiment with or adopt particular kinds of structures, particularly those having to do with community policing.

The acquisition of organizational structure, behavior, and knowledge. This refers to the deliberate choosing of organizational elements by particular organizations. The rapid gains in the contemporary popularity of COMSTAT (an acronym for "compare statistics" programs are an example of acquisition. Managers want COMSTAT programs because they believe they can fight crime more efficiently.

The imprinting of organizational structure, behavior, and knowledge. This is the process by which new organizational forms acquire characteristics at the time of their founding which tend to remain into the future. The early emergence of policing, after the civil war, was tied to a militaristic command structure, largely because early police officers were drawn from the civil war. This form of command has been self-perpetuating in spite of a large quantity of evidence about its limitations (Guyot, 1979).

The incorporation of environmental structure, behavior and knowledge. This means that organizations will tend to internally map the complexity of structure that exists in their environments. This is not a coercive process, but reflects "a broad array of adaptive processes . . . ranging from co-optation . . . to the evolution of specialized boundary roles to deal with strategic contingencies . . ." (1979:179). This process emphasizes "unintended resultants, history-dependent causal determinants, and internal structural residues . . ." which is a complicated way of saying that organizations tend to fill up with the same institutional facts as their environments. They contain all the junk, logical clutter, and ethical complexity that typifies the settings in which they exist.

This notion makes sense if we think about it practically. Imagine the following setting. A commander at an orals board is considering the hiring of a recruit. She is being interviewed by six people, including one prosecuting attorney, the police legal counsel, a union representative, and a university professor. She is interviewed about police issues, her comprehension of the law, and local police procedure.

Occasionally someone will throw her a sidewinder, intended to take her by surprise or to create pressure on her, as in the form "you have to make a decision—what do you do?" Her response will reveal both the extent of her knowledge about the issue and the ability to cut through the chaff and take a course of action.

Her knowledge consists of "institutional facts" (misdemeanor or felony law, how to deal with domestic disturbances, the ethnic make-up of the community, how to diffuse a crowd, etc.) and her decision to act is always balanced among these competing institutional facts. If she displays a broad sense of pertinent (and often competing) institutional facts, and can make a decision to act, he will be impressed. He is hiring someone who can anticipate a wide range of contingent circumstances.

If she is smart and learns how to be a good cop, she will move up the organization and put her knowledge to work for the organization at administrative levels as well as street levels. Hence, the organization itself will become the product that she and others like her want it to be. And this means that the organization, enacted through people like her (and like the commander), becomes a mirror for the complexity of its institutional environment.

If the commander hires her, he is hiring a person who carries the local institutional environment with her. He is not only hiring a person with known quantities, he is hiring a person with a full array of cultural predispositions—her views on the polity, family issues, and the like. She also will have in place an array of cultural competencies that enable and extend well beyond occupational work. Thus, the hiring will always carry unforeseen contingencies and unintended effects. In this way, the organization will carry the same sorts of unpredictable elements carried in broader society. The local police culture will be reproduced in the hiring process. And, through the officer's work and participation in the life of the community, the institutions that carry these cultural elements are likewise reproduced and sustained.

The bypassing of organizational structure. Meyer, Scott, and Deal (1992) noted that much of the orderliness and coherence in American schools emerged from institutionally shared beliefs. Shared conceptions, in this instance, have a direct influence on the beliefs and behaviors of individual participants. This is a profound idea. It is that the basic ideas and values that underlie an organization and enable its members to get along and carry out their work emerge from the environment and are largely independent of organizational influences.

Crank and Caldero's (2000) perspective on police ethics represents this kind of institutional to local view of culture transmission. They suggested that police officers are frequently hired who are fully committed to crime control goals such as "do something about bad guys, and "make the world a safer place to live." They called this ends orientation the "noble cause." The noble cause, they contended, was an ethic characteristic of groups from which the police were hired, and was a bond— a commitment—shared by all police officers. The "noble cause," they stated, was a value that motivated and justified police behavior and infused police work with purpose, independent of (and sometimes contradictory to) formal organizational policies and goals.

Institutionalization in action: the community policing movement. Ritti and Mastrofski (2002) provided an institutional perspective to explain the way in which community policing has been adopted by U.S. police agencies. The term "community policing" first emerged in the mid 1970s. Community policing initially was adopted by a few agencies in response to a growing dissatisfaction with the "reform" or "professional" model of policing. Corruption, rising crime and fear of crime, and perceptions of police ineffectiveness undermined the traditional legitimacy of reform notions of policing that had dominated American policing through the twentieth century (Crank, 1996).

Ritti and Mastrofski identified two eras on the community policing movement. In the first era the ideology and justification of community policing was explicit. Advocates argued for its merits to deal with a variety of known organizational and municipal problems, especially those having to do with minority relations.

The second era of community policing began in 1989 and continues to the present. In this era, the authors observed that the legitimacy of community policing was increasingly taken for granted. Instead of justifying community policing, police agencies were interested in the nuts and bolts of its implementation. From this pattern, the authors offered a theory of the transmission of elements of community policing across the United States, as outlined below:

1. Growing dissatisfaction with some problem—in the community policing case, this tended to be police-minority relations, coupled with widespread perceptions of increase in violent crime. Existing solutions are found inadequate. There is an emergence of a new way of thinking about the problem, called a new "ideology" about policing.

2. Growing consensus about what to do about the problem. The consensus emerged around the need to increasingly involve the police in their community. The term "community policing" becomes an umbrella term for addressing the municipal, organizational, and ethical problems with which the previous model of policing—called the professional model—seemed unable to deal.

3. "Early adoption by organizations whose characteristics best match the problem as earlier codified" (2002:26). This was a period in which a few large departments began the process of formal adoption of community policing. This was a period of intense assessment and evaluation of community policing. It was an "explicit ideology," linking kinds of police behaviors with desired ends.

4.   "Later adoption as the ideology becomes 'taken for granted' and the structural solutions become ceremonially recognized as characteristic of proper organization" (2002:926). Agencies begin adopting community policing as a preferred way to deal with a wide variety of problems having to do with drugs, public disorder, and crime.

Swidler (1986) provided a perspective called "culture in action" that provides insight into the process of community policing adoption described above. She noted that, in periods of social transformation, "ideologies—explicit, articulated, highly organized meaning systems . . . establish new styles and strategies for action." Existing cultural patterns, she noted are "jettisoned with apparent ease." This is consistent with Ritti and Mastrofski's observation that community policing met with surprisingly little resistance as it underwent the process of institutionalization.

Ideological models emerge in some "contested arena," in the case described by Ritti and Mastrofski (2002) above, increasing frictions between reform or professional policing and broad trends in municipal life in the United States. In such unsettled periods, culture directly affects action. This means that there are efforts by reformers to directly link police practices to the underlying logic of community policing.

During settled times traditions emerge and the rational for behavior becomes taken-for-granted. An explicit ideology is no longer necessary to justify behavior. This is consistent with Ritti and Mastrofski's finding that, in reviews of newspaper and magazine articles, justifications for community policing had largely disappeared in the second era—its essential "rightness" or legitimacy was no longer questioned. Instead, departments had settled down to developing implementation strategies. Culture, in this period, did not directly organize action—instead, it had become a cultural "tool-kit"—ceremonies, organizational structures, common sense ways of doing policing, recognized professionals, rituals, and behaviors—that provided a set of strategies, or what might be called a "sensibility" from which community policing emerged. Community policing, by this perspective, may be settling down to a period of relatively uncontested legitimacy. This is suggested in Ritti and Mastrofski's data by the decreasing frequency of articles about community policing in the major news sources investigated. Community policing is becoming taken-for-granted. There is no way of predicting how long this period of legitimacy will last, though some authors have suggested it might be relatively brief (Crank, 1995).

The Police and Multiple Subcultures Within an Organizational Setting

Much of the preceding discussion has viewed police culture or subculture as synonymous with the membership of a police organization. Such a notion of culture does not fully recognize the implications of occupational and role differentiation. People are located in organizational niches. People inhabiting similar occupational niches and facing similar problems represent a subpopulation who may be culture generating (Van Maanen & Barley, 1994). Because of this, an organization may have any of a number of subsubcultures. Van Maanen and Barley define organizational subculture as:

> A subset of an organization's members who interact regularly with one another, identify themselves as a distinct group within the organization, share a set of problems commonly identified to be the problems of all, and routinely take action on the basis of collective understandings unique to the group (Van Maanen & Barley, 1984:38).

Subcultures proliferate according to the degree that their representative subgroups develop their own "language, norms, time horizons, and perspectives on the organization's mission." Cultural emergence is indicated by a "consciousness of difference" in which subcultural units believe they are best positioned to control the work they do. A countervailing centripetal force occurs when managers respond by using coercive force to control expanding subcultural identity (Van Maanen & Barley, 1984:40).

The presence of subcultures within police organizations has been noted by several authors. Reuss-Ianni (1983), for example, observed the presence of two police subcultures. One of these she labeled the "traditional" culture. This subculture was carried by line-officers and tended to find meaning in the traditions of the department. Members of this subculture frequently discussed the "good old days" when officers could police without present-day restrictions.[3] The traditional culture was contrasted with the "management" culture, comprised of middle managers in a police organization. This culture carried a professionalizing ethos characteristic of police professionalism: it was concerned with command and control prerogatives of managers and the routinization of departmental behavior.

Manning, in a wide literature, has also explored cultural differentiation or "segmentation" within police departments. In his work on British policing he noted a two-tiered pattern of segmentation similar to that described by Reuss-Ianni. Senior officers (ranks above sergeant) identified with rational bureaucracy, while constables were socially organized around principles of individualism and traditional notions of police work.

Relations between the segments were often conflictual, and were mediated through patterns of rule and discipline enforcement. In other literature Manning (1989) has divided the senior officer segment into two segments that he called middle managers and commanders.

The accounts of segmented police culture presented by both Reuss-Ianni and Van Maanen above are images of occupational segmentation of police culture. That is, they represent an image of police culture that is segmented within individual organizations. But the pattern of segmentation is characteristic of the police occupation generally—all organizations tend to have this pattern of segmentation (Paoline, 2001).

Sackmann: emergent patterns of cognition. A different notion of cultural differentiation is put forward by Sackmann (1992). Sackmann does not describe differentiation in terms of subpopulation identity, but in terms of the organization of cultural knowledge. Sackmann defines culture as "collective sense-making." The activity of sense-making is defined as "an activity in which individuals use their cognitive structure and structuring devices to perceive situations and to interpret their perceptions (Sackmann, 1992:141). Collective sense-making—the we way we share our perceptions of the world around us—occurs when cognitions are commonly held by a group of people in a given organization. Commonly held cognitions accumulate into cultural knowledge. Cognitions are structured through four "cognitive devices:"

> **Dictionary knowledge.** This consists of commonly held labels, descriptions, and definitions. This refers to the "what" of situations, their content. "As such, the semantics or signifiers that are acquired step; by step in a articular social situations."

> **Directory knowledge.** This refers to commonly held practices. Directory knowledge delineates the 'how' of events and their cause-and-effect relationships.

> **Recipe knowledge.** These are prescriptions for repair and improvement strategies. "It expresses 'shoulds' and recommends certain actions." It contains recipes for survival and success, and is "closely related to norms." It tends to refer to the immediate chain of causation.

> **Axiomatic knowledge.** This refers to reasons and explanations that explain the ontology or causality of an event. "Axiomatic knowledge is about the 'why' things and events happen . . ." It tends to refer to underlying causation and may include taken-for-granted assumptions about things (Sackmann, 1992:142).

Sackmann used a thematic content analysis to identify cultural themes, which she defined as equivalent meanings attributed to different situations or events. Interviews were conducted to acquire respondents' perceptions of commonly held themes. Additional "validating" thematic analyses were carried out to confirm the findings. Using this analytic strategy, Sackmann noted the presence of nine cultural groupings across the four kinds of cultural knowledge.

Patterns of cultural participation were uneven across the different kinds of cultural knowledge. This meant that different subcultures emerged depending on which kind of cultural knowledge was assessed. Sackmann also found that the same functional domains of different divisions were more alike than different functional domains within the same division. That is, differences between functionally different units within the same organization were greater than differences between functionally similar units across different organizations. In Paoline's (2001) terminology, culture was segmented within organizations but not occupationally. This is compatible with the observations of both Manning and Reuss-Ianni described above, that police subcultures tend to form around line and management positions, and this pattern of subcultural differentiation is similar across agencies.

Chan: Culture and Reform in Australian Police. Chan (1997:3) extended Sackmann's work to police organizations. Lamenting "the failure of existing definitions of police culture to account for internal differentiation and jurisdictional differences," Chan used the four-fold typology of knowledge types to assess the New South Wales police organization. Using impressionistic data, Chan assessed how cultural knowledge in the organization was affected by a broad program of community-based policing reform. A broad package of reform proposals had emerged in response to concerns about the relations between the police and aboriginal citizens. Reforms included merit-based promotion, regionalization, redesign of training and education, and the development of a variety of community-based programs. Chan used Sackmann's typology to conceptualize the police response to reform. Her conceptualization is presented below:

> **Police axiomatic knowledge.** This was traditionally organized around the "war against crime." Assumptions associated with community policing quickly prevailed. "The new objectives gave priority to crime prevention, services that are responsive to the needs and feelings of the community, citizens' involvement in policing, and the minimization of corruption. . . . Once in place these assumptions guided strategies and processes of reform." (1997:19).

> **Police dictionary knowledge.** Community-based policing was viewed superficially and seen as a public relations exercise. Many traditional definitions prevailed, and ethnic stereotyping remained commonplace.

> **Police directory knowledge.** Often, officers found that they could carry out their tasks in the old ways, and real change in police practices were often unrealized. Where strategies were aggressively implemented by command, change in directory knowledge did occur.

Police recipe knowledge. Because many of the proposed changes in other forms of knowledge did not occur, recipe knowledge—the way things should be done in particular situations—generally was unchanged.

Chan described the community policing interventions as generally ineffective. Substantive change was noted only with regard to axiomatic knowledge. She attributed the failure of reforms as a failure of recognizing the importance of the "field," a term adopted from Bourdieu (Bourdieu & Wacquant, 1992). The field is defined as the:

Social space of conflict and competition, where participants struggle to establish control over specific power and authority, and, in the course of the struggle, modify the structure of the field itself (Chan, 1997:71).

The importance of the field was that it provided the social structure in which police culture operated. Because reform changes were aimed at the culture and not at the field itself, reforms were generally disappointing. The failure of reforms led Chan to conclude reforms must be aimed at the broader social structural environment in which police work occurs, not only at the police.

The changes adopted by the New South Wales Police Department were intended to improve relations with minority groups, particularly aborigines. However, the position of the aborigines in Australian society—the field—was generally unaffected by the reforms. Moreover, many of the external changes imposed on the organization were not enforced, leaving officers' existing use and interpretation of cultural traditions unchanged. Without field-wide changes, Chan concluded, reform efforts were likely to be frustrated and ineffective.

In a paper published in 2001, Chan extended her perspective on police culture to agency socialization processes. She argued that a theory of police culture should account for variations in socialization processes, recognize the active part played by recruits in socialization, locate socialization within the sociopolitical conditions of policing, and take into account broad social change in the field.

With regard to variations in the socialization process, she noted that the process was heterogenous.

Not only did recruits come across a variety of role models in the course of their training, the vast majority of the cohort thought that their learning experience varied according to the culture and workload of the local area command, and the personality and style of the local area commander, the shift supervisor and the shift partner (Chan, 2001:126).

Recruits took an active part in the process—they reflected on who they talked to and assessed the relative merits of information received from superiors. When asked about participation in police culture, recruits provided diverse answers, suggesting different modes of adaptation to local cultural dynamics. She also noted that the "field" itself was undergoing broad change. This change stemmed from reform efforts of the Royal Commission aimed at corruption in the police organization. Because of the change, the authority of many traditional officers was eroded—they did not have the economic and symbolic "capital" they might have had in more stable periods. These changing field conditions created a diverse socialization process, as both recruits and experienced officers struggled to adapt to changing conditions. It should be noted that Chan did not discuss specific behaviors in assessing the active part played by recruits, but focused instead on ideational elements of culture.

Paoline: Culture and Police Types. Paoline (2001) took a sharply different approach to the study of police culture. He used an empirical methodology, and allowed the definition of cultural differences to be determined by the results of statistical procedures. The differences between "cultural" and "subcultural" attitudes were determined according to statistical distributions of attitudinal scores. Attitudes that showed little statistical variation among officers, yet had overall skew, were designated "cultural." "Subcultural" attitudes were those that displayed significant variation across groups.

Paoline used a technique called cluster analysis, which is a data reduction technique, to identify group formations within the particular attitudes studied. Clusters produced by the analysis were the empirical basis for the identification of "subcultures," or differentiating patterns of attitudes. To the extent that the clustering technique identified distinct clusters, the officers associated with those clusters were described as a "subculture."

Analysis revealed the presence of seven clusters, suggesting subcultural differentiation. An interpretive review of the clusters suggested the following labels: the lay-lows, old-pros, traditionalists, anti-organization street cops, "Dirty Harry enforcers," peace-keepers, and law enforcers.[4] He identified cluster means that varied from group to group, indicating subcultural differentiation, and cluster means that exhibited little variation across groups, suggesting the presence of a more general culture. The identity and meaning of the "types" emerged from an examination of often subtle differences in "subculture" or "cultural" group central tendencies.

One of the interesting aspects of the analysis was the analytic separation of subpopulations from subcultures. An officer could be a member of several different groups, depending on the clustering pattern she or he matched. This is a fruitful finding, because it allows researchers to consider that an officer's identity is not subcultural per se, but is a composite social entity formed from subcultural elements selectively obtained from participation in a variety of subgroups.

Controversial in the mode of cultural analysis was the way empirical measures are used to generate cultural identity. All interpretation of cultural or subcultural identity were based on assessments of statistical differences, an analytic strategy at stark variance with ethnographic traditions in cultural analysis. Can a cluster analysis differentiate underlying attitudinal structure in a way that reasonably distinguishes between "cultural" and "subcultural" elements? Paoline's analysis moves cultural investigation into the empirical camp of quantitative methodology in justice studies, a move inevitably controversial yet important for the expanding arena of cultural research on the police.

Conclusion: Which Notion of Culture Is Best?

In this chapter, I have reviewed literature and research that suggested three frames for thinking about culture. The reader might reasonably ask *which of these frames most adequately captures elements of police culture?* However, there is no equally reasonable principle by which one of these approaches to culture might be selected over another.

Here is the problem. There is not a standpoint outside of culture from which I can "objectively" evaluate these different perspectives and say: *There. That one. That's the best.* Any criteria I use to select the "best" is itself a cultural point of view. For me to select a "best" is to reject the inevitability of my own reasoning—culture is a concatenation of institutional facts, and institutional facts are observer-dependent.

I might, for example, follow Paoline's (2001) lead and build a justification for a particular technique on the use of inferential statistics, widely legitimized in the social sciences. I might select ethnographic techniques to develop an image of group identity as it sees itself as did Sackmann (1992). Concerned with acquiring the fullest array of information about communicative information about the culture, I might select a semiotic strategy, as did Manning (1997). Or I might develop a theoretical perspective to help me understand the limited reach of reform efforts, as did Chan (1996). Each one of these models of inquiry is justifiable and can be fruitful. However, there is no exterior viewpoint to select "the best." The judgment of "which is best" is always from some standpoint, and is for that reason always inside culture.

I certainly can take a position inside culture, that is, recognizing that I am making a judgment from a prejudicial standpoint. The position I prefer has two parts. First, the decision about one or the other strategy of inquiry depends on and flows from the interests, skills and intent of the researcher or writer. The researcher can select the method or narrative style that best addresses the problem she is concerned with, or that provides the most elegant method of assessing her notion of culture. The reader might object that, using this logic, a Hollywood movie about the police is of equal worth in depicting police culture as methodologically rigorous social science. The reader would be correct.

Second is that the mode of inquiry a researcher selects is not some window on the truth, but simply another interpretation. The cultural interpretation is a sort of textual account of what we have observed, in which the text is the culture observed and written about. Once we view it as an interpretation, however, we are implicitly acknowledging the legitimacy of different points of view. Warnke advises us that:

> A text will refer to different experiences and issues for different genera-
> tions of interpreters and may have different meanings for different mem-
> bers of the same generation. Hence we can never claim eternal truth for
> our interpretations but must rather hold them open to changes in his-
> torical circumstances, in our concerns and in the issues that arise
> (Warnke, 1993:130).

From this recognition emerges what Warnke calls a hermeneutic con-
versation. Our goal is not to determine which is right, but to see what we can learn from each interpretation. Our efforts to learn from engaging the "text" of police culture are the same as the challenge facing our ethnographer in Chapter 1. We learn by trying to see the world as it is compre-
hended by members of the culture of interest. In the process we become "more" human, in that we acquire more of that special cultural quality that makes us human—our capacity to find meaning in the world around us. Accompanying this perspective is the notion that we may not end in consensus. Consensus—that is, the idea that in the end we can develop enough knowledge to generally agree on a particular way of looking at culture—is itself a standpoint, and may preclude ways of looking at culture that are not compatible with others. Warnke again advises us that the scope of our dialogue is unlimited. The conversation is always open to additional interpretations of culture, and recognizes that conflict is an essential ingredient in cultural analysis.[5]

The obligation of the researcher is, like our ethnographer earlier, to *engage the text on its own terms*. Research on culture should always be something more than the imposition of a preset language on the group studied. It is by engaging the text in its own terms—not the imposition of our own cultural predispositions—that we learn, adapt, and in turn contribute to the "webs of significance" from which we emerge.

Endnotes

[1] See also Paoline, 2001:11.

[2] For comparative similarities cited by Waddington (1999), Canada; Ericson, 1982; Great Britain, Brewer, 1990; Australia, Chan, 1996; White & Alder, 1994; continental Europe, Punch, 1979; India, Bayley, 1969.

[3] Manning (1997:133) similarly notes a traditional orientation of the "line" culture in his study of a British police department.

[4] See Paoline (2001) for a detailed discussion of these types.

[5] Warnke (1993) was specifically discussing political liberalism. Her core ideas apply with equal vigor to discussions of the meaning of culture.

3

Culture and Cultural Themes

This book is an exposition of police cultural themes. I view themes as the essential "building blocks" of culture, to use a construction metaphor, they are the way action is wedded to value in important areas of the working environment of the police. Part II of this book lays out the diverse police themes. In this opening section, I will provide some preliminary considerations on what I mean by a cultural theme.

The term cultural theme represents the joining of cultural elements in ways that, as Manning (1987) observed, highlight areas of shared occupational activity. They represent activities that tend to be widely distributed, that is, common to many police departments.

Themes tend to mix together many cultural elements. First, they are behavioral—they occur the ordinary "doing" of police work, and derive their meaning from routine, ordinary police activity. Second, themes are a way of thinking about that activity, the sentiment that is associated with the activity. Kappeler, Sluder, and Alpert (1994:108) use the term dynamic affirmation to describe the linkage of behavior and sentiment. Put another way, police do not approach each aspect of their work as if they had never done it before—there are traditions and ways of thinking that are associated with their many activities. Nor are the themes rule-bound—they are predispositive, applying appropriate customs and taken-for-granted assumptions to, in Shearing and Ericson's (1991) colorful phrasing, provide the sensibility for thinking about particular routine activities. Third, themes imply social and organizational structure. This can be seen in patrol strategies, which associate a commitment to territorial control with geographic assignment. Or it might be associated with police relations with other municipal actors, such as the courts and media, and their ways of thinking about them.

That the police share a culture united by common themes has been noted by many observers—Manning, 1989, 1977; Reuss-Ianni, 1983; Shearing & Ericson, 1991; McNulty, 1994; and Bayley & Bittner, 1984, to name but a few. Shared cultural themes—of unpredictability (Skolnick, 1994), "Assholes" (Van Maanen, 1978), management brass (Ianni & Ianni, 1983), and the liberal court system (Niederhoffer, 1969) have been cited so frequently as to seem ubiquitous in literature on police culture. Yet there is little consensus on even what the boundaries of a culture are, let alone what themes are and how we distinguish among them.

Below are some general considerations of culture and its themes pertinent to police culture specifically. These considerations have to do with cultural boundaries, and how I developed the boundaries of police culture used in this book.

Boundaries. When we think about culture, we tend to think in imaginatively primitive terms, such as some small group geographically isolated from other groups, perhaps some remote Indian tribe deep in the Amazon rain forest. The principle of geographic remoteness does not apply to the police—they are embedded in and surrounded by other groups. How, then, can we describe boundaries for police culture so that we clearly know who it is that we are studying?

A boundary central to police culture is rank. That a police organization may contain multiple cultures has been suggested by various scholars (Gregory, 1983; Van Maanen & Barley, 1982). Manning (1976) describes a three-tier image of police culture segmented by rank. Distinguishing cultural characteristics, he observes, can be noted at the ranks of line officers, at the middle-management ranks, and at the level of command. While granting that there are core values that mobilize all levels of the police, I will limit the focus of the current inquiry to elements associated with the segment at the bottom of the chain-of-command, line-officer culture. The audience of line-officer culture includes organizational management or "brass" as well as the courts, felons and misdemeanants, the public and the courts. As I discuss in detail later, line officers routinely interact with these audiences, and the routines officers have and values and sentiments that correspond to their routines comprise cultural themes and circumscribe their culture.

The selection of cultural themes. I have deliberately selected the most inclusive, but perhaps also the most undisciplined, means to answer this question, through the identification and discussion of themes identified by other researchers on the topic. This method suffers from problems of validity. Themes are described using writings both from quasi-scientific models of inquiry and from the anecdotal perceptions of police researchers or writings of former cops (see Van Maanen, 1978, for a description of this problem). Distinguishing fact from fancy is nearly impossible (and perhaps artificial). Consequently, I may at times be charged with mixing a fanciful blend of police anecdotes and researcher anecdotes together with more scientific research to create a story rather than to construct meaningful theory. I plea guilty to the charge, offering in my behalf the thin argument that police anecdotes may not be technically true in the sense that accurately represent historical fact or reality. Nonetheless, they may be an accurate reflection of the sentiments and values that characterize police cultures. The study of culture is not simply a pursuit of historical truths, but a search for meanings, values, and traditions as they are sensed, believed, and acted out by particular groups. In this context, anecdotal stories are more than conversational entertainment, they are the carriers of cultural history. To overlook their importance is to neglect a central device of culture itself—its oral traditions and its bases for action.

Theme inclusiveness. When a cultural theme is identified, can it be known if the theme represents only one particular culture in some particular organization, or if it is more inclusive, characterizing beat officers in municipal departments generally? In this book, I identify a diverse array of cultural themes associated with police culture. Yet the apparent pervasiveness of some of these themes undoubtedly derives from the process of academic reproduction of knowledge rather than from our knowledge of police culture in different settings. It is difficult to separate what we know about the police mystique from writings that reflect academic mystique of the police. I try to address this problem by citing a wide variety of materials to illustrate concepts and examples.

Though there are a great number of elements of police culture described in this book, I doubt that the list is comprehensive, or that all themes discussed below will be present in all organizations. Yet, if you step back and look at the picture constructed by the themes of this book, similarities between police cultures become visible, while differences recede into the minutiae of background. In other words, there is a sense of relief in which some themes are highlighted more prominently than others. Culture, in this sense, is a thematic topography. The organization of this book into particular themes is a way to create a working topography of a culture, so that one can think about individual items, concrete behaviors, and their relation to the whole.

Thematic dominance. It is my belief that far too much emphasis has been put on such heavyweight themes of police work as the use of force, coercion, danger, and corruption (Klockars, 1991; Bittner, 1970; see Kappeler, Sluder & Alpert, 1994; Skolnick & Fyfe, 1993). These themes are weighty ideological hammers and clumsy for the weight, too unwieldy to mete out the diversity and subtlety of police culture. That they are salient themes of police culture is beyond question, but they are only a few of many themes, and their meaning is embedded in the context of other elements of police culture.

The way in which culture uniquely characterizes the police does not reside primarily in these most publicly visible attributes of police work, but in the myriad details of occupational activity. Culture is a diffusion of the work-a-day world in which ways of doing work become habitual and habits become meaningful. Culture, like heaven and hell, is sustained, celebrated, and feared; in short, lived in the concrete minutiae of everyday work.

Culture can be thought of as a confluence of themes of occupational activity. The word "confluence" is a metaphor suggesting the emptying of streams and rivers into a common body of water. At a confluence, the particular contributions of individual creeks and rivers are no longer clearly recognizable—the flow is a blend of them all. Police culture is like this. Diverse aspects of organizational activity merge into a whole united by commonly held values and shared ways of thinking. Culture cannot be wholly explained by the presence of any particular theme (though it may be clearly visible through the theme) but rather by the unique mix of them all in a particular occupational setting. The texture of police culture—the entire body of meaning or worldview of its celebrants—lies in the way in which these themes join together in some particular encounter, play off each other, motivate and justify behavior, and are expressed in some story a police officer tells another after a long shift.

Thematic overlap. To what extent are cultural themes discrete entities? In this book I will try to separate them analytically, yet do so with the caveat that in practice they seem to be more like unintegrated congeries than distinct elements (Spradley & McCurdy, 1975). Cultural logic is an astonishing process of circular reasoning encompassing fluid situations: police-citizen interactions that progress unpredictably and rapidly, danger anticipated and resolved in a context of hurried decisions, reactions to potential threats, use of force and applications of street justice, and how to act, to avoid action and corresponding responsibility, or to simply lie in the face of sharply incomplete and inconsistent information from the public, the courts, and from their own superiors. The rush and tedium of everyday phenomena becomes overlaid with cultural meanings and values, general principles and guides for behavior that apply to individual, concrete encounters. Thus, by identifying and analyzing as discrete that which is fluid and highly interrelated I may well be obscuring what was in practice uniquely cultural about them—like explaining a tree through a description of its chemical properties.

There is substantial thematic overlap in the book. This means that many themes tend to be similar to other themes, or that an example that is appropriate to one particular theme may also seem to fit another theme. This teleological phenomenon is unavoidable—aspects of culture tend to a sharing of artistic form, or a sort of emotional and logical consistency. For example, were I to talk about common culture among American youth, I might talk about rock and roll and about rejection of authority. Both themes are powerful currents among young people in the

United States, and perhaps of the world. Yet they overlap considerably—rock and roll tends to be about rejection of authority, and many youths display rejection of authority by listening to (very) loud rock and roll. This suggests that an appropriate metaphor for the relationship between cultural elements and culture is not a construction analogy, where themes can be systematically linked and summed to form a culture, but a growth theme, where similar cellular structures of a single animal tend to subtly modify and shift as they take on different rolls for the group. The cells are all composed of the same basic stuff, sharing a fundamental similarity in nearly all of their characteristics, yet they contribute differently to the functioning of the whole. This is, of course, the classical organic metaphor, widely used among the social sciences. I think it is an appropriate metaphor for the way in which I view the relationship of elements to culture, and how elements come to be infused with purpose and meaning for a particular culture.

I argue that street cops everywhere tend to share some common cultural elements because they respond to similar audiences and share similar functional concerns. Put another way, at the municipal level they operate in similar institutional environments, where the expectations of important actors tend to be similar. By actors, I mean those groups with whom the police interact, and who have expectations about how the police are going to act around them. Police audiences—the public, criminals, lawyers, automobile drivers, the courts, and departmental administrators across the cities and towns of the United States have remarkably similar expectations of the police. These expectations provide the basis for large numbers of common elements among American police organizational cultures. In the following chapter, I will discuss principal audiences of the police, and how they contribute to a common definition of police culture.

Emotions and themes. Culture study is not simply a dry analytical exercise. At its core it is about how police express emotions. Police work is not simply a set of rules that guide what officers do, carried by a municipal bureaucracy that organizes police work. Police work is something more than a set of organizational structures, formal policy, tactics, and strategy. The "something more" is the powerful personal sentiments that officers feel about what they do. To be meaningful, a study of police culture must somehow look beyond overworked and tired ideas of organizational structure and look at the feelings police officers hold for each other and about their work.

The role of emotions are not somehow unimportant to the study of culture: they are part and parcel of the way in which we think about the good life. Emotions, Nussbaum (2001) reminds us, are central to our flourishing. Emotions are part of our "eudaimonia," our sense of flourishing, they "embody the person's own commitment to the object as a part of her scheme or ends" (Nussbaum, 2001:33). When we display emotion, we display it in ways that reveal a blend of social construction, blended with our deeply personal patterns of expression, what Nussbaum calls our "narrative history of the individual personality" (Nussbaum, 2001:173).

Grief for the police is like this. The death of a fellow officer, discussed at the end of this book, is deeply personally felt, a hole in the fabric of personal identity. In the grieving process we witness the reconstruction of the social self, absent the person lost. In police culture, with its clannish relations and close ties, loss is strongly felt and acted out through elaborate rituals. It is a collapse of the personal and social—the death of culture with in the individual, and its reconstruction:

> For as one reweaves the fabric of one's life after a loss, and as the thoughts around which one has defined one's aims and aspirations change tense, one becomes to that extent a different person. This explains why the shift does not take place without a struggle; for it is a loss of self, and the self sees forgetfulness and calm as threatening to its very being (Nussbaum, 2001:83).

If police work is meaningful, then this study of police culture must tap some of the feelings that constitute the social and narrative self. Accordingly, I strive to capture the unpredictability of the work, the seductions of street life, the efforts of officers to peer through the haze of the obvious, the bullshit of police administration, the ironic sense that works so well for officers in the field. And I discuss its moments of grieving. In the writing, I occasionally capture a glimpse of the secret heart of police culture itself.

Themes and the observer. Chapter 1 presented a central concern of cultural studies—any narration of culture is from a standpoint, and the view of the observer is always meshed with the cultural "text" observed. To a large extent, the image of culture herein is a distillation of the views of the many writers about culture included here. Is the image herein an image of "police culture" or it an image of the various cited writer's predispositions and hidden (and sometimes wide open) attitudes concerning the police? For example, do we tend to get a negative, distrustful image of the police from critical reviews of police culture because academic authors tend not to trust police and crime control policy? Do we get an over-sympathetic view of culture from former police officers who are supportive of the police? A curious student might state "I just want to know what's actually going on. Where can I go to get an honest, unbiased view of police culture?"

The answer to this question is the same as for cultural studies generally. There is no such thing as an unbiased or independent view of police culture. People who are wholly unbiased are perfectly uninterested, and they are highly unlikely to write on police culture. Moreover, we bring all kinds of presumptions to bear on police research—our existing knowledge of the police, what we have seen on so-called "reality police" television shows, our experience with the police and with criminal and victims, what we have read about the police, our polity predispositions toward liberalism and conservatism, police contacts our friends have had, and on and on. Writers on the police tend to be dense in these sorts of experiences. They are the least likely not to have some existing standpoint regarding the police. The only way to have a truly independent view of the police is to know absolutely nothing.

To engage the text, as Gadamer so eloquently put it, the reader should not view the themes as descriptions of "categorical information. " The reader should try to comprehend the police from the point of view of the writings in this book, or any other article or book. Knowledge emerges from engaging the text in its own terms. In reading about themes, the right question to ask is "what is the writer about this particular idea trying to convey?" The wrong question (and yes, there are such things as bad questions) is "is the writer right or wrong?" Intellectual growth cannot occur when disagreeable information is discounted. By the same token, it should be recognized that the thematic structure presented here is a creation of the author, not an actual "thing" that exists in police departments. It is a systematic way to think about the swarming babble and rush of social life. Like all cultural studies, it is an inseparable blend of viewer and viewed, cultural text and observer.

The onioness of culture. Think of police culture as an onion.[1] An onion is an apt metaphor—it has heart, but it is a heart shielded from the outside world by several layers of protection. It is a protective layer bitter to many and loved by a few. Crank and Caldero (2001) describe the heart of the onion like this:

> It has a heart that animates every police officer and gives meaning to police work. The heart is how police officers feel and think about their work, how they celebrate their victories and morn their losses It is how they do their work and how it is meaningful to them. Mostly, it is about their commitment to the noble cause and how that commitment is animated in training, in daily police work and in conversations with other police officers (Crank & Caldero, 2001:155).

The "heart" or officer's values, particularly their commitment to the noble cause and the belief that they can make a contribution to society, are imported from broader society. The heart is not an emergent property of police culture. It is brought in from the outside, a product of the institutional environment of policing. Officers are committed to police when they begin, a commitment learned from their families and from their personal and social backgrounds. Research has suggested that, in terms of broad "polity" and ethical values, officer's views are largely in place when they begin police work and do not change much throughout their career (Zhao, He & Lovrich, 1998; Caldero, 1997; Caldero & Crank,

2000). Police work tempers these predispositions and provides them with substantive meaning grounded in everyday circumstances, shared and accumulated in departmental histories.

The layers over the heart of the onion are emergent properties of local culture, which means that they come about from the daily experiences of police work and the ways the experiences are shared by officers. That they are emergent does not mean that they are unique to each department. Police tend to operate in similar institutional environments and face similar functional problems in those environments. That is, they have to deal with the courts, the law, suspects, and the public everywhere. Hence, compatibilities are evident across departments and we can describe police in terms of themes, which are recurring patterns of behavior and values. As Christensen and Crank (2001) remind us, however, departments are only similar to a point. Sharp local differences can be obscured by the seeming similarities in broadly interpreted cultural themes across departments.

That there are layers to the "onioness" of police culture suggests an insulation or a crescive embeddedness of the heart inside its protective shield. The layers of police culture serve purposes of identity formation, protection, and shielding. Each of the layers serves a particular purpose.

The first layer, the layer that encloses the heart and animates its pulse, is their assigned beat, romantically called the **street environment.** This is where patrol officers and detectives carry out their daily work and refers to the various kinds of people line officers come into contact with. Police territories—their assigned spaces—are viewed in a profoundly moral sense. All of its problems are their problems. Their reputations and self-esteem rise and fall on how well they control their territories.

Their territories include suspects, bad guys, and troublemakers. Cops do not see a lot of differences between criminal suspects and troublemakers, who are often believed to be criminal wanna-be's or whose crimes are not yet known to police. "Assholes" are troublemakers who openly criticize the police, who are deliberately rude, or who do not show adequate respect. Sometimes, in racially divided communities, police use ethnicity or skin color to identify who they think is an asshole.

For a few officers all citizens are assholes and potential criminals. These officers have what is called a "siege mentality." For them, there are no friends but, rather, brother and sister officers. The world contains no joy, only dark threats everywhere. For "siege mentality" officers, police culture has ceased to be a source of celebration and growth and has become a psychological prison.

The second layer around the heart of the onion is **uncertainty**. Manning (1989) recognized the central role uncertainty played in police culture. A psychological sense of uncertainty was intimately tied to the external world of disorder and risk. An officer's external focus on order protected him or her from the unpredictable. Crank (1998) identified five different aspects of uncertainty that he called "themes of the unknown."

The capacity to recognize the danger in the unknown is called suspicion. Officers not only deal with legal suspicion, but develop the special skill of sixth sense suspicion. This is the ability to identify wrongdoing from the most trivial of clues. It is based on intuition, not fact, though when it is highly honed it will produce solid evidence. This latter type is the special craft of police work, and officers who construct cases from the most seemingly innocent of clues gain a great deal of status in their organization.

Police officers confront not only real dangers, but operate in a working environment where danger can occur unpredictably. The threat of danger mobilizes much of what the police are about, and danger realized unifies the police unlike anything else. Situational uncertainty refers to the ambiguity police face both with regard to their daily work routines and with regard to the organization itself. The unpredictability inherent in all police work underscores the need for apprenticeship-type training. Common sense among the police lies in their abilities to negotiate their way through uncertain settings to a successful, injury-free conclusion. Police work, as Manning (1997) noted, carries a great deal of contingency. Activity unfolds unpredictably. Activities can become so turbulent that they are physically dangerous. Edge control, the skills police officers have to contain turbulence below the edge of significant danger, is a central skill to police work, and important to understanding the way police officers view danger.

The third layer around the onion's heart is the strong sense of **solidarity** that police officers feel. Their sense of solidarity, what we call the "mask of a thousand faces," is often attributed to camaraderie, the sense of coming together in the face of danger. The perceptions of real and potential danger are a shared bond among police officers. Solidarity is reinforced by the perceptions of many officers that they are isolated from and in conflict with many elements of the public.

Solidarity is a product of conflict with outside groups (Coser, 1956). Recognizing that cultural identity is often forged in conflict with other groups, this layer of the onion is seen as a product of the way in which the police view other groups with resentment and hostility. Some of the conflict is ideological, as when police fret and grouse about defense counsel and lawyers. Consider the following cite from the *New York Times*:

> The city council has put shooting victim Amadou Diallo's name on the section of the Bronx Street where he was killed. The 22-year-old West-African immigrant was killed two years ago when four police officers fired 41 shots at him as he reached for his wallet. The officers, who said they thought he was reaching for a gun, were acquitted of murder and other charges (*New York Times*, 2002).

In this example, the re-naming of the street carries implicitly a powerful condemnation of the police who killed him. The condemnation is from the city council, one of the institutional sovereigns of the police.

That the officers were tried in court also suggests that powerful legal forces were mobilized against them. This example shows that the conflicts facing the police are immediate, diverse, and influential.

Some of the conflict is physical and involves the use of brute and state force, as when the police deal with criminals. Indeed, a central theme of police officer training is officer safety, and officers are constantly reminded that carelessness (i.e., failure to follow cultural lessons) is hazardous. In this layer of cultural identity we see how conflict mobilizes group identity.

This layer is described by themes used by line officers to protect themselves from external oversight. These **are loosely coupling** themes—they allow line personnel to carry out what they see to be the organization's principal business—taking care of crime—while administrators deal with the placation of various groups in the institutional environment. These themes represent ways, widely observed in many police organizations, that line officers avoid observation and control. These themes emerge when line personnel think that particular groups interfere with their ability to do their day-to-day work. One such group is the court system. Police everywhere tend to believe that the legal system is soft on crime, and some of them develop a repertoire of "street justice" skills and techniques so that they can both punish offenders and avoid the courts. Police officers also develop strategies to get around due process constraints on their behavior.

The most important group that line officers protect themselves from are their own administrators and commanders, sometimes simply called brass. Officers tend to have a powerful distrust of their departmental managers (Crank & Caldero, 1991). The influence of influential outside groups, the mayor for example, or the press, is translated into policy through the department's chain of command. Consequently, many of the frustrations line officers have toward outside groups are also focused on the department itself.

In the heart of the onion we can see the way in which broad cultural elements are introduced to policing, indeed, make it possible. The heart is similar in principle to the institutional transmission of cultural elements called the "bypassing of organizational structure" in Chapter 1 (Meyer, Scott & Deal, 1992). In the layers of the onion, we see the emergent, or "individual to society" elements of police culture. Perhaps most importantly, in the play of the themes across all layers, we see the ubiquitous and relentless inter-penetration of individuals and their environments.

Endnote

[1] This metaphor is adapted from and follows closely the discussion presented by Crank and Caldero (2001).

4

Articulating Police Culture and Its Environments: Patterns of Line-Officer Interactions

   The purpose of this section is to lay out the boundaries and audiences of police culture. If police culture is to be understood in terms of grounded aesthetics, then it is necessary to explain the "grounding," that is, the daily situations they encounter and the audiences with whom they interact. Two preliminary observations will be stated and discussed below. First, local police cultures are embedded in and bounded by the departmental organization. Consequently, it is first necessary to discuss how the organization of the police provides the conditions in which line-officers become a cultural-carrying group. Second, the themes studied here arise from observable, every-day interactions officers have with other people. Whether they are criminals, the administration, or citizens, these other people interact with line-officers in recurring, concrete contexts from which the cultural identity of the police emerges. I will also discuss the common, everyday ways in which the police interact with these various groups.

   Police culture is embedded in and bounded by organizational structure. This book adopts Reuss-Ianni's (1983) and Manning's (1989) perspective that culture is differentiated in police organizations. I focus on common culture among line-officers. I argue that culture arises in similar ways across police organizations in large part because the occupational organization of line officers—the squad—is itself similar in all organizations.

   All departments, given sufficient organizational size, are organized at the line level into squads. Rubinstein's (1973:32-43) analysis of the organization of squads in Philadelphia could apply to any city in the United States. Squads worked a six-day week, and were assigned to work shifts at one of three times. Day work was normally from 8 a.m. to 4 p.m., while night work started at 4 p.m. and extended to midnight. The last shift, which Rubinstein called "last out," began at midnight and ended at 8 o'clock the following morning.[1] With minor variation, this shift pattern is omnipresent across municipal police organizations today.[2]

This working schedule, especially in departments where officers rotate across shifts, tends to isolate members of the squad from the public. Former non-police friends, who may work a normal 8-5 job, are unavailable for leisure activities. They frequently work weekends and holidays, and cannot commit themselves to outside engagements that might broaden their friendship networks. Officers are also isolated from most other police officers in the department. They are in contact with members of their squad, but less frequently have contact with officers working other squads and other shifts. Their circle of acquaintances and friends are limited to the fellow cops with whom they come into contact on a regular basis.

Squads are divided into platoons of around 25 officers, each of these directed by a sergeant. The sergeants are answerable to lieutenants, the highest-ranking officer with whom line-officers are likely to make contact. While squads are differentiated by shift, platoons are differentiated by geography. In Rubinstein's study, the platoons were assigned to the "east end" and the "west end," the informal division of the district. Each platoon had its own roll call, but members of the two platoons knew each other and were in frequent interaction during shifts and at the end of shifts.

The period at the end of the shift is a particularly fertile period in which to rehash the activities of the day, to pass on new information about problems, and to tell stories and exploits of particular officers. Pogrebin and Poole, studying a Colorado police department, noted the importance of end-of-shift discussion and interaction for officers. Officers remained well past the end of the shift to "'cool out' from a rough shift, . . . or to vicariously experience the highlights of fellow officers' calls . . ."

> It also provided an opportunity to discuss department policies, politics, and personalities. Rumors made their rounds at this time—with a few being squelched, several being started, and many being embellished (Pogrebin & Poole, 1988:188-189).

End-of-shift thus provided a fertile period for interactions that provided a basis for the emergence of police culture from the shared experiences that officers had encountered during their shifts.

Department-wide common culture emerges because officers are occasionally reassigned to new squads across the organization. Rubinstein noted the importance of the transfer of personnel across squads for the dissemination of common culture.

Occasionally a man transfers from one squad to another, bringing with him knowledge of ex-colleagues which he offers to his new colleagues, enriching their knowledge about co-workers who are frequently seen, greeted, chatted with, but rarely known in the personal way as are the (members of the) squad (Rubinstein, 1973:32).

The fundamental unit of local cop culture is the squad. However, because of transfers over time, and stemming from the inevitable gossip that characterizes the police locker room, squad information is transmitted across the organization and provides a common basis for culture across the organization.

Cultural themes stem from the everyday interactions of the police with their various environments. The members of a squad are in contact on a regular basis with people in their working environments in ways that are governed by particular rules and procedures. By environments, I mean that cops regularly come into contact with particular groups in their everyday working conditions. Cops interact with courtroom personnel in the courthouse and occasionally in the station house; the public, primarily on the streets in vehicular stops or at their houses in response to a call for service; and management, in their offices when they are called to the office to be chastised, or on rare occasion at the scene of a crime after a particularly violent incident. These environments tend to be replicated in similar fashion across municipal districts. Moreover, the work and the organization of squads is similar across jurisdictions. Finally, media influences—radio, television, the movies, newspapers, training films—carry common notions of police values and behavior and thus contribute powerfully to the cultural similarity of police organizations. Police cultures thus tend to be more alike than would be suggested by the sheer diversity of city characteristics, sizes, and types of municipal governments in the United States.

Line officers are not presented with a single monolithic environment in which they conduct their work, but instead confront a series of environments, each with its own particular expectations of the police. Expectations of the police vary across different groups in any particular jurisdiction, and line officers have to present themselves appropriately to different audiences, each of which may have sharply different ideas of the police role (Manning, 1977).[3] It is in the context of these environments, and the particular patterns by which the culture is articulated with the environments, that cultural themes become meaningful, and that we begin to gain an understanding of the powerful currents of solidarity that bind officers.[4]

The Street Environment

The street environment is the first and most salient environment. This is the officers patrol beat where the powerful themes of territoriality, force, and uncertainty are played out. Officers are assigned to a particular area, and become responsible for the production of police activity in that area. In this environment, police behavior reflects the interaction of their personal temperament, the circumstances of the encounter, and the attitudes of the individuals involved in the encounter (Black, 1980). The particular way a police-citizen encounter is resolved is an aesthetic through which officers play out their roles as police. This environment can be separated into the following activity-types that give rise to and sustain police culture.

Citizen-invoked interactions. Citizen-invoked interactions occur when a citizen telephones a department or when an alarm is sounded, and a patrol car is dispatched to the source of the call. This type of interaction accounts for the bulk of police-citizen contacts. It is a reactive style of policing, and powerfully shapes police-citizen relations. For property crimes, police can do little more than take a report. The likelihood of solving the crime is remote, and citizens know this. The police officer is often the verbal target of a citizen's frustration, and police are frustrated in their reactive role, locked into dealing with the problems caused by crime without being able to actually do something about the crime itself. Consequently, these encounters tend to be dispiriting for police and citizens alike; they tend to be perfunctory and ceremonial, satisfying the record-keeping requirements of crime reporting and the needs of insurance companies (Van Maanen, 1973).

Violent crimes tend to be similarly frustrating. These are typically felonies, and about 50 percent of these are solved, depending on the specific offense category. The higher clearance rate associated with these crimes stems from the presence of a witness (the victim) and surprisingly, the frequent presence of the suspect, who as often as not is a friend or member of the victim's family. These crimes are not particularly satisfying, either. As many observers of the police have noted, they involve rough, ordinary crimes of quick violence between friends and acquaintances (Felson, 1994). Instead of providing police with a satisfactory sense of work accomplished, they reveal the seamy, coarse, and destructive side of ordinary human relations. They tend to be repetitive, involving assailants and victims the police have been in contact with before and who are involved in violence over which the police can do little. Far from satisfaction, these contacts tend to breed cynicism and disillusionment among officers (Niederhoffer, 1967). Like property crime, police can do little to prevent violent crime.

For both felony and misdemeanor encounters, the decision to inter-vene is discretionary and affected by factors other than the presence of an apparent violation of the law (Kraska & Kappeler, 1995; O'Conner, 1993; Black, 1980). Police-citizen interactions in this context are some-times contaminated by the toxicity of power for both the police and citi-zens. Affronts to the legitimacy of police authority are commonplace in this environment. The reactive nature of police intervention insures that police activity will occur in the aftermath of crime. As Wilson (1968) noted, police will consequently be trying to do their work in an emo-tional, frequently hostile, and occasionally perilous, environment. In such an environment, distinguishing between offenders and victims is difficult. Because decisions must occasionally be made rapidly, mistakes involving due process, offender identification, and evidence are common. When offenders are present, their interest lies in hiding critical aspects of the crime, further complicating police work. The first layer of cultural mean-ing, coercive territorial control, emerges in this context, and is immedi-ately shrouded in task ambiguity.

Traffic Stops. Line officers routinely come into contact with the citi-zenry through traffic stops. Perhaps because stops are so mundane in the sweep of police activity, observers of the police have paid them scant attention. However, traffic stops are integral to the patrol task. Through the presence of formal and informal quotas, they are semi-articulated—officers are not assigned particular stops, but they often face departmen-tal expectations that they will issue a certain number of citations. Public response to citations is less than friendly. Even in that rarest of traffic stops, when a citizen responds to the news of their violation and impend-ing ticket with "You are absolutely right, officer. I deserve the ticket and will be more careful in the future," cops know that citizens are giving their best shot at appearing apologetic in the hopes that they will be forgiven.

Police-citizen interactions are articulated by the organization. Contact with the public is articulated through the organization. The decision to intervene is at the discretion of the officer, but problems associated with intervention are enveloped in department policy. And if the intervention is followed by an arrest, a panoply of organizational linkages—paper-work, court appearances, and the like—come into play. Dispatchers tell officers where to go, messages are taped, and a vast array of accountabil-ity mechanisms are activated when an officer is dispatched to a scene.

In spite of the seeming autonomy and low visibility of police attributed by many authors to contemporary patrol practices, police-citizen interac-tions are increasingly modulated through the organization. Consequently, much of what I describe herein as police culture—solidarity and loose coupling—stems from this extraordinary task ambiguity and the way in which administrators seek to control line officer-citizen encounters by controlling inputs and outputs through communications and dispatch.

Administrative Environment

The second environment is the organizational administration (Reuss-Ianni, 1983). Line officers are physically present at the police station during two periods each day, prior to and at the end of their shift. Pogrebin and Poole (1988:180) describe both the beginning and the conclusion of shift work, summarized as follows.

Roll call. Prior to the beginning of the shift, officers arrive at the station house and go to their locker room to change into uniforms. They then go to a briefing room for assignments and for roll call. The briefing session lasts for 15 to 20 minutes, during which time officers receive information on the activities of the previous shift, on the focus of the current shift, and on any new policy. Shift sergeants may caution officers on particular dangers, praise them for particular accomplishments, or call attention to particular problems.

Roll call may contain mild rebukes of officers. During roll call, particular officers may be singled out for unpleasant duty, may be given disagreeable temporary partners, or otherwise be the recipient of administrative "bullshit" (see Chapter 21). Jocular humor provides a way in which officers maintain face when subjected to rebuke during roll call (Pogrebin & Poole, 1988). The time periods before and after roll call, when officers are on their way to or from their cars, provide time to talk and exchange information. Police on duty exchange information, meeting covertly away from supervisors. The most important information of the day is sometimes shared among officers on their way to their cars, out of the hearing range of superior officers but not yet in their cars where their conversation can be monitored by radio dispatch.

Shift end. At the end of the shift, officers return to the briefing room to complete their paperwork. Their reports are reviewed by their sergeants, and time is spent debriefing. As Poole and Pogrebin note, officers often spend more time than necessary here, relaxing and exchanging stories about shift activities. Shift end is consequently an environment for the types of interaction and story-telling that contribute to the generation of local cultural knowledge. Officers also may extend the end of the shift to the local pub or to an officer's house, furthering interaction and story-telling—what some observers call bullshit sessions.

Sergeant supervision. During the shift, sergeant supervision is somewhat informal, occurring prior to and during patrol activity. Sergeants are the first link in the chain-of-command above line officers, and are responsible for the supervision of line officers during patrol. Though the sergeant is generally thought of as the most influential person over the day-to-day activities of officers (see, for example, Trojanowicz, 1980; Rubinstein, 1973), there is evidence that sergeants exercise scant control over line personnel (Kappeler, Sluder & Alpert, 1994). Allen and Maxfield (1983), studying arrest, citation, and warrant behavior of officers, found that sergeants had no substantive effects on officers' line activities, and only in a few cases did supervisors' emphasis on work quantity affect officers total output. Surprisingly, even the perception that they worked under arrest quotas had scant impact on arrest practices. Implications were clear:

> The influence of first-line supervisors in directing the behavior of officers is seriously limited. Even though supervisors emphasize a particular performance criterion or suggest that a certain level of performance be met, officers under their command do not seem to respond positively to these cues (Maxfield, 1983:82).

In other words, sergeants were themselves loosely associated with the police culture.

Internal review. Officers are articulated to the organization through internal review procedures. Review may be mandatory, for example, when an officer fires a service weapon, or may occur under subpoena, when an officer is being investigated for wrongdoing or as a witness to other wrongdoing. This is the form of articulation that is most feared by officers (Perez, 1994). It has been hoped that internal review would penetrate police culture and curb its excesses. Unfortunately, internal review is often perceived by line officers as an arbitrary tactic used by management to "hang officers out to dry" rather than as a tool for the uncovering of wrongdoing. Police reformers have failed to recognize that internal review is the source of loose coupling and a powerful stimulus for the development of police culture.

Standard Operating Procedure. The rules binding line officers with the organizational administration are called standard operating procedure (SOP), intended to guide police encounters in specific circumstances. They are written by the administration, and may reflect state and municipal influences over police behavior. Standard Operating Procedure is a typically thick manual that defines the vast array of rules telling officers what they should not do in various circumstances, representing, quipped one officer, "100 years of fuckups." Representing the rules by which the organization seeks to coordinate its functions, the SOP provides little insight into the creative process officers use to deal with their most intransigent concerns—unpredictable police-citizen interactions. Officers recognize instinctively, or from experience if instinct does not provide insight soon enough, that SOP is a tool used punitively, always in retrospect, and by managers who seek to protect themselves from line-level mistakes. For many line officers, SOP represents the systematic formalization of department "bullshit."

The Courts

When line officers make an arrest, they have linked the police with another component of the criminal justice system. The third environment to which the police are articulated is the courts. This articulation is of several types. In the first type, police are articulated through the warrant process. If the police suspect that a crime has occurred, and that evidence for the crime exists, unless there are warrantless bases to obtain information they must seek a warrant. This can be a frustrating process, as Sutton (1991) noted in the following case where a detective recreates his efforts to get an appointment to have a warrant signed:

Receptionist: . . . if that's the case, you don't want to find just any attorney, you want a search warrant. Just a moment, let me check.

Officer: (and I know what they're doing while I'm on hold.)

Attorney #1:   No. Can he come over at 2:00?

Attorney #2:   No. I can't cause I really got to go do this.

Receptionist: Sorry, we don't have anybody right now (Sutton, 1991:435-436).

A variety of additional circumstances articulate police with the courts. If an officer has made a felony arrest, he or she will have to appear at a preliminary hearing. An officer may face cross-examination and direct examination. More frustrating to a line officer is that the case may be postponed, and an officer will have to reappear multiple times during this and subsequent proceedings. Both work and time off may be disrupted at the whim of the court.

During the pretrial phase, the defense has the right of discovery, to find out about all evidence that may be used against the defendant at the trial. The trial itself may demand precious off-duty time. All testimony is recorded and available for reference by the defense for future use. An officer's legitimacy will be measured by the police report, by transcripts of earlier proceedings, the D.A. interview, and by the quality of the evidence (officers sometimes simply forget to bring important evidence with them).

Police legitimacy in the courtroom, based on the legality of their behavior, may be at odds with their street behavior. While on patrol, officers may rely on the presence of a wide variety of subtle cues in deciding where and how to intervene in the affairs of a citizen. Instinct, as much as the presence of articulable cause, may guide their behavior. And arrest may represent a desire to bring justice to some asshole rather than a calculated estimate of the presence of probable cause (Van Maanen, 1978). On patrol, officers learn how to use personal authority to handle situations. In the courtroom, legitimacy is an issue of the quality of the evidence and demeanor in front of the judge, and officers have to express obeisance to the judge.

In spite of high-minded rhetoric claiming that bad guys regularly beat the law because of liberal due process protections, courts operate pretty much like most people would like them to operate. Walker (1994) notes that, of the cases brought from the police to the courts, approximately 30 percent of all cases are rejected by the prosecutor during the pretrial period. That 30 percent are rejected should not be surprising: arrests have a lower evidentiary standard, probable cause (that the crime in fact occurred and the person did it) than do courts (beyond a reasonable doubt, or a moral certainty of guilt). The lower standard, and even lower for initial intervention into citizens affairs—reasonable suspicion— enables the police to conduct their work unhampered by the substantial rigors of proof beyond a reasonable doubt needed for conviction.

Of those cases that are carried forward by a prosecutor, about 95 percent of those result in conviction and some type of penalty. When prosecutors do not carry cases forward, it is for obvious reasons of evidence and witnesses. Due process issues are simply irrelevant to the day-to-day activity of the court. It is extraordinarily rare that a case of murder, robbery, or rape, for example, is rejected for due process reasons: statistically, less than one percent of such cases that are rejected are rejected for due process reasons (Walker, 1994:46-47). Why, then, do the police, who clearly value their common sense (and have a great deal of it) and who have a concrete and practical perspective of the world around them, so profoundly misunderstand and misstate the impact of due process on their ability to do something about "bad guys" in the courtroom, particularly when they are such active participants in the courtroom and should know better? This topic will be discussed in great detail in later chapters. The perception of due process leniency by the courts, a myth at the center of nearly all police beliefs, underscores a great deal of police culture (Kappeler, Blumberg & Potter, 1993).

Media

The fourth area of articulation is with the media, members of which are in frequent interaction with the police. Newspaper reporters are social control agents whose influence can both negatively and positively affect the police. The police know this, and seek their sanction through co-optive strategies. As Ericson (1989) has observed:

. . . the police try to incorporate the news media as part of the policing apparatus. They do so by giving journalists physical space within police buildings, by taking them into account in organizational charts, directives and planning, and by making them part of the everyday social and cultural practices in the police organization (Ericson, 1989:208).

News reporters, particularly the "inner circle," frequently carry scanners so that they, like police, can arrive at the scene of breaking crime events. These are often individuals who support the police and may have worked with them for years. Their values are the values of the police culture. At the scene of a criminal activity, police try to steer the flow of information to friendly reporters, and to avoid the release to others who might also look at the conduct of the police.

Police manage the release of friendly information through the inner circle when possible. They seek to otherwise tightly control the release of information that might ideologically disparage the organization. The strategic use of secrecy and silence enables them to control information to non-friendly press, while inner-circle reporters will censor themselves. Through articulating their relationship with inner-circle reporters, the police seek to assure the support of the media. The police avoid the release of much negative information in this way (Ericson, 1989).

Scandal ruptures the inner circle. Sometimes stories are too hot to be controlled by the inner circle, and pubic relations units cannot contain the sudden, massive investigation of what Ericson (1989) calls the "outer circle." The impact of scandal is massive and dramatic loss of legitimacy of the police. Such events are periods of uncontrolled articulation, chaos personified, formal relations between the police and other groups yielding confusing and poorly regulated communications. Departments are swamped by persons seeking information, officers in different circumstances, ranks, and degree of involvement provide inconsistent accounts of the department, and the veil of secrecy is widely breached, as managers and line personnel alike seek to strategically cover their butts.

In summary, the relationship between line-officers and these groups gives meaning to culture. The values, stories, metaphors, and meanings that give each police culture its unique identity stems from its relations with these groups. Because culture is grounded in the relations of line officers with these groups, culture had an immediacy and practicality often overlooked by students of culture. How police make sense out of, deal with, and pass on knowledge about these groups to recruits is what police culture is all about.

Endnotes

[1] In 1973, when Rubinstein wrote his study of Philadelphia, most major police departments were working rotating shifts, where members of the day squad would shift to the night squad after a couple of months, and then rotate to last out, completing a rotation cycle. In the current era, departments are increasingly abandoning rotating shifts.

[2] I conducted research in eight medium-sized departments in rural and urban locations in Illinois in the late 1980s. All of the squads were organized in the way described by Rubinstein.

[3] Manning (1977:317) describes police presentational strategies as follows: "The equivocation about the police role that characterize most communities permits and encourages the police, especially the administrators, to respond to this public ambiguity and to present and maintain multiple definitions of the police role and function. Typically, they maintain a "private" or covert, and a "public," or open and accessible, version of their policies and practices. Audiences are segmented in this way, and performances are differentially directed and symbolized. The police direct their public performances for the most part to those powerful segments of the community that are most able to legitimate them as an organization." In this book, I view segmentation that not only affects the administrators role but the line officer's as well, and in which one segment is the administration of the police organization.

[4] Some have referred to the criminal law as a relevant environment to which organizations must respond. In this research, I conceptualize environments in terms of interactional contexts. The environments contain people. Thus, each of these four environments may invoke the criminal or civil law, but the law in itself will not be conceived independently of an environmental context.

Understanding Police Culture

Part II

Coercive Territorial Control

The first topical area is what I call the coercive control of territory. I link three themes; dominion, use of force, and guns, each of which are briefly reviewed in this opening section. Coercive control of territory is a grounded aesthetic—grounded, because its meaning derives directly from normal daily routines of police officer activity, and aesthetic, because the use of coercion and control of territory are done in particular ways, reflecting officers' styles or behavioral preferences.

Coercive control of territory is presented at the beginning of the discussion of themes for several reasons. First, many observers of the police view coercion in its various forms as the core of police work (see, e.g., Bittner, 1970; Klockars, 1991). I do not take such a strong position; I believe that themes are comprehensible only in the context of the others. Yet coercion and territory, because they are of wide interest and are widely recognized as important, provide a basis for launching the general discussion of police cultural themes. By reviewing common conceptions of these themes, I accept a well-established starting point for thinking about police culture.

Coercive territorial control is defined as follows. The term coercive means that the police seek to gain control through practical applications of compliance when faced with someone who does not want to give compliance. This very general notion of coercion encompasses such diverse aspects of force as the use of lethal force, the use of pain compliance to control the behavior of suspects, lying to gain information when a suspect does not wish to provide that information, or thumping someone who refuses to accept the police definition of a situation. The legality or illegality of compliance is secondarily relevant to the imperative that it be obtained. Cops may strategically use symbolic elements of their authority as coercive devices as well—displaying their weaponry in an intimidating way, for example.

When I use the term territorial control, I am referring to the physical geography of police work—the beat, or the jurisdiction in calls for assistance or other emergencies, that pragmatically bounds the daily routines of officers. However, I prefer the term dominion to territory to better capture the relationship between police and their geographical assignments. Dominion implies a moral imperative that links an officer effectively to a territory (Van Maanen, 1978; Manning, 1978). The use of coercion is license bestowed by society to achieve that moral imperative (Klockars, 1991). Subjectively, it means to an officer that they do what they must to control their turf in face-to-face encounters with citizens.

Guns emerge as an important theme in this section because they are regarded by cops as the core element of an officer's capacity to protect himself or herself from the criminals. At the core of coercive territorial control is the idea of effectiveness in territorial control. Officers are taught to always use sufficient force to resolve situations, and often they learn informally to always use more force than is necessary. The notion that they would limit their use of force is incomprehensible. Cops do not cry uncle in the face of superior firepower. Anyone who has observed the authority of the range master, or the care and knowledge officers have of their weapons, will comprehend the importance of this infrequently studied area of police culture.

Coercive territorial control provides a historical basis for understanding the contemporary importance of law enforcement in police work. By carefully considering the three elements in this section—force, dominion, and guns—we can see how the contemporary emphasis on law enforcement has shaped police culture and we can gain some insight into one of the most profound though unrecognized changes in contemporary policing—the militarization of cop identity (Kraska & Kappeler, 1997). By studying force and territory as cultural themes, we also gain insight into limitations of contemporary efforts to control the so-called "dark side" of police culture, frequently described in terms of corruption, secrecy, and brutality against citizens (Kappeler, Sluder & Alpert, 1994).

Training provides officers with techniques and skills at different levels of force and provides knowledge in the use of pain compliance, both of which are techniques that weigh a police response against an offenders behavior and perceived danger. As officers develop street sense, they learn to bring more force to bear than is needed to control situations and to thus minimize potential resistance. Ultimately, officers develop particular tricks involving the use of force that simply overwhelm potential threats to their well being. Learning about the use of force comes from the sharing of problems, stories about their resolution, anecdotes, and examples concrete and metaphorical. They teach each other what to do in all kinds of police-citizen encounters, how to inform the brass of what they did, and how to cover their ass in a courtroom when they are held accountable for their use of force. Effectiveness in the use of force is thus a cultural commodity, a core of information about what works and against whom, traded in stories about what cops do and passed on to rookies by field training officers. Effectiveness not measured by some objective calculus of financial expenditure, but subjectively in terms of common sense, local values, and organizational traditions.

A common thread in all the themes is that they have concrete meaning, situationally applied, regarding the use of coercion in the control of particular territories. The themes in this section derive their value and energy from the way in which they harmonize with each other in the occupational setting of the police. Together, they provide the moral sensibility for thinking about cops' self-accepted responsibilities to wield crime control. These themes also provide an extensive litany of metaphors, stories, and ironies that provide a great deal of the common sense knowledge of policing.

5

The Moral Transformation of Territory

Dominion: (pl.) an order of angels. (*Merriam-Webster's Collegiate Dictionary*, Eleventh Edition, 2003).

In the heart of every cop is a sense of morality, strong in some and weak in others, but always present. In spite of all the statistical chaff used as hiring criteria in the contemporary era, morality is the bottom line—if they lack it they will not be hired, they will resign, or they will be weeded out. Cop culture works in large part because cops start out with a common residue of moral values associated with the traditional, small-town that symbolizes mainstream America. The fires of cop culture are not suitable for everyone—the texture of the clay has to be just so. Police culture transforms and unifies cops with a shared perception of social justice. Assigned to a territory for which they are responsible, they hold dominion over a shared vision of justice.

Bestowed with a specific beat assignment, working alone, and provided a portion of automobile-enhanced discretion, they act out their subjective, shared sense of morality every time they decide whether, how, and when to intervene in the affairs of the citizenry. They are granted moral dominion over a turf and act, insofar as they are permitted or can get away with, as sovereigns. That which interferes with their sovereignty stokes the fires of culture, be it the brass, the press, department policy, the courts, university educators, or the public. Details of control that we social scientists carefully ponder—for example, was the intervention for purposes of order maintenance, service, or did somebody actually break the law are simply irrelevant. It is their territory and exists to be controlled. To do less is to fail utterly.

Territory is, for cops, more than a geographical assignment. It is their prize for being morally righteous, a divine gift, placed in their care so that they can deal with the assholes and bad guys of the world. A cop's territory is theirs, not management's, not another cop's, certainly not the media's, those sovereigns of a darker order. And cops take it very seriously.

I use the term "dominion" rather than the more traditional term "territory" to capture the spirit of responsibility that is associated with a geographical assignment. The term territory is fertile in the wrong way, rich in intimations of geographical description that suggest a detailed practicality in police activity. What is wrong with that image is its inability to recognize that cops view their territory as a morally invested responsibility. The term "dominion" captures the divine responsibility over secular human activity that characterizes the special relationship cops have with a piece of earthly terrain. Because the more common term for this responsibility is simply called "territory" I will review literature on that topic.

Territories are spaces freighted with meaning. Were one to view territory from a operational or "management culture" perspective, one might use descriptors such as deployment effectiveness, neighborhood coverage, response-time, span-of-control, emergency responsiveness, and the like. One might further break out colorful tables derived from operations research techniques that show intersecting lines of available manpower, squad sizes, and variations in assignment, and speak about maximizing efficiencies.

Police reformers and executives have been doing this or related sorts of scientific management since the turn of the century, believing that such efforts will instill greater efficiency in police work. And they have completely missed the point. Territory is about dominion over people, those that live there, work there, recreate there, or commit crime there. Territory is freighted with human values and meaning, not the least of which are those values held by cops. Territory is, in a word, dominion.

Territory carries a great deal of meaning for the police. Police territories are infused with important values—commitment and responsibility—that surpass simple conceptions of spacial arrangement and population flows. Officers do not simply patrol areas, they control them, and they invest their energies and reputations in them. Areas are an officer's responsibility, a trust from the state and an obligation an officer accepts to keep the peace. It is a place to protect the weak, the kind, and the hard-working citizens from the predators.

Territories are normally organized as beats. A beat is an assigned geography, whose particular dimensions are historically based on common-sense divisions of community boundaries, the road and train system, the distribution of precinct stations, and geographic features of the jurisdiction. Larger communities are separated into sectors, and each sector is again separated into specific patrol beat assignments. Officers patrol their assigned beat, which usually means that they drive around in them, though sometimes they may ride a horse in them, walk in them, or bicycle in them. They stay within their beat and take total responsibility for maintaining the peace there. When a dispatcher sends out a call at a particular address, only the assigned officer will go, though other officers may be invited in to back up that officer. The first officer is in charge of the call—it is their call, and backup decisions are made by them. Unless invited, other officers never officially enter another officer's beat. They may occasionally see their sergeant in their beat, or encounter detectives when there is a serious crime. Except for those infrequent occasions, the beat is their exclusive responsibility.

Random preventive patrol enhances territorial control. The contemporary practice of police patrol, called random preventive patrol, is based on a philosophy of geographical crime deterrence. Officers are supposed to drive around unpredictably and randomly in their assigned areas, so that criminals will not know where they are. Absence of predictability is supposed to act as a deterrent to crime.

Random preventive patrol was founded in the early part of the twentieth century. August Vollmer implemented automobile patrol in Berkeley, California in 1914, and added radios in 1921. (Walker, 1977). Vollmer believed that automobile patrol would lead to an end of crime in the United States; that criminals would be preoccupied with the threat of a potential police encounter, that they would not know where the police were and would face an increased likelihood of capture. Today, random preventive patrol is a highly institutionalized form of police patrol whose effectiveness is unquestioned in most police organizations, and is widely practiced in police departments in the United States today.

Random preventive patrol is proactive police work. What some police managers and most academic researchers fail to understand is that random preventive patrol is a myth of operational effectiveness nowhere seriously practiced: Cops simply do not drive around randomly.[1] Officers certainly spend a large part of their days driving around in cars, but their driving patterns are intentional, not random. The phrase "random preventive patrol" itself is self-contradictory, without meaning. To suggest that an officer's driving pattern can be "designed" to be "random" or that officers will not seek out crime, hot spots, or troublesome individuals when they are driving around is nonsense.

Random preventive patrol has gotten a bad reputation in recent years, largely because it is said to force police into an ineffective, reactive or "post-crime" mode (Moore, Trojanowicz & Kelling, 1988). By random I mean that a police dispatcher receives a call from a citizen to deal with some problem, the dispatcher calls a patrol car, and the patrol car responds to the call. This is ineffective, reformers contend, because officers are thought to spend large quantities of their time as report-takers; showing up after unsolvable crimes have occurred, dealing with disconsolate victims, and taking hopeless reports. Contemporary advocates of reform contend that, to make the police more proactive, that is, to get them on the "front" end of crime rather than after the criminal event, the police must develop different types of patrol tactics.[2] This is typically called police proactivity, which means that the police use tactics that allow them to anticipate crime or track criminals.

What is often not realized is that so-called random preventive patrol permits many opportunities for proactive activity on the part of individual officers. Officers drive around purposefully, not randomly. Random preventive patrol is a way of doing police work that allows officers to control their territories as they see fit. From philosophy to procedure, it is tremendously liberating. Officers have the discretion to do what they want where they want it, guided by the cultural stipulation that they must control what goes on in their territory.

Officers on "random preventive patrol" are engaged in a great deal of proactive activity. They drive around in areas where there are problems that they want to monitor, and where there are people whom they want to track. The officers also check out alleys where hookers take their johns, and scope corners where gangs compete for turf. They know who the assholes and troublemakers are, and they look for them. They know who is getting out of prison, or where the family of an absconder lives, and they check out those places regularly. They repeatedly drive by known drug distribution areas, particularly houses associated with crack and heroin abusers. They carefully drive through projects, making a presence and checking automobiles. Indeed, on the beat, they are anything but automatons driving around randomly in the faint hope that they will inadvertently scare off a potential felon. They are cagey observers of dangerous people and places—they are not afraid to look or to intervene, and they know how to be devious. They put pressure on particular problems when the shift commander wants them to do so. When they do paperwork, they may park at hot spots, where they can make their presence known or where they can keep an eye on a troublesome area. In short, their work is not, by any stretch of the imagination, random or reactive.

Thus, in the strategic guise of randomness and deterrence, police are highly proactive. Random preventive patrol provides officers with a great deal of discretion, and that discretion is used to seek out and identify problems in their territory. That police are in a patrol car means that they can easily go to any part of their beat where there might be a problem— that there is no area that they cannot access because it is too far to reach. A car consequently contributes to a cop's dominion over their territory, and the illusion of randomness provides large quantities of time and discretion to invoke their sense of righteous control in keeping the peace. It would be difficult to provide more proactivity for police than is provided by the highly discretionary patrol behavior associated with random preventive patrol.

How Officers Use Patrol Time

In practice, random preventive patrol means that officers have a great deal of police discretion to determine if, how, and when to intervene in the affairs of the citizenry. In an insightful essay into patrol officers' use of discretion while on patrol, Greene and Klockars (1991) surveyed the Wilmington, Delaware Police Department, a medium-sized agency of 244 officers. They examined the agency's Unit Activity Files, the files of patrol units assigned to fixed district patrol areas in Wilmington. The single largest block of workload activity, coded "clear," accounted for 29.3 percent of officer's time and referred to time in unassigned patrol activity.[3] It is during this time that officers have the opportunity to be engaged in proactive patrol activity. Officers also spent three percent of their time investigating suspicious circumstances, also proactive activity. These numbers total nearly 33 percent of an officer's total time on patrol.

Greene and Klockar's (1991) findings are important for two reasons. First is their finding that police spend a greater proportion of their time on law enforcement than has been generally thought (Wilson, 1968; Eck & Spelman, 1987; Goldstein, 1987; Bittner, 1970).[4] Historically, police have been thought to be involved in order-maintenance and service activities, employing limited and generally ineffective practices to deal with problems of law enforcement (Wilson, 1968; Goldstein, 1979). The finding that officers spend the largest single block in "clear" time, that is, time wholly self-directed, lends itself to a different way of thinking about random preventive patrol. Greene and Klockars (1991) astutely noted that the workload represented value choices by police on patrol. Unfortunately, they did not discuss what the value choices were. A thoughtful consideration of unstructured time, representing nearly one-third of their work (as stated above), suggests that officers use free time to create "pressure" on identified crime problems, check on hot spots, look for gang activity, seek out known offenders or troublemakers—in short, to do all the things discussed previously that enable officers to exert proactive control over their territorial dominion.

Unstructured time fuses in a practical way the use of automobile patrol to the demands of territorial control, and provides police with the opportunity to exercise, as Greene and Klockars (1991) noted, value choices. Value choices, however, are not only between service, order maintenance, and law enforcement activity—a distinction more important to academics and managers than to cops—but in where they should be, in what they should do when they have arrived, and what sort of force will sustain their dominion over their territory.

Territory is practical knowledge. Police proactivity in patrol activity is also revealed in Rubinstein's (1973) enlightening discussion of territory. Rubinstein observed that the organization of a police officer's cognition—the way they viewed their working space—occurred in terms of immediate and practical considerations of territoriality. To understand why geography is so important, one had to consider what the geography of a sector looks like to an outsider: street signs may be lost or turned, and an officer does not know where he or she is. District geography, he suggested, made sense when one considered how a recruit learned about their working environment. The absence of a fixed territorial referent was particularly troubling to recruits, trained as they were to be fearful of the unknown and constantly pushed by their training officers to keep track of where they were in case they had to call for backup. The memorization of the street system occurred rapidly, under pressure from trainers and reinforced by the constant need to respond to calls for police service.

Officers learned that they could create private space for themselves at prominent public places. Fire stations and hospitals provided places where an officer could make a phone call, wash up, or simply relax for a few moments. Officers on day patrol tended to restrict their work to the main streets because there was little activity on less-used side streets. Back roads, Rubinstein noted, were of greater interest during the night. Intersections were of particular interest, because they were the scene of accidents, traffic violations, and sometimes marked gang boundaries.

Officers eventually memorized their sector assignments. Knowledge, Rubinstein noted, was detailed:

> He learns the names and directions of the streets, and he knows each intersection by its buildings. His knowledge of the streets is dictated by his concern to achieve maximum visibility with his car . . . he pays careful attention to the little connecting streets and alleys. He examines, in time, every empty space to see if he can drive his car through it. He carefully checks empty lots and fields to see whether he can drive his car over them (Rubinstein, 1973:137).

Knowledge of particular buildings was determined by the officer's obligations. Those visited regularly were those that were friendly, or that had required log sheets for the officer to sign. Officers learned the "name, location, and proprietor of each taproom, bar, and private drinking room . . ." (Rubinstein, 1973:140) as they were often the setting for his work. This body of knowledge was practical, and defined the limits of an officer's responsibility.

Geographical knowledge was also private knowledge. Officer's knowledge of their area was for their use only; they did not discuss it with other cops, and they did not inquire too keenly about things having to do with other cops' territory. It was not shared with other cops because the sector was the responsibility of the assigned officer—no one else had a right to it.

Officers learned what Rubinstein called a "highly particularized" knowledge of the people and activities in their sectors. This knowledge was normative, which meant that officers developed a sense of what was normal and acceptable, and what hinted at being out-of-kilter. Knowledge of local behavior and ideas of how the streets should be used transformed officers into specialists of the ordinary and commonplace. It is the ordinary in their dominion, the simple familiarity with people and places that indicated an absence of trouble—that all was well.

Territory is people. Territory has a distinguishing geography, and the geography provides the cognitive structure of an officer's knowledge. Territory is occupied by people, and the people define the way in which an officer acts out his or her sense of responsibility. Van Maanen provides us with an understanding of the link between territories of geography and of people. Officers, he noted:

> . . . come to know, in the most familiar and penetrating manner, virtually every passageway—whether alley street or seldom used path located in their sector. From such knowledge of this social stage comes the corresponding evaluations of what particular conditions are to be considered good or bad, safe or unsafe, troubled or calm, usual or unusual, and so on . . . these evaluations are also linked to temporal properties associated with the public use of a patrolman's area of responsibility . . . the territorial perspective carried by patrolmen establishes the basic normative standard for the proper use of space (Van Maanen, 1978:226).

The physical geography of an officer's territory is overlaid by a human geography, and normative standards regarding the human use of the sector or beat geography guide police behavior. When normative standards are not met, when someone is violating the law or disturbing the public order, the police intervene. Because intervention is a discretionary decision made by individual officers based on their subjective estimation of circumstances, the successful resolution of the intervention is a measure of their self-worth. Control of their territories, by whatever force necessary and under any and all conditions, is consequently a principal measure of their self-esteem, and efforts to limit their right to intervene will be resisted.

Officers view their right to intervene as an absolute authority in all circumstances. This is different from more civil libertarian conceptions of the police, in which the right of the police to intervene in the affairs of the citizenry occurs only when a law has been broken. When legal infractions occur, police tend to think of offenders as "bad guys." Yet, when the public order is violated, police intervention is as rapid and as righteous, whether or not a law has been broken. Violators of the public order may be labeled "assholes" and may be treated brutally, without the legal niceties of due process (Klockars, 1986).[5]

During a three-year period, Fletcher (1990, 1991) interviewed 125 Chicago police officers. The product of her interviews are police stories about police crime activity. The chapters of her book—the street, violent crimes, sex crimes, narcotics, property crimes, and organized crime, are an astonishing compendium of stories of real police work presented à la film noir. The following story shows an infrequently noted aspect of police behavior—providing assholes the opportunity to leverage themselves into trouble and justify aggressive police response.

> I try to deal with people on a human level, on the human side. Even the lowliest asshole that I'll confront on a day-to-day basis, I'll give him his due. "Good morning, sir" or "May I be of service to you?"—something to that effect. I let them go off on me. Because once you go off on me, or call me out on my name, or you're disrespectful to me, now it's my rules. Now we're gonna play this by my rules (Fletcher, 1991:283).

Intervention is also acceptable for service-related phenomena as well. A police officer will stop to inquire about the plight of a motorist with a flat tire in a bad neighborhood. The flat tire may be a ruse, and the officer wants to take a closer inspection of the circumstances. Or the officers may genuinely be concerned about dangers confronting the motorist. Either circumstance justifies intervention.

Importantly, many cops do not believe that they need a reason to intervene. Distinctions of service, order maintenance, and law enforcement, are useful for administrative pigeonholing their work, and useful to the unremitting and insufferable flow of social scientists who pick and prod at their work, giving them silly questionnaires full of nonsensical questions. Officers intervene because they want to intervene. They are sovereigns of their dominion.

The geography of a territory is given meaning by the flow of people through it, and problems are associated with the people that inhabit particular locations. Intersections, for example, become important because gangs may use them as boundaries, or because the pattern of the lights seems to invite an unusually high number of traffic violations or accidents. Certain bars are of interest because they generate many calls, perpetuate DUIs, or are a way to meet women. Older trailer parks may be known for the high numbers of child and spouse abuse calls. Subsidized housing projects are tricky because they are seen as always dangerous for cops—some police shun them, while others seek them out as a source of activity.

Herman Goldstein (1979) observed that a small number of locations accounted for most recurring crime. He argued that the police should shift out of traditional, "reactive" modes and focus on these "hot-spot" areas. Today his approach is called problem-oriented policing. His seminal work deserves all the accolades it has received. However, in some ways he was re-discovering what patrol officers had been doing already, though more informally because departments harbored illusions of patrol randomness—street cops were using their large quantity of unallocated time to deal personally with problem area. His work gave the stamp of legitimacy on administrative recognition of cop territories, and justified the investment of more resources to bear on problems than any single cop could ever be authorized.

Herbert's Normative Ordering of Space

The cultural dimensions of territory have often been overlooked. An ethnography of Los Angeles patrol by Steve Herbert (1997) begins to fill in this important theme of police culture. Social action, he noted, always occurs in space, and social, cultural, and spatial elements of police activity are "deeply intertwined" (Herbert, 1997:21). For this reason, observers of police culture must "pay attention not only to its social and cultural construction, but also to its intractable spatiality; in working to uphold socially constructed notions of public order, officers define and seek to control the spaces they patrol" (Herbert, 1997:21).

Herbert extended his analysis to a consideration of the values that characterize police use of territory. Use of territory, he suggested, was socially constructed in terms of a series of "normative orders," and linked the spacial nature of police work to social and cultural factors (Herbert, 1997:18). Normative orders provided a "range of rules and permissible practices organized around a central value" (Herbert, 1997:39).

Police work was characterized by several normative orders. These normative orders, Herbert observed, were each "centered on a celebrated value" and structured the use of police space. Normative orders and their celebrated value are as follows: The law focuses on preserving legal regulations. Bureaucratic control is about the maintenance of intraorganizational order through the chain of command. Adventure/machismo is a celebration of courage and strength. Safety values the preservation of life. Competence is the demonstration of competence and worthiness of respect. And morality is goodness through triumph over evil. These normative orders may at times represent competing or conflicting value systems. Herbert provided the example of an officer pulled off a high-speed pursuit by a superior officer. The officer chose between adventure and morality, on the one hand, and bureaucracy on the other. Herbert's important contribution is the recognition of the way in which culture, values, and space are deeply intertwined, and that value conflicts may arise in officers' social construction of territory.

Reuss-Ianni's Territory and Cops' Rules

Elizabeth Reuss-Ianni (1983), in her research on police in New York City, has provided an illuminating case study of the dimensions of police culture. She described the linkage of territory to responsibility as a process, defined as the "formal and informal relationships between environment and behavior within the precinct and between the precinct and other environments" (Reuss-Ianni, 1983:10). In diverse and rapidly changing street environments, decisions were made of necessity at relatively low organizational levels.[6] Organizational subgroups, usually squads, sometimes other detectives and other units adapted to the demands of particular territories. Their work was territorially specific, tailored to the social and cultural conditions of their assigned geographic responsibilities.

Management cop culture, Reuss-Ianni argued, has sought to provide universal principles of administrative governance and accountability to a police tradition of local autonomy and decentralized decisionmaking. This means that administrators have applied a wide body of rules and procedures to the traditional domain of local territorial responsibility, seeking to regulate and standardize what officers do in their territories. Bureaucratic efforts to control line officer activity have been poorly received by beat officers, who view the intrusion of management culture as ineffective, arbitrary, and self-serving. Management encroachment into local territories consequently drives a great deal of street-level culture.

Reuss-Ianni identified several fundamental elements of street cop culture. Following Manning's (1977) observation that cops' rules tend to be site specific, she noted several responsibilities having to do with territory.

1. Don't get involved in another officer's sector. This injunction means that other cops are accountable for their territory and "must live with the consequences."

2. Don't leave work for the next tour. This has to do with practical exigencies of work—putting gas in the car, failing to take a complaint.

3. Hold up your end of the work. Don't slack off, or someone will have to pick up the work.

Territory seamlessly fuses with line responsibility, and shared ideas of beat responsibility are a powerful cultural theme that seek to limit the intrusiveness of management brass. The following maxims reflect officers' efforts to limit management intrusion into their territorial autonomy.

1. Keep out of the way of any boss from outside your precinct. Officers develop accommodations with the bosses of their precincts. Bosses from outside are unknown authority figures, who are not to be trusted.

2. Know your bosses. "Knowing your bosses" means that you can adjust your expectations and activities for the tour to what you know about their expectations and style of supervision.

3. Don't do the boss's work for them. If a peer is shrinking from his or her responsibility, don't tell the boss about it.

4. Don't make waves. This is one of the ubiquitous maxims of police culture, and will be referenced frequently in this book. In this instance, it means "don't mess with the system." If you do, bosses will pay more attention to what both you and your peers are doing.

5. Don't give them too much activity. If you provide too much activity, that is, write too many tickets or the like, you bring unnecessary attention to both yourself and your peers.

These maxims place responsibility at the lowest organizational levels and bring peer pressure on cops to avoid management oversight. The discretionary demands of territorial decisionmaking, coupled with administrative efforts to control line behavior, consequently account for a great deal of secrecy associated with street culture.

The fusion of responsibility and territory has implications for media relations as well. The following story from Klein captured the keen sense of pride in accomplishment that officers hold over their ability to control their assigned territory. Klein's story reveals the moral indignation aroused when a cop's control over their beat is challenged by a negative press release.

> In 1961 I was assigned to command the Detective Squad in Central Park. As a native New Yorker I had made use of just about every recreational facility of the park as a child, youth, man. Now that I was to have a personal interest and responsibility for the protection of the users of this area, I set to work to learn exactly what the conditions were, and determined to remedy those that had brought about the park's bad reputation . . . The newly assigned captain shared my enthusiasm and determination to improve conditions, and together we designed programs to eliminate various evils that had affected the morale of the men assigned to the overall command, as well as the security of the public, who had become apprehensive about using the park and its facilities. Within a year we were able to point with pride to a record of solid accomplishment. Reported crime took a marked drop; few serious crimes had taken place, and the arrests for these crimes had increased apace . . .
>
> One day I was reading the newspaper with the largest circulation in the city. Upon reaching the editorial page I was shocked by the picture that graced its upper-righthand corner. There, over the signature of C.D. Bachelor, whom I considered to be the finest editorial cartoonist in the country, was a cartoon with the caption "Central Park—Shame of the City." It depicted two people seated on a lawn, surrounded by trees bearing snakes labeled, "Rape," "Robbery," and "Death." This was a foul blow. When I cooled off and permitted my reason to rise above my punctured pride, my desire to strike back was tempered by my respect for my adversary (Klein, 1968:166-168).

The storyteller subsequently contacts the cartoonist, who suggests that he write a letter to the editors of the paper. The author does so, and receives a handwritten note of apology and a promise to print his objections in the paper.

The next day my letter appeared in this newspaper's letters-to-the-editor column, and from then on very little appeared in print that was derogatory to "my" park (Klein, 1968:168).

Challenges to officers' abilities to control their territories are, as suggested by this story, a fundamental threat to their sense of self-worth.

The Future of Dominion: Morality and Community Policing

In recent years a new image of police territorial responsibility has emerged—a "community-based" notion of police, sensitive to and responsible for the preservation of local communities and neighborhoods. Traditionally, responsibility has been associated with an identifiable geographic context—the beat. However, contemporary efforts to rethink the role of the police have resulted in a mystification of this traditional notion of territory. This change has profound implications for dominion, and for police culture.

We are in what has been called a sea change in policing (Hartmann, 1988). The generic term for this change is "community-based policing," a term that covers a lot of strategic and tactical ground, but seeks in the most general sense to (1) expand the scope of legitimate police interventions so that the police can deal more effectively with issues of community protection, and (2) to build bridges between police and the public that will enhance police intelligence and involve the public in a more direct way in their own self-defense.

The expansion of the scope of legitimate police interventions was central to Wilson and Kelling's (1982) "Broken Windows" essay, in which the authors argued that police needed to re-focus their efforts away from an abstract and individualist notion of law enforcement and address the needs of specific communities.[7] In "Broken Windows," the need to protect local communities provided the justification for the intervention of the police into the affairs of the citizenry. Wilson and Kelling suggested that the legal bases of police intervention—including arrest authority—should be expanded beyond law enforcement situations to encompass circumstances where the public order is violated. Wilson and Kelling used an analogy that they called broken windows to describe what they perceived to be modern processes of urban decay. Houses, they argued, are generally safe until there are outward signs of disrepair, such as broken windows. The presence of these signs of decay initiates a period of rapid decay and deterioration.

Neighborhoods, they proposed, are the same way: once a few human "broken windows"—prostitutes, derelicts, drunks, and their like—appear the neighborhood will rapidly deteriorate unless the police intervene.

Police intervention consequently must begin early, and must focus on the problems of order-maintenance—the street people, to prevent the onset of serious criminal activity. Police, according to this perspective, become the means for the reproduction of informal social control in communities invaded by criminal influences. Savvy police officers, they argued, use their skills to maintain already existing ideas of community order, and thus protect communities whose informal standards of order are threatened.

The authors advocated for an expansion of the authority of the police to intervene in the affairs of the citizenry when the public order was threatened. As defenders of the public order, officers could use their unique sense of the "normal" in a community to determine how, when, and whether to intervene. Many researchers have commented on the mythic history of urban reform that underlies the broken windows essay (Walker, 1984). Nevertheless, the metaphor that undergirds it—community disorder, if left unattended, will escalate to serious crime—has become central to notions of effectiveness in community policing. By advocating an enhanced basis for intervention, the broken windows theory has expanded territorial authority to symbolic territories—previously moral communities on the edge of criminal collapse.

Community policing also appears to hold promise as a way to soften management-line hostilities, a widely cited condition of police organizations in the United States. Wilson, in an earlier work (1968), had noted that police managers who sought to professionalize their departments tended to put into place policies to control line discretion, an ill-fated move: it tended to alienate line officers from brass and intensify secretive elements of the police culture. The so-called "professional" style of management cops has been a principal grouse for street cops for years, who see management cops as too controlling and unsympathetic to realities of the "street." Because community policing strategies expand line discretion and decentralize organizational authority, line-brass conflicts might be diminished, and secretive elements of the police culture lessened (see Sykes, 1989). Indeed, advocates have suggested that under the discretionary model of policing associated with community policing, the traditional bases for police culture will cease to exist. It has been further suggested that police culture cannot survive where police have forged a close link with the public, also a central theme of community-based policing. Thus, both through a return to high levels of police discretion, and through enhanced and more positive police-citizen relations, community policing offers an end to police culture.

The end of police culture? Such an outcome is neither likely nor reasonable. It is more likely that enhanced police discretion under a community policing mandate will lead to sharply different outcomes: indeed, community-based policing may inadvertently contribute to the further entrenchment of police culture. In a recent article, Bob Langworthy and I (Crank & Langworthy, 1996) explored some of the practical implications of community-based policing for police culture. Our concerns principally focused on the "how" of community-based policing. If community-based policing is to be anything more than a rhetorical smoke-screen (Klockars, 1991), then street-level police must do something different from what they traditionally have done. The rub, we thought, did not lie in identifying what they would do that was different from traditional practice; that is fairly well established (see, e.g., Skolnick & Bayley, 1986). The more problematic issue was how cops were to be held accountable for what they did differently. We noted that:

> Community-based policing emerged in response to the perception that police were not accountable to urban problems, and is largely about being accountable to neighborhood needs, particularly in traditionally neglected minority communities. How, then, is accountability to be accomplished?

> Police organizations . . . draw from two internal accountability mechanisms: as bureaucracies they hold line officers accountable through standard operating procedures, and as quasi-military organizations, they hold officers accountable through [the] chain-of-command. Neither of these is likely to disappear . . . (Crank & Langworthy, 1996:225).

To the contrary, both are likely to expand as the work of the police expands. Yet it is precisely these accountability mechanisms that alienate street officers from managers, that spur the growth of police culture. Moreover, the maintenance of public order is an area of policing in which ideas of effectiveness are vague at best, lacking the relative clarity of action associated with law enforcement interventions. Cops know when a law is broken, but "out of kilter" order maintenance situations are much more vague. To expand accountability in an area considerably more ill-defined than the criminal code will inevitably invite a sharp growth in the police culture, as officers develop strategies to protect themselves from vague expectations for which they will be held responsible.

Community-based policing is not a solution for the "blue curtain" secrecies associated with the police culture. If not carefully implemented, the expansion of police organizations into community-based policing may inadvertently be the worst we can do to management—street culture relations. The inevitability of administrative oversight may undermine the best efforts of reformers to bring together management and line officers.

Thus, we arrive at the rub, a genuine conundrum. Should accountability for community policing be abandoned or expanded? What if police dominion over physical territory is extended vis-à-vis community policing to symbolic territories—the neighborhoods and communities celebrated by the COP model, and police values do not change (Caldero, 1997)? The answer may be dominion without accountability. Extend administrative accountability to expanded police public order responsibilities and darker elements of police culture flourish, building barriers to close inspection. Abandon accountability at the peril of democracy.

Endnotes

[1] Greene and Klockars (1991:274) recognize the distinction between administrative images of patrol and what officers actually do. They note that ". . . police activity, as presented in the official reports of a police department, may reflect only marginally the 'real' activities on the street." Craft norms, they suggest, are more influential in determining the content of everyday police work than administrative or command decisions.

[2] This is an over-simplification of proactive and reactive policing. Police proactivity is affected by the seriousness of the crime, for example. In misdemeanor crime, the police in most states must witness the crime to make an arrest. These types of encounters have been described as bald confrontations between the state and the citizen, and are highly discretionary (Black, 1973). The police seldom witness more serious types of crime, and their involvement and decision to arrest depends on citizen reporting and is affected by the predispositions of the plaintiff or witnesses. My argument here is that there has been a simplistic association of random preventive patrol with traditional, reactive styles of policing, an association that fails to take into account the way in which random preventive patrol actually occurs.

[3] Fifty percent of the remaining time was spent in crime-related activity, with the largest single category being the investigation of "not in progress" crimes, that is, crimes that had already occurred.

[4] Most observers of the police have focused on their activity in maintaining the public order, or public service activity of the police. Greene and Klockars (1991) found, however, that officers spent 49.9 percent of their committed time in enforcement-related activity, but only 16.4 percent in order-maintenance activity and even less, 7.9 in service activity.

[5] I will talk a great deal about the "asshole" later. This label is of sufficient importance to merit it's own category.

[6] Reuss-Ianni (1983:11) notes that "In day-to-day police work, however, responsiveness to the immediate territorial and behavioral environment and situation is more crucial, demanding more flexible parameters, and so decisions are appropriately made at lower levels."

[7] Wilson had earlier (1968) described policing as a craft characterized by the maintenance of public order, a view that caught the fires of idealistic researchers. His description continues to be widely held in spite of more recent work, like that of Greene and Klockars above, which shows that the police after all tend to do a great deal of law enforcement.

6

Force Is Righteous

> The use of force is not a philosophical issue for a policeman. It is not a question of would or whether, but when and how much. Therefore, the amount of force a policeman uses does not depend solely on himself but also on the character of the people he polices and the policies of his department (Rubinstein, 1973:323).

Few issues are so emotionally charged as the police use of force. In the United States, democratic principles propel our belief in law over order, and the police are expected to behave objectively and fairly as instruments of the law. We seek just laws, dispassionately enforced. We want police to use force when they must, but to avoid it unless absolutely necessary. Our distrust of force is so strong that we encircle the police with due process laws, internal review, education, training, militaristic personnel standards, and threaten them with litigation, public rebuke, and with loss of employment in even the most trivial misapplication of force against a citizen. We seek automatons of dispassionate law enforcement—"robocops" in blue.

We then ask cops to deal with our most profound social problems and to use whatever force is necessary to shelter us from the criminal and the uncivilized. We complain bitterly when police do not quickly resolve problems we ourselves cannot handle. It is a contradictory and impossible responsibility. When cops show too much passion, or do their work too well, display too much aggression, or exceed some bureaucratic guideline, we seek their punishment. We shake our heads in horror, failing to comprehend that they have done precisely what we expected them to do. Police culture provides a barrier of protection behind which they hide so that they can do what we want them to do without at the same time incurring our chastisement. In many ways and for all the implied contradictions and paradoxes, police culture protects us as much as it does them.

Media portrayals of the police frequently focus on their capacity for force. From favorable portrayals of the police such as in "Miami Vice," a popular television series in the 1980s, to *Prince of the City*, a movie about entrenched police corruption in New York, the capacity to use force makes the police a powerful source of media inspiration. We are simultaneously bewitched and terrified by the social presence of force and its destructive implications for human flesh. The police indeed have power, and the media know what sells.

What does not sell, and what we do not see, are the police living ordinary lives, facing the same daily myriad of petty problems confronted by the rest of us. As thoughtful, ordinary people, the police are invisible and we do not see them; they are known to us only through their evocative and sometimes controversial symbols: centurion in blue, sunglasses, nightstick, badge, and gun. We do not see their pain, their celebrations, and their humanity. We do not see the culture in which they, like all groups, wrap themselves. We know them as instruments of force, solvers of our most trenchant problems. Their display of visible and symbolic force frightens us, just as it is the reason that we invoke their authority. And when they have done our bidding they go away, back to their families, to their bosses, their circle of friends, to their ordinary lives.

Overview of Police Use of Force

The first national survey of the police use of force was carried out by the Bureau of Justice Statistics in 1996. A Police-Public Contact Survey was conducted in representative American households. Members in 6,421 households were interviewed in May, June, and July 1996 (Greenfeld, Langan & Smith 1997). The survey found that:

1. Approximately 44.6 million persons had a face-to-face contact with a police officer in 1996.

2. The authors estimated that 1.2 million people (.6%) were handcuffed during 1996.

3. About 500,000 people (.2% of the population 12 or older) were hit, held, pushed, choked, threatened with a flashlight, restrained by a police dog, threatened or sprayed with chemical or pepper spray, threatened with a gun, or experienced some other form of force (Roberg, Crank & Kuykendall, 2000).

From these numbers, the use of force appears to be relatively infrequent. Of those with a face-to-face contact, less than one percent encountered police use of force.

However, force may be defined in much broader terms. Force involves something more than violent behavior. Force can be defined as "any thing the police do to have citizens act in a particular way." A police officer asking for one's license during a routine traffic stop is certainly coercive—my failure to provide the license immediately brings the weight of state sanctions against me. How nicely she or he asks for my license is irrelevant—it is a use of force. In this way, we begin to see that virtually all police citizen actions involve some sort of use of force. An officer talented in the use of force will use his particular artistry or style to prevent the force from escalating.

That force occurs at the most casual interactions is recognized by trainers, who introduce trainees to "use-of-force" standards. A clear presentation of these standards is provided in Skolnick and Fyfe's excellent work on police and the excessive use of force. They identify the following levels:

1. Mere presence. This is the notion that the simple presence of an officer, the embodiment of the authority of the state, will deter dangerous citizen behavior.

2. Verbalization. When officers speak, they are taught to do so persuasively. This is described as an adult-adult interaction. If it does not work, officers move on to more forcible options.

3. Command voice. Command voice is more vibrant, and is in the form of an order. Skolnick and Fyfe's example is: "Sir, I asked you for your vehicle papers once. Now I'm telling you that you have to give them to me now."

4. Firm grips. These are physical grips on the body directing a suspect when and where to move. They are not intended to cause pain.

5. Pain compliance. These seek suspects' compliance by causing pain. They should not cause lasting physical injury.

6. Impact techniques. These may involve physical contact or the use of chemical spray or stunning weapons.

7. Deadly force. This is force that is capable of killing a suspect. Skolnick and Fyfe describe three such uses of deadly force: the carotid control hold (or sleeper hold), that induces unconsciousness in a suspect and can be deadly in practice, the bar arm control hold, in which the forearm is squeezed against the neck to cut off the flow of air, and the use of guns (Skolnick & Fyfe, 1993:37-40).

Police training provides exercises in the use of appropriate force. By the time officers have completed POST training, they have some skills in the use of force, a preliminary sense of appropriate levels of force, and have practiced some situations requiring the use of force—how to take down someone, to cuff a resistant suspect, how to use weapons, when to shoot and when not to shoot. This training is the linchpin of POST. We see in it that force is central to the craft of police work. It is a pervasive theme of police-citizen interaction. The artistry an officer brings to bear on a citizen encounter will involve a way of thinking about force in some way, how the authority that the officer has can be converted into citizen compliance. Make no mistake. The behavior of the police in police citizen encounters is about how to convert the authority of the state into citizen compliance.

The formal training of use of force is always in terms of resistance—force increases as resistance to the requests of an officer increases. However, many people have accused the police of using force in ways less self-defense based. The police are sometimes accused of using unnecessary force disproportionately on minorities. Caldero, for example, argues that police have fundamentally different notions of acceptable force when African-Americans are compared to wealthy Anglos. In the following example, he is talking to a roomful of officers.

> *OK. Imagine this, There's a [carful] of fat white men in $1,000 suits. The driver's license of the driver is expired. Now in your mind, imagine slamming these guys on the hood of the car, palms down. Kicking their feet apart. Screaming at them. Can that image, that CONCEPT even enter your mind? It's not even possible. The image doesn't work.*
>
> *Now imagine doping this to a car full of black teenagers with baseball hats on backwards.*

The audience laughs quietly. Mike laughs too, nodding his head up and down.

> *See. Now that works, doesn't it? You can imagine that. Now you understand that your officers are making value-based decisions about their work* (Crank & Caldero, 2000:85).

The capacity to conceive of such treatment during a routine stop of a carful of rich white men is simply absent. On the other hand, it is commonplace if they are black teenagers. In other words, use of force occurs within a cultural environment in which rich whites and poor blacks are viewed differently, and that difference is linked to predispositive behavior—in this case, sharply different levels of customary force for the same infraction.

One might counter that force is appropriately different in the two encounters, because the potential threat from the two groups are different. Put differently, police are acting reasonably to different kinds of threats. To assess these two ideas, Terrill and Mastrofski (2002) assessed use of force among two departments in their Project on Policing Neighborhoods (POPN) study. Force was measured as "acts that threaten or inflict physical harm on citizens" and included both verbal and physical force. Contacts were made with 6,500 citizens in Indianapolis and 5,500 in St. Petersburg. Systematic observations were carried out by trained observers and in-person interviews were conducted with officers.

Their findings showed that the decision to use force involved both what the citizen did and who the citizen was. The force used by an officer was often triggered by the resistance displayed by citizens. Officers' perceptions of the police role, their attitudes toward citizens and toward legal restraints had little effect on the use of force. However, the authors also found that force was more likely to be used against males, nonwhites, poor suspects, and young suspects, regardless of their behavior. Also, proactive stops were associated with higher levels of force. The authors cautioned that the use of force was disproportionately high on these vulnerable populations, even with resistance controlled statistically. The authors concluded that "while officers tend to respond to legal determinants of citizens' behavior, they also rely on extralegal determinants."

Force Is Central to the Literature on Police

The idea that force is central to the work of the police is common among academic studies of the police. Writers, seeking to understand the unique characteristics of police work and culture, almost always focus on some aspect of the use of force. The coercive use of force, more than any other idea about the police, seems to capture the unique role that the police play in contemporary American society.

Wesley and Force

Wesley (1970) was among the first of the police scholars to recognize the importance of force to the police and the paradox that implied in a democratic society. He argued that, as a nation, the United States was committed to the virtues of peace—virtues embodied in the law of the Constitution. So ingrained is the notion of peace to our social sensibilities that we not only seek peace in our social relationships, but we believe that social relations should only be maintained through peaceful means. We accordingly limit, as much as possible, the use of force by citizens to solve their problems (Bittner, 1970). This vision of peace is captured in the following quote:

> In ways wholly consistent with this aspiration to achieve peace through peaceful means as a condition of everyday domestic life, Western societies have sought to circumscribe to the greatest degree possible the legitimacy of the use of force by its citizens. Save for occasions of self-

defense from criminal attack and intra-family discipline of children by their parents, Western states have all but eliminated the rights of citizens to use coercive force (Klockars, 1991:530).

In order to eliminate violence as an acceptable way to conduct our affairs, society creates a "core institution whose special competence and defining characteristic is its monopoly on a general right to use coercive force" (Klockars, 1991:530). The police stand apart: their occupation is inherently offensive to democratic process, yet they and they alone can act as protectors of society.

How are we then to reconcile the offensive nature of routine violence in a democracy committed to peace? Bittner (1970) argued that we must conceal what the police do. The history of the police, he noted, was marked by a tradition of themes that served to hide the raw use of police force and surround the police with powerful themes more acceptable to a peaceful people. The militarization of the police at the turn of the nineteenth century and the police professionalism movement were both powerful themes that served to mystify the police use of coercion under more acceptable ideas, that the police were "militaristic," or that they were "professionals."

Bittner, Klockars, and the Mystification of Force

Bittner (1970) contended that police work became comprehensible in specific situations, when it was used to resolve particular problems. He called this "situationally justified force" (Bittner, 1970:39). Regardless of the activities police officers were involved in, the common thread that pulled them together was the use of coercion to rectify some immediate problem. Police alone had the legitimate use of coercion at their disposal. This uniquely marked the police as agents of the state, and set them apart from a public often uncomfortable with the use of force. The inherent contradictions of situationally justified force in a democratic society, particularly because coercion is acted out in concrete everyday circumstances of coercive problem-solving, irrevocably separated the police from the public.

Klockars (1991) extended Bittner's ideas to the contemporary community policing movement. Klockars argued that the community policing movement was simply another of the history of "circumlocutions" used by the police to obscure what they did—use force to deal with citizen problems.

Community policing gave police a new legitimacy when the police professionalism movement lost its credibility as a justification for police behavior. As both Klockars (1991) and Crank (1994) noted, community policing gained a great deal of headway with the compelling arguments that traditional police practices did not work. However, there was no evidence that tenets of community policing worked either—it gained momentum on a blind faith in the ability of the police to act benignly and favorably on behalf of local communities and neighborhoods. This, Klockars suggested, was simply another mystification of police work. The centrality of coercion to the police, hidden behind a smokescreen of police professionalism and community policing rhetoric, "circumlocuted" the true police role and made coercive encounters more socially palatable.

In the end, the public uses the police for one reason: so they can deal with situations in which "something ought not to be happening about which something should be done NOW" (Klockars, 1985:16-17). The first part, "something ought not to be happening," refers to illegal acts, but also includes a wide variety of order maintenance situations such as crowd control, removing disabled vehicles on the roadway, and calling on an elderly man who hears a suspicious noise at night. The second part, "about which something should be done NOW," means that the police deal with situations that need an immediate resolution. This is where coercive authority comes in. Klockars notes that, "despite resistance or protest by participants or observers . . . the general right to use coercive force gives police the right to overcome any and all opposition immediately." From this, Klockars concludes that coercion is at the core of the police role: In response to the question "Why do we have the police," he answers "We have them to deal with all those problems in which coercive force may have to be used" (Klockars, 1985:17).

Wilson and the Emotional Content of Force

The idea that police use of force is mystified behind ideas of peace is also embedded in the notion that police can act emotionlessly to enforce the law in an evenhanded way. The notion is nonsense. Wilson (1968) was the first to note that police work was carried out in a context frequently emotional, and that the police had to get personally involved in order to do their work. Wilson recognized that the dynamics of police work were sensible only in the immediacy of day-to-day interactions with citizens. To understand what police do, one had to recognize the actual circumstances of their interactions with the public. This, not a set of formal policies or job description handed down by department superiors, determined what police officers did in specific encounters.

Police, Wilson observed, were far more likely to deal with order maintenance situations—a family dispute, a loud stereo, a rowdy teenager—than with an actual violation of the criminal law. Police-citizen interactions in these kinds of encounters, he argued, were unpredictable in a way that had a disproportionate effect on officers. Police lacked clear guides to deal with order maintenance. Where, he asked, did one draw the line between order and disorder? The resolution of order maintenance rarely had clear administrative input beyond department policies that tell officers what not to do. Officers thus approached order maintenance situations from the view of "playing it by ear" or "handling the situation" rather than in terms of "enforcing the law" (Wilson, 1968:32).

The lack of clear legal guides in order maintenance situations meant that officers had to use personal authority. They had to get involved, to become emotionally engaged. Rubinstein (1973:317), citing an officer in his survey, noted "you wear a uniform and a badge, you got a gun, stick, and jack—who is gonna give you any trouble? Who would want to fight with you? You learn quick." As he, and many others since him, have noted, reliance on formal police authority is rarely enough to deal with problems—indeed, often the presence of a police uniform heightens hostilities. Officers thus become emotionally involved: they cannot do otherwise.

> The felt need to "handle the situation" rather than "enforce the law" and to assert authority and "take charge" leads the officer to get involved, but "getting involved" is the antithesis of the ideal—that is, being impersonal and correct . . . To get involved means to display one's personal qualities . . . (Wilson, 1968:33).

Wilson recognized that emotions were an inevitable part of police-citizen encounters. Many police-situation encounters, he noted, took on the character of contests, in which each tested the other to see who would control the situation. The uniform and authority that went with it were not sufficient to gain citizen acquiescence: personal involvement was necessary.

Wilson's way of looking at personal authority is sensible for understanding police-citizen interactions when citizens refuse to do what a police officer tells them to do. It utterly fails to explain police use of force in situations when suspects or citizens have come under police custody. Yet such circumstances are disturbingly frequent and repeatedly cited throughout the history of research on the police (Reiss, 1971; Van Maanen, 1978; Skolnick & Fyfe, 1993; Domanick, 1994).

Street-citizen encounters are marked by powerful and sometimes destructive emotional energies. To understand them we must look at how force links with other themes of police work. Officers are motivated by a need to maintain respect, a need not always acknowledged and often challenged by citizens (Skolnick & Fyfe, 1993; Kappeler, Sluder & Alpert, 1994). When a citizen fails to acknowledge the personal authority of the police, an encounter takes on a visceral life of its own, and officers' efforts to reassert the control overrides all other aspects of the encounter. Themes of machismo also bear on citizen encounters (Herbert, 1997). An officer's self-image is brought into question, and there must be an accounting when a citizen fails to acknowledge their authority in any police-citizen encounter (Van Maanen, 1978).

Emotional involvement is not simply a by-product of the failure of formal authority to resolve unsatisfactory police-citizen encounters, as Wilson implied. It is sometimes a desired way of dealing with particular types of troublesome individuals. Police scholars frequently miss an important characteristic of the use of force: its seductive quality.[1] In encounters with assholes and criminals, police act out a mythos—they are righteous, placed on earth to deal with assholes. They are culturally united by their identity as cops, the first line of defense against the evil in society. They are the hammer of righteousness.

Wilson (1968) recognized that the emotional nature of police-citizen interactions limited the extent to which officer behavior could be brought under administrative control. Management efforts to control line behavior, he wrote, would never be wholly successful, and chiefs of professionally oriented departments would never be accepted by their officers. The wisdom of his vision lies in the recognition that chiefs and line officers had to deal with different audiences, a principle central to this book as well.

Police coercion contributes to solidarity. Police use of force is a powerful stimulus for cultural solidarity. Van Maanen (1973) captures this conjunction of energies in his discussion of police training. Field training officers, he noted, often put training in risky positions to test their willingness to back up other officers. Rubinstein (1973) has similarly explored this relationship in his research on Philadelphia police. Force, he noted, was not an analytical construct for cops—it was a way to deal with fear. Consider the following statement:

A policeman understands the meaning of fear, the loosening of muscles in the midriff and the vision of terrible things happening to your body, and he does not condemn men for being afraid, but he does not want them around him when he is working. They are only a danger and a burden (Rubinstein, 1973:318).

Police officers must be prepared to use force, he argued, and those who are unable to put themselves in harm's way without giving way to fear are shunned. Officers make sure that all their colleagues know when an officer is hesitant to use force. "A man who is unwilling to use force is viewed as a danger to everyone who works with him, and he cannot be allowed to persist in his ways" (Rubinstein, 1973:319).

The linkage between force and culture is often viewed negatively, as a collusion among officers to keep quiet about abuses of force (Skolnick & Fyfe, 1993). According to this idea, the need to cover up abuses of force requires that officers cover for each other, and spawns a culture of secrecy impenetrable to administrative oversight. Culture, in this context, is a mask for deviant police behavior (Kappeler, Sluder & Alpert, 1994).[2]

The idea that force is a negative impulse for solidarity overlooks important aspects of force. Whether legal, questionable, or illegal, force is bound up in the day-to-day doing of police work and linked to other important themes of police culture. Force as formally taught in the academy, rule-bound by criminal law, and circumscribed by department policy, does not fit ordinary police activity very well. Department policy reflects administrative rather than street imperatives, and is typically viewed as more organizational "bullshit." Due process is simply a recognition of the fundamental incapacity of the criminal justice system to deal with criminals, a set of handcuffs that interfere with the ability of cops to do their work (Sykes, 1986). It is not that cops do not believe in the necessity of due process in a democracy or the imperatives of administration, nor is it that cops are, by nature, authoritarian. It is just that when things get wild, when an officer has to maintain the edge and is burning with energy and fear, other considerations become less important. A cop uses force in the street because it does the job, solves a problem. The law, from this perspective, is not a set of rules to bound police behavior: it is what legitimates police use of force.

Officers are not equivocal in the use of force. Ambivalence is dangerous, weakness where force is needed invites disrespect and encourages counter-force (Rubinstein, 1973:317). If tested, or in the event of danger, it is the officer's willingness to commit his body and weapons to the fray that may save him, that allows him to maintain the edge. Fielden captures this dynamic:

> July 1992. While on patrol, two Las Vegas police officers were ambushed and shot by four juveniles who later boasted the song "cop killer" gave them the idea, the motivation on how "to get even by killing cops." While in custody, the four chanted the song's lyrics over and over.

> Yes, I'll admit there are those in our profession who occasionally step beyond the boundaries of using reasonable force to make an arrest. But for every cop who does that, there are hundreds, literally thousands, who wind up getting injured themselves because they used too little restraint in apprehending a suspect (Fielden, 1995:164).

This example shows how the use of force is tied to cultural dynamics. In this short story are two important cultural elements—the mobilization of police energies around the threat of a police officer being killed, and the belief that officers often do not use enough force to deal with genuinely dangerous people. The song "Cop Killer" has been a powerful impulse toward solidarity among the police, who view it as an enemy and see in it a justification for increased use of force in ambivalent situations.

As a cultural element, use of force is not about the secret bonding of men from dark deeds they have committed and of fear that they will come back to haunt them. Culture emerges around the use of force because it is central to police work. Elements of secrecy emerge as areas of the use of force are forbidden. One only has to listen to the stories cops tell to recognize the importance of force to police culture. You will hear many stories about the legal use of force, many that cross the bounds of legality, and many that are simply legally indecipherable. The use of force, legal or otherwise, permeates police culture.

Illicit Coercion

> Do you think you can study evil without living it? How are you going to discover the attributes of the Devil without getting close to him? (Davies, 1975:57).

The use of coercion under legally questionable circumstances is often darkly described as the abuse of force. It is too often made simple; here is an officer gone bad, there is a cop that cannot keep his cool. Such simplicity is popular fare in the newspapers, stirring up pot-boiling emotions and polarizing colleagues. Sometimes victims are high-mindedly blamed— "the idiot had it coming," "they should have known better." These are all individual-level explanations that attribute agency, or blame, to use a popular and emotionally slanted synonym for agency, to individuals. Both explanations are wrong, as well—the excessive use of force is a cultural phenomenon, common among the police, stemming from common-sense solutions to recurring predicaments in their working environment.

Perspectives on Excessive Violence

Excessive force is a topic of extensive discussion in the criminal justice literature (e.g., Skolnick & Fyfe, 1993). Manning (1970:99) suggests that the use of excessive violence is one of the fundamental characteristics of American policing. The excessive use of force symbolically communicates the unquestionable authority of the state in the affairs of the citizenry. The recipient of a beating knows that they have acted in an unacceptable way, that their behavior will not be tolerated by the police. Victims of excessive force understand that they have little recourse, that they will confront difficulties in filing a complaint, that they invite further problems, and that the courts will likely look the other way.

The moral authority of the state is a theme is evoked by Van Maanen (1978) in his description of "street justice." He contends that cops mete out immediate punishments in the face of what they perceive to be behavior that denies the authority of the state. Street justice emerges in concrete encounters, in which the authority of an officer has been questioned, and where an officer's perceived disrespect is repaid in kind (Bouza, 1990; Fyfe & Skolnick, 1993). Those that are perceived to have known better and could have acted differently are labeled "assholes." Assholes are particularly vulnerable to rough justice. For this reason, assholes hold a great deal of moral and emotional meaning for cops—the righteous beating of a card-carrying asshole feels good.

Police violence is sometimes explained as an overreaction in the face of potential or real danger. In these instances, it is suggested that the scuffle was started first by the felon, and police only reacted in like measure to control the situation. However, Wesley (1970) referred to this phenomenon in terms of what he described as the disturbing tendency of the police to use violence against disrespectful citizens after they had been placed in custody. It is only after a suspect has been subdued that the police can convey to him the full enormity of what he has done wrong. Violence serves powerful symbolic purposes—it acts out the authority of the state on the body of the suspect (Foucault, 1995).

Suspects are particularly vulnerable to rough justice when they try to hide from or avoid the police after being approached. Instances in which suspects that try to outrun the police in a vehicle in order to avoid a routine traffic stop are high on the list of violence-producing events. Indeed, as Skolnick and Fyfe (1993) observed, no aspect of police work is more exciting than the chase: the apprehension of a suspect is real police work; it is invigorating, and cops live for it. Once the rabbit runs, the hunt is on. Once caught, it is difficult to resist a good stomping.

Street violence is sometimes associated with more traditional policing styles. Wilson (1968), for example, suggested that police approach their work from the point of view of maintaining public order, were more likely to tailor their behavior to the exigencies of the "street." If violence was the most direct way to resolve a problem, to rectify a dispute or to straighten out an asshole, then violence was likely. Violence, arrest, and other coercive tools were seen as among the diverse tools officers used to deal with problems on their beat.

Wilson contended that coercion was a mechanism for the distribution of justice to those who have earned it. Police violence was not gratuitous, in the sense that it is randomly distributed by so-called "out-of-control" cops. It was proportioned out to those who most deserved it (Wilson, 1968). An officer encountering a group of rowdy teenagers might roughly search, arrest, slap, or otherwise antagonize a particularly obnoxious youth, both to give that youth the justice the cop thought he deserved and to warn the others in the group. The use of coercion in such an instance maintained control of the situation and insured that those who deserve justice got it (Wilson, 1968).

Because police violence is associated with old-fashioned police practices, professionalizing reforms, particularly those favorable to education, seem to be a way to control it. There is little evidence, though, that this is the case. In a study of municipal police in medium-sized departments in Illinois in 1994, two colleagues and I sought to assess line officer "worldviews," or customary ways of looking at their work (Crank, Payne & Jackson, 1993). We identified two ways of thinking, the first a "professional" view that reflected commonly held views of what professionalism was, and the second a craft-oriented worldview that consisted of beliefs associated with traditional departments. We were curious if traditional beliefs were more likely to condone police violence, secrecy, and hostility toward due process. Indeed, this was the case; that officers that were more traditional consistently were more secretive and were more supportive of the use of violence. Equally importantly, we wanted to find out if more professional officers tended to reject those beliefs. They did not: there was no support for the idea that those with a professional outlook were any less likely to support police violence. Though the scope of the research was limited—medium-sized departments in Illinois—the implications of the research were clear. Efforts to increase the professionalism of police officers would have scant effect on the formation and sustenance of attitudes in support of police violence.

Distinguishing Legal and Illegal Coercion: A Line in the Sand

Legal and illegal coercion do not separate cleanly in practice. Consider the following encounter, described by Rubinstein (1973), in which an officer uses too much force. This encounter shows how violence flows from the circumstances of an unpredictably unfolding situation. A young white officer encountered an elderly African-American, and yelled across the street at him "Take your hand out of your coat." The elderly man ignored the request. The officer repeated the command, drawing his pistol in the process.

> Slowly the (elderly) man began to extract his hand, but he gave the appearance of concealing some intention which threatened the patrolman, who cocked his gun and pointed it directly at the man. Suddenly the man drew out his hand and threw a pistol to the ground. He stood trembling. The patrolman uncocked his gun with a trembling hand and approached. He was on the verge of tears, and in a moment of confusion, fear, and anxiety, he struck the man with the butt of his pistol. "Why didn't you take your hand out when I told you? I almost shot you, you dumb bastard." The man . . . said that he had no intention of using the gun, but was carrying it for self-protection. The patrolman recovered from his fright, but despite his regret for striking the man in anger, he refused to acknowledge any responsibility. "Are you wearing a sign? How the fuck am I to know what you're gonna do?" (Rubinstein, 1973:303-304).

This use of force was a clear violation of department policy. The behavior was not motivated by a rational calculus of crime prevention or law enforcement, but from fear stemming from the officer's subjective evaluation of a threat to his personal safety and the explosion of tension after safety was assured.

How would the department administration respond to this event? Predictably, through the invocation of administrative process—a review of department policy, perhaps a hearing, possibly a reassignment, and a letter in the permanent file. In other words, the agency would respond bureaucratically, addressing its concerns to a municipal audience concerned about the behavior of line officers to citizens, and invoking complex chain-of-command procedure as a corrective. If they found out.

They probably will not find out. Street cops will construct legality into the use of force, to cover their butts so that they conform to department policy and criminal law (Barker, Friery & Carter, 1994). When the use of coercion is questionable, or when officers legally reconstruct a questionable use of coercion in a more favorable light, essential self-protective elements of the police culture come into play. Coercive encounters are protected by loosely coupling themes, where officers devise strategies so that they can protect themselves in the event of civilian and department review.

A department review would contribute little to avoiding the events that prompted the misuse of force—the blow to the face. Those circumstances were out of the control of the administrative apparatus and chain-of-command protocols. To a certain extent they were out of control of the officer who struck the elderly man, and they were out of control of the elderly man, as well. The situation was characterized by unfolding contingencies, in which actions were based on subjective evaluations of previous events, in a cascading and unpredictable fashion. Replayed, the event probably would not unfold in the same way; history is only fixed and predetermined in retrospect.[3]

Police officers inhabit a world of unfolding contingencies. It is not easily amenable to control. As I will describe in future sections on suspicion and on situational uncertainty, themes of unpredictability are central to the formation of the police subculture, and wild, unpredictable violence is an irreducible part of this world. It cannot be brought under control of administrative apparatus. When administrators seek to control it, as of course they do, it only fuels the police culture.

Endnotes

[1] The notion of seduction was taken from Katz (1988) work. He believed that sociological perspectives of crime came up short on key elements—they failed to understand how crime feels good to its participants. He constructed a mythology of criminology: offenders were not presented as rational actors, but constructed and acted out a mythological image of themselves, a mythology from which they derived identity and pleasure. He reinserted the criminal actor into the center of the criminal event, rather than the criminal actors socioeconomic background, and he recognized that crime occurs in an emotional context. I argue here that a similar perspective also applies to the police in police-citizen interactions, and characterizes many uses of force.

[2] In this vein, Kappeler and his colleagues (1994:288) note that "A police officer who uses excessive force frequently requires the support of his or her peers at a minimum and, at the other extreme, the active assistance of supervisors to conceal the activities of the officer from detection." They further argue that, while the use of force is a separate analytical type, individuals involved in these activities tend to interact with other deviant police categories. Configurations of corrupt and deviant associations makes it impossible to introduce constructive change.

[3] The inconsistencies between occupational ideas of professionalism—for example, that professionals have autonomy, that they can't be immediately overruled by supervisors, that their every decision is subject to administrative review, or that their status is higher than that of line officers, who hold the lowest wrung of status in the police organization, have been discussed elsewhere. As Klockars (1991) has noted, the use of the term "professionalism" to describe the police during this era was little more than a mystification that disguised what the police did routinely—use force to accomplish the resolution of immediate problems. Yet, labels have a persistence that overshadows their validity.

7

Crime Is War, Metaphor

Theme: Militarism

"We don't have to deal with all that complicated stuff about bad guys. We just kill 'em."

Few notions seized the American psyche in the latter half of the twentieth century with as much vigor as did the idea of as "War on Crime." The introduction of a "war on crime" into federalist politics can be traced to 1966, when President Lyndon Johnson presented it as a political call-to-arms. Presidents since as Kraska (2001:19) noted, have continued to "ratchet up" the rhetoric of a war on crime. The metaphor "war" has continued to dominate electoral politics:

> The Reagan, Bush, and Clinton presidential administrations, along with the mainstream media, have further militarized crime control discourse by radiating the master metaphor of "war" into a flood of taken-for-granted martial expressions and submetaphors (Kraska, 2001:19).

The notion of a war on crime is an example of a metaphor that, in many ways, fits police work pretty well. Criminals become an "enemy combatant" and crime control becomes "military battle." In this case, the notion of "war" is a metaphor with dramatic organizing potential. War carries the full force of a vibrant, polyvalent metaphor, with auxiliary meanings about combatants, training, policing urban areas, weaponry, due process, and crime control (Angell, 1971). And when we are at war, complex issues are simplified. Warriors don't need to worry about all that due process stuff. You're with us or against us.

The war metaphor is warmly received by many police officers for several reasons. Many police are recruited from the military, and bring with them a military bearing and perception of the appropriateness of military discipline. The police and military often overlap, with family histories often blending police and military careers. Similarly, many police officers view military service as a rite of passage that they should go through prior to career work in the ranks of the police. Issues of personal weaponry overlap. Organizational hierarchies in the police and the military use similar rank designations. Shuffle the "war" metaphor into the mix and, well, it all makes perfect common sense.

The problem is that it is not common sense for everyone. To some, it is strikingly un-American. The war metaphor plays havoc with "posse comitatus" separatist traditions of the police and the military in the U.S (Dunlap, 2001). As Dunlap (2001:30) noted, Americans have historically distrusted the use of armed forces for internal security purposes. Some believe that the police are better conceived as a multi-service public agency, concerned with the provision of service. Others argue that the police should focus on ameliorating public order tensions associated with ethnicity, age groupings, economic status, and race.

Yet, that the "war" mctaphor has taken hold is increasingly apparent. One of the many dramatic political developments in the "post-9/11" era— the period after the terrorist destruction of the World Trade Center towers in New York on September 11, 2001—has been the reassessment of the relationship between internal security—local and national police— and the military. In the current period, the metaphor of "war" has dramatically extended its reach, in the following way—in the event of terrorist threat, the local police are the most likely to be the first on a crime scene, and consequently the first involved in any interdiction, prevention, or clean-up.

This chapter explores the theme "militarism." Militarism can be defined as the adoption of military procedures, attitudes, structures, and practices by the police. Post-9/11 militaristic tendencies among the police occur within a history and milieu of police/military interaction. This chapter explores many facets of this overlap.

Militarism, Professionalism, and Reform

Police paramilitarism as we know it today emerged after the Civil War. Lane (1992) attributes the emergence of paramilitarism to the prestige associated with the military after the Civil War. Activities such as morning roll call and the adoption of military titles followed almost naturally for the police. The remainder of the nineteenth century was characterized by convergence of organizational arrangements, particularly in the adoption of a paramilitary organizational style (Monkkonen, 1981).

Efforts to reform the police at the end of the nineteenth century led to the unlikely marriage of professionalism and militarism. One of the vexing dilemmas faced in the latter half of the nineteenth century by urban reformers was the vast power held by urban political machines, a type of municipal government characterized by big city bosses, pervasive corruption, and unregulated hiring and firing practices. "Good government" forces, led by progressives and the anti-saloon league, opposed political machines for several reasons. Progressives sought improvement in city government through administrative innovation, and believed that political machines were responsible for widespread corruption that characterized the urban milieu of the age (Berman, 1987).

In 1893, the International Association of Chiefs of Police (IACP) was formed by a group of police chiefs whose allegiance was reformist (Uchida, 1989). Dedicated to removing the influence of political machines, they correctly recognized that political machines would not survive of they did not have police jobs to offer loyal supporters (Fogelson, 1977). The agenda put forth by the IACP is widely regarded today as the foundation of the police professionalism movement.

Central to the agenda of the IACP was the separation of urban politics from the affairs of the police. They sought to make police departments autonomous from city politics and instituted a wide-ranging agenda in pursuit of that goal. The police were to have a mission: law enforcement. Officers were to be dedicated to that mission. The militaristic rank-structure, well established in police organizations, provided the form and the ideology for crime control. Thus, militarism and professionalism were joined under the banner of the "police professionalism movement," an unfortunate label for a police movement that was astonishingly anti-professional in its efforts to control the behavior of its employees (Walker, 1977),[1] and could have more properly been labeled a police militarism movement (see also Lane, 1992; Sykes, 1989).

Over the following 40 years the "professional" model gradually displaced the machine model of policing (Uchida, 1989). But the professional model was a model of quasi-military discipline and rank structure: what was called professionalization was simply a system for the importation of traits of outward military discipline (Bittner, 1970). It was a quite successful model for chiefs seeking municipal funding and political prestige: the militaristic image provided a powerful metaphor for politicians seeking election on a war-on-crime platform. The rhetoric of professionalism continues to have a stronghold on the police, and its unlikely companion—police militarism—is central to the way the police are organized and how they think today.

In the current era, police organizations are distinguished by their military bearing. Police wear uniforms, have adopted military sigils and rank insignia, and dress for combat. Departments everywhere now have military rank structures, with line officers on bottom and the chief (or in some places, the commissioner) on top, with the intervening ranks inevitably filled with traditional army labels. Officers parade in military style and occasionally have to make formation like military personnel do.[2]

Police departments are "paramilitary" complete with "chains of command," "divisions," "platoons," "squads," and "details." In many places, patrol officers are "privates" or "troopers." In virtually all places, officers report not to supervisors, middle managers, or executives, but to "sergeants," "lieutenants," "captains," "majors," and "colonels." In police training, much attention is devoted to "close order drill" and "military courtesy" (Skolnick & Fyfe, 1993:13).

Command officers today consistently agree with the notion that police organizations should be organized along paramilitary lines. An Illinois study of police administrators revealed that "more than 87 percent of the respondents agreed with the statement that a police agency functions most effectively if it is organized along paramilitary lines, and that their departments were so structured" (Auten, 1985:124). While these examples may seem obvious, they reveal the extent to which notions of militarism infuse the organization of American municipal police organizations.

Militarism and the Organizational Status of Cops

The "professional" paramilitary model has never been well suited for street cops, nor was it intended to be. The model has served the purposes of reformers throughout the century, whose goals were largely to bring the behavior of street cops under administrative control (Walker, 1977). Indeed, if one were to try to construct a personnel system intended to violate every principal associated with the spirit of true professionalism, it would be difficult to design a model more successful than the so-called professional/military model of policing that we have today.

That the professional/military model was about the control rather than in the granting of professional status to police officers has not been lost on street officers (White, 1986). In a twist of fate, the professional police officer, that is, the street officers who make everyday decisions on life and death matters, have the least status, lowest rank, and lowest pay. As Skolnick and Fyfe note, efforts to "shoehorn street-level officers' great discretion into the lowest level of a military organizational style has resulted in the creation of elaborate police rulebooks . . ." (Skolnick & Fyfe, 1993:120) Officers inevitably "devalue rules and find shortcuts" around administrative procedures. They believe they are isolated in their own organization, and in a real sense they are. The working habitat, they note, is perceived as "cops against bosses" (Skolnick & Fyfe, 1993:122). It is not surprising that the paramilitary model drives a great deal of police culture.

Line-officers have adopted elements of the military mind-set, what we call today the "war on crime" mentality. But as anyone who has been a grunt in the military service knows, a part of the mind-set is a gut-level dissatisfaction with the authority of superior officers (Fussell, 1989; Auten, 1985). Grunts—the term for GI's serving in Vietnam—know that superior officers sit behind desks and make unreasonable decisions that arbitrarily put line personnel in danger, have no knowledge about what is going on "out there" where the action is, play favorites, and endlessly seek to avoid responsibility for their decisions. If the mis-named police professionalization movement did not create the police culture, it certainly encouraged it (Lane, 1992). Outward military discipline, as Bittner (1970) noted, tended to displace misconduct by officers into areas difficult to regulate. In a word, it intensified many aspects of the police culture; secrecy, criminal activity by the police, deception, and line-administration friction.

The military model, while serving important symbolic purposes, limits reform (Sykes, 1989:292,293). Symbolically, militarism connotes an image of hierarchical police accountability and rule-bound behavior. Military symbols, Sykes suggested, function as powerful "myths:" they reassure a liberal society that it is "not in danger of unrestrained power." As he noted, it was the fear of unrestrained police power that led early reformers to support a militaristic model, in the belief that street-level officers can be controlled by military discipline.

The public, Sykes notes, expects the police to do more than solve crime, a task they do probably as well as can be done given the crime opportunities in mass modern society (Felson, 1993). The public wants the police to solve problems, a task considerably larger than law enforcement activity. Problem solving, the informal use of coercion to control those who violate local standards of decency and conduct, is the primary means whereby police are able to effect the maintenance of public order. Were militarism reforms to be wholly successful, police would be constrained to dealing only with violations of the criminal law. The peacekeeping role of the police would be lost, together with the capacity to solve problems and the ability to maintain informal social control. In an ironical outcome, the outcome of too rigid a militaristic control over the behavior of line officers might be the public's freedom to walk the streets unafraid.

Militarism and the Metaphors of War

Metaphors are powerful linguistic tools that at once organize thoughts and focus our attention on some aspect of the criminal justice system (Christie, 1994; Crank, 1996). Metaphors provide a way of thinking about something by likening it to something else that can highlight an important or distinguishing point. "Ecological niches," for example, is a wonderful metaphor for describing cities, because the use of an organic metaphor allows us to focus on the way different human populations socially transform the urban environment.

Militarism is such a metaphor for the police (Kraska & Kappeler, 1997). The police, of course, are not a military unit fighting a war—their principal clients are citizens, and their work is dominated by petty peace-keeping problems involving rowdy teenagers, angry spouses and neighbors, and other persistent social problems. Yet we have used the metaphor so many times that it is difficult to think otherwise. An inevitable outcome of the shift to a militaristic mission is that police officers come to believe it. The military metaphor instills focus and direction into tasks that are otherwise difficult to manage and logically unintegrated, primarily by labeling those who disagree with the police in warrior terms of "enemy." The military metaphor allows cops to take righteous pride in seeking, arresting, and thumping bad guys, and provides them with broad social and political supports for doing so. In the current era, police militarism has become much more than a set of paramilitary organizational structures that constitute the police personnel system. Militarism provides a moral-emotional identity for police as warriors in the war against crime.

The metaphor "war" has had explosive mobilizing potential. It provided a way to view the police as protectors of society (read "your wives and children"), and to view criminals as amoral enemies—less than human. It promoted a perspective—a slant on the metaphor—with enormous staying power, that criminals are enemies of the state, and therefore not worthy of state legal protections. And it stilled dissent. Anyone supporting a loosening of criminal sanctions was in league with enemies of the state. A consideration of the language used to describe police and criminals today reveals the taken-for-granted nature of the "war" metaphor. We are at war with crime. We have to fight crime. Police are outgunned or outnumbered by criminals. Police are the thin blue line that separates order from anarchy. It is them versus us. Police are crime-fighters. Police gather intelligence about criminals.

The language of war provides a vocabulary that unites officers in militaristic identity, and provides individual officers with a warrior persona. This identity is ever-present:

> Thinking of themselves as soldiers and crime fighters, all the police carry guns, even when working in the radio room or the juvenile division. They wear uniforms with badges of rank, like soldiers. They have military inspections and sometimes march as units in parades. They expect violence from the enemy and are ready to respond to violence in its own coin (Betz, 1988:182-183).

Betz further observed that the military model becomes embodied in cop identity and encourages violence:

> The policeman is tainted by his Janus-like position. He has one foot planted in decent society and one in the criminal underworld. He crys-

tallizes and focuses the hate of respectable society for the criminal, but he learns to think like the criminal and to make counter-moves in the criminal's own game . . . If his coercive force crosses the line to become violence, no one watches, or watching, no one objects (Betz, 1988:183).

Militarism, a model that has been celebrated for the discipline and accountability it provides for officers, has resulted in a paradoxical conclusion: today it provides a basis for many of the enduring features of the police culture. The "we-them" attitude fostered by a militaristic perspective has contributed in some departments to a siege-mentality in which the public is increasingly the "them." Technology has been used to gather detailed intelligence on citizens and to sophistication in weapons hardware, and has fostered strong linkages between the police and the U.S. military, particularly in the so-called war on drugs (Kraska, 1994; 1993). Resistance to the gathering of police intelligence is perceived in militaristic ideas of "what do they want to hide" instead of democratic deliberations of the relationship between government and citizens.

Kraska (2001:16-17) identifies several dimensions of police militarism and militarization in policing today. Below is his list, summarized:

1. Blurring external and internal security issues. Targeting of civilian populations as security threats. Focus on aggregate populations as potential insurgents.

2. Emphasis on information gathering and processing and surveillance work.

3. Ideology of militarism that emphasizes "problem-solving with state force, technology, armament, intelligence gathering, aggressive suppression efforts," and other ways of military thinking.

4. Special operations paramilitary teams, policing using military tactics.

5. Purchasing, loaning, donating, and using actual militaristic products.

6. Collaboration between the defense industry and crime control industry.

7. "The use of military language within political and popular culture to characterize the social problems of drugs, crime, and social disorder." (2001:17).

In each of these items, we can see the interpenetration, in material and ideational culture, of the military and the police. The military, Kraska advises, is an increasingly central metaphor for police in contemporary society.

In 2002 a new word with powerful metaphorical organizing power emerged: terrorist. Terrorist is a word difficult to pin down, and easily accumulates meaning for that reason. To be a terrorist is a status. It is not a crime per se. A terrorist is a person who commits crime. Any kind of crime can constitute terrorism, depending on how terrorism is defined. Prior to September 11, 2001, terrorism referred to home-grown radicals of the 1960s left and 1990s right.

After the attack on the World Trade Center towers in New York City, the word "terrorism" accreted a great deal of meaning. It conjures images of people in far-away places plotting the destruction of the United states. However, it is not difficult to imagine that any one who commits crime with intent is plotting the destruction of at least a small part of the United States. For example, are street gangs terrorists? An article in the *Los Angeles Times* certainly thinks so:

> Polls show that the U.S. public stands firmly behind the war on terrorism, but who will stand with Julia Zepeda? It didn't take an international terrorist to end her life, just a trio of home-grown ones.

> Eleven years old. A Times photograph captured the toll of this domestic war. There stood the family Christmas tree, unwrapped toys—a doll, a Santa, a daypack—not yet put away. There sat Julia Zepeda on the edge of the couch, hands clasped, head bowed, face sculpted by sorrow.

> It took an act of international terrorism on U.S. soil to make many Americans feel vulnerable for the first time in their lives. For residents in Southern California's poorer neighborhoods, it just takes getting up in the morning. When will the rest of us say this cannot stand? (*Los Angeles Times*, 2002).

The logic embedded in this article is clear. We are engaged in a domestic war with terrorism. When will we do what we have to do to win? The author's plea—when will we say this cannot stand?—is reminiscent of the movie character Rambo's complaint in Vietnam—why won't they let us win the war? By labeling law-breaking as terrorism we implicitly justify the wholesale abandonment of civil liberties, as we have already done for Americans accused by the executive branch of the federal government of aiding the Taliban or Al Qaeda.

The police, warriors for the forces of good, have become what reformers sought, though perhaps not what reformers wanted. Cop identity, tied into a military "us-them" sense of self-worth, watches "them" for "us." As Betz (1988:184) put it: "The police thus withdraw into themselves—another sense of us versus them. They observe their own comrades brutally mistreating suspects, and disapprove, but do not report them." Tenets of culture link the militaristic mind and violence: Cops protect their own. It is a war out there, be careful. Always cover for another officer. Don't back down. Always bring superior force to bear. Thus, many of the more coercive, violent, and secretive themes of cultural identity are intensified in a militaristic model of policing. Advocates of police militarism were successful beyond their wildest imagination. In contemporary society, militarism is a root metaphor that organizes a great deal of meaning and behavior for cops, both in terms of how they perform their occupational tasks and in how they view their own organizations.

The New Warrior[3]

In *Warrior Dreams*, James Gibson (1994) discussed a profound frustration, engendered by the Vietnam experience, that continues to haunt the memories of American veterans of the war (see Kraska, 1994; 1993). In Vietnam's aftermath emerged a myth of spiritual malaise: the United States lost, and did so because it did not try hard enough—it lacked the political will to fight. The troops were not supported at home. We lost, not from the absence of manpower, not because our troops did not give their all, but from moral weakness on the home front. We were not permitted to win.

A new warrior emerged from the war experience. Celebrated in the media, the warrior fought the righteous fight, but always carried the battle on two fronts. On one front, a firefight involved a small group or a lone operative in a jungle setting, seeking to right some wrong incurred by the Vietnam experience. Typically it was the freeing of prisoners secretly held captive long after the end of the war. On the home front, the new warrior fought against corruption and deception, and was often at odds with his own superior officers or political leaders. The new warrior, Gibson argued, was an outsider, dependent on his particular skills, loyal, always heavily armed, a true American (Gibson, 1994:290).

The new warrior re-fought the battle for Vietnam a thousand times, each time winning it decisively (Gibson, 1994:11). In high camp, he was acted out in the "Rambo" movie series titled *First Blood* and *First Blood, Part 2*. Rambo, a former green beret guard in Vietnam, in the first movie he burns down a small Oregon town. In the second, he returns to Vietnam in search of presumed prisoners of war. His question is always the same: Do we get to win this time? (Gibson, 1994:5).

Rambo, Gibson noted, was not an isolated, disturbed malcontent. To the contrary, he represented a core set of American values. He was "the emblem of a movement that at the very least wanted to reverse the previous 20 years of American history and take back all the symbolic territory that had been lost" (Gibson, 1994:14). Rambo fought his battles against former Viet Cong in Southeast Asia, and against corruption at home. He may have been an outsider, but only because he was the last of a breed—a true American. He was a symbol of the purity of spirit lost by our refusal to "go all out" to win a war, our weakness and lack of moral courage that we needed to "save our boys" in Vietnam. And in a powerful symbolic sense, he was back, bad, and mad—fixing what was wrong in the USA so that failures like Vietnam could not happen again.

The ideological shift from Vietnam to the streets of America was easy (Kraska & Paulsen, 1996). The permissiveness of the 1960s and the youth counterculture were implicated in the Vietnam War. Drugs became a symbol of moral turpitude on the home front—they represented a sort of moral laziness and absence of fiber, fertile soil for the end of the "American century." It is not surprising that the warrior culture adapted straightforwardly to a new battlefield fought on the streets of America: the war against drugs. Even the language of the new drug war was the same as Vietnam:

> An article in Soldier of Fortune contended that the drug war suffered from exactly the same flaws as did the Vietnam war. " . . . It's a war where the police, as the soldiers of the streets, aren't given the opportunity to win." Once again, "defeat" was cast as the result of self-imposed restraints . . . (Gibson, 1994:290).

The new warrior was wholly committed to the war. The warrior culture passed the banner to American paramilitary police, dedicated to stopping the Asian and South American influence from destroying our country through drugs. The law itself was seen as a repressive device keeping the new warriors from winning the war:

> When brave soldiers and policemen who are doing their best to stop dictators and criminals discover that the leaders of their organizations expect them to put their lives on the line while at the same time crippling them with regulations, they become outraged. In their righteous anger at the 'system,' they either ignore the law, disobey their superiors, or resign. At that moment they become paramilitary warriors. Rambo was not alone when he asked "Do we get to win this time?" The paramilitary warrior must fight outside the system even though the enemy threatens to destroy America and the values it represents (Gibson, 1994:35).

Kraska: The Iron Fist of Militarism

In a series of articles, Peter Kraska has described how the ideology of the new warrior is gaining a powerful foothold in American municipal police agencies (Kraska, 1994; 1993; with Paulsen, 1996; with Kappeler, 1997). This phenomenon, metaphorically described as the "iron fist inside the velvet glove" (Kraska & Kappeler, 1997) represents a poorly recognized but sweeping change in American police departments today.

In spite of a great deal of police managerial rhetoric about the velvet glove of community policing, an influential militaristic way of thinking is securing its place in American police organizations. Its structural port of entry is through police paramilitary units (PPUs). PPUs were originally organized by major departments as anti-terrorism, anti-riot, or special weapons and tactics (SWAT) units. Their popularity has sharply increased in the current era. They are increasingly being used by small and large departments alike, and they are taking on normal police functions of investigatory search warrants and proactive drug interdiction. They are often used to conduct crack raids, and sometimes they patrol high-crime areas (Kraska & Paulsen, 1996). Though actual numbers are not known, Kraska and Kappeler (1997) suggest that 89.4 percent of all city departments serving populations of more than 50,000 today have some form of PPU.

PPUs are changing the character of urban policing tactics as well. Modeling themselves as elite paramilitary troops, they adopt the training, the language, the planning, and the weaponry of warriors (Kraska, 1996). They import a sharply militaristic language to police activities, one that belies the municipal foundations of American policing. Their language is the discourse of the new warrior:

> In a popular police magazine, the Fresno P.D. claimed that the streets had become a "war zone;" they responded by deploying their SWAT team, equipped with military fatigues and weaponry, as a full-time unit to 'suppress' the crime and drug problem (Kraska, 1996:417).

This is a military vision of police work. It looks at America and sees the "enemy within." Its mission is tactical: search and destroy. It is promoted at the highest levels of government. Consider the following quote from Attorney General Janet Reno, speaking to a crowd of military and law enforcement individuals. "Let me welcome you to the kind of war our police fight every day. And let me challenge you to turn your skills that served us so well in the Cold War to helping us with the war we're now fighting daily on the streets of our towns and cities" (National Institute of Justice, 1995:35, in Kraska, 1996:419).

Kraska and Paulsen (1996) provided a case study of the way in which the use of paramilitary teams has become a normal part of police work. In a city they did not name, a PPU was first founded in the early 1970s, and was disbanded in 1976. Reorganized in 1982, the unit was "normalized," that is, it was increasingly used for mainstay proactive police functions. In its reformative years in the early 1980s, its use was primarily for SWAT-type functions—barricaded suspects and the like. By the late 1980s, its use had changed dramatically. Whereas in the earlier period it was called out on only two proactive calls, which were one felony arrest and a security detail, it was regularly used for proactive calls in the late part of the decade.

From 1986-89, the PPU was used for 43 drug raids, six arrest warrants, two civil disturbances, and one security detail. This level of activity was maintained in the early 1990s, and again escalated in the mid 1990s; in 1994-95, a scant two years, the number of proactive calls increased 110 percent, with 39 drug raids, nine civil disturbances, one search warrant, and one gambling raid. Moreover, these proactive calls represented 93 percent of all calls for which the unit was used. Thus, the unit had been almost wholly converted to routine police duties. And this was in a department that considered itself as having a community policing orientation.

PPUs are proliferating across the urban landscape, and increasingly they are spreading to the rural American environments: Kraska estimates that one of five of all departments has one such unit. They are accompanied by a way of thinking, and it is the thinking of the new warrior. The intensity with which the new warrior ideology is taking root in police units should not be underestimated. It is a vision that celebrates firepower, and PPUs occupy high status within police organizations. It carries a military vision, where a criminal is seen as the enemy, and the mission as search and destroy. PPU officers particularly focus on what Kraska calls "hyper-danger," a highly exaggerated form of the fear that characterizes all police work. Units always anticipate encounters with armed individuals, and the apprehension of serious injury is always present. This sense of hyper-danger fosters a "brotherhood of war," a level of support and camaraderie not found in ordinary team patrol activity. Kraska and Paulsen (1996) cite one PPU veteran:

> As far as I am concerned it's a very tight group, more so than anywhere else in the department because you depend on each other. You can say I depend on a back-up officer on a domestic call, and you do. But when you get out there, if the man behind you isn't looking out for you, then you could very well get shot. So we're very tight knit in that we count on each other.

That perceptions of hyper-danger are culturally based is revealed by the history of the PPU: Of 208 call-outs from 1982-1995, only 18 shots were fired, and 12 of these occurred in one call-out.

Max Weber is reputed to have commented on the remarkable ability of ideas to reverse their meaning during their intellectual careers. Community policing is undergoing such a transformation of meaning today. It began as a velvet glove, a community relations effort when police in the latter 1960s recognized that aggressive police tactics offended and alienated citizens, and that the ability to gather basic intelligence—witness and victim testimony, the stuff of successful prosecution—disappeared when the police were feared. With the publication of "Broken Windows" (Wilson & Kelling) in 1982, community policing was recast in terms of aggressive order maintenance policing. In 1986, Skolnick and Bayley presented six innovative police departments that had implemented community policing components. They described the policing philosophy on Denver's Colfax Avenue in terms of "find a rock and kick it." Of the six studies they provided, they observed that what they witnessed in Denver was the future of American policing.

In the mid 1990s the velvet glove is giving ground to a new image, one that has a powerful paramilitary component, and where community policing is measured in a department's deployment capability for drug raids and its capacity to shut down crack houses. It is an iron fist. Rambo has come home. And the tactics of the Vietnam war have followed him. In a revealing comment, the chief of the city investigated by Kraska described his vision of the relationship between PPUs and community policing: ". . . the only people who are going to be able to deal with these (drug) problems are highly trained tactical teams with proper equipment who go into a neighborhood and clear the neighborhood and hold it to allow community policing and problem-oriented policing officers to come in and start turning the neighborhood around" (Kraska & Paulsen, 1996:22). This is precisely what we did in Vietnam. We called it pacification. It was a horror.

The potency of the new warrior vision in police work was brought home to me in a recent class I regularly teach titled "Police in America." I sought to describe the complexity of the police function in the United States today, to provide the students with insight on the problems of policing in a democracy. After the lecture, one of my students approached me and mentioned that he was undergoing anti-terrorist training. And he added simply, "And we don't have to deal with all that complicated stuff with bad guys. We just kill them."

Endnotes

[1] Auten (1985:123-124) identifies 19 characteristics of the paramilitary police organization. They are listed here, for those who may be interested in more fully exploring what is meant by police paramilitarism:

1. A centralized command structure with a highly adhered to chain of command.

2. A rigid superior-subordinate relationship defined by prerogatives of rank.

3. Control exerted through the issuance of commands, directives, or general orders.

4. Clearly delineated lines of communication and authority.

5. The communications process primarily vertical from top to bottom.

6. Employees who are encouraged to work primarily through threats or coercion.

7. Initiative at the supervisory and operational levels neither sought, encouraged, nor expected.

8. An authoritarian style of leadership.

9. Emphasis on the maintenance of the status quo.

10. Highly structured system of sanctions and discipline procedures to deal with nonconformists within the organization.

11. Usually a highly centralized system of operations.

12. Strict adherence to organizational guidelines in the form of commands, directives, general orders, or policy and procedure.

13. Lack of flexibility when confronted with problems or situations not covered by existing directives, general orders, or policy and procedure.

14. Promotional opportunities which are usually only available to members of the organization.

15. An impersonal relationship between members of the organization.

16. Feelings of demoralization and powerlessness in the lower levels of the organization.

17. Concept of the administration and top command as being arbitrary.

18. Growing level of cynicism among supervisory and operational-level personnel.

19. Development of a we-they attitude among supervisory and operational-level personnel toward top management.

[2] Kraska (1994; 1993) also explored the link between Gibson's Warrior Dreams and the new police militarism and provided the stimulus for this section.

[3] This idea is not original, but simply an analogous use of Gould's (1989) theory of natural selection.

8

Stopping Power

Why didn't you blow the asshole away? I would have shot the son of a bitch full of holes (Scharf & Binder, 1983:40).

The harsh sentiment contained in the quote above is ubiquitous to cop culture. It is replayed in an astonishing variety of situations, a word of support to a husband or wife who unexpectedly finds their spouse with a lover, small talk to cool off a pal whose encounter with a felon brinked on the use of deadly force, support for a colleague that got suckered into a pushing match with a drunk and almost "lost it." The quotes hint at underlying predispositions: that the use of a gun can resolve disputes, that those labeled as assholes or sons of bitches deserve to be shot. There is in the quote a sort of noncritical acceptance of the use of killing force, even if it is only verbal acceptance and both speaker and listener know that an actual killing would have been much more personally and occupationally troubling. When cops receive encouragement along these lines they are being socialized into a way of thinking about guns. They are learning the emotions and the language of a culture that, due to necessity, overreaction, excessive zeal, or mistake, acknowledges the inevitability and righteousness of deadly force. Indeed, to put another cop into danger from the failure to use a gun dooms an officer to social rebuke and isolation. This is a way of thinking for those accustomed to guns.

Surprisingly, that the police are participants in a culture in which guns are key elements, though common-sensically recognized by observers of the police as well as by the police themselves, has been virtually ignored by police researchers. (For a wonderful exception to this absence of discussion, see Kraska, 1996.) Guns are integral to police training, and they are in a cop's thoughts in all citizen encounters, even if the encounter is not itself manifestly dangerous. A cop will always approach

127

a citizen with his or her weapon away from the citizen, and will scan or perhaps pat down a citizen for hidden weapons. In a world of chance encounters and unfolding contingency, guns represent the final reality check. The influence of guns on cop behavior and their importance to the police occupational culture cannot be overstated.

This section looks at the police guns from a cultural point of view. I provide a glimpse of the powerful influence guns have on how police think about their work. I argue that guns are more than a symbol—they are a powerful thing in itself, an embodiment of immense force. Surrounded by training rituals and ceremonies of law, they are the supreme authority of the state to intervene in the lives of the citizenry.

In the culture of policing, guns transform police work into a heroic occupation, providing both a bottom line and an unquestionable righteousness that pervades all police-citizen encounters. From training ceremonies to funeral rites, guns symbolize the danger of police work. The gun is the ultimate arbiter of the dangerous unknown. With the gun, the capacity of the police to deal with problems is not bounded by the physical strength and wiliness of an individual officer, though both are desired traits. With guns, police are not just good guys, but good guys with stopping power, a distinction that celebrates the use of all necessary force to resolve any dispute, however violent. The term "moral servants" has been used to describe the police, but this term fails to capture the spirit in which guns transform the occupation into a heroic enterprise. Police see themselves, not as servants, but as moral custodians.

Consider the following description of Denver:

> Working with ESCORT[1] highlights a quality in policing that is invisible to outsiders but profoundly affects the psychology of its practitioners. Policing in the United States is very much like going to war. Three times a day in countless locker rooms across the land, large men and a growing number of women carefully arm and armor themselves for the day's events. They begin by strapping on flak jackets . . . Then they pick up a wide, heavy, black leather belt and hang around it the tools of their trade: gun, mace, handcuffs, bullets. When it is fully loaded, they swing the belt around their hips with the same practiced motion of the gunfighter in Western movies, slugging it down and buckling it in front. Many officers slip an additional small-caliber pistol into their trouser pocket or a leg holster just above the ankle. Inspecting themselves in a full-length mirror, officers thread their night sticks into a metal ring on the side of their belt (Skolnick & Bayley, 1986:141-142).

The incongruity of the policeman-as-warrior is not lost on the authors:

> We give a massive pistol to these tender-faced children and ask them to handle people whose life experiences they can't begin to understand. Dressing them to kill, we expect them to keep order so that we may live

in security. What a colossal act of faith on our part; what tremendous responsibility on theirs (Skolnick & Bayley, 1986:142).

This is not a picture of American youth dressing for public servitude. These are warriors going to battle, the New Centurions, as Wambaugh calls them. In their dress and demeanor lies the future of American policing.

Guns and the Culture of Policing

To understand the relationship between cops and guns, one has to consider their background. Rarely are officers first exposed to guns during pre-service POST training. Most officers come from a broader cultural milieu where weapons are prized. They have typically been raised in families where guns are normal fare, and most have hunted and target-shot since they were children. Many recruits have military experience, and have trained for combat with many types of weapons. They tend to enjoy shooting and to be card-carrying members of the National Rifle Association. They not only recreate with guns, they believe in guns.

For many, the use of guns and the desire to be a cop have been shared notions since they were children. The following quote shows how, for children in police families, guns are an organizing metaphor for police work itself.

> I've watched this ritual at least a hundred times. At night when my father came home from work as a detective from the Bronx and stood in front of the hall closet, my imagination saw a wild west gun slinger. I can still hear the slap he made as he ripped the belt off and wrapped his belt and holster and placed them deep in the top shelf of the closet.

> I waited for a day when my parents were out shopping. I finally worked up the courage to get the gun. Currents of power and fright surged through me. My fear was not of the gun but of my father if he ever caught me. I held the gun only a minute or two as I watched my reflection in the living room mirror. The steel stub nose of the barrel of the .38 police special felt cool against my palm.

The author, a young child at the time of the incident, uses this story to introduce the viewer to the history of his family, a family with three generations in the New York City Police Department. Though not a police officer himself, the identity of his family past and present is stamped with the identity of the NYCPD.

Guns are central to a vision of American independence, summarized in the saw "God made men but Sam Colt made them equal." Guns are neither socially irresponsible or the cause of crime; to the contrary, when criminals use guns, the responsibility lies clearly in their behavior. In many ways, guns bring to the foreground issues of personal responsibility; individuals that cannot responsibly own a gun—that use it in a crime, or threaten a police officer with a gun—should be punished by the harshest means available. A positive disposition toward guns thus already exists at recruitment. Indeed, for some, the sight, smell, and taste of guns elicits an almost mystical high.

Guns and Occupational Identity

Rubinstein (1973:290) is among the few scholars to recognize the importance of guns for the occupational identity of police officers. Guns, he argues, occupy a central position in the arsenal of weaponry. They become second nature, a part of the psychology of survival. A police officer learns to "use weapons as extensions of himself." Skill in weaponry contributes to the police officer's authority among other officers. This is particularly evident in POST training. Recruits quickly learn that, outside of the chain-of-command, the apex of authority resides in the high status position of the range master. Failure to perform adequately with a firearm is the most likely reason for a recruit to fail POST training.

In Rubinstein's research—a scant 30 years ago!—the principal weapon was a service revolver. In the current era, service revolvers (now an anachronistic term) have been replaced by 9mm semi-automatic handguns. These weapons are categorically different from the other weapons in an officer's arsenal. Weapons such as a nightstick and a taser have as their object the disablement of a felon through the infliction of pain. They are not gauged for their "stopping" or killing power. Guns are, and they have it. Today we have 9mm Glocks, Heckler and Koch MP5s, 10mm Glocks, Remington 1187 tactical shotguns, to name a few (Kraska, 1996). They are not selected for their ability to protect the police from unanticipated danger. They are selected for close-in fighting power. Cops want effectiveness, and effectiveness does not occur with a limited arsenal. Service revolvers evoke a sneer in today's high-firepower world. A minimum of firepower includes a shotgun and a 9mm handgun.

Rubinstein recognized that guns were qualitatively different from other weapons. Guns have as their principal intention the killing of the felon. Officers are trained to "double-tap" (two shots) in the center of the chest in order to "stop" the felon. The likelihood that two 9mm shells in the center of the chest will in all likelihood kill the target is not lost on patrol officers. Officers are not trained in the romantic tradition of "wounding" suspects with a grazing shot. Grazing shots are bad shots. Guns are evaluated for their stopping power and cops for the accuracy of their aim, and the larger and more centered the hole, or the more the tearing action after entry, the more potent the stopping power is judged to be.[2]

Scharf and Binder (1983) described the contribution of guns to cops' occupational identity in terms of Goffman's (1962) "identity kit." Individuals, Goffman observed, surround themselves with totems of their occupations. For example, a construction foreman will wear a 25-foot Stanley tape measure on his or her belt—any other type or a shorter length is an indication that the foreman is a novice, and subcontractors will recognize this vulnerability instantly. Such "identity equipment" provides individuals with identity and self-worth, tells others about their interests and inclinations, and establishes their status. Moreover, its presence is associated with a variety of attitudes that compliment the status—a 25-foot Stanley tape measure, for example, suggests to subcontracting crews that their work will be carefully scrutinized.

The identity kit for the police is their uniform and its compliment of weaponry, cuffs, and other related hardware. The thick police belt with field weapon and holster is a prominent feature, capable of creating fear in outsiders and engendering respect among peers. Culturally, the identity kit signifies toughness. As one officer interviewed by Scharf and Binder (1983:32) noted with regard to his weaponry, "Any motherfucker comes at me, he gets this [his gun] up his asshole."

Advertising aimed at police audiences reinforces the importance of guns. At police conferences, most exhibits are devoted to guns and related items such as holsters, paper targets, gun sights, and ammunition. Magazines such as *The Police Chief*, *Police Product News*, and *Law and Order* devote many pages to weapon types, concealment, use, and "strategies of survival in gun encounters" (Scharf & Binder, 1983:33).

Guns fuse with police mythology. Righteous images of police stomping bad guys are carried in stories of marshals dealing with gunfighters in the old west, or G-men in the Prohibition era (see also Skolnick & Fyfe, 1993). The reality of nineteenth-century America, of course, was far less bloody than the stories carried in myth and saga, and armed confrontations with desperadoes were rare. Yet, the power of myth does not reside in its historical accuracy but in its ability to evoke strongly held values. Guns evoke a heroic cop image, a lone actor on the metaphorical street, protecting citizens and stopping bad guys. Guns symbolically transform street cops into the urban warrior elite.

The image of cops carried by contemporary media sustain the hero mythology. Television frequently portrays lone officers (whose partner or spouse has been killed) fighting a soft or corrupt criminal justice system in order to get rid of an unquestionably evil bad guy. A large number of television shows reinforce this mythology, showing cops as the last bastion of frontier individualism, armed only with courage, righteousness, and of course, a motherfucker of a gun.

Police officers are presented daily with media images of their profession (Scharf & Binder, 1983:28). And these images have an impact. It is quite common to see police officers between arrests in the station glued to the latest account of "Cops." Mass media feed the occupational preoccupation with weapons and violence. The role of guns in police work, sustained by a body of historical myth, popular media, a simplistic public conception of crime control, and a very real concern with unpredictable danger, nourishes police culture:

> . . . the police officer's concern with the gun is not an arbitrary cultural anomaly but rather reflects a core occupational reality: the legal right (and at times the legal obligation) to exert force against those who may physically defy his legitimate demands and who may possess deadly force themselves (Scharf & Binder, 1983:38).

Guns and Authority

The gun is a powerful totem of the police officer's authority to use force. It is not simply the extension of a cop's physical prowess, but takes on a symbolic life of its own in the officer's cultural cosmology. It is a pure manifestation of copness, embodying a dramaturgy of coercion and force, deterrence and finality. In the battle of good against evil it equalizes. With a gun, a police officer can be as righteously good as a bad guy can be dastardly bad. Chevigny opens his (1995) book with David Bayley's quote "The Police are to the government as the edge is to the knife." Guns hone the edge.

Guns are at the most defining moments of the police role: confrontation with a dangerous and armed offender. Deadly encounters are etched in the personality of the police officers forever—an unrequested rite of passage that leaves a stain on the personality of the officer. This sentiment is related by Klein (1968).

> Every once in awhile, under a headline such as POLICEMAN SHOOTS TEENAGE SUSPECT, there appears a news article that pictures the policeman as a sadistic monster who goes about firing his revolver recklessly in exercise of his "license to kill." . . . during the last sixteen years of my career, as a supervisor, many of the men assigned to my command were embroiled in shootings. It was my responsibility, along with the captain or the higher superior in charge of the precinct where the shootings occurred, to investigate each of these occurrences. After the investigations, the men return to work. Their efficiency appeared impaired, but they were different. Each of the men reacted in line with his own personality, but even in those to whom shooting a man was not a first such experience, there could be noted, if sometimes subtle, changes (Klein, 1968:230-231).

This is followed with a story of a detective who kills a suspect during a botched robbery. The suspect had fired at the officer simultaneously, but the weapon had misfired because it was loaded with the wrong kind of cartridges.

> The district attorney presented the facts before a grand jury, and that body found nothing wrong with the detective's actions. The Police Department's investigation (a most intensive one, as in every instance of shooting by an officer) declared the detective blameless. He was recommended for, and received, a citation for his exceptional performance. . . . But the change was already apparent. This man, always rather quiet, was now prone to a certain moodiness. He drank more at social functions, and this seemed to produce a false gaiety in him, rather than the light humor which had been characteristic of him before the shooting. When tired, he tended to become irritable.
>
> What happened to this detective is not the exception. The troubled hearts of hundreds of living policemen and the hundreds of names listed on the memorial plaques in police stations throughout the country give the lie to the do-gooders, "civil rightists," and bleeding hearts with their denunciations of "kill-happy" cops (Klein, 1968:233).

Why have guns been overlooked by researchers? For some, they may be too "gritty," dealing with a hard and uncompromising edge of reality. The consequences of using guns are serious, intense, and final. They lack the sentimental flexibility that typifies the assessments of the police by social scientists. Guns are not for sentimental people. Moreover, police do not normally talk to outsiders about their weapons—guns are a topic that is personal. Talking about guns is like talking about a member of the family. It is too central to the heart of police work, too vital for words.

Guns embody the most thrilling aspects of police work, the reason police do what they do carried out at its highest, most intense moment. Guns deter. Nevermind that many police officers may not have a violent felony encounter in their career: The lovingly attended gun, the careful training, the stern warnings, and stories of lonely death that tarnish careless officers, insure that the presence of the gun will dominate a police officer's attention in all encounters with the public. Guns, protection against deadly force and violent criminals, are the ultimate edge in any encounter.

The controlling power of guns has not been lost on female officers, who quickly learn the equalizing power of weapons when dealing with potentially dangerous felons. Some police women, Martin (1980:176-177) observes, play on the fact that many suspects fear women with guns, thinking they will be "trigger-happy." One of Martin's respondents noted that she had an edge over male officers because she was not first obligated to use her fists to control male suspects. She was "freer to employ 'tools of the trade' which give her a clear psychological advantage in such situations." As one respondent told a suspect, "I'm so confident that I couldn't beat you up I'd shoot you if you hit me. . . . I'd probably go berserk and shoot you."

Police Infrequently Fire Guns on the Job

Despite their high profile in the psyche of individual officers, guns are used infrequently in real work situations. Geller and Scott observe that the popular image of cops as gun-wielding enforcers differs from what actually occurs:

> To take a single example, the average police officer working in Jacksonville, Florida (a city with a high rate of police-citizen violence) would have to work 139 years before he or she would be statistically expected to shoot and kill a civilian (Sherman & Kohn, 1986), 42 years before nonfatally shooting a civilian (Blumberg, 1989) and probably about 10 years before discharging a firearm at a civilian. Observational studies of New York police note similar patterns of infrequent use of guns, with guns used against civilians only in five of 1,762 police-citizen encounters (Geller & Scott, 1991:449).

The infrequency of gun use belies the emotional intensity of encounters where guns do come into play. Gun encounters are scary, and few cops look forward to them. In all weapons training, bravado is discouraged as a dangerous attitude. Cops are not taught to be brave but to cope with their fear. A two-handed grip, for example, is taught as the most effective way to aim when the hands are shaking (Adams, 1980). William Doerner, an academician turned police officer, provides a glimpse of the bright fear of an encounter where survival may not extend beyond an imminent use of deadly force.

> As I rounded the corner of a house and headed up the driveway, the suspect wheeled around the other end of the house, startled to see me just 30 feet away. I drew my revolver, aimed, and ordered him to put up his hands. While the butterflies waltzed in my stomach and my heart pounded like a jackhammer, I realized that I had no cover. I felt naked. The man began talking and slowly walking toward me, all the time keeping his right arm behind his back out of my view. Despite two more commands, the man kept moving as if I were not even there. In what seemed like a time-warp, a slow-motion series of frames, he turned slightly at the hips and was bringing his right hand forward. My stomach soured as my hand began the squeeze. He was about to be dead. Suddenly, something clunked to the ground behind him, and he raised both hands over his head. I eased off the trigger and the cylinder rotated. He was a half-pound pull away from death (Doerner, 1985:397).

Guns Are Central to Police Training

Training in POST carries large blocks of time devoted to weapons use and care. Officers learn about types of service weapons, how to clean them, to fire them, to wear them, and to care for them. A common training ploy is for the range master (the police officer in charge of the shooting range) to reveal to an academy class how he or she has carefully hidden five or six guns on his or her body. Long training discussions involve types and effects of ammunition, use of weapons and levels of force, types of weapons, their costs, and where they can be purchased, the diverse accessories related to service weapons—the belt, clips, handles, holsters, and related weaponry. Anyone that has ever observed the dynamics of a training class cannot help but notice the intensity of interest, focus, and discussion that develops around gun discussions. Hours are passed in the range developing the capacity to fire accurately. Many POST agencies use simulated firearms training devices.

Rubinstein is one of the few researchers that has written about police firearms training. The importance of the revolver, he observed, was emphasized at the outset of training. Though revolvers are badly outdated in the current era, the message he brings is as relevant today as it was when he wrote it. The firearms instructor warned the recruit class that "As long as you remain in the police department, the revolver you have just been issued is yours, until either it or you is destroyed. Well, fellas, it happens, you know." (Rubinstein, 1973:286). Recruits were then provided a week of weapons training, with the instructor emphasizing "the fatal character of the weapon and the intimate circumstances with which most police shootings occur." Live ammunition was used, and recruits in the training academy he attended were taught "point-shooting," shooting to survive. Point shooting was described as follows:

> In point shooting there is no aiming, the gun is simply pointed in the direction of the target and fired. You are shooting to kill. The patrolman is instructed to bend forward slightly as he draws his gun, placing his free arm across his chest. This is done to make the target he offers smaller and to use the large bone in the forearm as a deflector of any bullets that may be coming in his direction . . . The instructors realize that many men will be terrified when they draw their guns and tell them not to be worried if they are shaking. They are shown a two-handed grip which allows a man to steady his gun with his free hand, permitting him to shoot more accurately (Rubinstein, 1973:290).

Weapons training is used to demonstrate the sheer unpredictability of the working environment. Officers learn that they can trust no one, and the failure to anticipate all circumstances may result in their death. Adams, in his training manual Street Survival, summarizes the way in which officers are taught to think about guns:

To wait until you need to draw and fire your gun to think about survival tactics is like waiting until you're coughing up blood to think about annual physical checkups. You should have survival in your conscious thoughts the moment you receive an assignment . . . (Adams, 1980:45).

Ragonese tells the following story about his police training in New York city. This example provides a sense of how guns are used to train officers about unpredictability in police-citizen confrontations.

The training was designed to make us think about every conceivable possibility we might encounter. An instructor gave me and my partner, Charlie Johnson, a situation to handle, saying, "The precinct got a call on a family dispute, they went to the apartment and heard a woman inside hollering, 'He's gonna kill me.' Now you guys go to it."

My partner and I put on vests, jumped in our truck, and said on the radio, "Adam One's responding." We pulled up to the building and got out. I took the shotgun and Charlie grabbed a coil of rope, a sledge-hammer, and a psycho bar. Two instructors were waiting on the side-walk posing as precinct cops. They told us we had a family dispute that had escalated into a possible hostage situation in apartment 2H. Our job was to secure the area—seal the apartment—until the hostage negotiat-ing team arrived.

"We went upstairs and, as directed, moved in a low crouch toward apart-ment 2H. We were some fifteen feet from it in the wide hallway when we heard a woman yell, "Don't shoot me!" Then a man yelled "I'll kill you, you bitch!"

"I dropped down on one knee ("make yourself a small target," as instruc-tor had said) and trained the shotgun on the apartment door down the hall, concerned about the armed man inside. Charlie went down on a knee to my right and slightly behind me, his revolver aimed at the door. Then the door suddenly swung inward and a woman came flying out toward me. I motioned her behind me, keeping my eyes on the open door. In an instant I felt the muzzle of a gun against the back of my head—and the click of a hammer falling on a firing pin.

"You're dead, Ragonese," said the instructor . . . (Ragonese, 1991:162-163).

Ragonese trained in the early 1970s, more than 30 years ago. Since then, the sophistication of training technology has increased dramatical-ly. Yet guns continue to be at the core of a police officer's carefully trained skills in uncertainty and danger recognition. In all POST, when danger is presented, and it is presented daily, it is demonstrated in the most deadly form possible—unpredictable events, seemingly non-dangerous suspects, unanticipated but explosive, deadly gunfire.

Consider the following training exercise. An interactive video called F.A.T.S. (for firearm training instruction), popular among recruits and staff alike, provides a series of interactive videos that train recruits in the use of deadly force. A training officer initiates the video and controls the flow of events on the screen that simulates an offender about 20-25 feet away. Each video encounter displays a potential offender, involved in a situation that might or might not turn deadly. Trainees are given a Smith and Wesson with laser device inserted, and standing about 15 feet from the video screen, are told to react as if they were in a true encounter. In other exercises they might be provided with a similarly modified shotgun. The screen is capable of registering the shots fired by multiple weapons.

In one video, a male officer exits his patrol car and approaches a suspect spray-painting a wall. In another he approaches two vagabonds sleeping on a park bench. In a third, he peers around a corner of the roof of a building and finds a sniper. In each encounter, the officer must approach and (if necessary) disarm a suspect. In a fourth, he backs up his partner who is approaching a woman screaming at a her husband in a station wagon. A suspect or someone else may turn and fire unpredictably.

Trainees will face a series of gambits in which they try to take control of the situation. Sometimes they should not fire, and sometimes they must to survive. If they fail to return deadly fire and only wound a suspect, the suspect may suddenly fire again. Moreover, officers are taught to continue to fire their weapon even after they are hit. The training officer controls the behavior of the suspect and scores the firing accuracy of the recruit. Through these interactive training scenarios, officers are taught the mechanics of deadly force encounters, and learn how and when to react to unpredictably deadly force. As a technology to prepare officers for the potential danger in citizen encounters, the F.A.T.S. is an elegant heuristic. Officers not only learn when to anticipate and how to react to deadly force, but they also develop skills for learning when not to use deadly force when it might at first blush seem appropriate.

Recruits also learn that they should take nothing for granted, that no one is to be trusted. Interactive training, a more sophisticated version of the training described by Ragonese, is adapted to late twentieth century video technology. Both training episodes share in common a desire by trainers to recreate simulated deadly encounters in as realistic a way as possible, and to reinforce the uncertainty and untrustworthiness of suspects.

Gun training has changed over the years. Officers have traditionally taught to aim for the largest mass—the center of the trunk. Today, officers are increasingly taught to aim for the head as well—to take head shots. Barker describes this change as follows:

> This is a more difficult shot because because the head provides a smaller target, but the shot has greater stopping power. This shot has been deemed necessary because of an increase in suspects using bulletproof

vests, and because drug-intoxicated suspects (especially those on PCP) can take several shots and continue to resist for prolonged periods of time, according to police lore (Barker, 1999:68).

Gun training thus brings concerns of officer safety and survival to their highest pitch. It is no wonder that, by the time officers have graduated from POST academy, they think similarly about danger and survival. The intense focus on unpredictable danger that characterizes each of the above examples is typical of training, and is a powerful stimulus for the "we-them" attitude at the core of police culture. And in these examples we begin to learn something about the "them" in the we-them distinction that is central to culture and that I will talk a great deal more on later in this book—"them" is not about a definable population, but about a population of unknown membership. And the focus on guns elevates the unknown to its most primal concern—the ability to survive encounters. It is no wonder that, by the time cadets have graduated POST training, they are already utterly conditioned to a world where no one but another cop can be trusted.

Police Shootings of Police

When people think of police shootings, they typically imagine police shooting suspects, or felons shooting police. People infrequently think of police shooting police. Yet police deaths at the hands of other police, whether accidental or suicidal, are as common as police-suspect shootings. Fyfe (1978) noted that, from 1971 to 1975, nine cop shootings involved mistaken identity of police by other police. In 1988, five of 53 officers shot were by fellow officers, and two of those were fatal. As Morris (Geller & Karales, 1981:iv) noted, "It is the armed robber, and paradoxically, the armed policeman who are the threats to the life of the police!"[3]

Accidental police shootings and killings are among the most emotionally disturbing events that can happen to a police department. That big city police have moved into super-enforcement, undercover, multi-task force anti-drug mode where strangers work in plainclothes and may be working together guarantees that mistakes of identity will occur. Yet cops, singularly focused on individual responsibility, always view mistakes as human error, by either the shooter, the victim, or brass. Regardless of the circumstances, some of the taint always spills on the shooter; an officer who accidentally shoots another wears the stigma for what's left of their career and sometimes for their life.

Suicides are also prevalent among the police, though their relative frequency tends to be overstated. Fyfe (1978) noted that nine of 12 New York City officers who died by guns in 1987 took their own life, as did eight of 10 in 1986. He wryly noted (1978:476) that police are as "likely to be killed by themselves, their acquaintances, or their colleagues as by their professional clientele." Similarly, of 294 Chicago police officers who were struck by bullets, 100 shot themselves (Geller & Karales, 1981) (see Geller & Scott, 1991).

Recent research has found high levels of police suicide (Arrigo & Garsky, 1997). Police rank among the most occupationally prone groups to commit suicide (Violanti, 1995; Hill & Clawson, 1988). Arrigo and Garsky, citing ongoing research conducted by the National Association of the Fraternal Order of the Police, found that suicide was the number one cause of accidental death among cops.

The tendency of police to commit suicide by gun is usually explained by the proximity of weapons and the effectiveness of the police in using them. It is more than this. It is a part of yourself turning on you. Baker quotes a cop describing a 12-year period when he was, in his words, "cracking up:"

> I was trained to use a gun. I saw cops who tried to blow their brains out and still lived because they put it to the side of their head. The oral sex, the making love to the gun is to put it in your mouth, put it inside your head so that way you won't miss. And I started to think about it an awful lot . . . I've seen myself stop the car, get out, empty the gun and throw the bullets across the field. Then I felt safe (Baker, 1985:357).

The gun is described as if it were a potent self, experienced as an aspect of the officer turned inward, against him, Kali-like, in an orgasm of hate and destruction. Guns are the most potentially violent element of the police culture, the ultimate expression of its authority. Sometimes their potency is too much, a toxin that burns into the brain. In the end, for some they are the only way out.

Endnotes

[1] ESCORT is an acronym for Eliminate Street Crime on Residential Thoroughfares. It was a force of about 21 officers assigned to the Capitol Hill district in Denver, Colorado.

[2] Even in Rubinstein's time the stopping power of ammunition was an important consideration. Consider the following quote from his book:

> Every large department has special sharpshooter and anti-sniper units whose members are trained to use all types of ammunition, are allowed to carry Magnum revolvers, high-powered 38s, and have available to them semi-automatic and automatic weapons. Some of these men carry shotguns in their car loaded with rifled slugs called "pumpkin balls," which can blow open a heavy wooden door at close range. Some departments even acknowledge that their men are allowed to carry the

hollow-pointed Super-Vel bullet, and several federal police agencies have made this ammunition standard. These bullets are prohibited under international treaty because "dumdum" bullets, as they are called, are considered too ghastly for international warfare (Rubinstein, 1973:288).

[3] Cited from Geller and Scott (1991:453).

Themes of
the Unknown

If there is a cosmology that ties officers together, that unites all elements of the police worldview, it is a paradox: the cosmology of the unknown. The unknown in all its forms, whether it is a call for service that hints at danger, an automobile stop when an officer cannot see the hands of the driver, the bulge in a coat pocket of a teenager, or a strange car in a familiar neighborhood, the unknown haunts police officers. It is most likely something trivial, sometimes a hassle, perhaps dangerous, unpredictably deadly. It is always a dilemma to be resolved.

This section is about the experience of the unknown and how adaptations to it unify the police culture. Police cultural adaptations to the unknown are in a real sense a product of our fears of it. A colleague and former California Highway Patrol officer explained it to me in the following way. When facing the unknown, our expectations for the police are fundamentally different from our self-expectations. We run away, or at least we probably should, when confronting something unknown, potentially dangerous, perhaps threatening. We expect cops to run toward it (Caldero, p.c.). The public mandate is that cops identify and resolve that which is unfamiliar. We want them to do what we would not do. We want them to be different from us.

A number of investigators have commented on the unpredictability of police work and its implications for administrative control over line officer behavior. Wilson (1968), a keen observer of police behavior, argued as follows. In spite of public beliefs that the police primarily do law enforcement, order maintenance situations tend to dominate day-to-day police work. Yet these situations are legally vague: the task of maintaining

141

order suggests that there is a condition of disorder that can be brought back to order. This is quite different from law enforcement, which is a relatively straightforward assessment of violations of the criminal law. Because judgments about community order are always subjective and require a good deal of street sense to resolve, it is almost impossible to bring them under the control of department policy.

Nor is line-level discretion limited to misdemeanor activity; Black (1980), in an observational study, noted a great deal of discretion among felony crimes. In follow-up research I observed a great deal of community variation of arrests for felony crimes across offense and race categories, even controlling for reported crimes (Crank, 1992).

Literature consistently attributes the inability of administrators to control line officer discretion on inherent vagueness of order maintenance circumstances. What has been overlooked is the mediating influence of police culture on the relationship between unpredictable encounters and police administration. Officers deal with the unknown on a daily basis, and develop broad cultural adaptations to unknown situations. The popular adage "officers should take a four-foot leap over a three-foot ditch" suggests, for example, the need to bring more than sufficient force to bear to control police-citizen encounters. The metaphor, leaping over a hole, implies that the use of more than adequate force is necessary because officers can't be sure what is in the "hole." The hole is a metaphor for the unknown. The perimeters of real holes, however, are visible—the boundaries of the unknown are not.

This section is about cultural adaptations to the unknown. The unknown is treated with predictable formulas—cops tend to fall into patterned behavior during traffic stops and other routine encounters. The key phrase, though, is "tend to:" at the outset of all citizen encounters a police officer never knows for sure whether his or her action will resolve a situation, and this absence of certainty motivates a great deal of police cultural activity. Day-to-day situations, both trivially and dangerously unknown, contribute to a way of thinking about work and about citizens. Shared, this way of thinking becomes an important part of police culture. The following five themes—(1) suspicion, (2) danger and its anticipation, (3) unpredictability and situational uncertainty, (4) interaction turbulence and edge control, and (5) seduction—are different aspects of the way in which everyday unknown encounters shape cop culture.

9 The Twilight World

Theme: Suspicion

> Suspicions among thoughts are like bats among birds: they ever fly at twilight.
>
> Francis Bacon

The quote above was presented as a definition of the term "suspicion" in Webster's Unabridged Dictionary. The definition continued as "the act or an instance of suspecting; a believing of something bad, wrong, harmful, with little or no supporting evidence." The shadowy imagery provided by Bacon more correctly approaches the nature of suspicion than the technical definition. In suspicion lies the dark metaphor on which police work rests; an irony that converts a bright, safe world into a "twilight world" fraught with danger and hostility, where nothing is as it seems. Suspicion is the ability of the mind to create a world parallel to yet morally opposite the one in which ordinary people inhabit, and in which the greatest danger of all is to take things as they appear.

Writers on the police have frequently identified suspicion as a characteristic of the police personality (Skolnick, 1994; Swanton, 1981; Rubinstein, 1973). In this section, I suggest that it is a feature of the culture rather than the personality,[1] that it is a widely shared attribute of the police worldview, and that it is driven by everyday characteristics of cops' occupational environment.

Suspicion is a product of broad legal and political factors. Legally, the craft of suspicion, the ability to ironically convert the seemingly "safe" into the darker world of lawbreaking, is a craft demanded by the criminal code. As creatures of the law grounded in due process under a democratic constitution, police are required to have an articulable basis for noncasual citizen contacts. Constitutional pressures over the last century have endeavored to hold police accountable to the rule of law. In prac-

143

tice, this means that the police have to be able to say clearly why they decide to constrain the liberty of a citizen. As Skolnick (1994) has recognized, suspicion is central to the demands of the criminal code.

When an officer screws up an arrest, when they fail to show a legal basis for a search or a seizure and a citizen takes formal action, the impact of the screw-up is passed through some complaint procedure. It may come through a complaint from a citizen to his or her city council representative. City councils sometimes act as grievance bodies when police overstep their legal boundaries with citizens. A person who felt that she was inappropriately detained and questioned by the police may find a voice of support in the membership of the city council. Or a complaint might be filed directly to the police department itself. In some cities the complaint may go to a citizen review board. A citizen may sue the department and the officer. Legal challenges to the police and mistakes of individual officers are ultimately passed down the chain of command by the chief in the form of policy. The question all groups respond to is: Did the officer have a legal basis for intervention? Was reasonable suspicion present?

Over the past 40 years, interpreted by the courts, molded by municipal politics, and ultimately transferred through the police chain of command as policy and training, suspicion has been transformed from an inarticulate guessing game into a legal craft of the highest development. Today, the art of a carefully honed suspicion, couched in all necessary legal mumbo-jumbo, focused on officer safety, and practiced by a skilled police officer is an element central to both the police organization and to the police culture.

The Legal Bases of Suspicion: Reasonableness

The defining issue in a democracy is the boundary between the authority of the state and the rights of the individual. In the United States, the police enact the government's authority to intervene in the affairs of the citizenry. It is not a whimsical authority, but a matter of written law. The behavior of the police under rule of law, for all of the frustrations that it causes the police in the short term, is among the enduring strengths of our democracy. Police may not detain a citizen without clear reason. The courts have consistently rejected the use of inarticulate hunches as a basis for the detention of a citizen or the investigation of a citizen's property. A police officer must have an articulable basis to stop and interrogate a citizen. This basis is called reasonable suspicion.

An officer cannot respond "I had a hunch." When officers respond in this manner, the courts do not look favorably on the contact.

Once reasonable suspicion has been established, the police may (1) conduct a pat-down search, which is something less than a full body search and is intended to check for weapons, (2) ascertain the identity of the person, and (3) conduct a brief field interrogation. With these three techniques, they must decide whether to escalate their involvement with the suspect, that is, to inquire specifically about their culpability, to read them their rights, and to arrest them.

The importance of field interrogation to contemporary police procedure has been widely cited. Reasonable suspicion is the legal basis for many initial contacts between the police and the citizenry. Developed from *Terry v. Ohio*, the notion of reasonable suspicion means that cops may approach someone and investigate the possibility of criminal activity without having to fully satisfy the demands of probable cause.[2] Brown (1981:161) notes that field interrogations make up 40 percent of all onview (what police actually see occurring) stops. Reasonable suspicion is one of the primary bases for the involvement of the government, vis-à-vis the police, into the affairs of the citizenry.

The idea that there is a legal basis for suspicion is wholly inconsistent with cultural dimensions of suspicion, what I will call sixth sense suspicion. The skill of sixth sense suspicion lies not in the ability to gather enough evidence to make an arrest, but in the ability to identify wrongdoers from the most meager of cues. It is in the inarticulateness of suspicion that an officer's true skill comes into play and is recognized by their peers. An officer or detective who can use their "sixth sense," or construct a case from the most seemingly innocent or meaningless information, is the officer who gains status and recognition.

Suspicion is the special craft of policing. It is the stuff of stories and traditions. A cop's talent is in seeing what is hidden or disguised, not what is there. Evidentiary considerations become important after the officer is on the trail, to use the old adage, after the "game is afoot." When the case is legally constructed for the court drama, the evidence will be carefully weighed for its contribution to a guilty verdict. But this all comes later, and offers scant support for an officer on the scent of a wrongdoer. These are technical considerations that back up the craft of sixth sense suspicion. The following section shows how the craft of suspicion is learned in the daily context of police work. The section borrows extensively from Rubinstein's work in 1973. Though the writings are old by today's standards, the ideas about suspicion in the daily work of the police are as current today as they were 30 years ago.

Rubinstein: Suspicion as Craft

Suspicion is not a friendly sort of social attribute. To observers it looks like a distrustful psychological disposition, which of course it is. It is a behavior that sets police apart from conventional people who are put off by obvious displays of distrust. Yet it's an irony of occupational life, a nonsocial attribute that furthers cops' abilities to do their work. As Skolnick (1994) notes, it is a trained predisposition.

Rubinstein captures the flavor of this behavior from one of the officers in his study.

> Paul studies the people on the street. He'd learned to hold their eyes. Many glanced at him and turned away quickly. Others held his eyes for a moment before turning away. Then there were the defiant ones, but eventually even they were stared down. As each one turned away there was a look of guilt on his face as though he'd revealed too much to the cop's prying eye (Rubinstein, 1973:221).

Used as an inquiring technique, suspicion can be a powerful tool in the police officer's armamentarium, a psychological ploy by which cops assert their authority to peer into the private domain of an individual's psyche, to probe the shadows of another person's gaze for hints of wrongdoing. The suspicious stare intimidates; it seeks out wrongdoing and asserts police authority.

> Whatever others may think he is looking at or for, when he stares at someone he is expressing his special rights as a policeman . . . He knows, too, that it is unsettling to be stared at; but he need fear no reprimand . . . It is his way of telling those people at whom he is looking of his claims on their behavior in public (Rubinstein, 1973:221).

The suspicious stare is a display of power. It is the absolute right of a police officer to take an interest in you, no matter who you are or what you are doing. It is a form of inquiry that is less intrusive and below the "reasonable suspicion" standard, but one that nonetheless unequivocally displays the power of the state in citizen affairs.

A patrol car can also be used as a psychological ploy to probe suspicious circumstances and determine whether or not to act further. Like Van Maanen's (1978) process of "asshole" recognition, the relationship between suspicion and action may involve a series of decisions by an officer that identify the type of person with whom he or she is dealing. The following example describes this process.

> Instead of stopping and staring or riding on past, he (the patrol officer) drives the car toward the suspects, openly displaying his interest in them . . . As he comes even with them, he turns his head to look at them, not concealing his interest in any way. He does not halt nor does he stop looking. If he is successful, they will be following his actions intently. He is making a play and they are responding to it . . . When he has gone past them, he suddenly hits the brake, causing the car's wheels to screech, and shifts the wheels into reverse. When he does this, he is watching closely for any movements in the group, someone throwing something to the ground or a person moving to block off his direct view.

They might run and he will not chase them, but if he has been successful, he might find a knife, drugs, or even a gun in the gutter (Rubinstein,
1973:241-42).

Suspicion is precipitated by cues. Suspicion arises in everyday situations and is aroused by behavioral clues. A person who averts their
gaze from a patrol officer, as if he or she is looking elsewhere, is always
suspicious. Forms of concealed concern, staring overhead and reading a
newspaper for example, may be matched with an underlying tension on
the body that makes the person appear unnatural (Rubinstein, 1973:235).

Suspicion is aroused by a person who purposefully ignores an officer
when he or she should take notice. The intimation of flight, or initial
furtive movements away from an officer, are particularly powerful stimuli
that arouse suspicion. Persons who move suddenly are noticed. In the following story an officer describes behavior that kindles his suspicions.

> If you see a woman rubberneck, she's usually a pickpocket or a whore.
> Whores rubberneck. They know what's going on. As a rule, whores
> know more about what's going on in the street than anybody.
>
> The guy whose head is on a swivel, the rubberneck, that's the guy who's
> probably looking to commit a crime. When you see a guy looking all
> around him, the trick is not to be seen by him, just to kind of lay back
> and let him look around, follow him to where he's going.
>
> For spotting burglars, the old one used to be "Look for the guy carrying
> a pillowcase that looks full." Now it's "Look for the guy carrying a gym
> bag." We stop them most of the time. Mostly, they're legit. But you'd be
> surprised how many times the guy drops it and runs (Fletcher, 1990:23).

Suspicion is honed through training. New hires marvel at the
ability of old-timers to "see things," as Rubinstein (1973) puts it. Stories
about officers who identified a felon or discovered a crime with their wits
are prized in local police cultures. These stories illustrate the art of suspicion, the rare, special police skill in recognizing the unknown. It is not
learned, but is taught through stories, field training practices, and on-the-
job learning. It is a product of concrete practice, a self-taught art, a true
craft. In many ways, suspicion is the craft of policing.

> During his training period, the recruit is encouraged to patrol with his
> windows open, alert for any unusual sounds and smells. Under the com-
> mon law he is considered a sight officer who may arrest for any crimes
> he sees being committed. The law interprets his sight to include all of
> his natural senses. If he smells something he feels reveals evidence of
> criminal activity—a still or drugs—it is sufficient cause for him to inves-
> tigate without a warrant (Rubinstein, 1973:224).

Suspicion is the art of "exceptionality"—the capacity to recognize unexpected variation in otherwise routine activities" (Skolnick, 1994:77). Officers first learn to recognize the normal in things. The "normal" is a silhouette, a backdrop against which officers can identify that which is out of place. When officers learn the daily routines of their beat, they slowly become adept at recognizing the presence of normality, what should fade into the background. Only with a fully etched silhouette of the ordinary can officers recognize when something is out of place, when something should attract their attention. Citing a former student that also worked as a police officer, Rubinstein noted that time spent cruising a sector or walking a beat is not wasted. "During this time, the most important thing for an officer to notice is the normal . . . only then can he decide what persons or cars under what circumstances warrant the appellation "suspicious."

The Working Context of Suspicion

Characteristics of the working environment stimulate suspicion and how suspicion in turn becomes the basis for citizen contact. Suspicion connects cognition with action; suspicion is the legal gambit through which an officer's observational skills become the basis for an intervention into the life of a citizen. Rubinstein noted several varieties of ordinary work activity where suspicion becomes the basis for police action. These varieties of activity are what I call the "working context of suspicion," in which suspicion emerges as an occupational response to commonly occurring events in their working environment.

Crime Report

Police officers on patrol often receive crime reports. Yet, the likelihood of catching a suspect is low, and officers learn that they probably will have brief moments before the opportunity disappears. Cops consequently tend to look for cues that are easy to spot and allow rapid action. The make and model of the car are the most important cues; these are easy to spot from a patrol car. If the car is garden-variety, police look for highly visible characteristics of occupants—manner of dress and the like. If the suspects are on foot, he looks for two specific things: identifiable clothing and distinguishing characteristics. These cues are often meager and chances of a successful interdiction are slim.

> He is making a stop on the odds, and his suspicion is low. Since he knows that he has only a few minutes to capture a suspect, any hint of culpability is sufficient for him to make an inquiry . . . It is common for the same person to be stopped successively by several patrolmen with-

in a few minutes of a reported crime, each man being attracted by the same distinctive feature of the person's appearance (Rubinstein, 1973:28).

Pedestrian Stops

Officers develop extensive repertoires of behavioral cues among pedestrians that lead to further investigation. Furtive glances at a police officer, staring overhead, and other efforts to conceal concern are noted by officers: "These efforts to conceal concern, while not daring to convert into motion, frequently cause the whole body to tense, giving the person a rigid appearance that is wholly 'unnatural' and making him even more apparent" (Rubinstein, 1973:235). Shoes provide information: ex-convicts and other institutionalized individuals are accustomed to walking with their toes curled and absent shoelaces, which are denied to inmates. A person with a limp in a gang-infested area might signal a shotgun strapped onto the leg. The list of pedestrian cues is long and tends to vary from beat to beat. However, these cues are likely to mobilize further investigation by an officer.

Car Stops

Rubinstein notes that most car stops are made for violations. Frequently, however, these reasons are incidental to the officer's true reasons for stopping the car. Officers, he notes, are interested in "finding stolen cars, cars carrying contraband, illegal armed people, and persons sought by the police" (Rubinstein, 1973:250). When they make a stop, they tend to have done so by approaching the car from the rear. Most of the cues they seek are consequently at the rear of the car. Temporary license plates, a tag fastened by wires or on only one bolt, a dirty tag on a clean car and vice versa are suspicious and may lead to a traffic stop. A missing trunk lock (suggesting forced entry), signs of pry marks, and the absence of a rear bumper (suggesting that the car was stolen from a repair shop) may also cause suspicion.

If an officer's suspicion has been aroused, the officer will check out the driver and passengers of the car. The presence of several teenagers in a suspicious vehicle will almost always lead to a stop because a police officer will wonder if the car is being used for a joyride or to carry contraband. A woman driver with male occupants in a high-crime neighborhood will be frequently stopped, he suggests, because this is an odd combination that is sometimes found in robbery situations. A suddenly cautious driver is as suspicious as a driver that makes a sudden turn; both have suddenly and inexplicably changed their behavior to avoid contact with the police.

Suspicion, the talent of ironically converting safe areas into perilous ones, mobilizes much police behavior. Officers know that, unless a complainant and a suspect are at a scene when they arrive, their chances of solving the crime are almost nonexistent. The only chance they have to catch a perpetrator is through a keenly honed suspicion. Consequently, "The setting of every call to work is momentarily contaminated in the patrolmen's view. Every person in that setting is contaminated by simply being there" (Rubinstein, 1973:230).

The Expansion of Sixth Sense Suspicion in the Contemporary Age

In the current age, formal training for police has expanded, and the craft of suspicion is facilitated by a wider knowledge and legal base. POST training courses provide trainees with practical information on field interrogation techniques aimed at uncovering wrongdoing. Types of suspects, gang paraphernalia, and other aspects of their work environment are identified as areas that should arouse suspicion.

The legal and organizational foundations that justify the employment of a cop's notion of suspicion are also expanding. This is particularly evident in many contemporary changes in the police: the expanded formal training requirements in place in many states today, the expansion and legitimation of drug interdiction activity, the good faith exemptions to due process that legitimize a wide variety of police interventions, the increasing tendency of the courts to accept an officer's experience as a basis for reasonable suspicion.

An area where the threshold for intervention has been lowered in the current age is in the use of drug courier profiles. Traditionally the basis for an automobile stop has been probable cause. This is because stopping a vehicle is itself a seizure. Increasingly, the courts are permitting a new basis for automobile stops: the drug courier profile. As a technique for intervention, drug courier profiles lower the threshold of automobile interdiction[3] from probable cause to a standard sometimes called "articulable suspicion," in practice, to virtually no standard at all. In *New Mexico v. Cohen*,[4] for example, the court recognized the following profile characteristics: appearing nervous, driving a rental car with Florida license plates, driving cross country, carrying a small amount of luggage, driving a rental car paid with cash. *New Mexico v. Mann*[5] extended this list to driving too slowly and carrying items in the back seat that would normally be carried in the trunk. Moreover, as currently practiced, profile stops are used to provide a basis for a subsequent search, a principle wildly inconsistent with traditional practice, where a stop itself did not provide a basis for a subsequent search. California Highway Patrol, for example, routinely pulls over drivers and, announcing that they are conducting a profile stop, routinely conducts a subsequent search of the vehicle. Through this and similar practices, inarticulate or sixth sense suspicion is becoming a legal basis for police intervention into citizen affairs.

Sixth sense suspicion in courier profiling is tied to another powerful theme of policing—officer safety. With Lee Rehm, I conducted an examination of a program titled "Operation Valkyrie," an Illinois State Police program initiated in 1985 with the assistance of the DEA (Crank & Rehm, 1994). Operation Valkyrie was designed as an "officer safety and awareness" program. Drug trafficking, the state police argued, was inherently dangerous and officers had to take extra precautions in case they should encounter a violent occupant or a second vehicle protecting the lead vehicle. Searches of the vehicle were justified in terms of officer safety.

In drug interdiction training, officers are trained to recognize suspicious characteristics that justify a search after an initial stop—torque marks on a screw in the side of a door that might indicate that the panel had been pulled off, for example, or hollow-looking areas in seats that might suggest that they had been de- and re-padded. Training also may include the use of drug-detecting canines, conversational approaches to suspected couriers, observation and stopping techniques, and methods used by couriers.

Into the home: The unpleasant reach of suspicion. Skolnick (1994) suggested that suspicion was an attribute of the police "working personality." Many of us, however, tend to take our work home with us. Officers sometimes carry elements of their work into social and personal settings. Consider the story of "the blade," a sergeant, trainer of recruits in New York.

> "Blading" describes the physical stance or posture of an officer who may, for example, be interviewing someone on the street. The object of taking a bladed stance is to remain balanced and alert, so that if the other person makes a threatening move, the officer will be prepared to counter it. When bladed, an officer is turned slightly sideways with the weapon away from the citizen. . .
>
> When the officers at the party nicknamed him "The Blade" it came as a surprise to Tom Michaels. He took his training role very seriously and was shocked to learn that his inability to turn off his radar was so noticeable to people in normal business and social conditions. And while he tried to make light of his new nickname, the rookie officers received a show of support from an unexpected source. Michael's wife happened to be at the party that night as well, and she pointed out that he had unconsciously been blading her and her three young children around the house for years (Carlson, 2002:41).

Crank and Caldero (2000) present a thought experiment of an off-duty officer who, suspecting that his wife is having an affair, uses well-honed "tricks of the trade" to uncover guilt that he "knows" is there. The incident develops as follows:

Police Training	Jealous Behavior
1. Falsely tell a suspect that he has been identified by an accomplice.	1. A friend called and said the wife was seen with another man.
2. Present faked physical evidence.	2. Takes out a pair of her panties and says he found evidence of semen on them.
3. Tell suspect he has been identified by an eyewitness	3. A friend saw the wife having lunch with a man.
4. Stage a line up in which a witness pretends to identify the suspect.	4. Husband says: "I followed you and saw you with him. Will you admit it?"
5. Lie detector: Tell the suspect that the test proved guilt.	5. He says: "Look me squarely in the eyes and tell me you're not having an affair."

Ah, sad suspicion. It is a well-trained art, and it seems to work so well on the job. Take it home and things just fall apart. The hidden warning, Crank and Caldero suggest, is that maybe all the tricks used to uncover guilt sometimes beget its illusion. The art of suspicion, carried out by a well-trained but distrustful officer who is convinced of someone's guilt, erases the line between unmasking guilt and creating it. In summary, suspicion is central to the police occupational worldview (Skolnick, 1994). Suspicion derives from the police preoccupation for potential violence and the development of perceptual shorthand to identify symbolic assailants. As a cultural theme, suspicion links the territory of police work and its inhabitants with police perceptual skills to recognize danger. In other words, suspicion represents a set of learned cognitive skills for recognizing potential danger and is a precursor to the use of coercion to resolve the danger.

As an occupational predisposition, suspicion will always stand out, a sour though necessary veneer for the working personality. It is, as Goffman (1959) once described personality, an occupational cuticle; a visage presented to the world, provided to adapt to work expectations and the demands of the occupational environment. As a social skill, it is not pretty; no one would list "suspicious" on their top ten list of admired personality characteristics. This element, so important to a police officer's craft, will never endear them to outsiders. It is not surprising that the more skilled officers become in their craft, the more they tend to retreat to their own kind for social and emotional support. The skill that makes them so good at what they do is one that separates them from those of us who abhor direct confrontation and prefer the knack of indirection for communication and inquiry. In a cruel way, their ability to pierce the veil of misdirection, to find the truth behind the lie, forever marks them different from us. And what does that say about us?

Endnotes

[1] Skolnick (1994) has described suspicion as a characteristic of the policeman's working personality. Semantically, the distinction between a "working personality" and an element of a culture is vague. Both concepts suggest that the element is common among line-level officers, and both suggest that it is driven by characteristics of the working environment.

[2] Probable cause means that:

    1.   The officer has a reasonable belief that criminal activity is about to take place.

    2.   The person that is detained is connected to the criminal activity.

[3] An automobile stop is a seizure, therefore probable cause is required for the stop. Any subsequent search of the vehicle requires a different probable cause, based on an officer's inspection of the interior of the vehicle. However, if the courts accept that the second search was based on considerations of officer safety, the probable cause standard may be waived.

[4] 711 P.2d 6 [N.M. 1985].

[5] 712 P.2d 6 [N.M. 1985].

10 Danger Through the Lens of Culture

Theme: Danger and Its Anticipation

Danger is a poorly understood phenomenon of police work. Academicians will paint a picture of work that is rarely dangerous, characterized primarily by monotony. Police will describe a darker picture, danger and violence as an endemic hazard of their environment. Well, which is it? Part of the answer lies in how danger is measured, and part of the answer lies in the way danger is viewed through the lens of culture. Consider the following story:

> I reached the doorway, peeked in, and the apartment was pitch black . . . Fear surged through me when a shot rang out in the apartment. Then I saw a flash as another shot was fired. The four housing cops came crawling out of there as fast as they could, and one dove right between my legs.
>
> I reached with my left hand to close the door, and a shot rang out. I got hit by a bullet between my thumb and index finger, in the fleshy part. It felt like a burn. A fourth shot hit the door jamb before I got the door closed. A fifth shot passed through it and struck the metal frame on the door across the hall.
>
> I turned to Sgt. Conroy and said, "I've got to get to the hospital."
>
> "What's the matter?"
>
> "I got hit," I said, holding out my left hand, which was bleeding. When Richie Michael heard his partner had been shot, he grabbed Jake Simms, saying "You sonofabitch!" Two cops pulled Richie away . . .

Richie got behind the wheel of Adam One, me in the passenger seat . . . He burned rubber and raced toward the FDR drive, weaving in and out of traffic like a stock-car driver.

"Easy, Richie, don't get me killed," I said. "I'm only shot in the hand."

Richie got on the radio and screamed, "My partner's got a gunshot wound and I'm taking him to Bellevue, heading north on FDR. ETA at the hospital in five minutes." When we turned onto the FDR, we were met by some twenty police cars, which had shut down the Drive to other traffic. They escorted us, lights flashing, sirens sounding.

"Holy shit, Richie, I'm embarrassed," I said. "With all this, I shoulda been shot in the chest or somethin'."

Father laughed and said "Look up." There was a police helicopter overhead.

(Later, after arrival at the hospital.) I was told that the governor's wife, Matilda Cuomo, was on the phone to me. Mrs. Cuomo thanked me . . . and said that she was terribly sorry to hear that I'd been shot (Ragonese, 1991:200-202).

This story was told by Paul Ragonese in his autobiography titled *The Soul of a Cop*. It colorfully captures both the emotions of real danger and the powerful, evocative symbolism that danger holds for police officers. In the following section, I will try to show that danger in the sense of an officer killing is an uncommon occurrence, but that smaller dangers such as assaults and batteries are common. It is a blend of the symbolism of deadly danger and the reality of common, but real, small dangers that account for the pervasiveness of danger as a cultural theme of the police.

Assessing the Dangerousness of Police Work

How dangerous is the occupation of policing? The public perception of police work is that of an occupation that carries considerable danger (Kappeler, Blumberg & Potter, 1993). Television, movie, and newspaper media provide an unimaginative public with a fattening diet of sound-byte-mentality story lines involving shoot-outs, swarthy bad guys with big shiny automatic guns, and violent crimes committed by smirking child molesters. Police are inevitably presented as risk-takers, which sometimes they are, but which they invariably try to avoid being such.

Police believe that their work is dangerous as well, though their perception differs from simplistic media fare. Officers will describe brief moments of terror in the midst of long periods of routine activity. Danger is not sought and not liked, but recognized as an inevitable accompaniment of their work.

Danger is a central theme of police work, and thinking about and preparing for danger are central features of the police culture. Perceptions of danger are underscored in POST training, where "police vicariously experience, learn, and re-learn the potential for danger through 'war stories' and field training after graduation from the police academy" (Kappeler, Sluder & Alpert, 1994:100). Evocative symbols of danger—a razor hidden on the side of a driver's license, a .22 caliber weapon that looks like a pen knife—are common training fare. Officers are constantly reminded that in citizen encounters they can trust no one. A popular training film shows an officer murdered during a vehicular stop on a Texas highway. Training instructors provide stories of dangerous encounters and personal experiences to convey a focus for occupational danger. Training is in many ways like "being prepared to be dropped behind enemy lines to begin a combat mission"[1] (Kappeler, Alpert & Sluder, 1994:101).

When one looks at statistics, the apparent dangers of police work seem to melt away. Researchers have noted that, when compared to other occupations, police work just does not look risky. The relative infrequency of line officers killed in action is often cited as supporting evidence. In 1994, for example, 76 officers were killed in the line of duty. This number is surprisingly low, given the estimated 842,805 employees in 15,513 police agencies in the United States, or less than 1 in 10,000.[2] Moreover, available evidence suggests that the risk of harm for officers has declined over the past decade (Kappeler, Blumberg & Potter, 1993). How, then, can we reconcile the seemingly low numbers of officers killed with the perception, widely held within the police culture, that police work is exceedingly dangerous?

Cullen and the Paradox of Danger

Francis Cullen and his colleagues (1983) identified what they called a "paradox of policing." On the one hand, they noted that concern over violence and physical risk was a distinguishing feature of the police occupation. By all official counts, however, police work did not seem particularly hazardous. Actual incident counts of bodily harm to police officers seemed to be infrequent. What could account for the imbalance between the seemingly infrequent threat of danger and widely noted perceptions of physical risk?

The researchers conducted a survey of five suburban departments of a large midwestern city. They found that officers recognized that the real likelihood of danger was not particularly high. On the other hand, their research revealed officers' keen knowledge that their work put them in the path of harm. Statistically, they noted that almost four-fifths of the officers believed that they worked in a dangerous job, while two-thirds believed policing was a dangerous occupation. It was not the actual danger that caused fear so much as the potential for danger that infused their working environment. Daily work activities, from routine traffic stops to calls to investigate suspicious circumstances, contained in them the seeds for violence against officers and produced deep concerns over officer safety. Though the chance that an officer would be hurt was slight, they argued, the potential for injury was present in a great deal of ordinary police work.

They concluded their discussion with a second paradox: that fear of danger was both "functional and dysfunctional." Very real hazards of police work, they commented, make it essential that officers remain vigilant to the potential risks of their work. However, police concerns over danger contributed to heightened work stress and a depressive symptomology. Officers recognized that there was a great potential for injury, and that it came from individuals who sought to deliberately harm them. Officers were consequently preoccupied with danger in police-citizen encounters.

Rethinking Danger in Police Work

Today, when researchers think of police danger, they tend to adopt the Cullen et al. perspective and its persuasive argument that fear is associated with potential danger. And indeed, the chances that an officer will be killed in the line of duty are slim. I believe, however, that this perspective needs to be broadened to account for the garden variety of dangers to which officers are exposed, not simply the extreme case of loss of life. There are many reasons why the use of loss of life as a measure of occupational danger may underestimate the dangerousness of police work and thus fail to capture the importance of danger to cop culture.

First, police have rapid access to medical care, thus decreasing the likelihood that a life-threatening injury will end in death. If violence is measured in terms of death, then police access to medical care will underestimate the violence of police-citizen encounters. Second, and perhaps more importantly, police officers are trained to minimize the threat of genuinely dangerous encounters; they are armed, they work together, and officers in areas thought to be dangerous usually wear body armor. They hide behind corners if it will protect them. They are absolutely focused on the threat of bodily harm, and have spent a great deal of time learning how to protect themselves in dangerous encounters. They are trained to be warriors. Consequently, a simple measure of police officers killed in the line of duty is a poor measure of real danger. Officer killings

are more realistically a measure of the presence of real danger unsuc-
cessfully recognized or countered. Police killings are closely scrutinized
by officers for mistakes made by their brethren.

A more realistic measure of danger experienced by police officers, I
think, is a count of the number of assaults on officers in the line of duty.
This number might more accurately reflect danger in the presence of real
bodily threat because it includes injuries of all types. When we look at
assault data, we find large numbers of incidents: 1994 data on assaults, for
example, show that 66,975 officers were assaulted in the United States, a
number substantially higher and seemingly out of proportion to officer
killings and more revealing of the real violence that characterizes their
occupational environment (Maguire & Pastore, 1995).

Even this number may be overly conservative, because assaults are
probably underreported by police officers. Police, like most people, are
less likely to report assaults when the injury is trivial. They do not want
to take the time to fill out a report, visit a doctor, and file an insurance
claim. Moreover, as discussed elsewhere in this monograph, themes of
bravery and masculinity are important cultural themes, and both of them
discredit as weak or feminine the reporting of minor injuries.

Consider again the opening example. The real injury in this case, a bullet lodged in Officer Ragonese's hand, was not life-threatening; to a casual
observer, the response of the department might seem dramatic and exaggerated. Yet, the circumstances under which the injury was received were
perilous by any standard—six officers were involved in a shootout that,
but for the vagaries of chance, could have resulted in the killing of one or
more of them. The encounter was deadly in intent. If the ceremony of the
department is overstated when gauged against the actual results of the
encounter, it was not for the gravity of the incident itself. Moreover, but
for the training of the officers, the number of injuries might have been
higher. For all the reasons cited above, then, even the seemingly large
number of assaults reported above probably fail to encompass the magnitude and frequency of real dangers confronted by police.

Finally, to grasp the full impact of dangerous events on a particular
police culture, recall the organizational structure inhabited by line-officers. The squad system keeps officers in close contact to each other as
well as isolated from the public. Members of a squad are in frequent face-
to-face contact both at the beginning and end of a shift, occasionally see
each other during a shift, and communicate by car phone according to
their needs and desires. They may be colleagues for years, they form
cliques, and they socialize after work. In such an intimate social environment rumors of an assault on an officer are transmitted with astonishing
rapidity, as in Officer Ragonese's story above, across an organizational
culture like the waves of a stone skipping across a lake, touching all members of the group, and contributing to a cultural reservoir of memories
and stories of dangerous encounters.

Danger is neither uncommon nor trivial. Police culture is grounded in common-sense reactions to real events, and cultural preoccupation with danger stems from real threats to police officer safety. Danger and police officer safety carry enormous symbolic weight because the work is seen as genuinely dangerous. The threat of danger mobilizes much of what the police are about, and danger encountered—the shooting of an officer— brings together the police as no other event can. Danger realized brings together the police culture; it is its most fundamental glue.

In Ragonese's story, it is clear that Ragonese is not seriously injured after the incident is over. The rapid self-mobilization of the police on his behalf—even closing off a section of the highway to escort him to the hospital—is an event he experiences with a certain degree of embarrassment. But given the occupational individualism and masculine orientation of police culture, his sense of embarrassment is itself a cultural element. Ragonese is a highly professional self-effacing officer who views danger as something that officers simply must deal with in their daily activity.

Danger, Culture, and Skolnick's Symbolic Assailant

Danger is a ubiquitous cultural theme. From academy training and field experience, officers "vicariously experience, learn and re-learn the potential for danger through 'war stories'" (Kappeler, Sluder & Alpert, 1994:246). Stories and heroic episodes shared among officers insure that danger holds a central place in the ideology of police work (Martin, 1980). Potential danger shapes police work, converting daily activity into a craft of identifying threats to public and officer safety. The powerful reality of danger converts it to a puissant unifying theme of police culture. The reality and the symbol interact in Skolnick's (1994) idealized notion of the "symbolic assailant."

According to Skolnick (1994), police routinely encounter particular signs that suggest that a person may be dangerous. Signs include the way someone is dressed (suggesting gang affiliation), their gait (suggesting that they are carrying a weapon), their talk (lack of respect, a troublemaker). Over time, from the gathering of common experiences, officers learn to recognize potentially dangerous persons. Such clusters of signs become a sort of "symbolic assailant"—an individual who carries characteristics that indicate danger—and rouse an officer's suspicions that they are engaged in a potentially perilous encounter. The symbolic assailant is a composite individual that arises from common experience and serves as a perceptual shorthand to rapidly identify and cognitively process potentially dangerous individuals. The following story is a description of a symbolic assailant.

> You can tell if somebody's just out of prison just by looking at them. They've got what we call the "joint body." They do the prison strut when they walk down the street.
>
> Say you're a young fellow, you're 5' 10," weigh only 160 pounds. You go to prison. You're fresh meat, baby. You're gonna be breakfast for these cons.
>
> The first thing you do—you start pumping iron to have strength to survive in the joint. You get a big chest, huge arm muscles. It's an attitude you want to give off to people; it says, Get outta my way, don't mess with me.
>
> These guys get out of the joint, they come at you down the street, they look like gorillas. They swing their torsos when they walk; they look menacing. You see somebody like that walking towards you, you get out of the way, right? He's got the joint body, the prison strut. You can spot an ex-con in a second that way (Fletcher, 1991:24).

Symbolic assailants may also have racial characteristics. As Kappeler and his colleagues observed (1996:98-100), because police tend to be homogenous in values and attitudes, and because their routines may put them in regular contact with ethnic groups different from themselves, the symbolic assailant may take on characteristics of economically or ethnically marginal groups in their jurisdictions.

For some officers, danger is not limited to symbolic assailants. A so-called "siege mentality" haunts some officers, convinced that distinctions among criminals, victims, and citizens are an illusion of circumstance. I have experienced this phenomenon when dealing with a police manager who, convinced that my findings would be published and made available to criminals, refused to provide me with interviews that might provide insight into ongoing police practices. Manning (1978b) tersely noted this phenomenon in the following tenet of police culture: "people cannot be trusted; they are dangerous."

Geographies as well as people are converted into potential threats. These "assailant geographies" are public and private areas that show signs that experienced officers recognize as potentially perilous (Crank, 1996). Playgrounds on weekends are assailant geographies—they represent areas where drugs are exchanged, gangs meet, and oldsters are mugged.

Assailant geographies, like symbolic assailants, are a powerful trope called an irony. Through the irony of suspicion, safety transforms into danger, and involve the transformation of seemingly safe areas into dangerous landscapes. The ironic conversion is accomplished through the craft of suspicion—and in this way the theme danger is closely linked to the previous theme suspicion. Danger transforms suspicion into both a characteristic of police personality (Skolnick, 1994), and an element central to the culture of a police officer's working environment.

Endnotes

[1] Kappeler and his colleagues (1994) are not denying that police work is dangerous. They are arguing that the police cultural focus on occupational danger overshadows real threats to police officer safety.

[2] The total number of employees includes both civilian and sworn personnel. If we were to focus only on municipal police agencies, the respective numbers are 493,930 personnel in 11,989 departments. Of these, approximately 21.7 percent are civilians (Walker, 1994).

11

Anything Can Happen on the Street

Theme: Unpredictability and Situational Uncertainty

Tales of the Ridiculous (McNulty, 1994).

Police work is unpredictable. Periods of boredom are punctuated by moments of action that can be wild and evilly whimsical. Unpredictability makes the endless hours of scant activity meaningful. The driving around is not so bad if the wait pays off. When it does, officers gain new insight into the logic of the street and sometimes a good story about the dark side of human affairs. The accumulation of these stories uniquely identifies police cultures. The following anecdote captures the kinesis of unpredictability.

> Practically anything can happen in the street. My partner and I stopped a fellow speeding down Lake Shore Drive; the ceiling's forty-five; the guy must have been doing a hundred. "Stop that son of a bitch!" So we turn on the blue lights, pull him over to the side. And he ran back to the car—we didn't even get a chance to look out, this is how fast he came back to the car. He says, "Look. I know I'm speeding. You've got to help me out." He says, "Please don't—I don't have time to get a speeding ticket. You see that girl in my car?" We say, "Yeah." "That is the greatest sexual experience I've ever had. She lives at the YWCA at Oak and Dearborn. If I don't get her back in five minutes, she's never gonna be able to go out with me again. I'd love to talk to you—if you stay here, I'll be back in ten minutes, you can write me up then, but I don't have time for this now"—he runs back, jumps back in his car, and zoom!—off he goes at a hundred miles an hour (Fletcher, 1990:6).

This unpredictableness, sometimes called "situational uncertainty" (McNulty, 1994), is different from circumstances where officers encounter danger. To a certain extent, danger haunts all of police work. Situational uncertainty, however, refers to the ambiguity police confront both with regard to work activities on the "street" and with regard to the organization itself (Manning, 1977). Van Maanen (1974) contended that unpredictable elements infuse patrol work with meaning and interest, and provide important breaks from otherwise monotonous routines.

In research I conducted on parole and probation training, I found that recruits were taught about the way unpredictability marked all elements of their work. Unpredictability infused daily work with unanticipated complexity and provided stories that acted as light-hearted heurisms. One such story was of a routine house visit, conducted by parole agents accompanied by the police, that progressively expanded.

> Instructor: This is a big case that was picked up on TV. We had an offender and we thought that he was changing VIN numbers on cars. Asked him if he had any weapons. Well, he did. There were 43 weapons, 34 loaded. Thought it would take 15 minutes, and it took 7 hours.

> Next, someone called the media. They came out and took pictures. We filled a marijuana bag with peat moss, and we let them take pictures. We never claimed it was marijuana. Nothing wrong with a little favorable media coverage. The media zoomed right in on that bag. There was a safe upstairs, and he (the offender) said it was his mom's and he couldn't open it. So I went upstairs and I said with a real loud voice "Get a locksmith and get him over here. Get Florida on the phone; if we find anything in there, I want his mother picked up within the next 4-5 hours." He started cooperating after that. The safe was full of drugs.

> I seize everything. We seized the house, then discovered it was in his mother's name. We had to let it go. Then we found out that it had been paid off and the deed for sale was signed from his mother back to him. We grabbed it again. Then we found out he had forged the document. So we let it go again, then added charges of forging the document.

In this example, through a series of unexpected findings and psychological gambits the officers were able to uncover a great deal more activity than they initially thought they would.

Only the common sense of individual police officers—not "book learning"—can prepare them for the pervasive uncertainty of police work. Because common sense deals with the unknown rather than the known, it cannot be taught in recipe fashion as a "book of rules," providing individual officers with cognitive maps of their work. Common sense is a sort of poetic logic that allows "activity to be both orderly and improvisational" (Shearing & Ericson, 1991:483). It provides a way to think about situations rather than recipes to follow in particular encounters. Common sense conditions officers to be flexible and creative, so that they can adjust to unknown, unpredictable encounters.

The Tediously Unpredictable

Unpredictability has a street ambience of wildness and danger. But it can be less than this as well: unpredictability can be tedious and boring. Consider traffic stops. The behavior of officers at traffic stops varies across a wide set of contingencies, very few of which include danger. Bayley and Bittner (1989:99) identify 10 actions that officers may select at the initial contact, seven strategies appropriate during the stop, and 11 exit strategies. In all, this is an astonishing number of contingent permutations (10 x 7 x 11 = 770) that may characterize a stop. Consider the exit (behavioral) strategies listed by Bayley and Bittner. Officers may

> . . . release the car and the driver, release with a warning, release with a traffic citation, release with both a citation and an admonishment, arrest the driver for a prior offense, arrest for being drunk, arrest for crimes associated with evidence found during the stop, arrest for actions during the encounter, impound the car, insist that the driver proceed on foot, help the driver arrange for other transportation, arrest the passengers for the same reason as the driver, transport the driver someplace without making an arrest, and admonish the passengers (Bayley & Bittner, 1989:98).

The selection of a particular action depends on the way in which the encounter unfolds, the behavior of the citizen, the seriousness of the infraction, the need to control the situation, the potential threat to the officer, highway safety and traffic flow, the presence of backup; in short, a host of factors contingent on the specific circumstances of the stop. In its fashion, unpredictability can be overwhelmingly mundane. It is precisely the dense varieties of outcomes that occur with mundane unpredictability that makes real danger so difficult to recognize when it happens.

McNulty: Common Sense and the Extraordinary

Common sense is highly valued among the police. Yet the idea of common sense is somewhat anomalous, given the unpredictability that characterizes much police work. Most people, when they think of common sense, think of aphorisms that guide a person to act in a particular way. McNulty (1994) recognized that common sense among the police was different. Working with a police department in Arizona, she noted that police used common sense to provide a way to think about uncertainty—a sort of mental framework that allowed officers to think about and gauge their reactions to unpredictability as it emerged in their work setting. She hypothesized that, by stressing situational uncertainty that characterizes the police working environment, police generate common sense knowledge.

McNulty's interest was in how uncertainty shaped officers' common sense. Participating in the police department as an outside observer, McNulty spent 16 weeks with a training class, conducted interviews with staff members, and did ride-alongs with many of the graduates. Through her research she assembled a picture of how police officers construct common sense.

McNulty observed that, with the police as with other groups, common sense derived from action; that is, police developed their ideas of human nature from things they had done in citizen encounters and how their colleagues reacted when they discussed those encounters. What characterized the police was that the stories they replayed to colleagues, like their work, involved situations that were, at their outset, unpredictable or uncertain. Officers' stories about what they had done led to the formation of vocabularies of common sense that focused on the uncertainties of police work. Common sense ways of dealing with uncertainty in turn were passed on to recruits, to prepare them for the unpredictability of police work. McNulty provides the following "interactive scenario" that introduces recruits to the idea of uncertainty.

> Several police officers re-enacted a crime scene as the recruits watched and offered comments. The setting was a convenience store where a robbery had just occurred. Two police officers were both claiming (loudly) to be the clerk who had just been robbed. Each actor tried to convince the recruits that the other "victim" was actually the "bad guy." Distraction was aided by another actor who portrayed a meddlesome and obnoxious witness. When this 'witness' was 'interviewed' by the officers in the scenario, his occupation (lawyer) drew insider laughs from the audience. A final note of confusion was added as the actor who was being 'arrested' turned and asked (referencing the "victim"), "Why did you let my partner go?" (McNulty, 1994:284).

This exercise, McNulty noted, was designed to bring uncertainty to areas normally taken for granted, particularly in distinguishing victims from offenders. Uncertainty was explained this way:

> . . . citizens often assume that those who commit crimes look different from victims and that only offenders would lie. Casting an attorney in the role of troublemaker, who may pose a substantial risk to the offender, further illustrated that danger could appear in appear in varied and unanticipated forms. Lastly, the scenario illustrated to recruits that dangerous and ridiculous components are neither rare nor mutually exclusive, but that both stem from pervasive uncertainty (McNulty, 1994:284).

Uncertainty may torment a police officer when it is associated with life-threatening circumstances. However, unpredictability in other job-related circumstances can be a source of wild sensations, energy, the stuff of cultural celebration. Nor is this sort of unpredictability uncommon. McNulty (1994:285) noted that "the ordinary always as the potential for becoming extraordinary." Both danger and sheer craziness stem from the same causes: pervasive uncertainty in the police working environment. She referred to the latter type of uncertainty as "tales of the ridiculous." The following story provided by McNulty characterizes this sense of craziness that pervades the working environment of the police.

> The officer responded to a call regarding a cab driver with a fare who wouldn't pay. In the parking lot, the cabby was standing outside his cab yelling at two prostitutes. In the front seat of the prostitute's car was a third prostitute who was naked, except for a red leather jacket that she somewhat used as covering, although as she got angry and got out of the car to scream at the cab driver, she didn't bother with the jacket. The cabby had picked up the naked prostitute and now she claimed she couldn't pay. All four of them were screaming at each other. The cabby was screaming for his money, the naked prostitute was screaming that she had been raped by a john, and the other two prostitutes were yelling that the cabby should have known that she had no money when he picked her up naked (McNulty, 1994:285).

Real Police Work

Both Manning (1977) and Van Maanen (1973) have described police work in terms of an underlying tension. The tension is between rookie expectations of what police work is, and its day-to-day reality as experienced by seasoned officers. This tension takes a related form as well; officers balance their activity between time spent laying low and avoiding trouble, and time spent seeking or doing real police work. It is during the latter that rookie expectations of excitement are fulfilled, and that sustains cops' interest in their work.

Real police work is the sudden blast of the unpredictable infusing an otherwise routine shift with excitement. At any moment on a shift, officers may hear over the radio "officer needs backup" and feel their adrenaline surge in anticipation of chase, danger, confrontation. Real police work, what Bittner (1990) calls "the huff and the puff of the chase," merges rookie fantasies with daily activity; the sudden call for a crime in progress, the chase of a felon—in short, all the stuff displayed on "reality police" television shows, bring the work of the police to life. Real police work engages the vital self, invokes warrior dreams to make a difference in the battle against crime. Officers have the opportunity to use the special skills that derive from their unique experiences and enforcement training—the powerful themes of danger, officer safety, weapons training, protecting other officers comes into play during real police work. Real police work is the "symbolic rites of search, chase, and capture" (Skolnick & Woodworth, 1967). Such work gives the police a sense of self-worth absent in the give-and-take of normal everyday routines.

Police work is perceived by officers as adventurous, regardless of the literature to the contrary (Hunt & Magenau, 1993). Patrol holds endless promise for activity. The following example provides a sense of this adventure.

> We had a string of cat burglaries in high rises along Sheridan Road. . . . It was really goofy. We'd check, and they all had double-locked doors, deadbolt doors, no signs of any forced entry.
>
> There was a detail put on it, and we had guys stationed various roofs of these high rises. Middle of winter—it was cold up there, and we got the wind coming right off the lake . . . We'd get a guy on a roof across the way, with the binocs, trying to see anybody coming up.
>
> So one night, a guy appears on one of these roofs, about two o'clock in the morning, a cold and windy night—carrying a bike. We later found he came up through the high-rise stair-wells. Takes the bike, puts it on the roof. He then takes out one of these . . . a rope, like mountain-climbers use, hooks it on the roof, and he—rappels—down three floors off the top, and drops onto the balcony. And he goes in through the sliding doors. The majority of people never leave their balcony doors locked—who's gonna think somebody's gonna come in from outside the fiftieth floor?
>
> He came back out with some camping stuff, climbed back on the roof. That's when we caught him. He's going to the bike he rides to and from the burglaries. "What'd you bring your bike up for?" He says, "I don't want nobody to steal it" (Fletcher, 1990:223-224).

Contemporary authors have sometimes observed that most police work is uninteresting (Walker, 1990), an idea strikingly at odds with the notion that police work is exciting. Because writers on the police do not want to overstate the limited quantity of real excitement in day-to-day police work, the importance of other, more interesting activity is downplayed. Police tend to, as Van Maanen (1973) observed, lay low and stay out of trouble.

Reuss-Ianni has questioned the idea that police work is boring, suggesting that such a conception is a "management cop's idea" of line activity that fails to catch the thrills and excitement that evolved spontaneously out of mundane activities (Reuss-Ianni, 1983). As seen in Fletcher's example, unpredictability does not have to be hard-hitting action-filled danger; almost any crime-solving activity is revered as real police work. Perhaps the idea that best sums up the meaning of real police work is the following, related to me during a field research project:

"Every night, when you start out, you never know when something special is going to happen." Some of the pleasure and the celebration is in the anticipation.

Grit Is the Policeman's Lot

Stories of the unpredictable sometimes carry a coarseness toward the human condition. The events that constitute good stories have a quality of grit, not frequently acknowledged in more scholarly tomes on the police. By grit I do not mean pluck or spirit, but rather the sense of being coarse, full of hard particles of dirt and sand. Grit is a metaphor that suggests the grinding or abrasion of smooth and comfortable textures by hard, stony material. Police deal with the grit of social relations, the coarse, rough outcomes that accompany the collapse of human affairs. Stories highlight police perceptions that they "have seen it all."

The following story of a suicide captures the gritty unpredictability of police work.

> One time we had a jumper; this guy jumped out of the 19th floor of the YMCA. He hit the ground, and his head hit, and the top of his head popped off, and his brain fell out. And it was perfectly intact. I'm walking all around it; I can't get over how it's just a brain laying there, complete and perfect as can be. It's laying right on the gutter. It didn't splatter-it wasn't icky or anything. It was like somebody just placed a brain on the gutter. Like an egg yolk. It was just perfect.

> So now the paramedics come. And this one paramedic goes, "Look at this brain! Do you think we should put it in the chest with ice?" I'm looking at him like "Sure, pal, go ahead and transplant this on somebody" (Fletcher, 1990:3).

Grit is not simply a way that cops cope with their work, though it is certainly that. It is a reflection of the work they do. Cops see the human body in ways that we do not normally see it. We are profoundly social creatures, and we normally see the human body adorned with personality and expressing itself with socially accepted mannerisms. We see and interact with our friends in full cultural dress; wearing facial expressions appropriate for particular circumstances, providing reassuring nonverbal communications, and wearing clothing fitting the station. Indeed, those that do not outfit themselves in appropriate social attire are rapidly abandoned as friends and colleagues—we self-select to be around those that are like us. Our connection with others is mediated, in short, through a complex set of institutions that constantly remind others what we are about and us the same about them.

Sometimes cops see something different. They see human flesh unadorned by custom. They see it for what it is, vulnerable, weak, sometimes hideously damaged, occasionally putrefying, desiccated and maggot-filled. Cops are true outsiders—they know what humans look like without benefit of social trappings. A Hans Christian Andersen fable speaks of an insightful clown, honest and naive, who sees the King wearing no clothes and has the audacity to mention it. Cops know what people look like with no skin on them.

In the summer of 1996, I rode along with a police officer, a young man of about 30 yet already tough and street hardened, through the tough and violent streets of Savannah's second precinct: the inner city, dangerous and brutal. We passed by a residence, a condominium comprised of four units, the upstairs of each painted a different pastel.

> In there was where Robby Robinson was killed. He was a civil rights worker. The whole front of the building (he nods toward the condo) was blown off with a nail bomb. Tore off a leg and an arm.

> "Was he killed?" I asked.

> Oh yeah. They stuffed his guts back in him and sewed him up, but he kept bleeding, so they opened him up again. Now I know that the body's a machine. I've seen it.

Violent death was common on the beat. In a six block area, he made several observations:

> Over there was where a hooker was found under the house. Over there (two blocks down) we found another hooker under the house. (Across the street) Over there, two burglars broke in and shot a woman in the face, killed her. (Around the corner, down three blocks) Over there was where I found my first mummy. She had her panties stuffed down her throat. She was full of maggots. The neighbors were complaining about the smell.[1]

For those that have witnessed such as this, the thinness of the social veneer will always be too visible. The human body stands revealed for what it is—a watery sack, perishable, stinky, given to release of bowel and bladder at the moment of extreme fear and death, always too close to evil forces that would shred it. On the brief shift I was with him, we witnessed a young woman, face gashed and bloodied, dark skin peeling back, and stomach with a deep puncture wound swelling even as we were looking at her. Her clothes were pulled back to provide room for the work of the medic team. "Blood and breasts" one officer observed. The meaning was contextual: her bra was a deep crimson color, except for one small white patch under her left arm, well away from the wound.

The white patch shined, as if to mock in its cleanliness the brutal blood-letting surrounding it. There is little opportunity in work such as this to celebrate the human spirit.

For many officers, grit is a staple of their humor, giving it a characteristically dark cast. The following story is particularly gritty, revealing the unpredictable in a humorous way and provides an exemplar to close this section. (Fletcher, 1990).

> See, you have ghoulish policemen. I tell you, though. It kind of goes with the territory. See, we have a sense of humor that to somebody who doesn't know cops would seem terribly gruesome. To us, it's extremely funny.
>
> Back in '72, we had a plane crash. A plane caught the telephone wires, went down, took down a couple of houses, killed a bunch of people on the plane. The pilot looked so natural sitting in the seat that they thought he was still alive, and he was dead. One of the victims was decapitated. And what happened was, the ambulance crew got there, they had a young female on it—and a wagon man told me this and swears it is true: He holds the head up and says to her, "Want to take this one?" She screamed and ran off. This brought howls, peals of laughter from the cops. This was the funniest thing they'd ever seen. Now this is sick, but that's how it is with cops (Fletcher, 1990:43).

Endnote

[1] Fletcher (1991:68-69) observes the reluctance of police to respond to calls regarding suspicious odors. One story tells of suspicious odors as the "most feared call of them all," another of the way in which officers adapted to bad odors, for example, "Wagon men are famous for smoking cigars at scenes."

12

No Animal Out There Is Going to Beat Me

Theme: Turbulence and Edge Control

"I'm not going to let any sonofabitch out there get me. No animal out there is going to beat me. You'll have to cut my head off to stop me."
—POST training class, 1995

This statement was presented in a training video, played in a POST training class for Probation and Parole officers that I attended. The sentiment, what the instructor of the class called a "positive mental attitude" applies with equal vigor to municipal police work. If a situation becomes so wildly unpredictable that events are life-threatening, he will triumph. The instructor, the range-master, then turned the lecture over to an officer wearing a T-shirt with the following in large letters:

Attack Me
I Need the Practice

The officers in this training situation are displaying the sentiment elsewhere called "maintaining the edge." This theme was described by Van Maanen (1978:312) as a key to understanding the "how to" of patrol work. Maintaining the edge means two things, both practical. First, make sure that you have more firepower, skills, training, or back-up than the bad guys. Second, bring decisive force to bear on encounters with bad guys, colorfully described by Shearing and Ericson (1991:492) as "taking a four-foot leap over a three-foot ditch."

Turbulence and Control

Control is one of the central elements of the police culture. Strecher stated the principle of control as follows:

> In every encounter police officers must gain control in the sense of initiating and orienting each part of the situation and maintain that control; they must prevail; psychological and strategic advantages must be maintained (Strecher, 1995:217).

In this section I describe edge control as a phenomenon associated with the contingent (or unpredictable) nature of police-citizen interactions. These interactions carry the potential of a great deal of turbulence, whether it is argumentativeness or hostility from a motorist, citizen deceptiveness, the fortuitous uncovering of wrongdoing, physical roughness, the sudden formation of hostile crowds during an arrest, or life-threatening danger that accompanies encounters with armed individuals. By turbulence, I mean two things—that a great deal of activity may occur in short bursts of time, and that the activity does not unfold predictably, but seems to run at its own demonic pace. Consider an arrest. With a pliant lone suspect, an arrest is not particularly turbulent; an officer can control the encounter without a great deal of difficulty. The formation of a crowd during the arrest, though, represents a sharp increase in turbulence—unpredictable contingencies emerge, and an officer has to adapt swiftly before some unforeseen development leads to an uncontainable event.

A variety of stories, gambits, and training strategies prepare officers to control the edge in these encounters. Officers learn quickly that police-citizen encounters are unpredictable, and that they cannot control all possible contingencies. Indeed, it is the unpredictability of outcomes that makes police work fun, interesting. Officers never know what is going to happen next.

Edge-Control vs. Maintaining the Edge

Unpredictability has a down side—blinding fear. Among a cop's most disturbing fears is being caught physically or psychologically unprepared in a serious, potentially life-threatening confrontation with an armed felon. Officers learn gambits that allow them to control the most dangerous excesses of police-citizen encounters, the edge of those encounters that carry the greatest potential for unruliness and violence. Experience teaches officers where the edge is, how to recognize it, and how to act in its presence. This is the phenomenon I call edge control. Consider the following example: Officers have responded to a domestic call, and the landlord warns them that there is a gun. They enter the apartment.

When we walked in, this woman was yelling; she's going off on us and she's getting up and down and stuff. All of a sudden, she sat down real fast . . . She has her arm down by her crotch, so I grab her arm . . . she's a big woman—she pulls out this six-inch-barrel revolver, a .22, and it's staring me right in the puss.

The only thing I could think of to do was grab it by the cylinder. See, if you can grab the cylinder, as long as the gun doesn't screw up, if they try to pull the trigger on you, the cylinder doesn't turn. That's with a good gun . . . OK, so I grab it—she's trying to pull the trigger, right?—I got it by the cylinder. I give her a whack in the puss with my other hand and pull the gun away.

I was lucky she didn't have a bad gun. If you get one of those and grab the cylinder, you're out. You lost. You're dead (Fletcher, 190:30).

The edge of this domestic call slides rapidly toward uncontrollable turbulence, possibly toward death. Only the quick action of the officer kept the encounter from sliding over the edge.

Muir (1977) has eloquently observed in his study of coercion and its ironies that there is a limit to the extent to which a police officer can control someone's behavior. Edge control occurs at the dangerous "edge" of unpredictability—in this instance, when the woman is displaying highly agitated behavior. Her behavior shifts to the chaotic edge when she grabs a gun. The officer's ability to control the edge is a product of his knowledge of weapons, his ability to act rapidly, and a large dose of luck. Failure to control the edge, in this situation, is life extinguishing.

I have selected the term "edge control" instead of the more popular phrase "maintaining the edge" (Van Maanen, 1978). The phrase "maintaining the edge" suggests that the focus of our assessment of police danger and its anticipation should be in terms of the skills that an officer has, that we look at a perspective and training style that over-responds to threatening and dangerous police-citizen encounters. The edge in this context refers to the level of skill carried by an officer.

The phrase "edge control," on the other hand, re-focuses police behavior back on its working environment. It is recursive, describing the nature of police work and the way cops try to cope with unpredictability. Edge control is a way of looking at danger that links police behavior in a direct way to the fundamental unpredictability of police-citizen encounters.

Police work sometimes demands that officers navigate a course of action through unfolding contingencies. Edge control refers to police efforts to prevent the greatest excesses of unpredictability, the chaos threshold, at which encounters become so unstable that neither control nor influence is possible. Officers learn strategies and gambits to "maintain the edge" because their work contains a great deal of edge control. Edge control is the effort to dampen the turbulence so that it does not reach the chaos threshold, put plainly, to keep things from getting out of hand.

Central to police training is learning to recognize when things are getting out of control and developing skills that enable action in chaotic situations. A high level of fear of injury associated with police-citizen interactions account for the intense focus on police officer safety that occurs during training. Officers are not always advised to intervene, but instead are recommended to trust their "instincts." This is problematic: on the one hand, edge control is learned through experience—it is not that it cannot be learned in POST training, but POST training is so short that there is simply not time to cover a great deal of ground on any particular topic. And new officers do not have experience. So they are taught to try to sense when things are not as they appear, and to get help if this seems to be the case.

Consider the following example from my research on POST training for parole and probation (Crank, 1996). Recruits were provided a sheet of instructions for home visits. Midway down the first page, and brought to the attention of the class by the instructor, was "JDLR. See p. 5." JDLR stood for "Just Don't Look Right." On page five, the instructor pointed out, was GTHO. In small letters, this was defined as "Get the Hell Out." This was a lesson for recruits; there will be time enough to learn to recognize and try to contain the edge.

Edge Control and Edgework: Lyng and Voluntary Risk-Taking

Lyng (1990; Lyng & Snow, 1986) has provided a way of thinking about the "edge" that is similar to the way I use the term here. Why, Lyng asked, in a society where so much emphasis is put on safety and predictability, do some individuals deliberately seek out dangerous, life-threatening situations? It could not be to accomplish some goal because those individuals that sought such encounters did so for the experience itself, not for some valued end. The pursuit of the edge, which he called edgework, he defined as the negotiation of the boundary between chaos and disorder. Why are some individuals drawn to the edge of chaos, the point at which life itself is threatened?

Edgework activities share a central feature: they involve a "clearly visible threat to one's physical or mental well-being or one's sense of an ordered existence" (Lyng, 1990:857). The edge is a metaphor that suggested a limit to an ordered, predictable existence. He described it as the border between "life versus death, consciousness versus unconsciousness, sanity versus insanity . . ." and later as "the boundary between order and disorder, form and formlessness." The archetypal image of edgework activities, he suggested, is the situation where the failure to control the edge ends in death.[1] The skill involved in edgework was the ability to maintain control "over a situation that verges on complete chaos, a situation that most people would regard as entirely uncontrollable" (Lyng, 1990:859).

Edgework, he observed, was grounded in irony. Edgeworkers believed that they had an innate ability to survive, that there was a direct link between their skills and the likelihood that they would survive. Each successfully negotiated edge was further proof that an edgeworker had unique skills that were unfathomable to an outsider. In a word, their luck was taken as verification of their skill.

Edgeworkers did not acknowledge that the risks might be unmanageable. If someone was killed or injured during edgework, "it is taken as direct evidence that he or she never had the 'right stuff' in the first place" (Lyng, 1990:859). Yet, this logic was inconsistent with the notion of the edge itself. The draw to the edge was in its proximity to chaos, to the unpredictable. It was attractive because survival became problematic. Consequently, "success in negotiating the edge is, to a large extent, chance determined" (Lyng, 1990:872). Survival did not depend on skill, but on a favorable alignment of chance encounters out of the control of the actor.

Control of the edge was an illusion. The notion of control defied the nature of the edge itself, conditions of instability and unpredictableness. Edgework was desired not because it allowed its practitioners to display a skill—if it was skill that edgeworkers sought, they could build cabinetry or grow a garden instead—but because it was wild and unpredictable. It brinked on the realm of chaos, where deadly endings sometimes occurred in spite of all the skill players bring to bear on the circumstances.

A pervasive paradox characterized edgework. An unsuccessful outcome was taken as evidence that the individual did not posses the basic survival skills required for edgework (Lyng, 1990:874). When edgework collapsed into chaos and death, edgeworkers blamed the outcome on the faulty skill of the failed player. In an astonishing denial of the nature of their activities, edgeworkers disregarded the feature that drew them to edgework—its wildness—and attributed death to failed skill.

Lyng's research led him to explore the emotional contours of risk-taking. Why, he asked, would someone be drawn to situations in which the orderliness of things is breached? What does exposure to danger offer to its participants? He thought that edgeworkers were attracted by a sense of mastery, an illusion of a particular facility to control chance itself. The introduction of skill situations into encounters where outcomes were unpredictable created an "illusion of control" (Langer, 1975). Individuals became mythic warriors, surviving in spite of the odds, believing in their special ability to do the impossible. They were an elite corps, a special group. They had the "right stuff."

Edgeworkers experienced what might be best described as self-actualization—they felt purified and strengthened by the act. Edge experiences induced a sensation of 'hyperreality,' a sense that the experience was intensely authentic. As a climber once mentioned to me "after being on the edge, the rest is just waiting." Day-to-day existence is mundane, boring, lackluster. Indeed, the sensation of hyperreality may be so strong that some edgeworkers deliberately increase the odds. The need to avoid paralyzing fear and the ability to focus on the task at hand are critical skills involved in edgework. Edgeworkers see themselves as mentally tough. Edgeworkers consequently have a high regard for their ability to deal with danger, and a correspondingly low regard for outsiders' skills.

Lyng's work focused on voluntary risk-taking. He did not discuss circumstances in which occupational necessity might require individuals to confront the edge. How does Lyng's edgework analysis illuminate our understanding of the culture of policing?

There are many parallels between Lyng's description of edgework and police work. Perceptions of occupational danger are ubiquitous to police culture. Nor are images of danger uniquely perceived and transmitted by police officers. They are played out every day in the newspaper, television, and films. A recruit would have to be raised in an isolation chamber to imagine that police work was not fraught with substantial, recurring danger. Such perceptions are further reinforced by training, with its intense focus on officer safety. Officers are repeatedly told stories about occupational dangers; the way in which particular officers negotiate extreme danger is part of the cultural lore of the occupational culture. In other words, the idea that officers do edgework occupies a central place in the culture of policing.

Officers' perceptions of their work are not unlike those held by edgeworkers. Both share the illusion of control—the belief that they, with adequate training, can survive the uncontrollable. When a police officer fails to negotiate the edge, when she or he is killed, cops refuse to acknowledge that the situation was not survivable. There are always dark rumors about the inadequacies of the cop that was injured or killed.

Moreover, many cops are drawn to the edge. A colleague once explained it to me this way:[2]

> There are two kinds of people in the world. Imagine that there's a sniper in a building, on the top floor, and he's shooting at people on the ground. What will a sane person do? They'll run as far and as fast from the sniper as they can. However, some people will not run away from the sniper. They'll run toward the sniper. That's the kind of person that becomes a cop. Which way would you run?

This perspective suggests that occupational dangers are not simply passively accepted as a part of the occupation. They may be aggressively sought by particular cops that enjoy edgework.

Edgework has psychological implications for the ability of administration to control the behavior of line officers in hazardous situations. Lyng draws on the literature of Mead (1950) to distinguish between the "I," the active, unreflective ego, and the "me," the social element that resides in the self, the product of our socialization, that allows us to reflect on what we do and to consider how others see us. Lyng suggested that during edgework the social "me," the reflective self, was inactive. The edgeworker had to instinctively and rapidly rely on personal skills and training in order to survive. Time for reflection was not present in true edgework encounters. Edgework was intense, hyper-real, because it was a purely egoistical experience. The social self was wholly irrelevant, perhaps even counterproductive to survival.

The absence of a reflective, social self in a police-citizen encounter may put fundamental limits on the ability of administrative policy to control police behavior. If officers find themselves involved in an unpredictable encounter, or one that contains substantial danger—in short, edgework—the capacity to reflect on departmental policy of any stripe may simply disappear. The reflective capacity, the social "me," is irrelevant to the encounter. At the border of chaos, other dynamics are in play. Indeed, as Lyng suggests, the ability to describe the encounter at a later time is itself problematic when the reflective capacity is not present.

Consequently, precisely those situations most likely to result in public controversy—deadly force encounters—are those where the working psychology of the edgeworker makes policy efforts irrelevant. To survive, the mind is working through other conduits, focused, acting instinctually. Its vitality is in the realm of the spontaneous, where a player acts and reacts to turbulent, often destabilizing, and sometimes life-threatening circumstances. Constraints such as administrative policy, in Meadian terms, are for the "me," the reflective, social entity. The "me" does not exist here. This realm belongs to the edgeworker. Others do not belong and are not wanted. For this reason, the ability to administratively corral line behavior in violent citizen encounters will always be limited.

Officers work with the edge, and they develop survival skills and containment logics. The following discussion describes various ways in which cops come to terms with edgework.

Bayley and Bittner: Injury Control, Fastidiousness, and the Well-Planned Lay-Back

Bayley and Bittner, in a loose-flowing and tightly packed discussion of police socialization, argue that the police are pervasively concerned with personal injury. They note that the police, though rarely in mortal threat, "continually deal with situations in which physical constraint may have to be applied against people who are willing to fight, struggle, hit, stab, spit, bite, tear, hurl, hide, or run." The reality of their work is the occasional "broken nose, lost teeth, black eyes, broken ribs, and twisted arms." In such an environment, police develop an anxiety about their personal well-being, and anxiety that, according to Bayley and Bittner, can appear to be fastidious to an outsider.

> . . . Officers develop an instinctive wariness, what one officer called a "well-planned lay-back." While they never want to give the impression of being afraid, especially to their peers, they try to avoid having to struggle with people. Since they are obliged at the same time to establish control, they feel justified in acting with preemptive force. In effect, they learn to act with a margin of force just beyond what their would-be opponents might use. One officer likened it to taking a five-foot jump over a four-foot ditch.[3] Never cut things too closely; if personal injury is likely, strike with just enough force to nullify the threat (Bayley & Bittner, 1989:93-94).

Bayley and Bittner describe stories told by officers about how they diffused potentially dangerous situations without injury. In these examples we can see the common-sense transmission of culture, through the development of a creative repertoire of stories. One story tells of an officer that gained control in a domestic dispute "by sitting down indifferently in front of the television set and taking off his hat. The husband and wife were so nonplussed at this lack of concern for their fight that they, too, lost interest" (1989:97).

Such stories, Bayley and Bittner suggest, are so prevalent that they are part of the mythology of policing and should be taken with a grain of salt. The suggestion not to take the story too seriously fails to recognize the power of myth as a vehicle for the transmission of values in the culture of the police. What counts is not whether the story is true but whether it is told. Once told, it becomes part of the cultural reservoir of common-sense knowledge for thinking about ordinary problems and their solutions, in this case, while minimizing potential risk to self.

Bayley and Bittner note that the stratagem described above is infrequently used. There is another way to think about the story, though. Culturally the story does not serve to provide a "rule-like prescription" telling officers how they should act. It suggests a sensibility out of which action can emerge (Shearing & Ericson, 1991). In this instance the sensibility is that the solution to the problem lies not in the officer's use of force but in the officer's keenness to manipulate the somewhat uncontrollable circumstances in which they find themselves. The message was not a rule-like "sit down and do nothing," but rather a sensibility that suggested that officers do something so unexpected that it changes the interpersonal dynamics of the intervention.

Van Maanen: Edge Control and Moral Responsibility

The literature discussed above focuses on the control of dangerous situations. There is another dimension of edgework. Maintaining the edge is an imperative that applies to interactions that are morally as well as physically hazardous. Van Maanen (1978) has discussed the moral component of edge control. He suggested that "maintaining the edge" stems, not primarily from issues of safety, but from ideas of beat control and moral responsibility. Any activity that threatens the perceived order of things, he suggested, is acted out at the line level as a pragmatic issue of beat control, and cannot be countenanced.

Because an officer's responsibility was framed both in terms of the moral rightness of lawful activity and dominion over the patrol beat, issues of control and morality tend to blur. To fail to respond to any challenge to authority was to invite "disrespect, chaos, and crime." Thus, officers believe that they must take control of all situations having to do with the public order, whether or not actual lawbreaking occurs. Police-citizen interactions were guided by the principle that "you (police) must make people respect you" (Manning, 1978b:11). When citizens displayed disrespect, officers invoked a wide repertoire of responses to correct the situation, including rough street justice and arrest.

Reuss-Ianni: Show Balls but Don't Be Eager

Few researchers have focused as sharply on the conflicts between managers and street cops as has Elizabeth Reuss-Ianni (1983). Her study of a New York City precinct in the late 1970s yielded a harvest of cultural maxims rich in meaning and implication. She identified 21 principles that mapped values central to the officers she studied, two of which are relevant to the idea of edge control. The first trait she called "show balls," which describes the moral righteousness of controlling citizen encounters:

> This enjoins an individual to be a man and not to back down, particularly in front of civilians: Once you've got yourself into a situation, take control and see it through (Reuss-Ianni, 1983:14).

Her research included management culture as well, a culture whose values conflicted with street cop culture. A corollary trait to "show balls" revealed an underlying predisposition to not go too far, to not be too visible. The trait is "Be aggressive when you have to, but don't be too eager." She described this trait as follows:

Old timers will tell new men that when a situation develops, get on it, but don't be too eager and go looking for trouble. If you get on a radio run . . . on a crime in progress for example, it will probably end up being a "past" crime, or unfounded, by the time you get there anyway, so don't break your neck getting there (Reuss-Ianni, 1983:14).

These two precepts of police culture, according to Reuss-Ianni, should be considered in relation to each other. On the one hand, officers were expected to handle whatever kind of problem came their way. The first precept emphasized the use of personal skills to assert control over whatever problems confronted them on their beat. The second advised officers that they should not compound existing problems. Officers that gave "too much activity" brought additional attention to themselves, and in the process might increase performance standards in the area.

White, Cox, and Basehart: Command Presence and Obscenity

White, Cox, and Basehart (1994) discussed how officers used profanity and obscenity in order to maintain control in formal citizen contacts.[4] Offensive language gained the attention of its target, established social distance between the target and the police, and had a powerful alienating effect on the target (White, Cox & Basehart, 1988; Cox & White, 1987).

The use of language to control situations is taught to officers at the lower levels of use of force, and the use of obscene language might simply be an extension of this training. As White and his colleagues (1988) noted, officers were trained to display command presence and command voice to maintain control and dominance. However, local cultural norms may justify the additional use of obscenity in particular circumstances; when officers are taking "shit" from citizens, and to deal with "assholes." The use of obscenity may simply be a cultural extension of organizationally acceptable use of voice command to dominate police-citizen encounters.

Profanity may also be a planned rhetorical strategy (Rothwell, 1971). An officer, in the presence of a target and another police officer, the strategic use of profanity can be used to create or to identify allies. By identifying like-minded colleagues, and by provoking disliked groups, the use of profanity can identify both in-group and out-group members. In this way, offensive language serves the purpose of reinforcing cultural solidarity (Van Maanen, 1978).

Edge Control and the Context
of Ordinary Police Work

Cops exhibit a wide range of techniques to control situations not particularly dangerous. On the one hand, officers cannot always predict what situations are dangerous, and edgework is expressed in a set of skills aimed at preventing situations from ever getting to this point. Second, edge control stems from the sheer unpredictability of police work, in which officers seek to avoid unpleasant encounters that are not particularly dangerous. Consider the following three examples. The first is a recruit reminiscing on his partner's admonition about car stops (Van Maanen, 1978:302):

> Keith was always telling me to be forceful, not to back down and to never try and explain the law or what we are doing to a civilian. I didn't really know what he was talking about until I tried to tell some kid why we have laws about speeding. Well, the more I tried to tell him about traffic safety the angrier he got. I was lucky to just get his John Hancock on the citation. When I came back to the patrol car, Keith explains to me just where I'd gone wrong. You really can't talk to those people out there; they just won't listen to reason.

The second example describes a situation that emerges periodically for Parole and Probation agents. Among their duties is the compilation of detailed records on offenders. Occasionally, they will encounter a person that is clearly innocent. The following recommendation, in a POST training class, notes the importance of maintaining control of an otherwise unconscionable situation:[5]

> We've all seen people who go through the system who were ultimately innocent. Sometimes you'll find someone who will plea bargain even though they are innocent in order to avoid an extensive period of incarceration. Sometimes you'll look through the case record and you'll see that there's no way that they could have been guilty. Your first temptation will be to ask them "How could you have pled guilty?" Don't do it. You'll lose control of the interview, and they'll use it against you up the road.

Third, in one of the few thorough discussions of the complexity and contingent nature of traffic stops, Bayley and Bittner (1989:98) discuss a variety of "gambits" used by officers when approaching a driver. The following gambits describe edge control.

> Some [officers] tell the driver why he was stopped before asking for his license and registration. This satisfies the driver's curiosity and puts him on the defensive. Others first ask for documents, thus ensuring that the driver will not escape and demonstrating that information will be given

only when the officers choose. Still others like to begin with the question "Do you know why I stopped you?" hoping that the drivers, most of whom drive on the edge of the law, will admit an infraction even more serious than the one that led to the stop. The officers can then be magnanimous, agreeing to forgive the more serious offense in favor of the lesser that the officer was going to ticket anyway.

These examples show how edge control is a way of thinking about unpredictability. In all of the examples cited above, edge control is a calculus that officers use to limit turbulence in police-citizen encounters. This police cultural theme is driven by the practical nature of everyday police work—the rough-and-tumble of everyday work, as Bayley and Bittner characterize it. In the form of the stories shared by officers, for example, the story above of the officer instructing the rookie about traffic stops and the rookie re-telling the story to the reviewer, edge control becomes a theme central to police culture.

Endnotes

[1] He cites Hunter Thompson (1971) as the source of the idea of edgework. For Thompson, edgework consisted of the use of large and mixed quantities of drugs at a level that threatened both his sanity and his life.

[2] Caldero, personal conversation.

[3] Interesting that this phrasing should appear both here and also in an earlier cite from research conducted by Shearing and Ericson (1991). This suggests the prevalence of this trope and the clarity by which it metaphorically captures edge control.

[4] As they note (p. 235), "Common attitudes among officers, reflecting the strength of this informal norm, are that officers should not take any 'shit' from citizens or go on duty to see what the 'Assholes' are up to tonight."

[5] This quote came from my 1996 study of a POST academy for Probation and Parole officers (Crank, 1996).

13

Seductions of the Edge

Many writers on policing have observed an emotional polarity in patrol work. This polarity has been described in terms like the following: Police officers spend a great deal of time in boring, routine activity during which they lay low and stay out of trouble. Van Maanen (1973), for example, describes this as a central element of the final frame perspective, the way in which cops view their occupation. Boring routines are punctuated by moments of intense activity, activity that frequently involves real police work. Police work shifts unpredictably between boring activity and quick-paced, exciting adventure.

The characterization of patrol as "boring" misses an important property of routine activity. It is not so much that officers are bored, though they may be. It is that they are waiting. And what they are waiting for is not exactly "real police work." They are waiting for excitement. They are investigators into the sociology of the wind. They are seduced by the edge.

Seduction brings out the brightest and darkest elements of police culture. At the brightest, officers ride the winds of unpredictability, flowing with changes in citizen moods and situational contingencies, using dodges, games, and hedges to control the flow of unpredictability and bring complex encounters to satisfactory conclusions. As an officer once said to me, "I like the calls. They are wild and unpredictable."

The bright edge of seduction has been overlooked by social scientists. To a large extent, the reason for this oversight does not stem from dark intent or anti-police bias, but from the way in which social scientists, particularly those with an empirical bent, have thought about police work. Patrol activity has been seen as an organizational problematic, a discre-

185

tionary way of working inconsistent with bureaucratic regimentation. Researchers have investigated police work with the traditional tools—we have prodded, pushed, and gauged the police using scales that measure items such as stress, cynicism, and role conflict. We have conceptualized the police in terms of friction between organizational layers, relations with other units of the criminal justice system, and in terms of corruption and abuse of discretion.

There is certainly a place for these ways of looking at the police: I use much of this type of literature in this book, and believe that it informs our knowledge about the police in important ways. Yet, if I review question-naire surveys that I have developed and distributed, and compare them to others with which I am familiar, I recognize a pattern. I ask questions such as "What is your primary source of stress?" From such measures, of which there are a great many, I develop relations between stress, cynicism, role conflict, perhaps including other measures as well. Even where I have looked at police professionalism, I find that I have sought its dark-er rather than more optimistic implications. There is nothing wrong with this—too often criminal justice policy has proceeded blithely ignorant of shadowy ramifications, and when put into practice self-destructs, or worse, aggravates real-world problems.

For a study of police culture, such dark analysis is common, but only provides one-half of the picture. If police work looked and felt like it was described by social scientists, then who on earth would do it? Clearly, many officers will, when asked in a dark mood, recommend that students get a degree in something other than criminal justice, so that when they get tired of the bullshit they will have something to fall back on besides police work. I myself have heard this from officers on more than one occasion. However, these same officers celebrate moments that are personally rewarding, righteous, or simply fun. Fun and pleasure are overlooked in more scholarly work—maybe it is we who are too serious. There is an overabundance of measures of the problems. Cop problems, I suspect, are theoretically over-determined. Who has asked the simple question "What do you like about your work?"

The drawback of social science imagery is not that it is dark, but that it is unremittingly dark. Life is not like that. It is not consistently bleak: it is dark at times, light at others, and partly sunny (or somewhat overcast, depending on your mood) almost always. Tragedies are balanced by celebrations. Boredom and wildness are joined in awkward linkages, and drudgery and fun mix without reason. For all but the truly unfortunate, life is not simply barren or bleak. Life is astonishingly, well, human.

Consider the following comment from Officer Tansey of Chicago.

> I remember, when I was in college, I had a summer job in the loop. It always impressed me, seeing the armies of commuters coming out of their offices every night at five, fighting their way across the bridge to

the train. It seemed like prison to me. From home to train to office to train to home. What did they ever get to see?

After I joined the force, I realized these people were still coming out of the offices, sitting in the train, going home, sitting in front of the TV, watching the things that I was part of. And it was all because of the magical star, that gave me the access to this world that nobody ever sees . . . (Fletcher, 1990:6).

The term "excitement" does not wholly capture the sentiment in this quote. This officer is describing a sense of fulfillment, of participation in a venture from which most people are excluded. Nor is his perspective that of the "hot dog," the young, overeager officer seeking a high-speed chase or a dangerous felon, naïvely believing that his daily routine will be filled with "real" police work. The hot dog has to learn to be patient, to wait. The view above is from a retired officer, casting his gaze over the city and back across his career. It is a view that still triggers in him a brief surge of adrenaline, a sense of being in special places, dark corners, dealing with wild things, and riding the wind. It is seduction, utter and complete.

Another of Fletcher's (1990) stories provides a sense of how delivering a search warrant can provide an opportunity for mirth. Under ordinary circumstances, preparing for a search is a nervy, occasionally hazardous activity. When delivering a warrant, officers will move in quickly to minimize their ever-present fear of danger, particularly if there is a suspicion that they might encounter an armed suspect. Fear is balanced by the need to move quickly before evidence is hidden, swallowed, flushed, or destroyed. Danger, speed, and real crime are a cop's adrenaline cocktail.

In the following example, officers were seeking a way to deliver a warrant to the manager of a fish market so that they can search for illegal weapons. An informant had warned that he would be dangerous, and had suggested where weapons might be found. So they developed the following strategy, adopted from the "William Tell Overture."

Four of us went to the fish place. We had two guys go in earlier; they're sitting there eating. Her and I walked in together, walked up to the counter, the guy's behind the counter, we asked him his name, he says, "Yes, that's me." So I say, "We have something to say to you." We both had the words with us; I had a pitch pipe with me; I blew on it—hmmmm—and we started singing:

> Because we're great and we're the best
> We got a warrant for your arrest
> And just because you're such a louse
> We're even gonna search your house.

And he was, like, startled. I tried to hand him a copy of the search warrant, but he wouldn't take it. He backed away, and he starts running back toward the kitchen. The informant had told us he kept a gun back there. So with that, myself and one of the police officers climbed over this fish cooler and then jumped over it, and one of the other officers went through where there was a door to the back, and we trapped him. He was going for the gun (Fletcher, 1990:44-45).

Seduction and Undercover Work

Seductions of the edge have been associated with particularly exciting forms of police work. Marx (1988) captured this excitement in his research on police undercover work. Agents thrived on their ability to mimic the behavior of the bad guys. The work was exhilarating.

> . . . the work is very intense; the agent is always "on." For some operatives, the work becomes almost addictive. The agent may come to enjoy the sense of power the role offers and its protected contact with illegal activity (Marx, 1988:109).

What is seductive about undercover work? As Marx pointed out, psychological studies of undercover officers do not exist. The seduction was that of living life on the edge, a stimulant unrecognized in research on the police. I have heard rock climbers express a similar sentiment: once you've been on the edge, everything else is waiting.

A second seduction was the freedom to use virtually unrestricted tactics to get someone to commit to a course of action that would result in their arrest. An act, Marx (1988:105) observed, was no less legally criminal because it is in response to a very attractive temptation. Undercover cops tended to shift their focus and efforts from determining "Is he corrupt?" to "Is he corruptible?" Officers developed the art of temptation through strategic mixes of coercion, entrapment, and trickery.

Nor were agents concerned by the possibility of entrapment; what they could not legally do they could induce an informer or third party to do. They were limited only by their inability to figure out some way to trick someone into wrongdoing. Temptation could be facilitated by coercive efforts to get participants to play.

> In a case growing out of a Washington, D.C. fencing sting, former assistant U.S. attorney Donald Robinson was accused of taking money for information from persons he thought were organized crime figures, but who were actually police. (He eventually won his case on entrapment grounds.) Robinson at first ignored their approaches, but became involved only after persistent phone calls, a threatening call to his wife, and a warning that he might end up missing (Marx, 1988:105).

Seduction, the Slippery Slope of Crime, and the Sensuous Dark

Police sometimes engage in illegal activity; theft, the sale and distribution of drugs, locker room merchandise, burglary, and the like. A logic that I call slippery-slope materialism is frequently used to explain their involvement in crime. According to this kind of logic, illegal activity is encouraged by financial rewards, which can be large. Gambling and narcotics can provide large payoffs in untraceable bills. Because police work is low visibility, with few observers of police-citizen encounters, chances of being caught are minimal. Officers take payoffs because their chances of being caught are low compared to the financial rewards. If an officer steals from a drug dealer, who is going to report the crime? The seduction is powerful when an officer can take a wad of bills from a drug dealer's wallet and put his kids through college.

This is a materialistic argument with a powerful moralistic component. Most forms of the materialistic argument start from a position of moral innocence, followed with some form of the "slippery-slope" metaphor. The slippery slope suggests that "taking" starts small, with tacit acknowledgment from other officers (Sherman, 1988:255). Officers become accustomed to small takings, and eventually become connected with other officers that are involved in graft of whatever stripe. Early grafting desensitizes them, and they graduate to increasingly serious crimes. The process of becoming bent ends with the officer involved in the most morally despicable form of graft, narcotics corruption.

As an explanation of crime, slippery-slope materialism has weaknesses. It rests on a quasi-theological assumption that human nature is essentially greedy and that, having tasted small corruptions, men begin to lust for larger ones (Feldberg, 1988:269).[1] It is a theological metaphor with implications of innocence lost. In its most simplistic form, this argument is that "bad guys" or "rotten pockets"—officers already ruined by the taint of corruption—are ruining our good recruits.

Slippery-slope materialism overlooks the powerful similarities of criminal activity and police work and their implications for corruption. Police work shares much in common with criminal activity (Manning, 1978). The criteria for achieving success in both police work and criminal activity are similar. Skills in dealing with darker sides of human nature are useful for both the police and for crooks. The ability to keep cool in unpredictable circumstances makes for both a good lawbreaker and a good police officer. A healthy dose of suspicion and the ability to react quickly to changing circumstances facilitate survival for both undercover officers and drug sellers. Both are preoccupied with danger and potential danger. Simply put, police officers receive superior training for crime— why should it surprise anyone that they occasionally seek its dark fruits?

Why should a good police officer also not be a good crook? Therein lies the dark seduction.

The seductions of criminal activity do not fit rational, high-minded conceptions of police ethics. Like criminals, police are sometimes enticed into it, seduced by its allure, intrigued by the presence of opportunities to test their mettle, to move comfortably into the emotional, seamy side of life—to find out how far they can go. They are certainly well trained for it. They know where the targets are. They know how to avoid the casual witness. They can get away with it, and they know it. Who are the victims going to call, the police?

Katz: Seductions of Crime

In a brilliant exposition of the seductions of crime, Katz (1988) captures nonmaterial or, as he calls them, "seductive" elements of criminal activity. Katz argues that much street crime does not fit the "sentimentality" of materialism. Katz quotes one of his respondents:

> Straight people don't understand. I mean, they think dudes is after the things straight people got. It ain't that at all. People in the life ain't looking for no home and grass in the yard and shit like that. We the show people. The glamour people . . . hear people talking about you. Hear the bar get quiet when you walk in (Katz, 1988:315).

In what is not a particularly literate way, this confidant is capturing the seductions of wild behavior. The seductions are not about material goods, though material goods may buy them. It is this non-economic dimension of corruption that research has overlooked.

Academic research, Katz argues, has failed to recognize that there are emotional attractions of crime. Sterile measures of attitudinal predispositions utterly fail to capture the energy of street-life. Katz' book captures the explosive sense of being catapulted into crime, the sudden, searing violence, and rapid retreat. Readers can feel themselves propelled into the crimes he describes, seduced by the undefinable, captivating characteristics of the situation, the target, a mythical calculus of opportunity and allure.

For the criminals he describes, the propulsions to commit a crime can vary dramatically: "the range of sensual dynamics range from enticements that draw a person into shopping to furies that can propel him to murder" (1988:5). Katz seeks a vocabulary uncommon to the empirical sciences for describing what he sees. Terms like badass and royal mind-fucking, blended into simple description, are used to capture the nonmaterial elements of crime. His research is profoundly subjective; he recognizes the importance of fantastic elements in the production of violence.

Crime feeds the imagination, and the imagination enjoys the criminal event: a person conjures up a spirit that allows him to seek out violence, and the spirit sustains him or her through the event.

If a fantastic conception of violence sounds distant from police work, bear in mind Van Maanen's article on the relationship between violence and perceived slights to police authority by those labeled assholes (1978). Katz's work seeks an everyday vocabulary to describe what he sees as well. The "badass" is one who challenges a furtive glance with "whachu-lookinat" and follows with a "royal mind-fucking" if the victim makes the catastrophic error of responding "nuthin" ("you calling me nuthin?"). In an explosion of wild violence, an enemy is mystically conjured and destroyed. One suspects that the badass would not respond well to a questionnaire pre-coded to measure occupational stress.

For a police officer, the moral seduction is clear—they have the opportunity to hurt the bad guys. It is a personal score, an affront to dominion, to personal morality and to pride. It is an insult that must be avenged. Slamming around a bad guy or an asshole is fair practice— besides, police officers may reason, these bad guys will be treated leniently by the courts anyway. The nonmaterial temptations of crime and violence are strong for those that already have the skills. They are beckoned by its sensuous allure, the seduction by dark, secret places and violent revenges, to be princes of the city. To walk down Colfax Avenue in Denver and watch the pimps crawl back into the shadows, not just because you are a cop, but because you are one tough mother in a uniform.

Sapp: The Seductions of Sex

Life on society's edge is seedy. Officers share the streets with hookers and their pimps, teenage runaways, drunks, peep-houses, massage parlors, drug dealers, the mentally ill homeless, gangbangers, and small-time hustlers. For some officers, their goal is simple: "find a rock and kick it" (Skolnick & Bayley, 1986). Officers have power here. It is not much, but to them it is enough to control some of the worst excesses, when the sleaze begins to invade surrounding areas, or when unknowing travelers inadvertently stray into these areas and are rapidly targeted. And it is an easy place to bust small-time pushers.

Officers work this environment and know it very well. They walk the streets and people watch them. They are watched intently though not directly, like wolves moving through an area where there was a recent kill. Women approach them, sometimes offering sex in exchange for petty favors, simple protection, sometimes sexual taunts. Arrests are easy here— and so is sex; like drugs, it is the lifeblood of the street. A runaway, alone and desperate, needs a ride, protection, a meal, wants to avoid arrest at all costs. Vulnerability is everywhere. Sapp notes the sexual seductions of the street:

I've been assigned to the vice squad. I believe every one of them has gone beyond the rules on sex with prostitutes . . . I'm not saying I did but I've been in this business ten years so you draw your conclusion. The prostitute squad isn't the only way vice officers get action. I've been offered, and I'm not saying I took the offers, understand, but I've been offered sexual services from barmaids, gamblers, narcotics addicts and dealers, and damn near every other kind of case you run into. Most of those cases are just between you and the suspect and they will do almost anything to avoid arrest (Sapp, 1994:194-195).

One scenario in which seduction could occur involves officers on patrol, who frequently stop women who are alone in their vehicles, perhaps women that have had too much to drink. The woman is attractive, and the officer hits on her. She is vulnerable—she does not want to say no outright and have to deal with a husband haranguing her for receiving a DUI. The officer takes the woman's demur as acquiescence. He gives her his number, or if he is lucky they rendezvous at some remote location.

Another example of a seduction situation would be one in which an officer follows up on a victim. The woman is lonely, she does not know how to meet decent men, and on a lark, offers the officer a drink. He declines, taking a rain check. He comes back when he is off-duty. With luck, he builds a quiet relationship that he can sustain.

These vignettes show how characteristics of an officer's job—low visibility, power, and dealing with vulnerable people, provide a climate designed for the seductions of sex. Consider the following example, in which an officer is talking about his first exposure to sex on the job.

I really didn't have any offers or even really think about it until I was assigned to a 1-man car and one night I stopped a female subject for running a traffic light. She was really first. The way she acted I just kind of hinted that maybe we could reach an understanding and she picked right up on it. Well, she had enough moving violations that another one could take her license and I guess she didn't want that to happen. Anyway, I met her later that night and [we] had a wild session. I called again a few days later and she wouldn't even talk to me. Yeah, I've had a few similar type experiences since [then] but I'm real careful (Sapp, 1994:195).

The give-and-take of favors in this example was an exchange between unequals. Sex was exchanged for the momentary abeyance of power—the officer sets aside his official authority to write a ticket, and the woman reciprocated with the gift of her body, offered sexually for an evening. That it was a coercive encounter was not well understood by this officer; it was taken for granted, a given. Police departments are imbued with a powerful male ethos stimulated by the flow of testosterone—why should police-citizen interactions reflect a different pattern of male-female relationship?[2] Given his efforts to continue the relationship by calling her on the phone and her refusal to respond, she appeared to have a better understanding of the forced nature of the exchange than did the officer.

Illicit sexual behavior by the police has recently received a great deal of attention (Kappeler, Kappeler & del Carmen, 1993; Dobash & Dobash, 1992; Edwards, 1990). This focus has brought forth some of the coarse aspects of police abuse of authority. One cannot help but be repulsed on reading Kraska and Kappeler's (1997) account of *Parrish v. Lukie*, 1992), a re-telling of the case of a police officer who forcibly sodomized a woman he had pulled over in Houston. In the following section, I will review empirical evidence that bears on this topic.

Research on Police On-the-Job Sexual Activity

Available evidence, though scant, suggests that sexual activity is widespread among patrol officers and detectives. Barker's (1978) research, one of the few efforts to assess this issue, was conducted in a small southern city with a department of 50 officers and civilians. He found that officers believed that 31.84 percent of their fellow officers had sex while on duty. Fifty-six of Barker's reporters also thought that sex on the job would rarely or never be reported, while only 19 percent believed that it would be.

Two recent studies provide some illumination into the frequency with which officers themselves have witnessed sexual harassment. In response to the question "Over the past 12 months, have you personally observed a police officer . . .?" Six percent of the officers surveyed in Ohio stated that they had witnessed sexual harassment, and 8.6 percent of the respondents from Illinois also agreed (Knowles, 1996; Martin, 1994). These percentages may sound relatively small until one recognizes that these are incidents where one officer (1) witnesses another officer display this behavior, and (2) is willing to tell an interviewer that they have witnessed the behavior. In other words, situations where officers will not come forward, and incidents where officers acted alone—a more likely occurrence, as suggested by Barker's research—are not reported. Moreover, these surveys were randomly drawn from 1,269 and 700 officers in the states of Ohio and Illinois respectively (Sykes, 1996), and thus represent the responses of 118 officers. Ohio has about 25,342 municipal and county officers, and Illinois has about 36,925 local officers. Extrapolating back to the original populations we begin to comprehend the magnitude of this activity. These numbers represent approximately 1,520 incidents in Ohio and 3,175 in Illinois, not including estimates for state police.

A different type of analysis was used by Kappeler (1993:93) to analyze police sexual misconduct. They defined police sexual violence (PSV) as "those situations in which a female citizen experiences a sexually degrading, humiliating, violating, damaging, or threatening act committed by an officer through the use of force or police authority." Intensity of PSV ranged from unobtrusive behavior such as viewing victims, photographs, and sexually explicit videos, to criminal behavior, including sexual assault and rape. Using this definition, the authors reviewed all media cases in a national newspaper between 1991 and the first six months of 1993. The authors also reviewed published cases decided by Federal District Courts between 1978 and 1992 in which the police were sued under 42 U.S.C. Section 1983, alleging some form of sexual violence (Kappeler, 1993:92).

News sources, not surprisingly, focused on the big-ticket items, criminal cases. Of the 33 cases reported by the newspaper, two-thirds were criminal cases. Federal litigation cases revealed a different pattern. Of the 91 litigation cases, 73.6 percent were obtrusive. These cases included custodial strip searches, body-cavity searches, warrant-based searches, illegal detentions, deception to gain sexual favors, provision of services for sexual favors, and sexual harassment (Kappeler, 1993:94). The authors argued that the prevalence of these incidents in the legal database stem from the wording of civil rights law: officers could confront civil litigation for criminal acts, but not for illegal strip searches and body-cavity searches.

Two perspectives, Kraska and Kappeler (1995) note, have sought to explain sexual violence committed by police officers against women. The first deals principally with the issue in high-minded ideas of "boys-will-be-boys," and attributes more aggressive forms of sexual behavior on "rogue police." Sapp captures the boys-will-be-boys genre in the following quote:

> There are three or maybe four addresses here in town that everyone knows when a car is dispatched it's another call from one of the 'lonely heart's club'. . . . one of them is pretty young and fairly good looking. She always answers the door in a nightgown that is nearly see-through and is scared or pretends to be so scared [and says that] she wants you to stay for a while. I answered one call, not one of the known addresses, and the woman just had a towel around her and she claimed someone was trying to get in her window while she was taking a shower. Well, when we looked the place over, the bathroom wasn't wet, the bed had been slept in and this was 3:00 in the morning . . . The brass really stresses the known addresses and we all have been warned about them. They don't know the others though (Sapp, 1994:197).

In the current era, academic research tends to focus on power differentials between women and police officers in police-citizen interactions. The image of consensuality, it is suggested, is illusionary, fostered by the victim's vulnerability brought about by the substantial power differential brought to the exchange (Kraska & Kappeler, 1995). Support for this position is provided by the litigation success of plaintiffs in sex abuse cases: Kappeler (1993) found that the police lost 69 percent of the sexual abuse cases against them, a large number compared to the average 10 percent for all other forms of civil litigation.

Cultural Bases for Sexual Seductions

Academic research seeks out the cultural, structural, legal, and ideological supports for police on-the-job sexual activity. It has particularly focused on the differential power exchange in police-citizen encounters to account for sexual activity. Studies of power differentials among the police and between police and citizens are important contributions—theories of the nature, distribution, and use of organizational power have been generally and unfortunately neglected in criminal justice research. A limitation of this literature is, I believe, its failure to capture the seductive aspect of sex-seeking, and how illicit sexual activity takes root in local police cultures. Like crime, sex holds powerful subjective, emotional seductions not fully understandable in terms of ideas of power exchange. The pursuit of sexual adventure is profoundly existential: it is fun, a wild ride, life on the edge, sheer raw pleasure. Power, authority, and simple propinquity—the presence of attractive potential partners in routine citizen encounters, provide the opportunity. Cops seek sexual adventure because, simply put, they can. As many observers of the obvious have noted, the human capacity for sex, in any encounter, in whatever circumstance, is insatiable.

Through stories told, games of one-upmanship, braggadocio, and the exploits of particular officers, sexual aggression becomes an element of police culture. Themes of dominion and of masculinity, discussed in previous chapters, loom large in police culture. The theme seduction mixes with these powerful themes of police work to culturally legitimize on-the-job sexual activity (Kraska & Kappeler, 1995). Inevitably, stories of sexual promiscuity and conquest are widely shared and become part of the lore of the organization. Accounts of individual officers become informal standards, and provide a sensibility out of which officers think about sexual relations in their work.

Efforts to separate sex from the working life of patrol officers and detectives, though perhaps ennobling, fail because of a litany of factors beyond the control of management and legal reform—the sexual energies involved in meeting potential partners in any work environment, the relative youth of patrol officers, and the lack of suitable opportunities to meet available females off work, the authority inherent in all police-citizen encounters to grant the favor of police discretion, the fires of human sexuality. Placing bureaucratic controls on sexual activity among line officers and detectives make as much sense as trying to put out a fire with a court order. Yet we must, driven to this unlikely goal by our simple desire that police-citizen interactions be marked by fair play.

Endnotes

[1] Marcus Feldman further observes that "My experience with police officers is that they are rather sophisticated in the arts of inducement and deception, and that they each have a clear idea of where to 'draw the line' between petty gratuities and open bribery."

[2] Kraska and Kappeler (1995:91) note that the "link between the institutionalized sexist ideology of the police and occupational sexual harassment is well established."

Cultural Themes of Solidarity

One of the most powerful aesthetics of cop culture is the sense of solidarity shared by its members. The extraordinary solidarity displayed by the police has been widely and frequently observed (Manning, 1978; Christopher, 1991; Skolnick & Fyfe, 1993; Crank et al., 1993). Explanations have been diverse, and have frequently focused on corruption and other "dark" aspects of the force (Kappeler, Sluder & Alpert, 1994; Knapp Commission, 1986; Stoddard, 1968).

The high degree of social solidarity displayed by police officers is, I believe, a product of conflicts and antagonisms with diverse out-groups, of which criminals are only one type (Coser, 1956). As a grounded phenomenon, solidarity is based on cops' perceptions of grievances that they have with various groups, and on how they form social bonds in response to those grievances. As an aesthetic, solidarity is carried in shared beliefs and actions whose purpose is to display solidarity, from training practices organized around protecting other officers to funerals that display overwhelming police unity in a "sea of blue."

That social solidarity is produced by conflict with outside groups is a perspective with a long and colorful sociological tradition (Durkheim, 1966; Simmel, 1919). Efforts to comprehend police solidarity using principles of group conflict put forth by Coser (1956) inform the perspective I use here. Coser (1956) used a functional perspective in order to integrate a diverse sociological literature on conflict.

Coser sought to explain how conflict stabilized and preserved particular social relationships. Conflict, he contended, had a powerful "group-binding" character that sustained group identity and marked group boundaries. Conflict could be in the form of overt behavior, or could be expressed as "sour grapes" antagonism, a sentiment Coser (1956:36) called "ressentiment." The emergence of antagonisms across different groups contributed to the mutual recognition of group boundaries and prevented their disappearance. Even in the absence of overt intra-group conflicts, covert antagonisms sustained group boundaries.

The idea that powerful themes of police solidarity emerge from group conflicts and antagonisms begs the question: what conflicts or perceived threats are faced by the police that would give rise to such themes? One possible answer is that solidarity derives from the dangers of police work. This argument can be summarized as follows: the sheer danger of police work, like combat, encourages strong loyalties, an "all for one and one for all" sense of camaraderie, and a military sense of combat-readiness and general spiritedness. Powerful loyalties emerge in the commonly shared and perilous effort to control dangerous felons. The danger hypothesis, however, fails to explain why police solidarity is particularly evident in other circumstances, for example, with regard to the courts and the provision of evidence, or why cops will not give up another cop, even with regard to law-breaking colleagues. In other words, the danger theme, in and of itself, is insufficient to explain the high degree of police solidarity. It also fails to explain the presence of solidarity in departments in jurisdictions where crime levels are low.

Themes evoking social solidarity, I argue, emerge in response to perceived challenges to police authority to do their work that emerge from members of their institutional environment—citizens, the courts, the press, and administrative brass, to name a few. Various organizational and external groups question police authority over their dominion and over the way in which they do their work. Police solidarity emerges as an affirmation of identity in the face of these challenges. Conflict with its various outgroups, even when the conflict is no more than "ressentiment," serves the powerful group-binding function of promoting police solidarity.

The powerful sense of solidarity displayed by the police mobilizes their cultural identity. Social solidarity is practical and concrete, a grounded phenomenon that emerges in everyday activity as a response to suspected and real antagonisms with real groups. Solidarity is experienced and understood common-sensically in the everyday doing of police work. Its strength comes from, and is in direct proportion to, the strength of perceived external threats to the police.

Solidarity themes serve an important ideological end: police officers see themselves not as selfish actors, but as members of a group struggling for a higher purpose. Borrowing Coser's (1956) terminology, individual police officers unite with feelings of power and purpose from their identification with the police generally. This powerful bond is the glue of cultural solidarity.

Five themes are presented below. These themes share in common the message of unity of purpose. Each theme in its own way celebrates a shared sense of purpose, and together they help to understand the way in which the "brotherhood" looks inward for cultural identity.

14

Angels and Assholes: The Construction of Police Morality

Theme: Police Morality

> We both deal with the evil in life—but the difference is, with priests, there's a big distancing from evil. Priests only hear about it in the confessional and the office. For the priest, it loses about nine-tenths of its impact and its, its *wham*.
>
> But with the police officers, with their experience of evil, there's an immediacy. They stand in it. They touch it . . . they taste it . . . they smell it . . . they hear it . . . they have to handle it. The priest only knows about evil intellectually; the cop knows it in his gut (Fletcher, 1991:5).

In his vocabulary of good and evil, a priest accustomed to working with the police describes similarities between his and their work. Though police may describe their work in grittier terms than such eloquent abstractions of good and evil, the sense of righteousness is present and clearly visible to those who work with and around them.

By morality, I mean that police see themselves as representatives of a higher morality embodied in a blend of American traditionalism, patriotism, and religion. As moral agents, police view themselves as guardians whose responsibility is not simply to make arrests but to roust out society's trouble-makers (Sykes, 1986). They perceive themselves to be a superior class (Hunt & Magenau, 1993), or as Bouza notes (1990:17), people "on the side of angels." Morality is the sentiment that transforms cops' territories to dominions.

Cops' morality sometimes carries with it a judgment of citizens as different and sometimes childlike. Klein provides an example of an encounter that begins with a challenge to the authority of the police, and concludes with the moral authority of the police reasserted. The challenge begins during a normal tour of duty as a desk lieutenant.

> One quiet Sunday afternoon I was the desk lieutenant on duty on a West Side precinct when a popinjay of a man of about 60 years of age came bounding into the station and up to the desk. "I want to file a complaint against Patrolman Santos," he announced. Before the man could continue, I interrupted with "Just a moment, please," reached for my scratch pad, and then asked the man for his name and address, noting the time above the date on my pad. The man became livid, and the next few words he uttered were accompanied by an openhanded pounding on the desk that practically made them inaudible. . . . Fearing that the man was working up to a heart attack, I resorted to my most unctuous manner in an effort to calm him. That only seemed to infuriate him more, so I picked up the big 'blotter' that lay before me, brought it down with a resounding crash on the desk, and yelled, "SHUT UP!" at the top of my voice. It worked.

The story continues with a discussion of the alleged brutality carried out by patrolman Santos, in which it is apparent that the patrolman did his utmost to resolve an argument between the complainant, his girlfriend, and a rescuer.

> After getting this part of the story, I told Mr. Serene he should be grateful to the officer, not complaining against him, for after all hadn't Santos saved him from a likely beating at the hands of the would-be rescuer?

> "Grateful! He took my girl away from me! I called her up this morning, and she says she never wants to see me again! Santos made me look like a bum, hauling me away in the police car!"

The officer informs the complainant that, under the circumstances he saw no basis for a complaint and was not going to file one, further inflaming Mr. Serene.

> As Mr. Serene continued, fortissimo grosso, I walked out from behind the desk, grabbed him by the elbow, and propelled him toward the door, repeating firmly, "You will have to leave; you are interrupting and interfering with our duties."

At this point in the encounter, Mr. Serene refuses to accept this outcome, thereby elevating the encounter to a new level.

> I will not leave; you can't make me. Where's Santos? He made me lose my girlfriend; I won't leave until you bring him in. I know the law; you can't make me leave.

I took him up on the last declaration, trying a new tack: "You're absolutely right: I can't make you leave. But if you don't leave, I'll arrest you for causing a disturbance and preventing the orderly business of the precinct." The discourse ended a few minutes later with the arrest of my would-be complainant, who remained adamant to the bitter end, which consisted of an escorted ride in the patrol wagon to Night Court.

The story concludes with the acceptance of the moral authority of the police by the complainant.

Some weeks later, a very chastened Mr. Serene signaled a general release before a magistrate, and received a suspended sentence after apologizing to the sergeant, the detective, the clerical patrolman, Patrolman Santos, and this writer, all of whom had to appear in court before the judge could be convinced that this apparently sane man had caused so much trouble just because he had been embarrassed in front of his lady friend (Klein, 1968:37-38).

This story serves not only as an example of the assertion of police moral authority over a particular individual but of a particular *kind* of individual—the person who complains about the *way* in which police do their work. It is a story with archetypal dimensions—a citizen complains about the behavior of a cop, and a police officer uses both his formal and personal authority to reassert his authority, to make the malcontent acknowledge his uninformed and inappropriate behavior.[1] The behavior of the citizen is shown to be child-like and in temper misdirected. The officer is wholly vindicated.

Morality as Dramaturgy: High-Mindedness

This narrative will, indeed, be one of progress. Starting from beginnings as humble as those of the infant city itself, it will, by an unbroken series of steps, arrive at a breadth and perfection of system commensurate with the modern glories of the American metropolis. This will be the most remarkable feature of the story, that—speaking broadly—there is neither defeat, failure, nor stagnation to be chronicled (Costello, 1972:1).

In these clear, simple terms Costello begins his chronicle of the history of the New York City police department. First written in 1885, 15 years before the turn of the twentieth century, the spirit is noncritical, supportive without question. His 572-page history does not mention the rampant corruption that characterized police practices in New York City in this era, nor does he discuss the electioneering violence carried on by police throughout this period. The mood he conveys is not complicated, not disturbingly realistic. Its ardor is that of rallying around the flag, of the celebration of Fourth-of-July patriotism. It is 100 percent pure high-minded morality.

Morality is sometimes viewed in noncritical, categorical ideas of right and wrong. In its simplest form, the evilness of those in the wrong—the other, *evil*—is under attack by the purity of the *us*, the angels (or vice versa). Possible taint of that which is good is not considered: if good is questioned, the credibility of the complainant is challenged. Fussell (1989), developing the idea of "high-mindedness," captures the clear and wonderful simplicity of high-minded morality in his description of the nonjudgmental public declarations of support for the allies in the Second World War:

> If elementary logic—the only kind that wartime could accommodate— required the enemy to be totally evil, it required the allies to be totally good—all of them. The opposition between this black and this white was clear and uncomplicated, untroubled by subtlety or nuance, let alone irony or skepticism (Fussell, 1989:164).

Fussell referred to this uncritical perception of forces of good and evil as the quality of "high-mindedness," that is, a belief in the "successful pursuit of uncomplicated High Purpose."[2] High-mindedness satisfied the wartime need of the home front to justify the slaughter of British troops on behalf of the "good cause." Literary repositories of high-mindedness, he noted, tended to become so uncritical as to be banal in their simplistic acceptance of the virtue of the troops. In the press, the rhetoric of military leaders, and among the civilian population, the moralistic dualism was "total, without shading or complexity" (Fussell, 1989:164)

The thin art of high-minded rhetoric is often present in public descriptions of the police and their adversaries. It typifies the often uncritical way in which the police are presented to the outside world as good guys, waging a war against the bad guys, criminals, or whoever fails to unequivocally support the police. The common-place term "bad guy" reveals this high-mindedness. Lawbreakers are rarely perceived to be ordinary people that have committed bad behavior: they are themselves wicked. The label is harsh and uncompromising.

The high-mindedness that we witness so frequently, coming from legislators, from police executives, from other police representatives, from telephone salesmen for the police charity ball for handicapped children, and from city mayors and council, is dramaturgy. It is a way to gain the support of the police for groups and individuals who want or need their support. That high-minded rhetoric is vapid is not a weakness when one considers its intent. It is pure high-purpose uncomplicated by shades of moral uncertainty—a show of unwavering support.

Morality is more than a dramaturgy of high-mindedness. Morality is also acted out daily by cops on the beat. The expectation that the police will control crime at the societal level is enacted at the individual level as the ability of the police officer to control his or her beat. The beat of an officer is thus transformed into a moral responsibility, the officer's dominion. The notion of beat control is an imperative with a powerful moral thrust. Only an asshole could disagree with how a police officer does his or her job (Van Maanen, 1978).

The moral dimension of police practice is the heart of police culture (Caldero, 1995). Morality is the first theme of solidarity; it is the theme that energizes and makes imperative the aesthetic of coercive territorial control. It justifies all that police do to control their turf, including righteous abuse of suspects and malcontents.

That the moral mandate and the use of coercive violence are inexorably interwoven in the same social fabric—territorial control—is beyond question. The relationship between morality and coercion, however, is perceived differently by the police and their various audiences. There has been an embarrassing though predictable tendency—sometimes less pronounced among the police themselves than among their political advocates—to exploit the high-minded aspects of police morality to justify the misuse of coercion and the abuse of police authority for political gain. The media are guilty of this (Ericson, 1991). Crime re-enactment television shows "which combine news films of events, re-enactment, voice-over narration by actors and actresses, and grainy video filming with handheld cameras," profess to simulate reality. In pure high-mindedness we see television shows with titles such as "America's Most Wanted: America Fights Back" and "Cops." Nowhere, of course, is mentioned the moral dilemmas engendered by the use of police violence in a democratic society (Manning, 1995:376). Media constructions are inevitably high-minded, offering simple contrasts between good and evil, black and white (literally and figuratively), us and them.

The police are implicated in the media's narrow vision, of course, in that they tend to manipulate the flow of information to develop the good-bad contrast, revealing particular aspects of their work and obscuring others (Ericson, 1989:139-140). The police may manipulate the image of their work to fit supportive social sentiments.

> Because society has come to learn that drug use is dangerous; that drug dealers are well organized and heavily armed; that certain deviant segments of society are less deserving of the full protections of the law; and that undefined "others" present a threat to the social and moral order, casting police actions within the context of fighting these groups makes the concrete actions of police, even deviant actions, more acceptable to the audience . . . For the larger public, the victim of police violence must be cast in terms of dangerousness versus the stereotypic depiction of the police as the "thin blue line" between order and anarchy (Kappeler, Sluder & Alpert 1994:106).

Kappeler and his colleagues suggested that police condone the perpetuation of such high-mindedness to obscure a closer inspection of rough and brutal police behavior in police-citizen interactions. High-mindedness, with its hidden stigmatization of classes of citizens as bad guys, justifies over-aggressive police behavior and provides the police with retrospective justification for reprehensible behavior. Who can question heavy-handed police behavior when it is against some scumbag that probably deserves it anyway and just might think twice next time? Not considered is whether the scumbag actually did something that broke the law, threatened the public peace, whether the law itself should be questioned, or if the police should have free-wheeling authority to use violence at whim.

Police executives, speaking to a public audience and to the troops themselves, frequently implore such high-mindedness. Through moralistic exhortations, they try to show that they are "one of the boys." Consider former Chief (of the Los Angeles Police Department) Daryl Gates' speech to graduating recruits.

> "I have chiefs all over the country with these badge collections," says Daryl Gates, now nearly shouting as he reaches the apex of his address. "And they're forever coming up to me and saying, "Hey! Can I get a badge from the LAPD? It's the only one I don't have." And I tell them proudly, "That's the only one you're not going to get. Unless," says Daryl Gates, pounding the podium, "you wanna go through the Los Angeles Police Academy—If-You-Are-Qualified-Chief! . . . If you are qualified" (Domanick, 1994:17).

Such exhortations are not wholly innocent of underlying motive. That chiefs have limited control over the day-to-day behavior of line officers has been widely cited. As Chief Gates was to discover in early March of 1991, when the first news of the Rodney King police brutality case splashed across the nation's airwaves, the way a chief finds out about what officers are doing is often like the rest of us—through the newspapers. Control over the behavior of line personnel during field duty is meager at best, and the wide influence of police labor representation has given them a means to resist bureaucratic oversight. Chiefs have to display their loyalty to the troops in appropriate ways to insure support:

> The modernizing chief is constrained, therefore, to make at least symbolic obeisance to police solidarity by demonstrating that (he) is a "cop's" cop, as well as a devotee of systems analysis . . . One of the ways he does this is by emphasis in his dress and bearing—the policeman's chief social tool—the ability to command personal respect (Bordua & Reiss, 1986:34).

Muir: Maturity in the Face of Paradox

In spite of the high-mindedness of police advocates, the police themselves wrestle with a morality substantially more complex than good-guy bad-guy distinctions. Morality is easy in the abstract and in the extreme case, when the bad-guys are known and what they have done is clearly reprehensible. Such post-hoc arm-chair moralizing, however, is no prescription for the bulk of police-citizen encounters. Police-citizen encounters are not characterized by certainty, but uncertainty. Offenders do not advertise their identity to the police. Police-citizen interactions, in which the citizen may also be an offender, are characterized by secrecy, suspicion, and unpredictability.

Most bad guys are not heavyweight predators, but bantam-class misdemeanants and, to use Van Maanen's (1978) terminology, viewed as "assholes" whose culpability lies in an officer's interpretation of vague laws such as interfering with an officer or creating a public nuisance. In such encounters, where and when is the use of coercion morally justified? This is a more difficult question, yet an everyday one that defines much of the police culture. To ponder morality at this level is to begin to understand what the police are about.

Muir (1977) has put forth an eloquent model of police morality. Muir recognized that police confronted situations that did not fall neatly into fixed moral categories. Simple ideas of good and bad provided little direction for officers, who frequently had to balance their moral convictions against the ordinary problems that overwhelmed many of the people with whom they came into contact. Categoric codes of right and wrong, conceptualized as officer safety, might justify the use of deadly force in a confrontation with an armed bank robber, but such principles provided little insight into, for example, more common family conflicts, where outcomes were unpredictable and simple ideas of right and wrong provided scant direction on what to do. A more complex idea of morality was needed to help cops think about such encounters.

Muir created a model of police use of force that he called the extortionate transaction. In a brilliant epiphany, he manipulated the model into four incongruities he named the "paradoxes of coercion." The first of these is the paradox of dispossession. "The less one has, the less one has to lose." The paradox in an antagonistic encounter is that the victim with nothing is less vulnerable to coercive threats: "In bargaining, weakness is often strength" (Muir, 1977:38-39).

The second, "the paradox of detachment," states that "the less the victim cares about preserving something, the less the victimizer cares about taking it hostage." This paradox deals with the victim and reveals the problematic nature of unfolding contingencies in an encounter: A victimizer "can't always perceive clearly what value a victim places on his own possessions" (Muir, 1977:40-41).

The third is the paradox of face: "the nastier one's reputation, the less nasty one has to be." This paradox is "elementally psychological. The successful practice of coercion is not to injure but to employ the threat to injure." Paradoxical is that violence is effective, not in its presence, but in its absence. All is threat and bluster. The risk, of course, is that someone will call the bluff. Unfortunately, this can destroy either party: to save face in the calling of a bluff "is to manifest malevolence and respond cruelly and destructively, even if it means risking one's own destruction" (Muir, 1977:42). The paradox is based on the threat of behavior that, if carried out, destroys the extortionate transaction.

The fourth is the paradox of irrationality: "The more delirious the threatener, the more serious the threat: the more delirious the victim, the less serious the threat." The paradox is that "being sensible and appearing so may be a liability in an extortionate world, and not knowing enough to know better may be an asset" (Muir, 1977:43).

Muir observed that these four paradoxes turn conventional ideas of morality on their head. Categoric ideas of right and wrong became problematic. Where is morality to be found, if the simple use of coercion to achieve good ends is thwarted by circumstances that contradict its effectiveness? Morality was to be found in an officer's talent in manipulating coercive authority to achieve good ends, without being overwhelmed by either the passionate pursuit of good ends or by an overwhelming sensitivity that he called perspective and that turned all issues of right and wrong into shifting shades of uncertainty.[3] Passion, he argued, enabled officers to integrate coercion into their morals. The limits of moral passion were in the unprincipled abandonment of ethical concerns of civilized life. Without guilt, he noted, there could be no conscience. Officers, he admonished, also needed to develop perspective, "a comprehension of the suffering of each inhabitant of the earth, and a sensitivity of man's yearning for dignity . . ." (Muir, 1977:50). The principled balance of passion and perspective promoted maturity, a moral balance that reflected an officer's ability to reconcile himself to the use of force without being overwhelmed by its corrupting effects.

The strength of Muir's formulation is linking the four paradoxes to his adaptation of Weber's professional political model. The use of paradox was an eloquent statement of the unpredictability in police-citizen contacts. One of Muir's underlying themes, the ability to envision outcomes precisely the opposite than intended, was a skill that enabled an officer to adapt to the cascading contingencies that characterize many police-citizen encounters. Muir's paradoxes were ironies. They implicitly asked "Is there a way in which what I am doing is going to have precisely the opposite effect from what I intend?"

Morality flows from police officer's abilities to adjust their use of coercion to these paradoxical encounters. Morality, like heaven, is in the details, in the moment-by-moment adjustment to changing circumstances, without losing control in an explosion of coercive force. Morality is played out as gamesmanship, and officers develop strategies to minimize their use of force in order to maximize their effectiveness.

Muir's model is a powerful heuristic, strong medicine for advising future officers about the corrupting effects of power. It is also an admonition for cops to sharpen their senses for ambiguity, misunderstandings, the unpredictable, and the ironic. Ultimately however, Muir's model fails as a guide for understanding police culture. His model is intended to teach officers how to think about their use of coercion in terms different from simple ideas of right/wrong, moral superiority, good guy/bad guy imagery. But the morality is post hoc, constructed in the replay of events past. When officers approach an ambivalent encounter, their behavior is not conditioned by paradoxical ideas of morality. It is conditioned by edge control, minimizing threats to personal danger, resolving the encounter, avoiding excessive paperwork, and getting on with something more interesting. Police work is more righteous than Muir's typology suggests, as Van Maanen (1978) recognized in the following article on a topic of eternal police interest: what to do about assholes. Muir sought an ideally moral officer, comfortable yet hesitant to use force when other solutions would achieve the same goal. Van Maanen (1978) recognized the ritualistic aspects of the use of force, and gained a better understanding of police culture.

Van Maanen: Righteousness and the Asshole

Van Maanen's classic paper titled "The Asshole" (1978) represented a fundamental rethinking of police use of coercive force. Van Maanen challenged the prevailing belief at the time that police use of force was directed primarily at criminal suspects. In his analysis of police overuse of coercion, he noted that police tended to focus, not on suspects, but on big-mouths, individuals who had not committed a legal violation but who, in their behavior, displayed resentment about the intrusion of the police into their affairs. His seminal paper captured the moral dimension of the use of coercion—police believe that they exist, in part, to protect the world from assholes.

Assholes, Van Maanen argued, represented a type of individual that organized a great deal of police activity. But a cop could not know who an asshole was until he encountered him or her. The process of labeling someone an asshole emerged in concrete encounters with citizens. The consequence of the label was an increased likelihood of street justice.

Van Maanen argued that the label "asshole" arose in the context of immediate situations, and was tied to observable social action. These situations were everyday police-citizen encounters. The stigmatization process—by which individuals were stigmatized as assholes, had three phases. The first phase was called *affront* and occurred when a police officer's authority was questioned by a citizen. A beer-guzzling citizen in a city park that responds to a police order to pour out the beer by pouring it over the officer's shoes, for example, has initiated a process that carries the risk of being labeled an asshole. This is a critical juncture in the labeling process:

> any further slight to a[n] officer, however subtle, provides sufficient evidence that he may be indeed be dealing with a certifiable asshole, and the situation is in need of rapid clarification (Van Maanen, 1978:229).

The second stage, *clarification*, represents the officer's effort to determine what sort of individual they are dealing with. Clarification involves the resolution of two implicit questions: (1) does the citizen know what they are doing? and (2) could they have acted differently under the circumstances? If the answer to both of these questions was yes, the person risked being labeled sub-human in a scatologically specific way, and became vulnerable to street justice. The third stage, remedy, was a typology of police behavioral responses that flowed from the clarification of the incident. Those that were labeled assholes were the most likely recipients of street justice, by which Van Maanen meant placement under questionable arrest, violence, and other rude attention-getting behaviors.

The asshole, Van Maanen argued, was a term that contained a great deal of meaning for the police. The label emerged from the need to maintain control in street encounters, and from a moral imperative to assert the authority of the state when it was questioned. The asshole thus organized much police work, and provided police with an expressive outlet in the absence of so-called "real" police work.

The term *asshole* may be the most ubiquitous celestial body in a cop's gritty cosmology. A major city in the southwest maintains a list of individuals that are perceived to be troublemakers on police calls for service. This list is located in the filing cabinet under the letter "A." Can you guess why? Bouza (1990) also noted the special utility of disorderly conduct statutes for those whom the police have defined as "assholes." One would be hard-pressed to encounter officers from any city in the United States that did not share a common vision of who assholes were.

I have frequently described to students Van Maanen's (1978) vision of the concrete way the label "asshole" arises in street encounters. I have been as frequently chastised by student-cops for failing to understand the term. I now suspect that Van Maanen, while providing an excellent (and titillating) example of ethnography, subtly missed an important aspect of the labeling process. Van Maanen's ideas of the process by which citizens are labeled assholes makes perfect sense, but only under the condition that an officer begins an encounter with a naïve or neutral state of mind. Officers, however, do not do this. When they enter into a situation involving a citizen, they already have a pretty good idea about who is an asshole; more than likely they had this idea before they became cops. Nor are police-citizen encounters neutral events; police talk to citizens because something has gone sour and the police want something they think the citizen has; witness testimony or criminal involvement, for example.

Van Maanen, I think, overlooked the way in which police culture reinforces a common moral sensibility in a circular logic of asshole identification and subsequent retaliatory action that verifies that the individual was indeed an asshole. Some cops may wait and see what citizens do before labeling them in some way. However, after thousands of encounters cops have a pretty good read of citizens. Many citizens are labeled assholes before the encounter even begins, and a self-fulfilling logic will verify at some point in the encounter that they indeed are assholes.

Van Maanen suggested that wrongdoers were not necessarily assholes; they frequently wanted to minimize problems with the police. Yet the police frequently treat lawbreakers roughly, justifying abusive treatment of suspects in terms of police officer safety. Anyone that has witnessed a police bust of a so-called drug house could not conclude that the police were treating inhabitants any kinder than Van Maanen's police treated assholes. What Van Maanen missed is that all lawbreakers are assholes, not just those who disagree with an officer's definition of a situation. Because an offender has violated the law, they have pretty much established that they have a different idea of appropriate behavior from the legal ideal cops are expected to uphold.

As a colleague pointed out, "people don't end up being assholes. Everyone starts out as an asshole, and cops will let some people off the hook, depending on their behavior." In other words, Van Maanen (1978) had the labeling process backwards. Within a few years after joining the force, some cops will see all citizens as assholes. Every situation is confronted with the presumption that an officer is dealing with an asshole. One of Fletcher's confidants captures this sentiment in the following comment:

> People lie to us eight hours a day. Everybody lies to us: offenders, victims, witnesses. They all lie to the police. It gets so bad, you go to a party, somebody comes up to talk to you. You're thinking, "Why is this guy saying this to me? What's his game?" You can't turn it off (Fletcher, 1991:278).

Before long, other police officers are assholes too. You are at roll call and hear your buddy make the same wisecrack for the one-thousandth time, and you think "Jeez, that guy's an asshole." One morning you look at yourself in a mirror and you realize that there is an asshole looking back at you. At this point the term *asshole* becomes so universal that it loses all meaning. Even the angels are assholes. So what.

Endnotes

[1] The Lieutenant in this example noted that there were valid incidents of police abuse, but that they were in the statistical minority. Generally, I have observed that officers will acknowledge the existence of police abuse in the abstract, but specific incidents that implicate known officers are generally denied or questioned.

[2] Quoting Eric Severeid 20 years later, Fussell (1989:163) notes that the high-minded spirit continued unabated: "If that fight was not holy, if it was not absolutely true that the contest was between good and evil, then no battle ever was such."

[3] Muir adopted this perspective from Weber (1946).

15

Common Sense and the Ironic Deconstruction of the Obvious

> One must have a certain disposition for irony, but it does not come without practice; like really good violin playing, it must be practiced every day (Davies, 1994:150).

This chapter is about common sense and irony. In it, I seek to describe how police common sense emerges, and how irony is central to police ideas of common sense. The chapter opens with a consideration of common sense, and I discuss how it differs from ordinary forms of rational knowledge. Irony is presented as a special case of common sense central to police work—indeed, one could say that irony is the craft of police thinking. It is a way of thinking that allows police to see danger in safe places, to uncover wrongdoing when obscured by suspects.

Irony is an art, and police work is the craft of irony. It is learned on the job from other police in concrete encounters with suspects and in ambiguous circumstances. The skill of a police officer is not in recognizing what is there, but in recognizing what is not there.

Police and Common Sense

It is astonishing that the police should characterize their craft, as unpredictable as it is, as a world that makes sense if one simply uses common sense. Defined in Webster's dictionary as the sense that at one time was thought to unite the five known senses, common sense implies the ability to bring a practical knowledge, obvious to any sensible person, to bear on a situation. Common sense works because a person's training enables them to apply principles learned in a previous situation to a current one, the art of historical analogy. Common sense, as Geertz (1973) observed, is what any clear-thinking person would do in the same situation.

That the police put a high value on the application of common sense has been widely cited, and the ability to use common sense is a source of pride among officers (Manning, 1976; McNulty, 1994). Police place great value on common-sense knowledge, "holding it to be crucial for survival on the street" (McNulty, 1994:282; see also Fletcher, 1990).

The notion of common sense suggests that we can apply our clear-minded practical experience to our work. But what if our work is unpredictable—indeed, that unpredictability is one of its most important aspects? As I have suggested previously, there is little about police-citizen interactions that is predictable. Encounters are like water moving over unknown terrain; they flow across cascading contingencies, and guides for action used by a police officer at the outset of an encounter may be useless or even counterproductive to its resolution. Indeed, police work is so unpredictable that theorists have used it as an exemplar of the improvisational nature of knowledge (Shearing & Ericson, 1991; McNulty, 1994; Sacks, 1972).

There is a paradox about police work and common sense. Police work is characterized by unpredictability, not by rule-ordered predictability (Shearing & Ericson, 1991). Common sense implies some notion of a natural order of things, not a natural disorder. Yet disorder is central to police work—without disorder, without rule-breaking, there would be no reason for the police in American society. And as we have seen, unpredictability, situational uncertainty, and turbulence are central aspects of police work. How can common sense (e.g., the ability to apply experience to police-citizen encounters), be reconciled with a fundamentally unpredictable task environment in which police-citizen encounters tend to cascade unpredictably and the control of events is always somewhat askew? The answer to this question is a conundrum, an ironic inversion of the obvious into its opposite, an affirmation of common sense through a denial of the senses. It is the conversion of the seemingly safe into the ironically dangerous.

Common sense is the lifeblood of the police culture. Police ideas of common sense are steeped in organizational culture (Manning, 1989).[1] The entire body of common sense in the occupational culture of the police—its stories, predispositions, collective moods, preferences, and dislikes—is its world collective sensibility, and it is grounded in local habits and the everyday work. Like other elements of culture, common sense derives from real events and the habits and ways of thinking that have accreted over time (Ericson 1982; Crank, Payne & Jackson, 1993). In police organizations, common sense is the accumulated wisdom of line-officer culture, carrying the wisdom, history, and traditions of the department. It is the "what works" in particular cases, and how to think about what works.

What is common sense, and how do we make it? In the broadest sense, common sense is the way in which a local culture views its work (Geertz, 1983). Common sense comes about from a culture's particular habits and routines, its taken-for-granted ways of doing things (Shearing & Ericson, 1991). Routine practices, accepted as how to do things by their membership, come to be accepted as natural ways of doing things, a fixed element of the environment (Manning 1989). Though practices may appear arcane to outsiders, to insiders they are what any perfectly sensible person would do. The repeated, shared actions of members of a group become customary.

Common sense derives from the informal and routine ways of solving problems, and is taught through example (Manning, 1970). This idea is summarized in the frequently repeated dictum, heard by every recruit upon being assigned to a field training officer, to "forget everything you learned in (read POST or school). I'm gonna show how we really do things out here." Common sense is passed on by training officers as the craft of police work, in which "learning comes exclusively through experience intuitively processed by individual officers" (Bayley & Bittner, 1989:87). Thus, common sense is more than a simple set of unspoken propositions about the occupational environment; it is a tool-kit of cultural repertoires, including verbal and nonverbal behavioral skills, for understanding and successfully negotiating both the street environment and the police culture.

How can a person describe common sense? It is difficult, and much of this difficulty lies in the way in which common sense is taught to police officers. Consider the following example, from a discussion of a Parole and Probation POST class (1996). The following brief exchange shows how informal organizational processes become common sense, by adding new charges for drug violators.

> Instructor: We rarely do these (file new charges). I did three over the past year, and that's a lot. For example, you might have a pregnant mother using drugs.
>
> Trainee: Is that a case where we don't do this?
>
> Instructor: No, that's the kind of case where we usually make an arrest (Crank, 1996:281).

Common sense about body searches, and by implication the nature of offenders, is revealed in the following quote.

> Lean him over and spread his cheeks so that you can inspect his anal cavity . . . You might have them stand on a newspaper. Keep in mind that these people have been in jail and are dirty. When they bend over all kinds of stuff might come out of their anal cavity. You don't want to have to clean that stuff up.[2]

An officer experienced in anal searches quickly learns to recognize the obvious—it makes perfect sense that a person undergoing an anal search stand on something like a newspaper. The search routine thus became a part of the vocabulary of common sense, and the label "scumbag" for offenders achieves its full metaphorical meaning. You can also note that the communication portrays an image of the offender as inherently foul. The clear causation of the foulness, stated in the quote itself—that the person is foul not because of who they are but because they have been in jail—is easily overlooked.

Common sense is different from technical knowledge. When we think of language, we tend to think of the rational organization of words that have clear meanings. We convey information by explaining precisely what the meaning is of the words we are using. If someone asks me, for example, what time it is, I can respond "it is 4:50" and most people understand what I am saying. Similarly, a police trainee in a POST class can learn how to recognize bomb paraphernalia, how to break down a 9mm pistol for cleaning, or how to conduct a body search. These are technical considerations, and are founded in rational ideas of the organization and meaning of knowledge.

Common-sense knowledge is fundamentally different. It not based on the clear meanings derived from rational-technical knowledge. Common sense is experienced by members of a police culture as something different from such meaning—it is the way in which the world itself works. It is the essence of the world perceived by its actors (Lakoff & Johnson, 1980). If the response to the question "What time is it?" was "It's about time to get a beer," the response carries social meaning—about the sentiments brought forward by the approach of the end of the working day, about the sort of social relations we have, about how we entertain ourselves. It carries no technical information, yet the response carries a great deal of meaning. Its meaning is common-sensical, obvious. If I were to respond "What do you mean, beer time?" my co-workers would look at me like I was from a distant galaxy.

Common Sense and Tropes

If common sense cannot be understood in terms of rational vocabularies, then what is it? Perhaps the best way to think of it is as a form of story-telling (Shearing & Ericson, 1991). An ingredient soup of tradition, heroes, metaphors, ironies, bad guys, trickery, assholes, coincidence, survival, and surreal events is what makes stories interesting, what gives them a larger-than-life quality. Stories highlight the actions of particular individuals, and tell about what they did, what they did not do, or something that happened to them. Stories are knowledge by example, concrete and specific—in response to a "how-to" question, stories provide a concrete example about what someone did in the past.

Stories may be very short, providing a way of thinking about some area of organizational activity. In addition, stories tend to carry the traditions and the history of the department. Officers who know the stories of the department know several things—they know what the department is about, they know how particular individuals have done things in the past, and they know what is meaningful. Through common-sense knowledge, police acquire a way of thinking about thinking, a way that marks them forever and irrevocably as cops.

Common sense is a story-telling form of knowledge that carries powerful images and histories about the nature of the work done (Shearing & Ericson, 1991). It is made up of metaphors, or terms that describe things in terms of something else. In occupational cultures, this metaphorical "something else" is often a story, irony, or some combination of these constituted from everyday experience. The accumulation of metaphorical images makes each organizational culture unique, depending on its work circumstances and the collective experiences of its members.

Consider the previous examples presented in this section, filing drug charges and searching prisoners. Both stories suggest routine ways to handle particular types of cases. The first story, framed as common sense, conveyed the message that drug offenses are to be treated as harshly as possible. The second, the most powerful of the two stories, communicated more information than the idea that officers ought to be concerned with cleanliness. The story conveyed the scatological metaphor that offenders are shit—disgusting creatures.

The role of metaphorical imagery for comprehending police behavior was first elaborated by Manning (1979). Manning suggested that metaphors provided an imagery through which the world of the seer fit the language system used to describe that world. Manning argued that the world of the police was constructed tropically, vis-à-vis the four master tropes, called metaphor, metonymy, synecdoche, and irony. Extending his work to parole and probation, I described tropes as follows:

> Tropes are processes of "analogous reasoning" or "cultural repertoires" that "allow action to be both orderly and improvisational" (Shearing & Ericson, 1991:482). Tropes provide a tool-kit of culturally acceptable ways for organizing knowledge under ideas of common-sense. The craft of policing, for example, has been characterized as an extensive repertoire of tropes that enable officers to move easily from one ambiguous situation to the next, practicing their craft according to commonly held ideas, embodied in a story-based vocabulary, of what policing is (McNulty, 1994). Each of these tropes is a way of looking at the world in terms of something else.

Four types of tropes are cited (Eco, 1984). Metaphor, defined as a "way of seeing something as if it were something else" (Manning, 1979:661), has been called the master trope, in that other types of tropes are special types of metaphors. Stories are metaphors in that they provide an explanation of something in terms of personal, concrete experience, although stories may themselves be constructed of strings of tropes. The other tropes are special cases of metaphors. Synecdoche refers to seeing a part for the whole. Burke (1969) defined synecdoche as representation, that is, one thing is presented to represent another.[3] Metonymy takes a whole and reduces it to its constituent parts Turner (1974).[4] Ironies convey meaning through their opposites[5] (Crank, 1996:271-272).

Police stories are synecdoches. As stories, tropes have wide significance about how the police organization works. Stories are a synedcoche: a specific instance that provides a way of thinking about the general area of interest. They provide a vocabulary of precedents that construct an appropriate intersubjective way of seeing the world (Mills, 1940). Stories enable police officers to act based, not on fixed rules, but "rather the sensibility out of which she or he ought to act" (Shearing & Ericson, 1991:493). Stories enable officers to generalize from concrete encounters, to think and adapt, to not be limited by rule-like prescriptions. Story-logic thus resonates well with police work, where success lies in the ability to adapt to unfolding contingencies in police-citizen encounters.

Common sense is tautological. Common sense, the sacramental knowledge of experience, does not tell officers what to do. It alludes, suggests, orients, intimates, and seduces. It provides ways of thinking through things (McNulty, 1994). It enables officers to ponder what they are doing in terms of how another officer did something else. It references without ordering, and arises from the doing, the outcome of its own motivation. Common sense allows action to be improvisational, and improvisational action keeps the story alive, renewed. Common sense begets stories that affirm common sense, and culture seeds itself.

Common sense is communicated in story and hyperbolic form. It is unfortunate that stories told by police officers are often perceived to be glosses arising from a lack of technical knowledge, reflections of cops' inabilities to make clear why they do what they do. Research on the police has overlooked a great deal of the process of cultural transmission because stories were seen as simple work tales or "war stories," without wider significance.

Stories are not crude approximations of technical knowledge. They are reservoirs of values and information. A more careful consideration of stories will reveal perceptions of work and the bases of activity in terms of common sense. Suppose I were to ask a police officer about due process procedures for conducting a drug raid. I might receive a practical, common-sense answer similar to the description of a raid.

Defense attorneys sometimes try to get us on a no-knock. But we do knock—we have to knock and identify ourselves, wait for a response- and then we're out there knocking with a battering ram or a sledge- hammer. And we do identify ourselves as police—if you had a tape recorder on one of those things, you'd hear "Police!" yelled about 20 times on entry. It cuts your chances of getting killed by about 90 per- cent. We don't want them to think we're the stickup men. We want them to know that we're the police (Fletcher, 1990:198).

How should I interpret this explanation? The officer is not explaining technical issues of due process. He is describing how defense counsel misrepresents his work as it is concretely practiced. To treat the story as no more than a gloss of usual activity would be to miss information cen- tral to how officers construct their images of bad guys. This image is that police officers on drug busts encounter armed individuals and deadly force, and by implication that officer safety is the primary consideration in the way in which raids are conducted. The message is clear—drug raids are dangerous.

Is there any evidence that the police are particularly vulnerable to vio- lence during a raid? There are no findings that suggest this, and categori- cal data from "Law Enforcement Officers Killed in Action" (National Insti- tute of Justice) does not support this presupposition. However, suppose we start from the assumption that houses where drugs are sold are full of armed and dangerous dealers. If this is the case, then tactical entry makes clear sense. Officers might argue that detailed preparation enables them to deal with these confrontations with armed and truly dangerous bad guys in a way that minimizes the likelihood of injury or death. Rapid entry with weapons drawn, use of command voice on entry, tossing a smoke grenade to confuse the suspects, grabbing to control anyone encountered in the room, are tactical strategies to rapidly overwhelm an armed and dangerous enemy.

This approach to anti-drug activity is an example of how common sense begets common sense—preparation and a quick tactical operation results in officer safety. How do we know? Because police officers pre- pare themselves for these encounters and hit them with overwhelming force, and officers are not injured. Listen to this story and you can see how preparation prevented serious injury. Additionally, this story reveals officers' hostility toward legal counsel. Legal counsel will raise funda- mental due process issues in court—they may fail to clearly announce themselves, or they sometimes obtain warrants using questionable sources, or probable cause for the seizure of the property will be suspect.

Finally, and central to the construction of common sense, the story communicates to other officers how they can defend themselves against charges that they had violated due process protocols during a drug raid. Any clear-thinking judge hearing this explanation from a police officer could not help but believe him or her—the story is perfectly sensible. It makes common sense that drug dealers would be more reluctant to kill a police officer than a suspected robber. How could anyone imagine that they had not announced themselves before entering? The problem, of course, is that the explanation does not make sense. It is inconceivable that someone that is armed and with large quantities of drugs in plain sight is going to invite a police officer into the house, particularly facing a sentence of life in prison. The notion is silly and absurd.

The following story shows the power of stories in training. Van Maanen described this story as an example of how departmental traditions were handed down as a part of the informal training process. However, this story is more than department traditions and informal camaraderie—it provides a particular way to look at the criminal law. The tale conveys more information than a simple venting of the instructor's frustrations: it contextualizes whatever technical information might have been presented in a lecture on criminal law with organizational spin, spin that is this context hostile to the criminal law itself.

> I suppose you guys have heard of Lucky Baldwin? If not, you sure will when you hit the street. Baldwin happens to be the biggest burglar still operating in this town . . . We've busted him about ten times so far, but he's got an asshole lawyer and money so he always beats the rap . . . If I ever get a chance to bust the SOB, I'll do it my way with my thirty-eight and spare the city the cost of a trial (Van Maanen, 1978:298).

This statement is not a gloss on an officer's frustration. It carries the weight of a respected trainer to a room of recruits. Officers "hear" that the organization has a high priority on doing something about this person. Implied is that extralegal considerations in dealing with Lucky Baldwin, particularly the use of extreme violence, might be acceptable to some people in the department. The statement also covertly sanctions the use of deadly force in nonlethal encounters.

The tale also is sharply critical of defense counsel. It is clear that his counsel is a bum with no respect for the police, of course, because he is devoted to getting this scumbag off. In addition, because the department has not been able to remove Baldwin legally, and because he is out there committing crimes, then other means must be used. The obvious interpretation for Lucky's continued freedom—that he has been busted and let off 10 times either because he is not guilty or because the police are astonishingly bad at evidence collection—is clearly outside the intent of the speaker.

Common sense arises from the doing of police work, what an officer sees and how officers act on and react to their working environment. It is the practical knowledge they use to do their work. As the previous stories demonstrate, common sense creates a "subjectivity" that is appropriate to the working world of officers. It is a particular way of looking at things, constructed of particular experiences and events in an officer's lore. Experiences accrete over time to form the intersubjective culture sustained by stories told and retold by members of the organizational culture. As Shearing and Ericson (191:489) noted, stories function as a "search-light rather than a spot-light, insuring that they (police officers) experience reality as a fluid rather than as a solid.

Common sense exists in a reciprocal relationship with action (McNulty, 1994). On the one hand, common sense can be seen as causal to action: common sense provides strategies or sensibilities for subsequent behavior. The replay of particular predicaments with other officers provides a shared framework for common sense to emerge. In this regard, common-sense knowledge emerges from the encounter and the way in which the encounter is interactively interpreted "in community with other officers." The replay of the story thus provides a perspective for viewing future interventions. In both the stories of Lucky Baldwin and of the knock announcement, common sense about the relationship between the police and criminals predisposed actions that in turn provided a justification for future action.

Tautology precludes objectivity. The tautology of common sense presents a paradox. If common sense predisposes behavior, and the behavior elicits a reaction that seems to justify the behavior, there is a causal loop in the use of common sense, as follows, in which a predisposition for a way of acting initiates a way of acting that elicits a response that justifies the original predisposition.

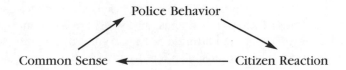

Common sense becomes the basis for common sense. How, then, can an independent, self-correcting, "reality-based" interpretation of events occur that allows for individuals to learn from their errors? For those who wish to pursue an objective understanding of behavior, that is, that there is a "truth" to events independent of the observer, the tautology between common sense and behavior is certainly uncomfortable—the clear indication is that knowledge, based on common sense, cannot be independently or objectively verified by participants, in this case the police.

Put another way, members of a police culture, acting on common-sense ideas of behavior and reconstructing events from that common-sense foundation, have a sharply limited capacity to see the predispositional biases in their behavior. This is not unique to the police, but a common phenomenon of humans—it is an accompaniment of our nature as cultural creatures. However, it seems to imply a subjective vision of police work in which police officers, as culture carrying agents, cannot also be rational, independent observers of the public and enforcers of the law. This subjective notion of police work is inconsistent with a vision of the criminal justice system as a set of procedures that seek to impartially and rationally invoke the criminal law based on objective, verifiable, strictly evidentiary considerations.

The subjective vision of the police is a dark one, at least for those who seek the lightness of clear, rational knowledge unsullied by predispositional passions. The vision of a police force that invokes a self-fulfilling set of common-sensical assumptions based on a story logic in order to carry out their role in the criminal justice process is inconsistent with the rational foundations of criminal law. How can we have a rational criminal justice system if the gatekeepers to the system are themselves creatures driven by subjective, common-sense concerns that harken more to organizational traditions and self-fulfilling logics than an independent quest for the truth?

This paradox is not limited to the police, but is central to knowledge itself. In a wide literature, sociologists of knowledge have sought the roots of true knowledge in a relativistic world (Mannheim, 1936). The paradox of the sociology of knowledge is that what we call knowledge is relative to its social setting (e.g., see Berger & Luckmann, 1966:1-18). This pertains to common-sense knowledge as well. The relativity of common sense comes from sharing and communicating in everyday life. Berger and Luckmann describe this process:

> . . . I know that there is a[n] ongoing correspondence between my meanings and their (others') meanings, and we share a common sense about its reality. The natural attitude is the attitude of common sense consciousness precisely because it refers to a world that is common to many men. Common sense knowledge is the knowledge I share with others in the normal, self-evident routines of everyday life. The reality of everyday life . . . does not require additional verification over and beyond its simple presence. It is simply there . . . self evident and . . . compelling (Berger & Luckmann, 1966:23).

That there may be an independent, objective reality that I can observe and record is at best questionable and in all cases problematic: even among the physical sciences, the profoundly distorting effect of the observer on the observed has been widely noted (see Whitehead, 1925). The police see the world in the only way they can, as do the rest of us. The problem with an objective search for truth is not the relativity of knowledge. The problem lies in the unfoundable belief that there is such a thing as clear, primal knowledge, independent of the observer.

Common sense is deconstructed from the obvious. Police culture is unique. Officers take great pride in their common sense. But their common sense does not come from the world as given. To the contrary, police common sense is expressed in their ability to see the world unseen. Common sense derives from an officer's skills in recognizing the hidden danger in the seemingly safe world inhabited by ordinary citizens. Consider the following story.

> B. Walked into the jail with a woman that they had arrested following a domestic incident . . . T. explained that the prisoner had given a false name and date of birth at a routine traffic stop. The information resulted in a "hit," indicating a felony warrant—in this case for a Chicago rape and murder . . . They focused on the one unusual aspect of the incident, namely the ages (30s) of the people involved. The incident had occurred in a retirement community (McNulty, 1994:290).

The key to common sense as used by an officer in this example is the trope "irony." McNulty recognized that the use of common sense resulted from the proximity of danger and irony. Through the trope irony officers were able to see through the image of normalcy to the danger underneath.

Irony derives its strength from the concrete practice of coercive territorial control. Police maintain the public order and enforce laws against bad guys who do not advertise their presence or behavior. Danger is unseen. Through irony, safe environments or normal encounters are transformed into circumstances sullied or dangerous, exposing criminal activity. Consider the following example.

> For the police, objects and places having routine uses are conceived in terms of favorite misuses. Garbage cans are places in which dead babies are thrown, schoolyards are places in which mobsters hang out, stores are places where shoplifters go, etc. (Shearing & Ericson, 1991:490).

In another example drawn from Shearing and Ericson, McNulty describes a "picture construction," in which an officer was describing a beat to a recruit, in a similar (ironic) way:

> 'There's where the house burned down with the transient in it." He pointed to another house and continued, 'This is where the suicide occurred, . . . and in this house [there] was the gas leak and in this house the old lady just died of old age'. . . . He showed me the location of the van accident, pointing out the field around which the bodies (of four children) were scattered and where the van had landed—at a very ordinary 4-way stop (McNulty, 1994:286).

Manning: Ironies of Organizational Structure

Through irony, differences are emphasized even when similarities may be striking. Manning (1979:666-667) discusses how drug enforcement agents use elementary common sense to distinguish themselves from drug dealers. Enforcement agents view the drug business as "immoral, improper, and certainly illegal." Because drug dealing and purchasing is usually victimless (this means that there is no citizen that reports a crime to the police and thus invokes the reactive intervention of the police) a particular model of police enforcement emerges. The first irony is that the organizational structure of police tends to mirror the organizational structure of drug sellers. Manning notes 15 structural and behavioral similarities between the drug-using system and the enforcement system, of which the following are a salient though partial list:

1. A mutual concern for security.

2. Pressures for sales and production.

3. Feudal loyalty.

4. Work demands that are episodic and sporadic.

5. Both caution and risk-taking are necessary for success.

6. Low, flat hierarchy where members on the bottom take the greatest risk.

7. Dealings based on personal relationships; trust central to the work.

8. Generally a young man's work, dominated by a young man's style of life and interests, on and off the job.

His point is that there is a striking similarity in the organizational and economic systems of both drug dealers and cops, a similarity that is obscured by the common-sense distinction between police as good guys and the stigmatization of drug dealers as other, different, evil. His discussion of irony could be written off as an academic drudge were it not for the ironic outcome of similar organizational structures, both focused on the control of drug distribution: at a certain point, it becomes impossible to tell who are the good guys.

> Ironically, undercover narcs do not look like police officers: they keep strange hours, hang out with the "bad guys," can drink, frequent bars, dress like criminals when on duty; are paid on a different basis; and attempt to become like persons for whom they were meant to be different . . . What ultimately distinguishes one from the other, . . .? (Manning, 1979:667).

That this other has real implications for police work has been noted by Marx (1988:108-109). Undercover work is, he notes, more fluid and unpredictable than regular patrol work. Agents tend to deal only with criminals and are always involved in deceptive practices. In such an environment, role models, that is, the roles to which he/she must adapt, are criminal roles. Effectiveness stems from the ability to blend in and be accepted. For the agent, being criminal-like means that he/she is doing a good job.

Ultimately, the toxicity of the role overwhelms the player. The game of irony ceases being a game, as the real world of the agent, undergone ironic transition, becomes the criminal world. The conversion is complete.

> A good example of this is the case of a Northern California police officer who participated in a "deep cover" operation for eighteen months, riding with the Hell's Angels. He was responsible for a very large number of arrests, including previously almost untouchable higher-level drug dealers, and was praised for doing a "magnificent job." But this was at the cost of heavy drug use, alcoholism, brawling, the break-up of his family, an inability to fit back into routine police work, resignation from the force, several bank robberies, and a prison term (Marx, 1988:109).

In a total ironic conversion, the ability of the police to do their work in a perilous, drug-dealing landscape leads to their perfect adaptation to the landscape. There ceases to be a way to tell the good guys from the bad guys. The ironic conversion of the police is complete, in a way never intended. Therein lies the hidden danger of irony: how can one tell the good guys from the bad guys? Indeed, as Pogrebin and Poole (1993) observed, even the good guys have trouble distinguishing themselves from the bad guys.

These examples show that police officers do not construct a working reality, but deconstruct the world as given in order to identify danger hidden therein. For them, common sense is the ironic deconstruction of the world as presented. The world as given is an illusion. The citizen's world is safe, tame, but unreal. Through irony, meanings reverse. The citizen becomes the victim or the criminal. Territories become perilous. Playgrounds become haunts for drug dealers. Human behavior hints at threat and danger. Through ironic conversion, police work takes on meaning.

The art of irony is suspicion. By what common-sense skill can a skilled officer convert an ordinary environment into an ironic one? The skill is suspicion. Consider the following use of suspicion to do good police work, that is coercive territorial control. A call had come in over the radio concerning a convenience store robbery. A brief description of the suspects was provided. The officer saw two males close to the store.

> D. shone his spotlight on them, looked intently, made a quick left hand turn into the street they were approaching and said 'I want to talk to this guy.' (This was followed by a fight between the suspects and the officer and arrest of the suspects.) Later, I asked D. 'What made you suspect that guy? He didn't fit the description?' D. said that he suspected that some-thing was wrong (underlined in original) when he shone the spotlight and the men did not react (McNulty, 1994:287).

Suspicion is a central theme of police work, derived from the ability to transform a safe environment—for example, the beat patrol—colorfully described as "the street," where the central organizing theme of police work is carried out. Suspicion is a true foundational or root metaphor, providing the basis for much police action. The consequences of police action in turn justify the suspicion. A bad guy does not have to be found every time an officer is suspicious, but each time one is apprehended the mythos of irony and suspicion is sustained by police stories. In story after story, officers acting on hunches or suspicions solve problems or save themselves, in a processual tautology of common sense and action.

Deconstruction is learned in training. Ironic training is highly visible in an academy and field training. Stories of peril and danger, role-plays, and films emphasize the threat and hidden danger in police work. Recruits, when taught the lore of police work, are simultaneously provided with a vocabulary of irony, danger, suspicion, and officer safety.

POST instructors are members of the police department, and as such arc participants in the common-sense language of the organizational culture. Their natural language is metaphoric and story-based (McNulty, 1994; Crank, 1996). Instructors provide insight into organizational culture when they are asked a question or when they feel compelled to provide an explanation of something during a class.

Explanations, drawing on the instructor's lore, will be drawn from the instructor's common-sense world-view, and will be expressed as a story or trope, usually an irony of some sort. In this way, instructors convey a cultural tool kit that enables trainees to organize the knowledge presented in POST training (Kappeler, Sluder & Alpert, 1994).[6] Because this tool kit is conveyed on particular topics being taught, trainees learn, to use Shearing and Ericson's (1991) phrase, the sensibility out of which to think about whatever instructional curricula is being taught at the time. Consider the following example:

> Police officers base action decisions, such as whether to stop someone, on incongruity—things out of place . . . The focus on incongruity was especially evident in the strategies that the staff recommended for initiating action . . . For example, they taught the recruits to avoid the abstract question, "Where does the truth lie?" Instead, they posed a more concrete question, "What's wrong with this picture?" as a means for recognizing whether things were "out of place." The class sergeant told the recruits that looking for something suspicious was less effective than looking for the unusual, because suspicious was so hard to define. One instructor used the analogy of a black and white picture to demonstrate the importance of contrasting the usual to the unusual. He explained that he began investigations of crime scenes by taking black and white photographs to establish contrast, highlighting the relative positions of items without the distraction that details provide (McNulty, 1994:286).

Thinking ironically focuses action. A trainee's ability to act in an uncertain environment is a task central to training. McNulty (1994:286) observed that officers in training learn quickly that they must act: she notes that "On several occasions, the class sergeant told hesitant recruits to "DO SOMETHING!" He told them "It's better to make a decision than to flounder around." By the time they are in field training, they have to be ready to do their work in environments perceived to be perilous. Here, recruits are expected not only to recognize danger, but to act in dangerous situations. This includes risk-taking.

> . . . testing the recruit's propensity to take part in the risks which accompanies police work goes on continuously in the police department . . . recruits are appraised as to their speed in getting out of a patrol car, their lack of hesitation when approaching a suspicious person, or their willingness to lead the way up a darkened stairwell (Van Maanen, 1978:203).

Always, through training, officers are told stories about the officers that made a single careless error and were killed. The message here was that danger was ever-present, and the only protection was vigilance against the unknown threat.

I have witnessed an intensely meaningful heuristic trope, a film story on unpredictability and danger during a routine traffic stop. This training film shows recruits that the gravest error they can make is to forget the perils of the environment in which they work.

> The film was taken by a video-cam mounted on the officer's car. An officer was engaged in a routine traffic stop of a car when he was suddenly and violently assaulted by its occupants. The dramatic footage showed the officer being beaten and murdered along a dark Texas road. The last few minutes of the film were of the officer laying dead on the pavement behind the patrol car, enveloped in the somber Texas night.

This story served as a powerful irony, transforming a routine traffic strop into one fraught with peril, and in which the greatest—life-ending—peril of all was that the officer took things as they appeared to be (Crank, 1996:278).

Officers thus learn customary ways of identifying territories and individuals as dangerous, and customary ways of responding to that danger. Common-sense identifications of danger lead to common sense solutions. By the time they are assigned to the field, their ironic repertoire is complete with stories, examples derived from other officers, dangerous locations, troubling people, behaviors made ironically sensible. The safe world of the citizen is razed, and police operate cannily in an uncanny world of their own construction.

Endnotes

[1] Berger and Luckmann (1966:57) describe this idea in terms of highly institutionalized belief systems that are composed of "taken-for-granted routines."

[2] Unpublished research.

[3] For example, a parolee or probationer may be referred to as a "bad guy," thus shifting the meaning of the status of the probationer from the relatively neutral term "client" to the negatively sanctioned term "criminal."

[4] Metonymy occurs when an instructor, attempting to respond to a "how to" question, tells what they did on a particular occasion (Shearing & Ericson, 1991). Manning (1979: 662) also noted that metonymy as the representation of a concept in terms of its characteristics, for example, describing an organization in terms of its size, its body of rules, or degree and type of structural differentiation.

[5] Umberto Eco (1984:87) has characterized four types of tropes as follows. The metaphor, the "most luminous" of tropes, is the master trope of which all other tropes are types. It is, he notes, impossible to define a metaphor since any definition of a metaphor is itself a metaphor and hence a tautology. A synecdoche is a substitution of two terms for each other according to a relation between them, for example, a part for the whole or vice versa. Metonymy is a substitution for a relation of contiguity (a definition he admits is "fuzzy"), and irony is substitution by something's opposite. By this definition, a story is always a metaphor, but may contain the other types of tropes as well.

[6] Kappeler and his colleagues (1994:101) noted a parallel phenomenon with regard to police training. Training instructors, they observed, used stories to reinforce the existing world-view rather than to provide recruits with education and new ways of thinking about their work.

16

No Place for Sissies

Theme: Masculinity

"I am convinced," he said on one (tape), that "because God has said that woman's role is to be submissive, that what they really want is for you to be the decision-maker . . . Wives ought be subject to their husbands in everything. That includes physical relationships." On another he discussed disciplining children: "I've spanked boys as old as sixteen and seventeen . . . I hit them with a boat oar . . . I tell them, if you use drugs, I'm going to spank you with a boat oar. But I don't do that with girls unless they've started puberty" (Domanick, 1994:325-326).

Bob Vernon, an assistant chief under Daryl Gates in Los Angeles, recorded these words on an audio recorder. The compilation of tapes was called *The True Masculine Role* (Domanick, 1994). That Vernon was recording these tapes at a time when he was a contender for the next chief's position was remarkable. That a deputy chief could consider doing such things in the late 1980s reveals the extent to which traditional ideas of masculinity pervaded the Los Angeles police department in the contemporary era.

Police organizations historically have been male in spirit and gender. Even as late as 1980, only 3.8 percent of all municipal police officers were female (Martin, 1997). The past two decades have seen inroads by female officers, and by 1994, 9.3 percent of all officers were female. Of communities with populations exceeding 50,000, 98.5 percent had female officers assigned to field operations (Martin, 1990).

Masculinity is not only a demographic characteristic of the organization, but a cultural descriptor as well. As a cultural theme, masculinity carries ideas of the appropriateness of men for police work—and by implication, the inappropriateness of everyone else. Masculinity is about the kind of work that police should do, how police work should be done, and about men's higher purpose in the maintenance of public order (Heidensohn, 1992). It is the paternalism associated with the traditional American male role, intensified through the lens of police culture into a guiding principal of social order and control. Masculinity is a theme that runs through the occupation, affects social status, reinforces group solidarity, and infuses officers' self-images as men's men (Martin, 1997).

As a cultural element, masculinity is emphasized in training. From the outset, recruits are expected to confirm their masculine images to others and to themselves by exaggerating the characteristics associated with manhood (Harris, 1973). Training emphasizes physical conditioning, fighting, weaponry, all skills that are associated with traditional male roles and are practiced as play in the early childhood of American males. Stories celebrating masculine exploits are also prized among the police. Stories of male bonding rituals have been colorfully explored in the writings of Wambaugh (1987). From crude slurs against women to the demonstration of an officer's willingness to put his or her life on the line for a fellow officer, themes of masculinity are pervasive to police culture (Kappeler, Sluder & Alpert, 1994).

Masculinity is associated with many negative aspects of police behavior. Sapp (1994) reports that a "boys-will-be-boys" attitude justifies sexual misconduct both within the department and with offenders and citizens. Citizens may be exposed to voyeuristic contacts, that is, surreptitious and systematic watching. More overt forms of sexual aggression include contacts with crime victims, offenders, and juvenile females, particularly truants, runaways, and delinquents. Custodial staff sometimes harass females and are unlikely to be observed. Some officers seek opportunities to see women in various states of undress, and a few may extort favors from female inmates. In the most aggressive forms of sexual exchange, officers exchange preferential treatment for personal favors.[1]

Martin and Masculinity

The study of masculinity involves an assessment of values and beliefs so deeply seated that their influence is sometimes difficult to recognize. Among the few to explore this aspect of police culture is Susan Martin. Her research, conducted among Washington, D.C. police, unfolded as an effort to comprehend the problems women confronted working for the police. In the course of her work, she recognized the far-reaching influences of American-style gender differences and their implications for police culture.

Masculinity among the police, Martin (1980:88-90) argued, was closely associated with traditional ideas, not just of police work, but of what it means to be a man in the United States. "Being a man" represented the fulfillment of a socially defined role, in which there were clear expectations regarding what a "man" is. This role was characterized by four themes: the avoidance of anything vaguely feminine, the attainment of success and social status, a manly air of toughness, confidence, and self-reliance, and an aura of aggressiveness, daring, and violence. The avoidance of feminine attributes was learned by men at quite young ages; to act like a woman was likely to engender the despective "sissy." Men were tough so that they could take care of the "weaker sex." The lessons of sports were to "stand up for oneself," or in the contemporary vernacular to "show attitude" or "stud up." It is his physical superiority that distinguishes a man. To be tough meant to refuse to change one's view in the face of opposition and adversity (and, some might add, overwhelming reason). Finally, men must be aggressive, by which was meant that they should attack first and act with vigor and violence to overwhelm the opposition.

Police officers have tended to come from working-class backgrounds where these attitudes historically received strong social support. Their models often have been from the screen and television, cowboy tough-guys, gangsters, and private eyes. The occasional excitement, danger, demands for strength and courage, and camaraderie were attractive features of police work and reinforced these existing stereotypes in a job otherwise mundane and boring.

Martin also recognized that attitudinal predispositions did not account for all displays of masculinity. She astutely recognized the way in which the working environment of the police encouraged masculine behaviors, even where the tendency toward aggressive toughness may not have been already present.[2]

> Officers must adjust to the values of the citizens they police in order to work effectively and thus come to be influenced by the "focal concerns" of the members of the lower classes. One of these concerns is 'toughness,' a composite of physical prowess demonstrated by strength, endurance, and athletic skills; the absence of sentimentality and the conceptualization of women as conquest objects; and bravery in the face of physical threats (Martin, 1980:90).

The cumulative influence of these factors creates a cultural milieu in which values associated with an exaggerated blue-collar masculinity are recognized and highly regarded. In other words, a masculine ethic contains values consistent with beat control. Masculinity seems to resonate well with themes of individualism and dominion.

In the contemporary age there are broad efforts to change the role of the police. Under the rubric of "community policing," reformers seek to move away from a traditional, law-enforcement conception of the police and into more service and order-maintenance activity. Such service-oriented changes, Martin comments, emphasizes skills that are not consistent with the "masculine" nature of law enforcement activity. These skills—the ability to reason through problems, to seek nonphysical and non-assertive ways of dealing with problems, the capacity to take interest in and effectively address the mundane problems of everyday people—are threats to the hard-boiled occupational identities of traditional police officers. She concludes with the recognition that there may be limits to change at the line level, where police work is produced. She suspects that "the core of the job—exercise of authority and the right to use violence in the face of resistance—will remain, requiring a person who, for some time to come, is more likely to be male than female." Police culture, with its powerful undercurrents of masculinity, is unlikely to change too far from a role conception rooted in the super-cop hyper-male identity. The implications for female cops are clear. Whatever external reforms police organizations go through, female street cops will continue to be pressured to "think like men, work like dogs, and act like ladies" (Martin, 1980:219).

At a cultural level, little has changed since Martin published her seminal work in 1980. In spite of increasing recruitment of women into traditional male police assignments masculinity continues to be a powerful theme of police culture (Martin, 1997; Herrington, 1997; Hunt, 1990). Today department policies do not permit gender abuse. This has shifted the location of bias, but has not fundamentally changed it. Herrington captures this change:

> Today, it's not very likely that those same blatant statements (sexist comments made to her by a colleague) would be made to my friends or to myself. Instead, they are made in the hallways or locker rooms or in more subtle tones and forms of behavior. You can't change attitudes through rules and regulations (Herrington, 1997:388).

The inability to change attitudes is not surprising, though it is troubling from a diversity viewpoint. Masculinity is a solidarity theme, as Martin (1997) has noted, a powerful bond linking men together in terms of a common conception of police work. Solidarity themes maintain group boundaries, and one consequence of the boundary maintenance function is that solidarity increases in potency in proportion to perceived outside threats (Coser, 1956). The implication is not favorable for those wishing to break into the male-dominated profession. Increasing the numbers of females in police work increases department gender frictions and intensifies cultural resistance (Martin, 1980).

Bravery: Masculinity Grounded

Bravery is a special case of masculinity. The idea of masculinity underscores particular traits associated with a traditional, paternalistic notion of American maleness. Masculinity is a trait that is also subcultural—I

mean that it is a cultural theme prevalent in the broader society, culturally transmitted to the occupation of policing vis-à-vis hiring processes controlled by middle-aged men and favoring young men.

By focusing on bravery, we can see how transmitted traits fuse with
police culture. Episodes of bravery provide just the right material for fascinating stories and traditions that energize police culture. Moreover,
bravery is associated with real activities in day-to-day police work. Its
meaning is not wholly comprehensible in processes of cultural transmission, though processes of transmission link it powerfully with masculinity. When one understands this, the sensibility that makes the theme of
masculinity so intransigent to change becomes more comprehensible.

To limit an explanation of bravery to a sort of blue collar predisposition toward toughness simply fails to acknowledge that police work is
occasionally dangerous and that danger is harsh on people exposed to it.
Bravery is an important element of the cultural ethos of police officers
because fear is profoundly debilitating, yet officers occasionally have to
place themselves in harm's way. When they do, even though such times
are infrequent, they are the grist of important departmental traditions.
They are regaled as episodes of solidarity.

Cops display bravery in several ways. Officers hide their personal feelings from others. Observers of the police state that officers do not talk
about their personal feelings, in any but the most banal terms. Cops do
not emote. Wilson (1968) noted how training officers test rookies by
putting them in situations that were inherently dangerous; writing tickets
in a particularly dangerous neighborhood. Will they stand up to the pressure? Will they back up another cop? Bouza (1990:71) notes that "coward
is such a powerful epithet that, even in a profession accustomed to the
rawest language, it is a word that is used very sparingly." Though Wilson
made this observation in 1968, it is equally true today. I once heard a
training instructor observe in a POST class that "When your partner is get-
tin' a lickin' you have to get a lickin' too." The expression of personal fears
is taken as a sign of weakness—a colleague may not be dependable in a
dangerous situation (Pogrebin & Poole, 1991). Officers that display emotional vulnerability are shunned by their brethren.

Well, then, what is bravery? It is a notion poorly understood—we
tend to think of it in bumper-sticker terms. The following discussion provides a sensibility for thinking about bravery, a linkage to themes of
unpredictability that infuse much of police culture.

Fussell (1975) provided artful (and dark) literary insight into the madness of war, and his works are to be read by anyone seeking insight into
the unremitting lunacy of military engagements in the first and second
world wars. A theme in his writing is that battlefield encounters tended
to develop their own maniacal logic apart from the intentions of field
commanders. All the best efforts of generals and planners to put a "rational" face on military encounters, or to make engagements appear sys-

tematic, logical, or in the 1990s engagement terminology, "surgical," simply failed to account for their inherent unpredictability. "Braveness" often marked the inability to recognize or avoid deadly peril in spite of circumstances favorable to its occurrence. In the lunacy of war, bravery is measured by the degree to which soldiers act against their best survival interests.

Situations in which police are involved, particularly perilous ones, can take on this same wild unpredictability. Ragonese (1991:262-264) describes the first time he handled a live bomb after being assigned to the bomb squad. He and his partner were called to a billiard parlor, where someone had left a pipe bomb inside a plastic bag. It was about three inches long, capped at both ends, with a fuse sticking out the middle. The fuse had been extinguished. Ragonese noted that a pipe bomb was a technicians greatest fear, because no one could tell what was inside the pipe.

The officers tied a rope around the bomb, and relocated it to the street. There, they used a remote mobile investigator, called simply the robot, a "chain-driven four-wheel machine about 30 inches wide and 60 inches high." The robot picked up the bomb and was carrying it to a containment unit when it malfunctioned. The following relates what happened next, in Ragonese's words:

> A crowd had gathered behind police barriers a block away. We walked out to the robot and carefully turned the 300-pound machine onto its side. The pipe bomb was wedged between the chain and the machine's undercarriage. Pete struggled with the pipe bomb, trying to pull it free. He couldn't. I joined him, both of us tugging at the bomb. It took us several minutes and a lot of effort to free the bomb. "The hell with this," Pete said. He took the pipe bomb over and placed it in the carrier. The crowd let out a derisive cheer (Ragonese, 1991:263-264).

The following morning, the officers found out that the bomb contained a pound of black powder, an extremely sensitive explosive. Ragonese related to his partner "Talk about the pucker factor, if I had known that my butt would've been triple puckerin'" (Ragonese, 1991:264).

Why did these officers engage in this extraordinarily dangerous, certainly unpredictable, and risky behavior? Contemporary literature on police culture, explaining bravery in terms of masculine predispositions of police officers, fails to account for the circumstances in which these officers found themselves. Ragonese's circumstance, like Fussell's observations of the madness of military engagements, permit us to dispel the idea that police work is uniformly predictable and safe. The officers found themselves in a circumstance in which the only meaningful actions they could take were sharply contrary to rational ideas of personal survival. In this example we can see how braveness, like other cultural themes, arises from characteristics of situations officers encounter in their everyday work.

Are police predisposed to seek excitement and confront danger? Do they always have to run towards the sniper in the tower? Or is all talk about toughness only bravado, a psychological ploy to try to overcome the more debilitating effects of fear in the face of uncontrollable, genuine danger?

Both fear and excitement are hopelessly mixed in displays of bravery. Bravery is fine up to a point. At the edge, where contingencies cascade over the point of control, fear takes a powerful toll on a cop's psyche. Yet the job requires that police officers act, even in the face of the unknown, even in spite of substantial danger. I use the word "act" rather than the words "act rationally." If one considers Ragonese's story above, the most rational behavior, at least to the extent that survival is considered a rational outcome, would have been to go home, turn on the television, and pop a beer. There is nothing rational about reaching under the carriage of a bomb-seeking machine to dislodge a bomb with an unknown fuse type and explosive content. But then, there is nothing rational about putting a bomb there in the first place. Bravery enables us to do mad things in an insane world.

Endnotes

[1] Sapp (1994) notes that the limited sample size in his research limits the generalizability to police generally.

[2] In a very interesting study, Storms, Penn, and Tenzell compared police officers' perceptions of the ideal officer with what they thought their respective communities' ideal officer would be. They found that the ideal policeman, as viewed by the police, was "more warm, emotional, responsive, flexible, considerate, and close than they think the community would like them to be" (1990:42). In other words, and consistent with Martin's view of community pressures for masculine police behavior, the police ideal was more emotional and less distant than what they thought their respective communities wanted.

17

Mask of a Thousand Faces

> The sense of "us vs. them" that develops between cops and the outside world forges a bond between cops whose strength is fabled. It is called the *brotherhood in blue*, and it inspires a fierce and unquestioning loyalty to all cops, everywhere. It is widened by the dependence cops have on each other for safety and backup. The response to a summons to help is a cop's life-line. An "assist police officer" is every cop's first priority. The ultimate betrayal is for one cop to fail to back up another (Bouza, 1990:74).

The loyalty of officers toward their own kind is legendary. There are a thousand faces for solidarity: camaraderie, cohesiveness, fealty, the brotherhood, honor, the blue curtain, esprit-de-corps, brother and sister cops. It is a principle that overrides individual differences and disagreements; fealty beyond challenge.

Solidarity, the "we" in the widely cited "we-them" attitude carried by many police, describes the extraordinarily close-knit and clannish nature of police interpersonal relations (Brown, 1981). The potential danger of the working environment, combined with a citizenry perceived to be unsupportive, contribute to the belief that cops can only count on "brother officers" for support (Skolnick, 1994). Solidarity is culturally transmitted through pre-and in-service training, where trainers frequently assess the ability of officers to follow protocols during a stressful officer in trouble call.

Loyalty, one of the faces of solidarity, was described by Brown (1981) as a core element of the police idea of value. Officers protect each other, not only against the public, but against police administrators frequently seen to be capricious and out-of-touch. The profound sense of loyalty that characterizes police culture is reinforced by POST and field training (Van Maanen, 1973). Officers learn through the training experience that when mistakes occur—and they always occur—only a fellow officer can be counted on. Solidarity emerged through trainees' reciprocal efforts to protect each other from the whims of departmental brass.

In the public arena, officers present a theater of unconditional support, a family commitment, loyalty and honor before all else, faith and fidelity to the brotherhood. That it is a staged presentation, carefully tailored to specific audiences by public relations units and brass, does not mean that the audience is limited to the public, or that it is any the less felt personally among officers. Solidarity is carefully cultivated, taught formally and reinforced informally through the first years on the job; for those that are raised in a police family, it is cultivated from a child's first breath.

Solidarity is dramaturgy. Solidarity has a powerful dramaturgical aspect. By dramaturgy I mean that the police have crafted a particular image of themselves that they present to their various audiences. Dramaturgy is acted out in powerful solidarity rites that are designed to display to the world unity and unswerving loyalty. The most powerful expression of these rites are funeral ceremonies, displays of police unity enveloped in symbols of social order and authority (Manning, 1970). I will have much to say about funerals at a later point.

Goffman (1959) developed the notion of dramaturgy in social interaction, later applied to the police by Manning (1970). Goffman (1959) described human interactions in terms of metaphors of front and back stage. Individuals have a front stage, where players put themselves on display for inspection, and a back stage, where individuals carefully guard that about themselves which they do not want others to know about. The back stage is kept hidden from the members of the audience. Manning (1970) extended this principle to police organizations, where the front stage described the management of the public image of the police, and the backstage or private aspect of policing was available for inspection only for other cops. A series of representational strategies was intended to convince the public of the unity of the police.

A dramaturgy of solidarity is fundamental to the police-citizen interactions. One could not imagine, for example, an arrested person approaching another police officer to get a second opinion. Nor can one imagine two police officers, responding to a call, openly arguing about whether a crime in fact occurred, or taking sides in a family dispute. That they might quarrel among themselves at a later time is a back-stage issue: the debate will not emerge on the front stage. The solidarity of the police will not be permitted to become a matter of public debate.

Presentational strategies allow for the police to display solidarity in the conduct of their work. Some of these are conducted at the occupational level. Manning noted that professionalism is one such presentation. Professionalism was the "most important strategy employed by the police to defend their mandate and thereby to build self-esteem, organization autonomy, and occupational solidarity or cohesiveness"[1] (Manning, 1970:127). Professionalism provided a sense of occupational solidarity by uniting police officers in a common definition of the kind of work they do, the attitudes they bring to their work, and the way the public should view them. Professional police officers provided an image of dispassionate law enforcement uncluttered by human emotion. Professionalism surrounds the police with the "symbols, prerequisites, tradition, power, and authority associated with the most respected occupations in American society" (Manning, 1970:129).

Law enforcement activities, Manning observed, were used dramaturgically by the police to promote an exterior image of police solidarity. Police uniforms, with sigils of rank, authority, and weaponry, were powerful reminders of the authority of the police. The way in which they recorded and distributed information to their audiences vis-à-vis the Uniform Crime Reports was heavily weighted toward the dramatization of violent crime, a statistically rare event in the overall body of crime and in their day-to-day work.

Dramatization of crime is played out in many ways. Consider the term "predator," popular in contemporary discussions of criminal activity and a powerful label in media and academic presentations of crime today. Criminals that commit felony crime are frequently described as predatory, thus invoking a metaphor derived from carnivorous behavior in zoological studies to describe a criminal suspect. The metaphor invokes community support in the name of "victims" of predators—a sort of "Peter and the Wolf" view of crime. As a metaphor, it leads us away from the recognition that criminal and victim populations overlap highly—that Peter put himself in harm's way, or that Peter himself may be a criminal. The metaphor also focuses our attention on the potential for violence in crime-control activities, and justifies aggressive and brutal arrest practices in the name of officers' safety. Thus, through a dramaturgy of predatory control, officer safety and victim protection, the police present themselves united in the protection of society, and invested of authority to use any means at their disposal to deal with threats to themselves and to the public.

Solidarity is sentiment. Manning's work focused on the symbolic and dramaturgical aspects of solidarity. There also are emotional dynamics, many of which are meanings geared toward officers themselves. Do officers feel an emotional "something" that can be labeled solidarity toward each other? Absolutely: it is a sentiment beyond question. It is more fundamental than reason. When an officer says "I'm all for the guys in Blue! Anybody criticizes a fellow copper that's like criticizing somebody in my family" (Brown, 1981:82) she or he is displaying unconditional support. This is something different from dramaturgical performance. It is a sentiment that places loyalty at a foundational level. When officers do not feel solidarity, they do not belong. They are usually weed-ed out by the end of the first year. Bonifacio captured this sentiment in the following observation:

> . . . it is important to bear in mind that being a member of the police fra-ternity is also a highly gratifying emotional experience in which the offi-cer sees himself as belonging to an exclusive group of men who are braver, smarter, stronger, and more self-reliant than the civilian popula-tion they serve (Bonifacio, 1991:39).

Wambaugh (1973:81) noted a similar sentiment of superiority among officers. He suggested that the increasing isolation of officers from the public stemmed from a sense of pride and self-reliance they obtained from doing police work. He noted that "You'll be able to come up with a quick solution for any kind of strange situation because you have to do it every day, and you'll get mad as hell at your friends if they can't." This sen-timent, that of being smarter than the public, derives from their percep-tion of the work they do, dealing on a daily basis with people who can-not get their life together. Solidarity is reinforced by a sense of pride interactively shared among officers in their ability to rapidly work through difficult human dilemmas to arrive at solutions.[2]

Solidarity does not mean lovey-dovey. Officers may quarrel and back-stab, fight with and play cruel pranks on each other, and they may com-plain bitterly about the favors received by some of their own. Sometimes they will hurt each other. If outsiders could really see what goes on inside the department, they would be amazed at the extent of the bickering within the organization. But, of course, an outsider will never see this. This view is not available for inspection and judgment. Outsiders do not peer inside the brotherhood.

Researchers have frequently measured their words to describe the dark side of solidarity. In their focus on corruption and deviance, they have missed the point. They know only the concept corrupted. They do not also see how solidarity is a celebration of the senses.

Cops dramatize their loyalty. That it is a dramatization does not mean that it overstates the emotions felt among cops, or the way in which that emotion is played out. That sentiments are linked to back-stage activities does not in some way weaken them. The contrary is true; the back-stage—where cops do their work—is the basis for the production of the strongest sentiments and for the rehearsal of our most important feelings later acted out publicly.

Cops share a backstage dense in memories. Such memories are mun-dane though common, gritty, and quintessential cop. Consider the fol-lowing story:

When my partner and I would go in on a burglary, I'd unscrew some light bulbs from the fixtures. My partner would be going down to check out the basement in an abandoned house. He's creeping down the stairs real cautious. I'd take the light bulbs and throw them—Pop! Pop! Pop! That would scare the hell out of him. I'd laugh my ass off (Baker, 1985:213-214).

Streams of ordinary events are punctuated by a few dramatically enacted ones, and a cop's life becomes crowded with partner memories. Police officers share a Philistine love.

The Impulse Toward Solidarity

Solidarity is taught and reinforced from the outset of training, as many observers of the police have noted. The impulse toward solidarity has traditionally been attributed to early socialization processes in the organization itself. In the following sections I argue that there is a broad "culture of policing" that predisposes solidarity among future recruits.

Solidarity Emerges Within a Culture of Policing

Investigators into police attitudes have tended to fall into two camps. The first camp are those who believe that a particular type of individual is drawn to police work. Of particular interest to researchers was the notion that those with authoritarian personalities were drawn to policing. Authoritarianism is associated with a host of distasteful personality characteristics: cynicism, bigotry, violence, conventionalism, and suspicion (Balch, 1977). Consistently, however, efforts to measure authoritarianism showed that police were not particularly authoritarian, or particularly anything else, either. They tended to be locals, drawn from individuals who liked outdoor work and were attracted to the potential excitement of police work and wanted to do something more with their lives. In a word, they were ordinary people.

The idea of predispositional attitudes among police recruits has gradually given way to the more popular contemporary "police socialization" perspective. According to this perspective, the "police personality," attitudinal dispositions that uniquely characterize cops, is something learned on the job. A number of observers of the police have contributed to this perspective (Skolnick, 1994; Walker, 1990). According to this idea, recruits are particularly vulnerable to peer group pressures in the early years of their career. Group socialization pressures associated with POST training and with assignment to a field training officer provide a model for the values and views held by recruits. A "final frame" perspective that is uniquely cop emerges early in a cop's career (Van Maanen, 1973). The police socialization perspective is dominant today.

I think that the police socialization perspective is also limited—it does not account for the presence of a wide "culture of policing" carried by many groups in American society that predisposes its members to accept police values and see themselves as unified with the police. Intended and unintended consequences of friendship networks, recruitment, and training practices reinforce the closeness of cops for each other. Yet, long before individuals become officers, many already have a high degree of esteem for and identification with the police and share many values associated with cop culture. Many prospective recruits come from families whose members number among the police, military, and fire professions, and have been involved since their earliest days in their occupational activities. A reservoir of solidarity is already well in place prior to formal recruitment.

Many prospective candidates, by the time they start police work, have been living and breathing police culture for years. Values and loyalties associated with a cop culture are shared by a wider social milieu, and a commitment to the police way of life is often learned early. Candidates tend to be drawn from a broad "culture of policing," made up of social groups that share cop values, similar ways of thinking about social morality, and a sense of solidarity with the police. They are already embedded in a social and ideological environment much wider than individual organizational cultures. It includes the American military institution, conservative groups that characterize small towns and rural America, business groups, police families, and other individuals who, for various reasons, develop a sense of solidarity with the police. Young members of the culture of policing commit themselves early on to the values of police officers, oftentimes in childhood. Components of the culture of policing are considered below.

Generations. Police families are powerful transmitters of the culture of policing. The desire to become a police officer is common among their children. Generational loyalties develop early and tend to be strong. A colleague, describing his children's police perspectives to students in a criminal justice class, noted that they had an "absolute belief in the good that police can give to society." His children, he noted, shared his belief that police represented a powerful moral force acting for the best interests of society. He feared that they would encounter a corrupt officer who would destroy their idealism before they had a chance to become wise about human nature.

A generational connection is not the only way young people become invested in the values of the police. An Hispanic officer in an Idaho County Sheriff's office told me about his childhood commitment to policing. He grew up working the hops fields in Southern Idaho with his family, who had migrated to Idaho from Texas. He would frequently watch

police officers working, and one day he met the Sheriff. After being introduced, he told the Sheriff "When I grow up, I'm going to be a county
policeman too." This goal was fulfilled when he reached early manhood
and was hired into the program. Today, he polices the fields that he
worked where he grew up, committed both to the particular needs of
Hispanics in Southern Idaho and to the crime control mandate that
accompanies his position. Thus, both through generational and more
casual, positive contacts with the police in early childhood, his activities
reveal the presence of a broader culture of policing. Young people connected with that culture may commit themselves early to the values of
police culture.

Small-town traditions. A culture of policing is also evident in many
small towns across the American landscape. The values associated with
small-town America, traditionally conservative and horrified by violent
crime, are part of the culture of policing. For children in small towns, a
position as a police officer may be attractive. Young people in smaller
towns frequently confront limited employment and educational opportunities. Moreover, rural areas tend to share a common idea of crime, asso-
ciating problems with teenagers and outsiders. It is not surprising to find
wide support for the police in rural America, where police are seen as the
last bastion of protection against the crime and decadence of large cities
(a vision supplied in megadosage prescriptions from television, newspapers, and the movies).

Military personnel. A third social group that shares the culture of
policing is military personnel. Personnel from the various military
branches share with the police a set of skills, sense of work organization,
morality, group loyalties, sense of camaraderie, masculine focus and tendency toward native conservatism; in these many ways the military culture mirrors the police's own.

The ideological compatibility of the institutions of the military and
police is strengthened by a variety of structural connections between the
police and the military. As early as 1893, the International Association of
Chiefs of Police, taking on the banner of police professionalism, suggested
that police leaders be drawn from the ranks of the military (Fogelson,
1977). Post-war periods have witnessed an influx of military veterans seeking employment with the police. The post-Vietnam focus on stress training in POST academies in the 1970s was frequently modeled after boot-
camp training experienced by ex-Vietnam officers hired into police
organizations in the late 1960s and early 1970s (Kraska & Kappeler, 1997).

In the contemporary age, police commanders occasionally are
assigned to temporary duty with various military units to engage in various international and covert national operations in a training or intelligence capacity. Military families provide an ideological predisposition,
sense of loyalty and solidarity with the police that prepares the way for a
career in American police organizations.

Thus, many police recruits are drawn from the culture of policing, and by the time they decide to go into police work, their loyalties and values are already aligned with the police. Recruits share a commitment to the values of the police, a distrust of the courts and media, a history of positive contacts with police officers, incipient knowledge of the working environment of police officers, and strong desires to do something about bad guys. Their participation in POST training is not marked by the sort of naïve vulnerability suggested by Van Maanen (1978). Indeed, before being hired as a police officer, many of them have begun the transition from a culture of policing to a specific police culture, already knowledgeable about local players and war stories.

The new cultural transmitter: universities. University criminal justice programs bring together large numbers of students seeking careers in criminal justice. Today in the United States, there are more than 1,000 criminal justice programs nationally and about 100 graduate programs. These programs carry the future talent for police organizations in the United States. Participating individuals often are already fully vested in the culture of policing, and they tend to have the self-motivation and testing skills necessary to move up through the ranks of the police.

Students tend to be drawn from several types of backgrounds. Most are young, drawn from the culture of policing and are already committed to a life in criminal justice. Some have been practitioners in criminal justice agencies and have returned to school to enhance their criminal justice careers; these tend to be two types. Some are retired individuals still sparked by criminal justice work and motivated to seek new opportunities in the field. Others are in-service officers trying to improve their position in future competitions for rank in their department. Finally, there are individuals that flounder across majors and now have settled in what they perceive to be an easy degree program. They are often right.

Criminal justice programs link students to the culture of policing in a variety of ways. In-service officers carry prestige in these programs, and students (and some faculty as well) prefer to associate with these individuals. Guest lecturers expose students to various aspects of local agency life. Internship programs place students in local agencies for a certain number of hours each week for at least one semester, giving students a more practical look at work they will likely be doing when they graduate. After graduation, many students are able to convert their internships to full-time positions.

Part-time faculty are drawn from local agencies, and provide in their discussions practical knowledge about the craft of their work. The quality of their instruction tends to be poor from an academic viewpoint. They tend to focus on local legal strategies for dealing with bad guys rather than analysis of fundamental issues in the field, and they frame moral issues in terms of loyalty to the police and prosecutors. However, these faculty tend to be popular with criminal justice students and they are indispensable for the running of most departments. Department chairs hire these individuals to cultivate and maintain preferred relationships to local agencies. In some places, criminal justice programs assist in POST training, and thus are directly linked into police pre-service training. Moreover, many tenure stream faculty have had experience in criminal justice at some point in their careers. Thus, in the contemporary era, criminal justice programs tend to be tied to local criminal justice communities in general, and particularly to local police agencies.

It is common for academically trained criminal justice faculty to rail against the deep native conservatism of their students; to grouse that the loyalties of criminal justice students are agency oriented and their allegiance in courtroom contests is fully committed to the prosecutor. An academician's pride is particularly deflated by students' preference for local agency part-time instructors over regular department faculty. This is because faculty do not recognize how criminal justice programs to which they are committed have become a part of the transmission of values associated with the culture of policing. In the contemporary era, college education often acts as a bridge for students progressing from the culture of policing to a particular police culture. Put simply, students use college to get jobs in justice agencies. One of the paradoxical social dynamics in the criminal justice education movement today is that criminal justice faculty, frequently trained in the liberal arts, skilled in research techniques, and by training and temperament critical of social and criminal justice policy, fill a critical link in students' transition from a culture of policing to police culture.

Each of the groups that we have looked at share a common characteristic: they represent the working class and its avenues of upward mobility.

Also, they produce a "type" of police officer, a type that is extraordinarily generic, quintessential American, altogether typical. Its roots reach deeply into working-class soil. But it is an unsatisfied, upwardly mobile working-class type, for police work is a way for ordinary American youth to move into the great American social-economic landscape of the middle class. By labeling police recruits, as academicians tend to do—individuals with limited vision, a desire to work out-of-doors, with hopes to remain in their community—we disdain them with intimations of mediocrity, of Archie Bunkerism conservative mindlessness. We hint that small-town cop fellows (and increasingly, ladies) lack inspiration to make a success of themselves in the competitive and intellectual marketplace—and we miss the point badly.

When one looks at a small town youth who has been hired into the police department in the big city, the black officer in Savannah who knows the tough streets too well, or the Hispanic officer in Idaho whose parents were itinerate farmhands, we see those who have boot-strapped themselves up and out of the working and the mis-named dangerous classes. We bear witness to the new entrants into the middle class, individuals who are using one of the scant legitimate avenues of social mobility available for their escape. As a sociological phenomenon, much like their immigrant colleagues that came from Germany, Ireland, and Scandinavia 100 years previously to take police positions in major urban departments, theirs are stories of achievement. They are the stream of upward mobility that uniquely characterizes American success. The river of working-class opportunity flows through American police agencies.

Early Organization Experiences Narrow the Solidarity Group

Early experiences in a police department fine-tune a recruit's knowledge of local culture and focus his or her loyalties to a small group. There are particular aspects of POST training and assignment to a field training officer that narrow officers' solidarity to other line officers, and particularly those in his or her squad. These have been discussed at length by Van Maanen (1973), and I will briefly review his observations here.

Van Maanen noted that POST training was characterized by enforced and harsh discipline. Trainee mistakes were common and were meted out to a training cohort rather than individually. Group punishments and rewards intentionally reinforced solidarity. The latent or unintended consequences of punishment for trivial behavior was an atmosphere in which recruits needed to cover for each other, thus validating secrecy as a central element of solidarity.

After POST academy, officers were routinely assigned to Field Training Officers for a period of six months to a year. Field training officers were their first partners, and they showed officers how to do the day-to-day work of policing. Field Training Officers demonstrated how to make their first arrest, how to deal with citizens, and how to survive the ins and outs of administrative procedure. Officers learned that only other officers covered for them in the event of a mistake. And mistakes were common. The unpredictable nature of the work environment, the hostile reactions officers receive from citizens, the exigencies of arrest, and the use of coercion made errors of procedure, paperwork, and due process common. Trainees learned that day-to-day police work is in-your-face activity, and that the public constantly challenged them. Their only protection was a brother or sister officer.

Today, almost all policing is done in single officer cars. Officers learn that they have to rely on other officers to respond to back-up calls. This pattern of back-up support sometimes leads to strong "partner-style" loyalties as some officers only want particular officers backing them up. In this way, solidarity is reinforced in the form of patrol modalities that encourage mutual protection and assistance.

Training has changed markedly since Van Maanen's seminal research. Stress training, popular in the era when Van Maanen did his research, was in large part a post-Vietnam phenomenon. It is increasingly disappearing from training regimens, though officers continue to make formation and are expected to maintain themselves in a disciplined way. POST today tends to focus on technical and legal issues, officer safety and self-defense, and paperwork, with frequent doses of weapons training sprinkled throughout the typical 10-week academy. Officers today rarely drop and "do 50," that is, give 50 push-ups for some uncontrollable and trivial error. POST trainees also have appeals processes that protect them from arbitrary removal from an Academy.

POST classes are organized in 1 to 4 hour blocks, each of which focus on substantive issues to the Academy class. Students take written examinations on various schedules and are usually tested at the end of each week. Training is increasingly academic in its format, content, and testing procedures, and less like the army boot camps of the Vietnam era. Moreover, officers are normally already hired into a particular organization when they go through POST, and deeply involved in the police culture.[3]

The arbitrary punishments of POST that pushed officers into a shared culture of secrecy 20 years ago are not characteristic of police training today. This is not to say that the impulse to solidarity is weaker today in POST training. It is not fed to the same extent by negative, brass-alienating dynamics that it was 20 years ago. Today, many aspects of training tend to focus on officer safety. Officers are taught the relationship between due process constraints and officer safety standards. They learn detailed techniques on safety defense in such areas as cuffing a suspect, making an arrest, transporting prisoners, bomb identification and disposal, and search and seizure procedures. As the use of weapons has shifted to the legal umbrella of self-defense, recruits learn these laws thoroughly.

The intense focus on officer safety that characterizes POST today reinforces the we-them attitude where the them is the public. All the outside world is dangerous, and only officers can identify the dangers there. This solidarity differs from the solidarity discussed by Van Maanen (1974). Van Maanen located solidarity in recruits' efforts to protect themselves from arbitrary punishment, and solidarity in the current age is grounded in concerns of officer safety and a parallel emphasis on unpredictable dangers emanating from routine police-citizen encounters. This is not to say that managers and line officers have become lovey-dovey, only that the dynamics that encourage solidarity are shifting from what they were 20 years ago. I will have a great deal to say later about management-line relations later, in the chapter on the theme titled bullshit.

My experience in a Probation and Parole POST unit revealed the impulse toward this safety-based solidarity that characterizes contemporary POST training (Crank, 1996). In that research, I noted how communications codes and techniques have become complex, and agents are expected to learn complex procedures to communicate by radio. Recruits were taught to use five types of radios, radio panel details, basic functions, and the 400 message code. To introduce officers to the use of the radio and the code, officers were asked to play out various dramas in class. These dramas always focused on code 444—assisting another officer.

> Dramas were scripted from known events involving officers in the department. The first drama was about a traffic accident that changed to a code 444 when an officer received gunfire and an armed suspect was chased on foot. The second concerned an aborted holdup that changed to a siege situation when the offender escaped to the roof and shot a medical officer . . . Through the administrative and technical complexity of police communications emerged one fundamental cultural precept: always respond to officer calls for assistance (Crank, 1996:282).

Thus, values involving officer safety provided an intensity and drama not attainable in purely technical discussions.

Dimensions of Solidarity

Once an officer is a member of the organization, he or she is a participant in the enterprise of solidarity. I call it an enterprise, for it is an ongoing affirmation of cops' identity. An examination of partner relationships in the current era of one-person patrols displays how solidarity has adapted to contemporary changes in policing.

The Solidarity of Partners. A powerful subtheme of solidarity, the partner is the most fundamental social unit in the police organization. Officers are expected to watch out for their partner before all others (Reuss-Ianni, 1983). The protection of one's partner supersedes all other responsibilities, as constantly emphasized during training. The partner is the cornerstone of officer loyalty and responsibility: stories are told and recounted in which mistakes resulted in peril or death to a partner (Brooks, 1975). Describing the strength of the partnership, Martin (1980:97) cited the following from an officer she interviewed: "I've been working with my partner for two and one-half years. I think I know more about him than his wife does. He knows everything about me. I think you get a certain relationship when you work together with a partner. If my partner were a female, I would have married him a long time ago."

Many researchers have noted that the most powerful stress for police officers is the death of a partner (Goolkasian, Geddes & DeJong, 1989). The shooting of a partner is a profoundly disturbing event with psychological consequences for members of the local culture; in its own way it marks the death of the culture itself. Funeral rituals following a killing are the way in which police culture comes to life again. Funerals are more than symbolic; through the massing of officers and invocation of powerful themes of loyalty, funerals are a dramaturgy of police solidarity acted out for the benefit of officers and their families, and thus police culture comes to life again. I will have much to say on this topic at the end of this book.

The enforcement mandate contributes to solidarity. Solidarity's shadowy side, shared secrecy and deceptions, are frequently associated with police violations of the law. What is overlooked is how the law itself is implicated in the sustenance of the darker elements of the police culture. Cops are under organizational and self-esteem pressures to do something about serious crime (Manning & Redlinger, 1977). If, however, their arrests do not hold up, if there are due process problems, or if the case is too weak to be sustained by the prosecutor, officers and departments are chastised. By covering up for each other to hide errors of due process, fabrication of evidence, or to conceal sloppy police work and the inevitable mistakes that accompany crime control activity, officers protect each other.

The intense focus of contemporary police practice on law enforcement also places officers in a particular relationship with citizens. To invoke formal processes of the law, officers have to make an arrest. Much has been written of arrest and its implications for police behavior. I will not rehash this large body of literature here, but instead refer the reader to the body of writings of Donald Black, Peter Manning, Carl Klockars, James Wilson, William Muir, and Egon Bittner, to list but a few very bright writers on this topic. I only want to make an observation—an obvious, but important one.

Arrest requires the use of coercive authority in an uncertain, contentive, and unpredictable environment, in a typically low visibility situation in which only one or two officers and equally few citizens are present. Important but overlooked is the banal consideration that, as a rule, people do not like to be arrested. They do not like turning their body over to the state for its will to be done. They are frightened both by the police and by the thought of being arrested and imprisoned, and this can make them dangerous. To expect anything else is to visualize a level of regimented public order that has not existed in even the most totalitarian of societies. The unanticipated presence of a cadre of black-booted, body armored, shotgun-armed police officers slamming through a door screaming, "Lie down on the floor NOW!" is more likely to engender uncontrollable bowel evacuation than tranquility. Such an inherently dangerous, irrational, and unpredictable situation does not lend itself to thoughtful social discourse.

Citizens are not only frightened, they carry constitutional protections. The tactics of the police are guided by safety concerns, but the citizen is surrounded by due process protections. There is no way that, in such circumstances, catastrophic legal errors will not be committed by the police. Wrong-address errors have been widely cited. The frequent absence of drugs in such encounters reveals the extent to which snitch-es use police raids to get even with people they do not like. Citizens have been inadvertently killed during questionable entry circumstances.

On the police side, fundamental principles of officer safety are extra-ordinarily difficult to maintain. The situations are so unpredictable that edge control requires extreme self-defense. In such situations, on the edge of chaos, the niceties of due process and law enforcement become trivial.

Due process considerations become compelling at a later time, when a prosecutor reviews an arrest. Questions such as "Was there some law that these people violated," "Were the officers at the right address," or "Why was a deadly strangle-hold used on a sleeping suspect" take on a salience in the courtroom not present at the time of arrest. The mission was a success, the defendants pissed in their pants, but was it legal?

Cop work is focused pragmatically on officer safety. The ability to safely and predictably manage scarcely controllable situations is neither possible nor reasonable. How is a police officer to make another person feel good about their impending arrest? How does a police officer com-pel a citizen to relax while their body is being handed over roughly to the state—cuffed—for indefinite keeping? How is a body search made into a comforting experience? For better or worse, officers have married them-selves to the law, and they will always be dealing with people that do not want to be arrested.

Officers find that they must "dress up" the arrest, mask back-stage problems, and prepare their dramaturgy for the courtroom. Due process errors are reinterpreted as good-faith misunderstandings, issues of officer safety are highlighted, drugs are flaked, and suspects are demonized. Offi-cers rehearse their testimony to conform to the expectations of constitu-tional law. Moreover, because prosecutors have first review of a case, abuses by the police may simply be dropped without explanation.

All police activity prior to arraignment is back-stage preparation for front-stage dramaturgy. The back stage is the realm of police culture, where officers sometimes mask legal violations or tacitly fail to acknowl-edge other officers' questionable behavior. The legal mandate, forcing officers into inherently unpredictable citizen-police encounters that can only be concluded when citizens ceremonially give up their bodies to the state, serves as a powerful stimulus to the onset and maintenance of police solidarity.

The darkness of solidarity. There is a dark side to solidarity. Loy-alty can be used to keep officers quiet in the face of corruption and law-breaking. Ahern describes the corruption of solidarity as a gradual process. A young, idealistic police officer finds his idealism vanishing in the face of petty corruptions, free cigarettes and meals, a scrap of change from store owners to keep an eye on their property. His peers participate in these practices, and if he will not go along:

. . . he soon finds himself ostracized from the only society that is left to him. He is asked whether he is 'too good' for the others. He is told that there is nothing wrong with these practices, that they are accepted by everyone (Ahern, 1972:13).

Peer group pressure, Ahern notes, is enormous. The former "straight arrow" begins to distinguish between legitimate gifts and dishonest graft. All this time, his former circle of outside friends is shrinking; his identity as a police officer makes him a less socially desirable friend, and rotating shifts, still common, increasingly separate him from the ordinary 8-to-5 world. He increasingly socializes with other cops.

When he gets off duty on the swing shift, there is little to do but go drinking and few people to do it with but other cops. He finds himself bowling with them, going fishing, helping them paint their houses or fix their cars. His family gets to know their families, and a kind of mutual protection society develops which the policeman is automatically entitled to respect (Ahern, 1972:14).

Ahern's account reveals a socialization process in which petty corruption and solidarity are intertwined. Peer pressures, combined with characteristic of the job that alienate outside friends, force police to depend on each other. Solidarity links with corruption when peers systematically pressure other cops to keep silent about illegal behavior.

Joined to petty corruptions, solidarity becomes a mask for deeper problems. The Knapp commission, an investigation into corruption in New York City, uncovered patterns of pervasive corruption hidden behind a wall of solidarity. Using the metaphors "grass eaters" and "meat eaters," they argued that the widespread presence of low-key, passive corruption (by grass eaters) provided an environment of secrecy in which graft-seeking predators or meat eaters could thrive. Serious corruption, the commission observed, flourished when large numbers of minor offenders were present but fearful of exposing their own petty criminality.

When supported by illegal behavior, solidarity is vulnerable to dreaded administrative review. When police solidarity is interleaved with criminogenic elements, culture can come to a crashing deconstruction under the harsh gaze of internal affairs. Suddenly, everyone runs for cover; even one's partner is not trusted. In a perversion of unity, solidarity, the social glue acted out in daily conversations and human contact between officers, becomes toxic, anathema. Consider the following description of a police department under investigation by internal affairs:

Eventually forty-three people that I worked with were arrested. One guy they caught taking money from a peddler on the street. He had over twenty years on the job. Here's what they did. "You're caught. You will be off the job. We might prefer criminal charges against you. You lose your pension. That's it. . . . Or we could give you a choice. We're going to put a wire on you. You go back out there. Don't let anybody know. If you tell anybody, we put the cuffs on you. No questions."

He says to himself, "There's no choice to make. I'm going to lose my pension. I'm not going to get a penny for all this crap. Oh, my god." They all go for the wire.

So this guy puts the wire on. What else is he going to do? The first day out with the wire, he gets his partner. They grab his partner and say to him, "Tell us everything you've done and don't let us catch you lying." The guy is pouring out his heart . . .

The thing snowballs. Guys start getting caught. That was the traumatic time. I was afraid to talk to the guy I rode with . . . He's your best buddy, the guy you hang out with before, during and after work. You know his wife and kids. Everybody's friendly. Now you got to sink him. And they did it. They did it. They sunk everybody to save their ass (Baker, 1985:241-242).

Solidarity, the mask of a thousand faces, can thus become a mask that hides a thousand corruptions. As the Knapp commission (1986) has revealed, patterns of illegal behavior can be sustained for decades by police organizations, though the "gold coast" days when assignments were handed down according to their lucrative opportunities, have largely faded. Aspects of police work that encourage police solidarity—social isolation, intense in-group dependence, the suspicions cops have of the public and the distrust they have of administrative brass, the powerful currents of safety and dependence on other officers in times of danger—become veils behind which corruption and illegal behavior can flourish. But it is solidarity that has grown rotten, weak. When Internal Affairs goes after corruption, solidarity can dissolve. No one is trusted. Even the culture itself can collapse.

Endnotes

[1] Manning (1970:129) further notes that "Externally, professionalism functions to define the nature of the client, to maintain social distance with the clientele, and to define the purposes, the conventions, and the motivations of the practitioners; internally, it functions to unify the diverse interests and elements that exist within any occupational or organizational group."

[2] I use the word "satisficing" to indicate that the solutions may not be the best, given the full knowledge of the circumstances, but they are the best given the knowledge at hand and the available materials.

[3] The Idaho State Academy is in the process of creating a program in which individuals on their own, unaffiliated with a criminal justice organization, can participate and be certified. If individuals are hired into a criminal justice department within three years of the training, the costs, estimated at $3,000, are charged back to the department. Otherwise the trainee has to pay for the training. The purpose of the program is to provide an opportunity for individuals to become certified and thus more attractive as prospective employees, and on the other, to provide agencies with a pool of prospective employees when they undertake a search for employees that are POST certifiable in Idaho.

18

America's Great Guilty Crime Secret[1]

Theme: Racism

> I tell people—when I came on this job I was preju-
> diced. Now I'm prejudiced against everybody: I
> don't care if you're White, Black, Hispanic, whatev-
> er—I want to know what kind of game you're trying
> to run on me (Fletcher, 1991:279).

One should not be comforted by the quote from one of Fletcher's
Chicago police respondents. His attitude reflects the inevitable convergence of values that mark the current national climate supportive of harsh
law-and-order crime policies, the "we-them" fostered by heavy-handed
law enforcement tactics, and the presence of geographically bounded
populations of economically ravaged minority groups. Dominion, the special providence of moral responsibility for an assigned particle of territory, includes dominion over minority populations that may live there.
When it does, cultural predispositions provide an opportunity for overt
and covert police racism. And one would be naïve or insensate to dis-
count the presence of racism in American police departments today.

How widespread is racist behavior by the police? The debate over its
presence in American police departments is an astonishingly polarizing
topic. The conditions of the debate are emotional and contentive. The
debate is played out in national politics: The "Mark Furmans" of the world
are weighted against the "Willie Hortons," the bad cop versus the bad
black.[2] Few citizens look beyond the emotionally satisfying sound-byte to
try to understand how and why the two are interrelated social phenomena, or care to know how we ourselves are deeply implicated in systemic
injustice, police racism, and violent crime.

Racism is an extraordinarily difficult concept to write to, partially
because the term is emotionally explosive, and partially because all its
connotations are negative. Is racism a description, or is it, as some have
suggested, no more than an accusation, a barrier prohibiting meaningful

dialogue? I hesitate to discuss it, knowing how offensive the topic will be to many readers. Yet I know of no way to broach this theme but head-on, as I have all others. Indirection is not a prescription for truth-telling, and the cops I know and respect, including some that I know who carry racist sentiments and sometimes act them out in routine traffic encounters, understand the world made plain. I will maintain the same standard here.

The role and culpability of American police in the preservation of racist social policies, both intentionally and inadvertently, has been widely documented (Williams & Murphy, 1990; Kerner Commission, 1968). Overt practices of racism are shielded by the "code of silence" (Stoddard, 1968), and efforts to investigate them are shielded from observers of police behavior (Powers, 1995). Outsiders have often accused the police of racism, a charge frequently denied by the police themselves. It has been argued that the police cannot be comprehended without understanding how they were embedded in a criminal justice system that supported slavery, segregation, and discrimination throughout America's history, and today continue to view minorities as second-class citizens (Williams & Murphy, 1990).

On the other hand, research supporting the presence of police racism is mixed. There is evidence that police arrest practices are not strongly affected by racial predisposition (Black, 1973). Wilbanks (1987) has provided detailed and systematic documentation that the presence of legal factors in police sharply outweigh extralegal factors of race in police-citizen encounters. In this book, I am primarily interested in the presence of racism as a theme central to police culture. An examination of the literature suggests that this is the case.

I conceptualize racism as a cognitive predisposition to associate particular ethnic groups with the commission of particular types of crimes or peace-keeping problems. Aspects of the work environment, mixed with shorthand strategies for offender recognition, lead to the development of de facto racial dispositions. Police in turn act on their dispositions in ways that are self confirming. Thus, police cultural biases against minority groups tend to become self-fulfilling in the doing of day-to-day activities.

I believe that a cultural conceptualization of self-fulfilling practice yields more understanding about racism among the police than other explanations. Consider the following problematic for those who seek to explain racism through subcultural predispositions. I have heard comments on several occasions that indicated strong racial predispositions by patrol officers. Striking was that these officers were frequently from the same minority group they were stigmatizing. Moreover, their attitudes were acted out in practice—an officer might be more likely to stop a Chevy "beater" with a Hispanic driving it, knowing that the likelihood was high that the driver did not carry insurance. Hispanics were thus stigmatized by this Hispanic officer as irresponsible in their driving habits. I have seen similar practices among African-American police officers. Such stories, and police organizations are full of such stories, seem to refute ideas of police racism. How can a person be racist against a member of his or her own group?

The answer to this question, I believe, is by recognizing that racism is a phenomenon grounded in local police cultures. Some officers may import racist values through a process of cultural transmission (Kappeler, Sluder & Alpert, 1994; see also Martin, 1980 for a discussion of the importation of cultural predispositions). However, cultural dispositions are learned and replayed in a process of concrete practice in police-citizen interactions. Cops develop common-sense prescriptions about the likely behavior of individuals with particular cultural, ethnic, or racial characteristics. Shared in the form of stories, warnings, and officer training and safety exercises, racial biases become fixed into departmental traditions and ideas of offender behavior. No ethics course can wipe away what every cop can see perfectly clearly on the street. In this way, cultural racism in a police organization is a self-fulfilling phenomenon that cannot be vanquished, perhaps not even contained.

A wide variety of research has provided insight into the sources and prevalence of racism in police organizations. The Christopher Commission (1991) discussed widespread problems of minority group harassment in the Los Angeles Police Department. The casual and common use of racial epithets was noted in the Commission's review of MDT transmissions. Moreover, the traditional police personnel system selects police applicants who are most likely to conform to conservative middle-class views, and are consequently unable to identify with marginal groups in society (Kappeler et al., 1994), fertile conditions for the emergence of covert and more overt forms of racism.

Police behavior is mobilized by characteristics of dress, behavior, and attitudes. These are often associated with membership in minority groups. The color of someone's skin, style of dress, or accent—symbols of cultural difference—become symbolic shorthand for identifying suspicious characters. Over time, they become common knowledge, accepted as the obvious way of doing things. Skin color or ethnicity can thus become a common-sense base for police investigation. The following story, from research in New York City, illustrates this phenomenon:[3]

One of the worst days in the police department is Good Friday. An awful lot of Gypsies steal on Good Friday. What's taught to the young Gypsy kids is that when Christ was put on the cross, they had four nails to nail him to the cross. A Gypsy kid came by and stole one of the nails. That's why, on the crucifix, Christ's feet are nailed with one nail and the other two are in his hands.

That's passed down from generation to generation. So, according to the Gypsy lore, Christ on the cross is supposed to have said, "From now on and forevermore, Gypsies can steal and it's not a sin."

Good Friday's a big day for them. When I was working the Gypsies, we worked them for ten years, we would never take Good Friday off because it was a day we'd have to get up early and be on the run with them because they would be everywhere (Fletcher, 1990:222).

Dealing with racism is not about identifying "rotten apples" in the police organization. It cannot be dealt with by re-educating officers who show prejudicial and racist attitudes, nor by making sure they have ethics training. It is about the work they do. One simply has to look at the history of police in the United States to understand how racism has been a pervasive characteristic since agencies were first founded. This section accordingly begins with a review of the history of racism among American police departments.

Williams and Murphy: The Historical Context of Racism Among American Police

In 1990, Williams and Murphy rejoined a published article on the history of police in the United States published by Kelling and Moore (1988). The authors argued that slavery, institutionalized segregation in the public and private sector, systemic discrimination, and overt racism are all powerful themes that have haunted the history of social relations in the United States. The police, Williams and Murphy observed, have not escaped the influence of these themes. In spite of the high-minded rhetoric of police professionals and reformers throughout the twentieth century, police departments had never been autonomous of their political environments. To the contrary, they often had been a social and moral barometer of the society they inhabited. When the communities they represented carried racist predispositions, the police tended to follow suit. A review of Williams and Murphy's history of the police in the United States reveals the way in which policing, in many places, evolved directly from efforts to control enslaved African ethnic groups.

The first American modern-style of policing, they argued, developed in the South. Cities such as Savannah and Charleston feared slave uprisings and developed foot and mounted patrols to prevent slaves from congregating (Richardson, 1974). Moreover, they questioned whether the first American-style patrol emerged from British patterns, and presented an alternative origin: they evolved directly from the "slave patrols developed by the white slave owners as a means for dealing with runaways"[4] (Williams & Murphy, 1990:3).

In the period after Reconstruction, blacks made dramatic gains in representation in police departments. But these changes were short-lived and had been largely abandoned by the late 1800s. The passage of *Plessy v. Ferguson* in 1896, with its acceptance of "separate but equal" public facilities, effectively ended Reconstruction. The authors noted that the impact on the employment of black police officers was dramatic:

> The disappearance of blacks from the New Orleans police department serves as the most dramatic example of this trend. From a high of 177 black police officers in 1870, the number dropped to 27 in 1880. By 1900, only 5 black police officers remained; by 1910 there were none. The city did not appoint another black to the police department until 1950 (Williams & Murphy, 1990:44).

The twentieth century witnessed broad police reform under the banner of the police professionalism movement, a movement committed to removing the interference of political machines in local municipal affairs. However, the movement had little effect on black Americans, already disenfranchised from the political process. Many of the changes implemented in the name of professionalism provided scant aid for African-American minorities.

The police professionalism movement, celebrated by reformers for its ability to remove the influence of political machines from employment practices at the turn of the century, was too successful: by the middle of the century large, autonomous police forces were out of touch with their constituencies, particularly those with dark skin. And it was in inner-city ghettos where there were the greatest levels of victimization and needs for police services. It was not surprising that the urban riots of the sixties were sparked by the actions of a police department, or that the urban riots pitted predominantly white police departments against black citizens (President's Commission, 1968).

The contemporary community policing movement, the authors suggested, held the potential to begin to respond to problems of police racism. Central to the movement was the principle of police-community reciprocity, or the recognized need of the police for community support so that they can do their work. The ability to accomplish fundamental police tasks—collect evidence, talk to witnesses, get victim testimony— in short, the fundamental ability of the police to do their work with the support of the citizenry in a democratic setting, disappeared when the police lacked community trust. Community policing has sought to reestablish this important bridge, particularly in communities where community trust has disappeared. Many of the most vocal proponents of the community policing movement, they observed, were themselves black police executives. As the authors noted:

> Their unswerving emphasis, in their statements of values, on the protection of constitutional rights and the protection of all citizens, gives us reason to be optimistic about the future of policing (Williams & Murphy, 1990:13).

Skolnick: Prejudice and Discrimination

Jerome Skolnick (1994) was among the first police researchers to closely examine dispositions of police culture.[5] In a study of two cities he called "Eastville" and "Westville," he noted that police officers frequently displayed prejudicial views toward black minority members. However, he carefully distinguished between prejudiced and racist behavior. Though prejudice—negative predispositions toward black minority members— was commonplace among the officers in his study, he observed that it was infrequently acted out in police work. Racist behavior was uncommon.

Skolnick noted that there was little in training that encouraged racist behavior: one might search a training manual from end to end and find nothing that suggested that black minorities should be treated differently from other citizens. Yet, "from the point of view of the African-American, or the white who is generally sympathetic to the plight of the black in America, most police officers—Westville and Eastville alike—would be regarded as highly racially biased" (Skolnick, 1994:77-78). The question posed by Skolnick was not whether officers were racially prejudiced, but whether prejudice influenced officers' discretionary judgments.

Skolnick noted that negative attitudes toward African-Americans were typical among the police that he studied. Officers not sharing this attitude would be resented by other officers. The following quote, from one of the officers he surveyed, summarized this attitude:

> When I came on this job, I don't think I was prejudiced . . . But when somebody hates you, you get to hate them. I used to work the Bowes Theater on my patrol beat. . . . First I didn't mind too much . . . Then after a while I began to see they hated me, just because I was a cop. It didn't matter what kind of a cop I was or what I did—they hated me (Skolnick, 1994:78).

Skolnick contended, however, that in spite of attitudes of dislike toward African-Americans, officers did not act against them in a way suggesting racial bias. He argued that, in practice, police officers probably did not exhibit prejudice against minorities. The delegation of authority afforded to police officers, he suggested, was more likely to lead to even-handed standards by the police to all groups, regardless of racial predispositions or skin color. Moreover, he suggested that police were more egalitarian to blacks than to other groups because of the extraordinary political power wielded by blacks in contemporary society.

> Indeed, as a result of the civil rights movement, police sometimes seem more color-conscious in an interesting fashion. They perhaps used to unconcernedly push a Black man around; the suspect was just another "nigger." Now, the police may think twice—An African-American suspect may appear to them not only as a person with rights, but one with exceptional political power as well.

It is unclear that African-Americans have exceptional political power, or that in ordinary street encounters with African-American suspects, police fear their political power. Skolnick concluded from his observations that racial predispositions did not have a large impact on police-citizen interventions, except in certain types of interventions.

Skolnick's work is a significant contribution to our understanding of police-minority interventions. Police attitudes toward minority groups are not simply an expression of predispositions imported from pre-rookie days, but should be interpreted through the lens of police culture and the way cultural dispositions are reinforced in self-affirming police-citizen encounters. Moreover, he made the important distinction between prejudice and discrimination, and reminded us not to commit the fallacy that predisposition translates straightforwardly into behavior.

Many aspects of police work have changed since Skolnick wrote his seminal work on the police. When *Justice Without Trial* was first published in 1966, the Crime Commission under President Johnson had yet to write its influential report on the police and the Law Enforcement Assistance Administration was only a twinkle in the eye of the congress. Today, as Kenneth Newman (Hartmann, 1988:2) commented, the police are in the midst of a "sea change," in which fundamental issues of role and purpose are being reconsidered. The contribution that local communities can make to police work is under consideration as never before. The police have undergone a "research revolution" and have become bedfellows with former antagonists, university programs of higher education. Finally, education and pre-service training have become a powerful force among the police. Surely, one might hope, all of these forces would be powerful countercurrents to discrimination and prejudice among the police. Yet, contemporary efforts to assess police racism suggest otherwise.

Measuring Police Racism

It has been argued that the presence of racism, the systematic withholding or selective disposition of justice for minority group members, stems from a few rotten apples in the police organization. This "rotten apple" theory is particularly popular with police executives who do not want the press or the public to look too closely into their departments. However, the evidence for widespread police racism is large and mounting.

In two statewide surveys conducted in Illinois (Knowles, 1996) and Ohio (Martin, 1994), officers were asked whether they had actually observed another officer harass a citizen based on race. One out of every four officers in Illinois (26.2%) and one in six in Ohio (14.9%) stated that they had. If one extrapolates these percentages back to the base populations from which they were drawn, one can appreciate the magnitude of the harassment and its potential for the alienation of minority citizens. According to the 1994 crime reports, Ohio has 18,721 sworn "local" or municipal officers, and Illinois, outside the Chicago police department (which declined to participate in the Illinois survey) has 16,131. Certainly not all of these sworn officers are active on the streets. We can allow a generous estimate that 50 percent of the police organization is in administrative support. This reduces our population to 9,360 in Ohio and 8,065 in Illinois. Calculating our population estimates from these reduced figures, we arrive at 2,113 instances of harassment in Illinois (8,065 x 26.2%) and 1,395 in Ohio (9,360 x 14.9%) in a single year's time, only counting municipal police and excluding the largest police department in either State, by any standard a conservative statistical estimate. It is unlikely that several thousand instances of minority harassment would go unnoticed by corresponding minority populations in these two states.

These numbers, moreover, are in all likelihood a substantial underestimate of the frequency of racial harassments, for three reasons: First, they only involve situations in which an officer has actually witnessed what another officer did, and hence do not include actions between a lone officer and a citizen. Second, they do not include those circumstances where an officer has witnessed a harassment and is unwilling to tell a survey researcher about it, which reasonably includes a large number of officers who would consider such telling as a serious breach of the code of silence. Third, they do not record the number of times an officer has witnessed such an episode over the previous year, but only ask if the officer has witnessed an episode. Whether an officer has seen one or 100 such incidents, the question only provides for a recorded response of one. Thus, in our two typical states, dominated by smaller police departments but with a sprinkling of big-city departments as well, police racism is by any reasoning a pervasive phenomenon. Nor are these figures in some way inflated by groups that harbor ill will against the police: keep in mind that these are numbers that the police are reporting about themselves.

Chevigny: Racial Violence in Los Angeles

When big city departments are examined, issues of racism become at once more complex and more palpable. Los Angeles has a particularly noxious reputation for racism by its police against civilian populations. One example of this was a police operation called "Operation Hammer," carried out in 1988. This operation was suppressive, aimed squarely at the stop and search of minorities. Consider the following description of the operation:

In April of 1988 alone, more than fourteen hundred minority youths were arrested, many of them only to be released later for lack of any charges. For two years, Black and Hispanic youths who ventured into middle-class neighborhoods were very likely to be stopped, forced to "kiss concrete," and searched (Chevigny, 1995:40).

Particularly troubling was the internal climate inside the Los Angeles Police Department, a climate that according to one witness for the Christopher commission, treated excessive force leniently "because it does not violate the department's internal moral code" (Chevigny, 1995:41). Officers were not punished for abuse of force against minorities, even when the abuse was widely known.

Dick Hansen's career in the LAPD is indicative. After the Rodney King incident, Hansen was successfully prosecuted by the federal government (the local district attorney having failed to prosecute) for violating the civil rights of Jesus Martinez Vidales, aged seventeen, whose skull he had fractured. After searching for Martinez Valdez, on a charge of driving a stolen car, Hansen, in the presence of witnesses, struck the youth repeatedly in the head with his baton, trying to pull him from his hiding place in the trunk. Hanson had a second federal case against him, again for brutality, that was dropped when he went to prison in the Martinez Valdez case. In addition, the city had paid substantial damages for his beating of a woman in 1986, and he had been cleared in the shooting of a teenager in 1983. Nevertheless, Chief Gates said he was inclined to give Hansen a leave of absence to serve his federal sentence (Chevigny, 1995:42).

What accounted for the extraordinarily high level of violence toward minorities in Los Angeles? Chevigny argued that the brutality witnessed for both the Los Angeles City and the County police stemmed from its intense focus on law enforcement, an "us versus them" or siege mentality, fostered by management and the chilling rhetoric of a "war on crime." It is easier to justify an "us versus them" mentality when the "them" is a different skin color, or speaks a different language. As a working basis for police intervention, racial characteristics dovetail with other elements of police culture. Where police exercise domain over geographically concentrated minority communities that are also poor and without political power, the war on crime becomes a military containment action. It is acted out as minority harassment, frequent intervention, and the occasional use of deadly force, inevitably justified by prosecutorial review, and frequently seen by mainstream whites as a way to keep minorities in their deserved place. Violence, Chevigny noted, was a very effective way to control people and maintain order.

The Future of Police Racism

The behavior of the police has broad support in a national climate increasingly fearful of minorities. The American public today seeks an illusory nineteenth-century small-town conception of personal security, an image that can only be sustained by keeping the dangerous classes away from them. In the nineteenth-century small town, everyone supposedly knew who lived on the other side of the tracks, as it were, and knew how to avoid them. The local police "watchmen" watched them closely and did not hesitate to intercede if they got out of line. They were troublemakers and had to be thumped, due process be damned.

Today, "war on crime" police actions reinforce the geographic and psychological distinctions between "safe" low-crime communities and the dangerous classes in order to "keep minorities in the districts where they live" (Chevigny, 1995:40). This has been popular, Chevigny noted, with many middle-class voters and with their city council representatives over the years. Informal containment policies have protected the economic status quo, locking minorities into inner cities where there are no jobs and no tax base, and consequently where the schools are sharply underfunded. As increasing numbers of minority group members seek illegal access to economic stability, institutionalized racism becomes a self-fulfilling phenomenon.

Broad social support for discriminatory policies, combined with the theme of racism that characterizes police culture and a "look-the-other-way" posture of police executive leadership, support an economic climate where particular groups prosper under racist policies. When we realize that containment means the preservation of property values in white neighborhoods, the financial well-being of rental/lease brokers, and that police harass minority individuals in downtown areas because more affluent white customers are too timid to shop there, the economic basis of racist containment is clear. The police do what we want them to do. They cannot change because we will not change.[6]

Efforts over the past two decades to increase minority hiring may have had the undesired effect of intensifying racial conflicts within police organizations (see Martin, 1980:12-15, for a discussion of organizational resistance to minorities). From a conflict perspective, this outcome is predictable. One consequence of increasing out-group efforts to establish appropriate personnel standards is the crystallization of in-group resistance. Today, widespread resistance in police organizations traumatizes the efforts of minority group members to gain acceptance in the informal organizational culture even when organizational membership has been assured.

Internal agency conflicts with racist overtones are a contemporary problem in agencies (Shusta et al., 1995:37). A police conflict in New York focused on a proposed civilian review board, while the Dallas police strike pitted black and white police officers against each other. Whether these policies in any way have diminished racism within police organizations is debatable; that there has emerged a powerful antagonism and resentment to affirmative action programs in their departments is not.

If we want to understand the theme of racism in police culture, it is not enough to only look at characteristics of the police themselves. To gain full understanding, we would be better off to look inside ourselves. Racist currents haunt American life, and to all but the ideologically oblivious, are apparent in the economic, social, and geographic organization of contemporary society. The police recognize this, and also understand that they are expected to reinforce informal racist norms in their community. If you are white and doubt this, put blackface on, stroll through a white, upper-middle-class bedroom community after the sun goes down, and see if you finish the night with your self-respect intact. As Chief Bouza notes, the police self-image as an "embattled fortress" comes from the problems they have with ethnic and minority groups on the one hand, and on the other, the "sub rosa" marching orders they have been given by the "overclass."

> The problem arises from the hypocrisy they see in a society that insists that they control "them." Them refers to Blacks, ghetto residents, the homeless, the poor, and all others who evoke a sense of fear or unease. These orders are implicit and indirect. The laws enabling control aren't there . . . The "offenses" of the group aren't crimes, but they do offend the overclass (Bouza, 1990:7).

Bouza observes that the racism exhibited by the police is not simply a mirror of racial patterns that exist in society. The link is more direct. It is police enforcement of broader, societal expectations, and the police know it. But it does not make them any fonder of financially secure white citizens, what Bouza calls the overclass. To the contrary, it contributes to the alienation of the police from that segment of the public as well. Perhaps the police are alienated from us because they know us too well. They know that our fear of the police is nearly as strong as our desire to contain the underclass—nearly, but not quite.

In the end, the police perform their task, and do so admirably. But is this good? In their fine performance of their work, the police permit us to look the other way. They permit us to avoid seeing what we've created. Bouza captures our deceit and the dilemma it poses for democracy:

> . . . as the only permanently present and invariably visible arm of government in the ghetto, the police, especially in the restive summer months, remained an army of occupation in a largely hostile land . . . The success of the police had ironic results. The better they were at coping with the problem, the less likelihood that society would ever come to grips with the roots of the matter (Bouza, 1990:78).

We arrive where we began three centuries ago: a self-described free society that is unable to cope with our most consequential problems of simple human equality, lacking even a common language that would allow us to speak about shared values (Bellah et al., 1985). Our politics too often a charade of moral righteousness and chastising zeal, we justify outrageous punishments for inconsequential crimes, destroying generations of Black youth through imprisonment, and through the panopticon of a growing urban gulag in many of our largest cities.

The police do their work as they should and as they must. They do it energetically; we dare not ask less from them. They control disorder, deal forcefully with bad guys, provide a critical function for society. Yet they permit us to hide the consequences of our neglect—our great guilty crime secret, as Bouza calls it—behind prison walls, allowing us to ignore the implications of what we demand and expect. The way in which we the people are implicated in the most profound problems confronting our racial minorities are masked by police effectiveness; the police know it, minorities know it, the rest of us hide from it. How could the police be anything but cynical about us, the public?

Endnotes

[1] Bouza (1990:280).

[2] Mark Furman was a Los Angeles police officer accused of racist manipulation of evidence in the 1995 trial of O.J. Simpson. Willie Horton was a black man on prison furlough in Massachusetts who was convicted of killing another man while on furlough, and whose act was used to attack Democratic candidate for president Michael Dukakis in 1988. I use their names for their symbolic value only, withholding any personal judgment over both individuals, neither of whom I know personally. I have not the least idea whether either person is even vaguely similar in personality and motive to the public images of them that have been played out in the national press for public and political consumption. To the contrary, my point is that they are played out for political purposes of polarization, intended to inflame emotions and mobilize political opinion.

[3] Though I use the term racism in this book, there are a variety of reasons why the term is inherently misleading that I must acknowledge. First, there is little credible scientific evidence that there is such a thing as race. Second, the term is so emotively loaded that rational discourse over the topic among antagonists is impossible. Once I label some statement as racist, for example, the person who has made the statement is rightfully offended and subsequent efforts to ameliorate tensions or to sustain meaningful dialogue about biasing predispositions is futile. The term is so emotionally charged as to preclude rational discussion. While the term "ethnicism" seems to carry similar emotive freight, and for even a wider audience, it lacks the connotative virulence that the term "racism" carries and may not be so immediately polarizing.

[4] In Georgia, for example, they note that "all urban white men aged sixteen to sixty, with the exception of ministers of religion, were to conduct such patrol on every night throughout the year. In the countryside, such patrols were to 'visit every Plantation with-

in their respective districts once in every month' and whenever they thought it necessary, 'to search and examine all Negro-houses for offensive weapons and ammunition.'" (Wood, 1984; see also Walker, 1977).

[5] The 1994 reference refers to the third edition of *Justice Without Trial*, initially published in 1966.

[6] Oliver and Shapiro (1995) provide a compelling picture of race and the structure of wealth in the United States. They distinguish between income and wealth, and argue that powerful systems of institutionalized economic discrimination—for example, exclusionary policies of the Federal Housing Authority for many years—have intentionally prevented the accumulation of wealth by blacks. The long-term consequences of these policies are inevitable, and intended (1995:151-152): "Owing to their severely restricted ability to accumulate wealth combined with massive discrimination in the private sector and general white hostility, black parents over several generations were unable to pass any appreciable assets on to their kin."

Loosely Coupling Cultural Themes

Section IV

The themes in the following chapters are loosely coupling themes, by which I mean that they function to separate police cultures from external influence and observation. In this case, external includes management brass as well. The idea of loose coupling is drawn from an institutional perspective. In the following section, I will first provide an overview of institutional perspective, and then discuss loosely coupling themes in police organizations.

Contemporary research on institutionalized organizations is typically traced to Meyer and Rowan (1977). Bureaucratic organizations are traditionally described as systems of coordinated activities organized around principles of efficiency and effectiveness. Meyer and Rowan argued that many organizations operated in highly institutionalized environments, and thus focused outward to the values and expectations of institutional constituencies and only were secondarily concerned with efficiency and effectiveness (Meyer & Scott, 1983). Primary and secondary education programs, for example, are expected to satisfy credentialing concerns of state boards and certification from appropriate authorities; more locally, they must contend with parent-teacher organizations. Municipal police organizations similarly have to respond to concerns of powerful constituencies such as the city council, mayor, media, and the courts.

In institutionalized organizations, goals and processes tend to become disconnected from the day-to-day activities of line personnel in the organization. Through this process, called loose coupling, the activities of organizational personnel responsible for the delivery of services to the public become shielded from formal organizational goals and processes

(Meyer & Rowan, 1977).[1] Consider Peace Officer Standards and Training, for example. POST is a powerful institutional influence over municipal and county police organizations. It is institutionalized in the sense that all states in the current era require it and the training and education it provides are highly regarded by executives. It is also loosely coupled from day-to-day police work, as every trainee knows who has been assigned to a Field Training Officer. How? What trainee has not heard the phrase, "Forget everything you learned in POST. Here's how we do it." In this example, the formal goals of the organization—training protocols will be transferred to day-to-day police behavior—are loosely coupled to what patrol cops actually do by the behavior of FTOs.

Loose coupling, I argue, may occur from the bottom up; that is, as a way lower-ranking actors mutually and creatively develop ways of doing things to shield themselves from administrative oversight.[2] That a police organization deals with issues in its institutional environment that are only incidentally related to crime control has been noted by researchers on the police (Klockars, 1991; Mastrofski, 1991; Crank & Langworthy, 1992). This observation has not been lost on line personnel. Loosely coupling themes emerge when line personnel perceive that particular problems interfere with their ability to maintain control over day-to-day police work.[3] By developing cultural themes that in some way obscure areas of police activity, cops maintain control of their assigned territories. Loose coupling of this stripe allows line-level officers to do what they perceive to be the important work of the organization when they think that the organization is unable or unwilling to do so.

For example, a cultural theme in police organizations is the set of common-sense tactics that have emerged in order to circumvent constitutional prohibitions on particular police behaviors. These tactics counter the organization's "outward" institutional focus on the courts, public pressure groups, and policy-minded administrators, all of whom seek to insure that the constitutional rights of defendants are fully in place during times of police arrest and detention.

This cultural theme emerges because at a pragmatic level, the police believe that their territorial dominion is undermined by the Fourth Amendment. Stories and examples of wrongdoing thwarted are shared by officers in order to solve concrete work problems caused by due process protections. Tactics include tricks to get lawbreakers to confess, lying on the stand, failure to report violations, covering for other officers, stories about bad guys who manipulate constitutional protections, ways to get PC (probable cause), and stories of lenient judges. These cultural "tools" mobilize cop sentiment and obscure the behavior of line personnel from formal organizational goals and policies (Klockars, 1980).

Loosely coupling themes thus allow line officers to focus on what they perceive to be crime control effectiveness in day-to-day activities when they think that the organization is obstructed from seeking effectiveness by conflicting expectations from their own managers or from influential outside groups. In a subjective, culturally based logic, loosely coupling themes re-introduce effectiveness into their work when management is focused on the demands of external audiences.

The following five themes are loosely coupling themes. These themes provide ways to think about or remedy situations where the police are constrained from acting out their ideas of effectiveness in peace-keeping and crime control activities. Because these are loosely coupling cultural devices, they allow the organization to deal with its institutional interface, while officers can continue the same basic daily routines they have accomplished largely unchanged since the beginning of the twentieth century. It is these themes that are often associated with negative aspects of the police culture (Kappeler et al., 1995).

Endnotes

[1] According to Meyer (1983:289) loose coupling occurs when "purposes and programs are poorly and uncertainly linked to outcomes; rules and activities are disconnected; and internal organization sectors are unrelated."

[2] In highly institutionalized organizations, institutional inspection is roughly equivalent to administrative overview.

[3] It is because police cultures share this common grounded aesthetic that they appear similar to the casual outside observer. Moreover, the more institutional expectations diverge from cultural perceptions of what it takes to "do something about crime now" the more the culture of policing separates from formal organizational processes, and the more it will appear as an insular subculture, unresponsive to externally imposed change.

19

On Becoming Invisible

Theme: Outsiders

> No good deed shall go unpunished.
> —Anonymous

Police see themselves as outsiders, different from citizens, apart and special. On its surface, the theme "outsiders" seems to mirror the theme solidarity. The two themes are closely related, but there is an important difference. The themes of solidarity and of outsiders pose different kinds of questions about culture. When discussing police solidarity, the central cultural question is "what makes us similar?" With regard to outsiders, one should ask "what makes us different from others?" The theme "outsiders" is thus in some ways a meta-theme of the loosely coupling topic. It has the potential to cover all the different ways in which police are different from other groups. In this chapter, I will focus on a few principal characteristics of outsider thinking—being secretive, lying low, and avoiding trouble.

The Outsider as an Occupational Disposition

Police believe themselves to be a distinct occupational group, apart from society (Van Maanen, 1974). This belief stems from their perception that their relationship with the public, with brass, and with the courts is less than friendly, sometimes adversarial. As outsiders, officers tend to develop a "we-them" attitude, in which the enemy of the police tends to shift from the criminal element to the general public (Sherman, 1982). This perspective is instilled through training (Van Maanen, 1973), and through hiring criteria that tend to produce a homogenous cohort of officers ill-equipped to relate to socially marginal groups that characterize most urban environments (Kappeler, Sluder & Alpert, 1994).

Cops firmly believe that the public does not like them. Manning (1978b) captured the essence of this theme with the brief cultural aphorism everyone hates a cop. The belief that they are outsiders is a basis for police secrecy, when secrecy protects cops from departmental directives and public oversight.

Outsiders are invisible. Police are haunted by accountability. They are in an occupation where situations in which they intervene are unpredictable, and sometimes they have to make rapid-fire judgments in emotional circumstances. Cops know that they will make many mistakes for which they would be publicly rebuked by any of a number of groups—the press, civic organizations, departmental brass, the mayor. Each of these is an influential actor in the cop's world—a rebuke from any of them might mean a letter in the permanent file, the start of an investigation, or public embarrassment. In institutional theory, they are those groups whose opinions count—they can disrupt the life and well-being of the organization and the people in it. They are the principal actors in a cop's institutional environment.

It is not that cops may know institutional actors personally that makes them influential in the life of a cop, but that any one of them, a newspaper for example, might find out a mistake and print it. Any one of them can make a cop's life a living hell. Cops are secretive, Chevigny (1995:141) notes, because "they are confident that whatever they say will be used against them." They live the aphorism that states no good deed shall go unpunished. They know that they are watched, that they are of intense public interest when they screw up. They know that suspects lie about police- citizen interactions to make them out to be liars. They know that brass cares about protecting its own rear; they know that the mayor wants to be re-elected. That city council members are politically indebted to their constituencies. That judges are unsympathetic to their working schedule. That defense council will do everything possible to humiliate them in a court room. The only way they can avoid trouble is by becoming invisible.

Police consequently stay low and avoid trouble. In most activities they are order takers; many of their tasks are routine, trivial, and involve completing paperwork. There is scant incentive for performance where there are few opportunities for arrest, and police are not rewarded for their speed in paper processing. And there are many opportunities to get into trouble, by roughing up an asshole that also happens to be an influential citizen, rousting some loud-mouth motorist, accidentally firing an unholstered weapon, using a warrant at the wrong address. Frequently, the best course of action is to do nothing at all. An invisible officer does not get into trouble.

Invisibility is learned as early as academy training (Bahn, 1984). The artistry of minimizing errors is taught from the outset. Officers learn that the only time training officers notice them is when they make a mistake.

By doing what they are told and no more, they avoid notice and the punishment that inevitably follows.

The ability to become invisible extends to routine patrol activity, where "real" police work is infrequent (Van Maanen, 1974). Police work tends toward routines, and opportunities for arrest are uncommon. Even felony crimes are rarely exciting; four-fifths of all felonies are property crimes, and cops can do little besides take a report so that citizens have written records for insurance companies.

Patrol activity is sometimes dangerous. Any intervention carries with it the authority of the state, and the parallel responsibility to not back down. Once an officer has engaged a citizen, the event can never become casual; even minor encounters have the nasty, unpredictable quality of escalating suddenly . . . what officer has not had a confrontation begin with the following comments, "What are you hassling me for? What'd I do? Why don't you deal with real criminals?" It is simply not in a cop's repertoire of responses to answer "excuse me, my mistake, I'll just go away now." Backing down is not an option. Cops have to pick and choose their encounters, and most of the time, they choose to stay invisible and avoid trouble.

Postulates of invisibility. Staying invisible is a general way of thinking about work (Kappeler, Sluder & Alpert, 1994). Kappeler and his colleagues, citing Reuss-Ianni (1983), suggested that this ethos was comprised of several specific beliefs. These beliefs were the "verbal links between a subculture's view of the world and their expression of that view into action." (Kappeler, Sluder & Alpert, 1994:110). That is, they described how the idea of invisibility was translated into ordinary activity, providing officers guides for protecting themselves and other officers.

1. Do not give up another cop. Regardless of the seriousness of the case or the circumstances surrounding it, never provide information to the public or to superior officers.

2. Watch out for your partner first and then for the rest of the shift. This means not only that officers must protect each other from physical harm, but also that they need to watch out for their interests. One, for example, informs a fellow officer if one discovers that he or she is being investigated by internal affairs.

3. If you get caught off base, do not implicate anybody else. If something happens and you are discovered in the wrong place or doing forbidden activities, do not involve other cops who might also be punished.

4. Hold up your end of the work. Malingerers draw attention to everyone on the shift.

5. Do not look for favors just for yourself. In other words, do not suck up to bosses for special favors. Line officers should not develop special relationships with superior officers.

Through these postulates, officers protected themselves from prying outside eyes. They particularly focus on departmental brass but, on the whole, they act as guides for avoiding scrutiny. An officer that fails to observe these tenets, that becomes visible, is a threat to all.

Outsiders Are Secretive

The "code" of secrecy is widely noted among police organizations (Kappeler et al., 1995). Secrecy serves several purposes: it protects line officers from organizational oversight (Wesley, 1970), it insulates them from the inspection of citizens who will not understand police situational use of violence, treatment of assholes, and frequent violation of procedural guidelines (Martin, 1980; Chambliss & Seidman, 1971). It hides due process violations and abuse of discretion review associated with ordinary street encounters (Manning, 1978). Secrecy is central to the police culture; those who violate principles of secrecy may encounter ostracism, loss of friends, and a shortage of backup in dangerous street encounters. Discussed below are two important dimensions of secrecy, toward the public and toward departmental brass.

Secrecy and the public. Ahern (1972:16) noted that many people who call the police manipulate them for their own purposes. People who hold grudges against others may use the police to take care of them. Theft and burglary reports written in good faith are actually intended to defraud insurance companies. The same individuals are arrested over and over for the same petty crimes: one alcoholic, Ahern observed, was arrested 140 times. And juvenile offenders become adult criminals, despite an officer's best efforts to intervene on their behalf. Police finally reach a point where they trust no one, and the secrecy of the police profession becomes a way of life.

Not all observers of the police have noted this secrecy. Baker did not find the police to be as secretive or unapproachable as he had anticipated.

> . . . the unwritten code of silence I had heard so much about was not the obstacle I had expected it to be. Maybe they were not entirely representative, but most of the cops that consented to be interviewed were gregarious. A number of them were downright charming. They seemed to enjoy talking (Baker, 1985:5).

This is not to suggest that Baker found the police in his Boston research to be totally open to external observation. He noted an "artless amiability coexisting with a skepticism bordering on paranoia" (Baker, 1995:5) and a constant sense of watchful suspicion that characterized his interviews. Fletcher (1990:iv) also observed that the Chicago police with whom she conducted her research were open. She noted that she was "stunned . . . of the generosity of the police I met . . . They gave freely of their off-duty time. Out of the 130 requests for interviews, I met with five refusals."

In my own research, I have consistently been permitted cordial entre to conduct research in police organizations. I have also experienced the sheer sense of being "other." I once visited a chief in an agency in a small community in Illinois, and had been given a tour of the department. The demeanor of everyone with whom I talked was courteous and friendly. As I finished, I stopped to look at a plaque on the wall that contained photos, badges, and insignia of fallen officers. Suddenly I sensed a presence behind me. Turning around, I saw three officers staring at me from behind a glass that separated the corridor from the deputy chief's office, about 10 feet away. Though I may have been guilty of mis-reading their expressions, the clear sense I carried from that encounter was as if they had said to me in this aspect of our lives you are not permitted entry. I have since penetrated that veil, but then again I am no longer the person I was at that time.

Secrecy and brass. The maintenance of secrecy from superior officers or "brass" is as important as secrecy from the public (Manning, 1977). Manning suggested that, in both Peace Officer State Training (POST) and Officer Field Training, officers learned that they cannot trust administrators. There were several consequences of POST training that encouraged secrecy, some intended and some not. The concern for detail was ritualistic, and discipline tended to be harsh and contrived. Punishments were meted out to the entire group for individual mistakes. Officers learned to lean on each other for mutual protection. The fabled loyalty of officers, noted in the chapter on solidarity, was motivated by a desire to keep information from leadership of the program. Field training similarly revealed a pattern of secrecy and mutual protection from administrative oversight. FTOs taught officers how to deal with the particular demands of the sergeants, and how other officers shielded them from the arbitrary expectations of command.

Recruits had in a short period of time adopted their characteristic perspective of police work: lay low and avoid trouble. Both the public and the brass, Van Maanen observed, were to be avoided. Without a relationship with fellow officers "that protects his interests and allows him to continue on the job—without their support he would be lost" (Van Maanen, 1974:306). Thus, both with regard to administrative oversight and with the public, a variety of intended and unintended aspects of their occupational setting taught officers to be secretive about their behavior. Knowledge was shared with only an elect group. The circle of an officers' friends were fellow officers, and even then only particular officers from his or her squad or department. The activities of this group were shielded by an impenetrable wall of selective silence that protected officers from the public, from brass, and from each other (Bittner, 1990).

Line-management relations are not always characterized by frictions. At times, charismatic chiefs may gain the support of line officers. The consequence is often positive, and some departments have good line-management relations. Alternatively, there may be a whole-cloth loss of accountability over the behavior of the police. A combination of insularity and the presence of a charismatic chief that has moved beyond accountability result in the intensification of activities corresponding to the dark side of the force (Skolnick & Fyfe, 1993:134). Secrecy, brutality, abuse, and violence characterize such departments. Frank Rizzo, former police chief of Philadelphia, represented such a case. In 1972, riding a wave of public support for the police, he was elected mayor. During his tenure the police department "answered to nobody but the mayor who encouraged officers to brutality and who backed up this invitation by insulating abusive officers from accountability" (Skolnick & Fyfe, 1993:135). This problem has not been unique to Philadelphia. Similar accountability dilemmas confronted by Los Angeles and Milwaukee are discussed in detail by Skolnick and Fyfe. In these circumstances, secrecy and insularity are themes of police culture that have overtaken the department. Legitimizing secrecy and isolation throughout the organization is a powerful way to move the police outside the realm of public accountability—loose coupling with a vengeance.

The veil of secrecy emerges from the practice of police work, from the way in which everyday events conspire against officers. The veil has no remedy. It may be desirable to penetrate the veil, but it is not reasonable. To look at secrecy in terms of good or bad, right or wrong, is to miss the point. It is a cultural product, formed by an environmental context that holds in high regard issues of democratic process and police lawfulness, and that seeks to punish its cops for errors they make. Secrecy is a set of working tenets that loosely couple the police to accountability, that allow them to do their work and cover their ass so that they can continue to do the work they have to do without interfering oversight. As long as police conduct law enforcement under a mantle of due process and accountability in the United States, police culture will be characterized by secrecy.

20

Individualism and the Paradox of Personal Accountability

Individual police departments are institutionalized organizations (Crank & Langworthy, 1992). This means that organizations exist because they are carriers of valued ways of doing things in their municipal occupational environments (Meyer & Rowan, 1977). The occupation of policing is literally the enactment of important values deeply held across the American landscape.

Police organizations are value-laden. Responsible for the maintenance of society's most deeply held moral sentiments—that which is so wrong that it is sanctioned by the criminal law—police organizations tend to carry very traditional values that are widely held in the general population. It is thus not surprising that individualism and the ethic of personal responsibility are central features of police work. In virtually all criminal justice cultures, this ethic is a key to understanding how officers think and act.

In the institutionalized occupational environment of policing, officers carry a profoundly individualistic perception of themselves and of work. They do not, and I cannot emphasize this strongly enough, view themselves as cogs in a bureaucratic organization, mindlessly carrying out supervisors' expectations of what they ought to do. Central to their work is the notion of personal responsibility, be it their responsibility for their own ability to control all circumstances or the personal dominion they have over the human landscape that is their charge on the beat. Responsibility for their dominion is absolute—to fail in one's individual responsibility is to lose face, to be seen as a bad cop.

Yet the individualism carried by street cops is paradoxical. In an occupation steeped in institutionalized values, that most fundamental of American values, individualism, limits occupational control over its own rank-and-file. The strongly held individualistic temperament of cops is a fundamental barrier to management efforts to hold them responsible to administrative oversight. They resist being bureaucratically controlled, cannot imagine working at a desk, and they loathe the idea that they are "company men."

In this chapter, I argue that the individualism felt by cops is encouraged by characteristics of their working environment. Like other themes, it is tied to concrete aspects of their work, particularly in the way police patrol and detective work is organized. Individualism is a loosely coupling phenomenon because it provides a sensibility that prohibits close managerial oversight. Cops exalt in their independence and resist efforts to bureaucratically corral what they do.

Individualism Is a Root Metaphor

In all fields of scientific endeavor, there are root metaphors, a founding analogy that is so central to the way in which a field looks at its work that it profoundly affects all scientific endeavor in that field. Consider, for example, the field of sociology. A great deal of sociological theory is based on analogies of plants and plant-life. Such ideas as "functional," "the city as a social organism," "ecological areas," "the whole is greater than the sum of its parts" and terms such as "growth" and "adaptation" reveal the pervasiveness of this powerful metaphor. It can be considered a "root" metaphor (itself a plant analogy) because it is fertile (there I go as well, using the plant metaphor)—it generates a great deal of thought on the relationship between society's diverse parts, and because it has wide-ranging implications for the relationship between individuals and government.

Individualism is a root metaphor at the heart of democratic process. It derives its analogic from the idea of the physical separateness of human creatures. The term "individual" is a way to characterize people in terms of their separateness from each other. By analogy, if we are physically separate creatures, then are we not also socially distinct, unique, each personally responsible for our own well-being?[1]

That individuals are responsible creatures and hence accountable for their behavior is a belief pervasive to modern life and a perennial source of intellectual debate over topics of agency, accountability, and obligation (Harmon, 1995; see McKeon (1957) for a discussion of the history of the idea of responsibility). In contemporary debates over the responsibility of individuals to society, in efforts to reform welfare, in economic theory; in short, in virtually all political, social, and scholarly debate we find the responsibility of the individual pitted against the needs of society.

Individualism, wedded to notions of personal responsibility, has sharply affected the way in which the police have addressed key problems. Consider police corruption. The way in which police agencies have responded to police corruption, for example, has been described by what has been called the "rotten apple" theory—that individual, rotten-apple cops are responsible for the onset and maintenance of corruption in particular departments. This logic implies that corruption can be corrected by weeding out particular bad cops (Knapp Commission, 1986). Where corruption or other organizational problems are pervasive, a typical political reaction is to hold the chief of police responsible for the whole mess and replace him with a new chief who promises to clean house (Crank & Langworthy, 1992).

The notion that corruption may persist because it contributes in some positive way to the social context in which police find themselves is utterly rejected by police and reformers alike. Bracey (1976) argued that, in spite of the best efforts of police administrators, the media, and city government to stamp it out, corruption flourishes in major departments today. It does so because it contributes in important ways to the peaceful co-existence of influential groups who otherwise would be in open conflict with each other. Her paper should have established a national research agenda into the causes and remedies of corruption. Instead it has been relegated to the dusty shelves of neglected scholarship. What a waste.

Individualism and Accountability

Within the police organization, the metaphor of personal responsibility is acted out in terms of line officer accountability. By accountability, I mean the extent to which street-level police officers are answerable to a higher authority for their on-the-job actions. Police organizations have elaborate accountability mechanisms: they try to control the behavior of their officers through a militaristic chain of command, through internal affairs units, through elaborate bureaucratic rules, and through complex standard operating procedures. Outside of a prison environment, it is difficult to imagine an organization that seeks more stringent control over its charges—or one that has such limited success.

Police organizations focus intensely on the accountability of the individual line officer, and hold him or her responsible for a wide range of ethical behavior. Then they create production and self-esteem pressures that push officers to commit violations of those same ethics (Manning & Redlinger, 1977). Our analogical biases, our focus on individual responsibility utterly fails to account for ethical problems that officers face that stem from their commitment to the police task itself, or how organizational factors undercut personal ethics. The notion that cops may confront problems that undermine the best efforts to be ethical has been too infrequently recognized.

The way organizational pressures contribute to ethical and legal violations has been studied by Manning and Redlinger (1977), who traced the many implications of police organizational power and authority for drug enforcement. They discussed how diverse organizational and ethical pressures accumulate in drug enforcement activities to push an agent toward corrupt behavior. Administrative pressures to get arrests push agents to use informants of highly questionable integrity and no clear understanding of the concept of honesty. Informants invert the hierarchy of sanctions: they traded information for light sentences or for drugs, and negotiated among prosecutors to see who would cut them the best deal if they were charged with a crime. Rewards for high production, which included raises, self-esteem maintenance, organizational recognition, and promotions, tended to offset concerns over violations of suspects' rights to due process. The importance of this work is in its recognition of the limitations of personal predisposition in the accumulation of pressures for officers to become "bent," that is, commit drug-related crimes, including the theft, use, and sales of narcotics. Organizational pressures for arrest, combined with personal desires for organizational recognition, outweighed personal ethical considerations.

In the following sections I will consider two perspectives that have looked at the individualizing notion of police work and the perplexing problems it creates for police accountability.

Brown: The Inner-Directed Cop

In 1981, Michael Brown published an insightful book on the way in which police thought about their work. His research was conducted with the Los Angeles police department and two other smaller departments in Los Angeles county. Among his findings was a recognition of the powerful role individualism played in the working life of street cops.

Brown observed that individualism was a core value of the police culture. Individualism, he contended, emerged from two elements of the working occupation. The first was a felt need to be inner-directed and aggressive. The inner-directed patrolman, he argued, "is a crime fighter; he values a "good pinch," and "police work is viewed as a game of cops and robbers" (Brown, 1981:84). His findings challenged Wilson's (1968) notion that police were "subprofessionals," or that police officers were primarily interested in job security. To the contrary, he contended, they thrive on the chase, "those instances in which it is clear where everybody stands, and the job is simply that of catching bad guys."

. . . skulking through alleys and back streets looking for miscreants and constantly monitoring the radio for the all too infrequent "hot calls" are the palpable manifestations of this role. A call that an armed robbery or burglary is in progress brings not just the assigned patrol car but any unit that is not otherwise occupied and can make it to the location in time (Brown, 1981:85).

Individualism, he suggested, legitimated the autonomy of patrolmen. Officers developed their own individual priorities and adapted their work to those priorities. Some officers, for example, tended to enforce all laws, and others, he stated, acted out patterns of selective enforcement. Individualism, he concluded, "allows each patrolman to pick and choose as opportunities arise" (Brown, 1981:86).

Issues of individualism and loyalty were most apparent with regard to partners. Officers backed each other up in questionable circumstances and covered for each other's mistakes; moreover, officers consistently felt that the responsibility for what occurred in a beat fell to the officer in charge of the beat and would defend the officer's right to make that decision. Loyalty and individualism were, in his words, two sides of the same coin: the police culture demanded loyalty but granted autonomy. Thus, individualism was closely linked with the cultural theme solidarity.

Other investigators have noted the importance of individualistic self-sufficiency in police work. Bittner (1990) suggested that their sense of individual responsibility was wedded to their idea of territorial responsibility. Responsibility, he observed, was a geographic phenomenon: officers did not involve themselves in another cop's beat unless invited, and even then their involvement was minimal. Whether working with a partner or alone, officers are compelled by the need to be self-reliant (Hunt & Magenau, 1993). Self-reliance extended to handling dangerous disputes; even though required to call back-up in perilous situations, officers believe that any problems on their beat are their responsibility alone (Bouza, 1990).

Manning: Entrepreneurship vs. Administrative Control

Few authors have focused as clearly or in greater detail on the police culture as has Manning. In a wide variety of articles, he has etched out the dimensions of police culture and the values carried by street cops. One of his observations is that a powerful individual responsibility infuses both officers' self-perceptions and the way they view their work. A cop's sense of personal responsibility, Manning suggested, was manifested in a tension between police rules and characteristics of everyday police work.

Describing London police, he noted that "Police work is seen as individualistic, entrepreneurial, practical, face-to-face activity involving particular people and their problems." Their perceptions of real police work stemmed from this self-perception: as one of his interviewees noted, "real police work is out there." Other aspects of police work were jaded, derivative:

> As a consequence, only the everyday activities of the constable even approach the form and functions of "real police work." Paper work, court appearances, administrative tasks, or report writing (even routinely required occurrence booklets) are considered ex post facto glosses upon the real work on the ground (Manning, 1978c:77).

In their everyday endeavors constables constantly faced administrative efforts to impose rules to structure their behavior. The different standard held by administrators was evident in the following statement:

> From the administrator's point of view . . . the execution of policy, the efficient achievement of organizational goals, and the maintenance of hierarchy and discipline are both required and a source of prestige and satisfaction (Manning, 1978c:77).

This idea of responsibility is sharply inconsistent with the independent, individualized approach characteristic of line officers.

Because street cops tended to have an individualistic approach to their work, administrative rules and department policy lost their proscriptive potency. Officers developed "tactical means of defending oneself against accusation, and a basis for counterattack if necessary" (Manning, 1978c:83). This attitude toward rules, seen in the light of individualistic perceptions of real police work, was perceived by Manning to provide one of the bases of police culture:

> The manipulation of the rules that takes place among horizontal cliques, typically partners in a area car, crew in the reserve room, or a team of people working plain clothes, allows lower participants to decrease the uncertainty in rule-enforcement and to protect themselves so that things don't come back (Manning, 1978c:87).

Clique formation became a loosely coupling mechanism for the avoidance of administrative oversight, and permitted the individualistic notion of police work to be sustained in spite of burdensome department policy manuals and SOPs.

The individualist conception of police work has also been described by Manning (1979) in his description of the "master detective" as a metaphor of police work:

> In detective work, the conventional metaphor is the 'super investigator' who encounters a crime, seeks clues, persons (witnesses, suspects, informants), motives, opportunities, weapons and other physical evidence, assembles the facts, correctly adduces a conclusion, and names a villain (Manning, 1979:665).

In related research, Manning distinguished between organizational and individual models of narcotics case management. Deeply seated ideas of individualism affected the way in which narcotics work was distributed in an agency. Cases were handled individually as special assignments. They were not "officially" opened and closed, but were assigned to and under the control of the investigator. Officers took pride in their individual skills in solving cases, and hoarded their work from other detectives. Cases were closed when detectives wanted them to be closed. They were "in effect self-initialed, self-defined, and self-closed." Informants were known only to particular investigators. Any advantage that might have accrued from organizational cooperation were absent in the individualized model of case management.

Manning juxtaposed the individual-centered investigation model against an organization-centered model, which he described as a sharply different image of case processing. In the organization-centered model, cases were routinely assigned, supervisors provided prior approval for buys and raids, and the use of informants required approval, while their performance was evaluated and maintained in a central file. From the point of view of effectiveness and efficiency, the organization-based model was a superior model, but from the point of view of the investigator, the individual-based model was consistent with cop cultural norms.

Manning's distinction between organizational and individual models is central to understanding the extent to which individualism infuses police work. The organization model stresses efficiencies of bureaucratic control, in which the individual is at best accorded a quasi-professional status in the organization. It is a model in which ideas of organizational design and structure coordinate (read "are intended to control") the behavior of members of the organization.

The organizational model is, by cops' individualistic credo, most emotionally unsatisfying. Officers are motivated, perhaps actualized is a better word, by their ability to use personal skills to identify and capture a bad guy. They want to see, feel, taste, and smell the world around them, and they want to act on their sixth sense of things. They loathe the thought of spending their working hours behind the partitions of a cubicle. The image of the frontier cop, the lone sheriff protecting Dodge City with his six-gun, carries freight with this crowd. Cogs in the machine they are not, and cogs they will not become.

The ideological combatants are clear: on the one hand is the bureaucratic organization, ubiquitous in the public sector because most people strongly believe that bureaucracy is the appropriate form for public service delivery. Yet, cops are often conservative to the bone, and individual authority and responsibility are central to American style conservatism. Their task environment plays to their individualism: it is characterized by unpredictable events whose resolution are sometimes facilitated by quick thinking and metaphorical shooting from the hip. Further, contemporary police reformers have inadvertently increased the need for individual officers to be self-resourceful in their daily activities: the shift in the United States from two-person to one-person patrol cars, done in the name of organizational efficiency, places a heavier burden on individual officers to be on-the-spot problem-solvers.

It might appear odd to think of cops, perhaps the occupational group most ideologically associated by large sectors of the public as a potential threat to traditional individualistic liberties, as a bulwark of American individualism. Yet it is their fierce sense of individual turf control, dominion, and beat responsibility that has challenged, and had held at bay, the encroaching authority of mass bureaucracy across the policing industry throughout the past 100 years.

Today, individualism is a way of thinking that is making a dramatic comeback in managerial police philosophies. Advocates of community-based policing prevalent in any police departments celebrate creative, customized police work, as Skolnick and Bayley (1986) colorfully described the new policing. The metaphor of the individual cop has endured among American police, and in the current era enjoys a resurgence of support: a myth in the process of actualization.

Gamesmanship and the Paradox of Accountability

In this concluding section I will present the accountability problem in terms of games theory. This perspective allows us to see the profound problems that we create in contemporary accountability efforts.

Police organizations have a historically abysmal record of accountability (Kappeler, Sluder & Alpert, 1994). Indeed, it might be said that accountability has been the central problem of the police throughout the American history of police organizations. In this section, I will discuss accountability in terms of gamesmanship. I do this to develop the argument that accountability is a chimera, that is, that accountability cannot occur in precisely those circumstances that mobilize citizen frustration and distrust. Consider the following description of a game-theoretic situation (Harmon, 1995:182):

> At each stage each of us will simultaneously trying to render himself or herself unpredictable to the other; and each one of us will also be relying on the knowledge that the other will be trying to make himself or herself unpredictable in forming his or her own predictions (MacIntyre, 1984:97).

As Harmon (1995) further notes, in the ordinary give-and-take of social and work relations, there is not only one but several games going on at the same time. Their relationship to each other renders unpredictable the outcomes for each one of them—oftentimes success in one is deliberately occluded by the winner; one does not want to reveal a winning strategy to a competitor.

This game metaphor is particularly apt for street-level police work, in which police seek out wrong-doers and traffic violators, investigate suspicious circumstances and question hostile people, and try to differentiate between suspects who would prefer that their wrongdoing go unnoticed and citizens that want to be left alone. The game is played out in an interpersonal field of unfolding contingencies, in which the behavior, guilt, or innocence of a suspect—and the potential for danger—is often revealed grudgingly, a piece at time. The behavior of the police is heavily contingent on the actions that unfold around them.

The problem of the game, of course, is that those unfolding actions are not known ahead of time. Simply put, the problem is this: How can a cop be held responsible for his or her behavior when there is not a clear idea of what behavior is expected? The paradox unfolds: the greater and more elaborate the accountability systems for police officers, the greater the likelihood they will be violated, and the greater the likelihood that cop culture will loosely couple itself from management culture in order to protect officers from accountability.

The way in which police managers respond to this paradox is itself one of the central problems with police accountability systems: they tend to try to control police behavior by telling police what they should not do. Standard Operating Procedure (SOP) manuals provide extensive guidelines regarding what police should not do in particular situations, but are not constructive regarding what police should do (Walker, 1990; Wilson, 1968). Yet SOP manuals are the primary means through which individual officers are "held accountable" for their actions; through written guidelines they provide a basis for the sanctioning of officers when guidelines are violated. Consequently, police personnel systems tend to use punishment strategies to enforce departmental procedures and policies. Put plainly, they try to scare cops into behaving in predictably appropriate ways in the face of fundamentally unpredictable situations.

Internal affairs and citizens' review boards tend to generate similar problems of accountability. Both review mechanisms operate with a similar logic: officers will behave if they are threatened by sufficiently severe sanctions. But deterrence, like accountability, only makes sense if cops are involved in predictable, controllable situations, which they are not. The inevitable outcome of deterrent oversight of the police is a more insular street-level culture, as cops put it, more cover your ass.

Individual-level accountability has profound implications for the development and sustenance of police culture. First, it misdirects problems away from structural or organizational sources and toward individuals. As subsequent reviews of the Knapp commission have noted, every 20 years New York confronts a dramatic, headline-making exposé of police corruption and a commission is called that uncovers widespread wrongdoing. A few individuals are punished, and things return to normal until the next wave of corruption is splashed across the front pages of the *New York Times*. The intense focus on individual responsibility prohibits structural assessments of problems that might create the conditions for their resolution.

Second, to protect themselves from external prying into their affairs, line officers must develop strategies to protect themselves. Control is in terms of personal accountability and is inevitably punitive. Cops, of course, will try to protect themselves. Efforts aimed at the external imposition of accountability will always engender the paradox of personal accountability: the more officers are held responsible for the outcomes of police-citizen encounters, the more difficult it will be to hold them administratively accountable. The corollary paradox is that administrative and citizen-based efforts to control accountability of individual officers will result in increased strengthening of the police culture and diminish the ability of administrators to hold individual officers accountable for their behavior.

Endnote

[1] See Lakoff and Johnson, 1980, for a discussion of the metaphorical relationship between the physical self and the way in which we envision our social and physical world.

21   The Truth Game

> When I was younger I used to play the truth game . . .
> The object of the game is simple: I have to explain
> to an imaginary black-robed square (His Honor) how
> Officer William A. Morgan *knows* that those men are
> committing a criminal act. If the judge finds that I
> didn't have sufficient probable cause to stop, detain,
> and search my man, then I lose the game. Illegal
> search and seizure—case dismissed.
>
> I usually beat the game whether it's imaginary or for
> real. My courtroom demeanor is very good, pretty
> articulate for an old-time copper, they say. And such
> a simple honest kisser. Big innocent blue eyes. Juries
> loved me (Wambaugh, 1973:3).

In his fictional account, Joseph Wambaugh provides a glimpse into
the way a street officer reconciles his instincts, his ironic common sense,
with legal constraints embodied in due process laws. How does an officer convince a jury that his knowledge, though not articulable, is sure?
He continues:

> I could explain to my imaginary jurist but never to a real one about the
> instinct—the stage in the business when, like an animal, you can feel
> you've got one, and it can't be explained. You feel the truth, and you
> know. Try telling that to the judge, I thought, try explaining that some-
> time (Wambaugh, 1973:3).

There are many variations to the truth game. Questionable consent,
the timing of the arrest, harassment, illegal searches, judge-shopping, perfunctory review, and police falsification and misrepresentation of evi-

289

dence, all may be used to circumvent due process provisions of the Fourth Amendment. In this chapter I will explore these dimensions of the game and their place in police culture.

Why does the truth game occur? Sutton (1991) has discussed in detail the dimensions of the game, and his work merits consideration here. Officers develop elaborate subterfuges in order to acquire a warrant signed by a magistrate, showing particularity and probable cause. The formal search process is embedded in administrative process, and some officers simply do not have the patience for bureaucracy—they want to be engaged in crime-fighting activity, not waiting around for signatures and making appointments with court officers. Administrative process was particularly difficult for older officers. Citing one officer, Sutton noted that younger officers were accustomed to the formal process: they grew up with it. However, "If they operated under the law twenty years ago, then search warrants are kind of winked at more than anything else, and I think they gripe about it" (Sutton, 1991:435).

The conflict was not simply generational. At the most fundamental level, Sutton argued that it was a conflict between the police's "crime control" values and court pressures for legal justice. Cops' values put the apprehension and conviction of criminals foremost, and the court's administrative model of justice placed emphasis on legal considerations that weighed the behavior of the police against unwarranted invasions of privacy.

Cops develop strategies for circumventing the legal rigors of due process. Consider consent. Consent is one of the exceptions to the warrant requirement. Consent is a common defense by officers when they have not received a warrant. Sutton related the following exchange by a judge and a police officer, in which the officer had used consent to enter a house:

Judge: What did the man say, when you said that you wanted to come in and look around?

Officer: [He said] Oh, be my guest, come on in.

Judge: What happened?

Officer: Well, I walked in.

Judge: And what did you see on the coffee table?

Officer: I saw an ounce of heroin, fifty condoms, and a scale.

Judge: So it's your testimony that this man gave you consent to enter?

Officer: Oh, yes, your honor! (Sutton, 1991:438).

Many judges, Sutton observes, are concerned about the truthfulness of the testimony they obtain from officers. Yet they realize that they have limited control, that officers will protect each other on the stand. Moreover, some judges tacitly support the use of tainted testimony, and are complicitous in illegal police testimony.

Dimensions of the Truth Game

Barker, Friery, and Carter (1994) identified three general patterns of police lying (see also Barker & Carter, 1994). *Accepted lies* are those that are deemed necessary because they assist in fulfilling the police mission. *Tolerated lies* are those that simplify the explanation of police discretionary decisions. *Deviant lies* are those that violate the procedural or substantive law, or departmental regulations, and may protect officers in the pursuit of illegitimate goals. In research conducted by Barker and his colleagues, 83 percent of the police respondents thought lies and deceptive practices were moderately acceptable, and 58 percent found deviant lies to be acceptable when told for legitimate ends. Striking in this finding is that such a high percentage would reveal this secretive element of the police culture through a questionnaire survey. The findings reveal that support for deception is widespread among the police. The truth game—the subversion of truth for a righteous purpose—is common and culturally legitimated.

Lies are a multi-purpose tool for police officers. Particular types of lies are sufficiently pervasive to be considered as cultural elements (Manning, 1978). Lies are verbal strategies in a police officers cultural tool kit for solving disputes dealing with circumstances otherwise difficult to resolve. Manning (1978:248-249) has noted several such circumstances: when legal constraints or public attitudes prohibit officers from what they perceive to be proper action, when police are required to successfully intervene in disputes, and when patrolmen seek to avoid disciplinary action. Lying also provides a means to cover for oneself or another officer in circumstances where the truth would invoke administrative wrath. Placebos—generally harmless lies that are in the best interest of the person duped by them, and blue lies—lies to control the behavior of an individual, serve to extend the police officer's ability to control their beat.

Skolnick (1982) observed that deception of the courts, defendants, defense attorneys, and even prosecutors is a routine practice in some agencies. Deception, he argued, is a culturally supported norm, and has an important place in police work.[1] He suggested that lies allowed police to resolve inherent tensions between crime control and due process. A typology of deceptive practices, composed of testimonial, investigative, and interrogatory types, enabled officers to maintain the legal illusion of due process while maintaining their crime-control focus. All served the same point: to increase the likelihood that a suspect will be found guilty in a court of law in order to justify an arrest.

Arrest Lies

The police, Chevigny (1969) contended, are of necessity involved in ambiguous arrests. Yet they have to construct legitimating accounts of their behavior when the arrest is reviewed by the prosecutor. He argues that three cover charges, disorderly conduct, resisting arrest, and felonious assault, are legal lies that are used to cover instances of street abuse. Cover charges contribute to police solidarity: all officers have, he argues, shared the experience of using cover charges to "CYA"[2] in legally ambiguous police-citizen encounters.

Media Lies

Police may lie to further their crime control efforts. The following story is a type of lie—information withheld—told to reporters in order to make an arrest and solve a wider conspiracy. The story begins with an accident case:

> The man crossing the street had just drawn $5,000 in the form of 50 $100 bills from a bank on the south side of the street, intending to deposit this sum in another bank located on the north side of the street. His head down, busy counting his money, he had rushed directly in the path of a four-door nondescript car occupied by four young men. At the moment of impact, $100 bills went flying in the air. The driver of the car jammed on his brakes, stopped, and ran to the downed figure almost at once. The man sitting beside the driver opened his door, took one look around, observed a police car, jammed his fedora down on his head, and just walked away. The occupant seated behind the driver started out his door, spotted the approaching police car, and moved toward the driver, who was then bent over the fallen figure. The fourth occupant alighted from the right rear door with a suitcase in his hand, and started walking past the front of the car toward the sidewalk, when he spotted a few of the $100 bills. He retreated a few steps, stooped to pick up the bills closest to him, stuffed them in his pocket, and hurried to the sidewalk. He started up the block in an easterly direction and right into the arms of a foot patrolman, who turned him around, bag, bills, and all, to return to the car.

A subsequent investigation revealed that the suitcase contained both money and marijuana, and that the rear luggage compartment contained more such suitcases. Later, the author was questioned by news media.

> As I answered the reporters' questions and faced the newsreel cameras, one of the sharper newsmen asked about the fourth man—"You know, the one who got away"—and I promptly replied that there was no fourth

man and that as far as we were concerned the case was closed and the arrest of the three and the recovery made. The other reporters present took down the story as given, but I thought I caught a wink from my questioner.

After the news broadcast, a "tall, slim man wearing a small fedora walked into the squad room" and, identifying himself as the brother-in-law of one of the arrestees, asked what he could do to help his brother. Because the individual fit the description of the suspect, the storyteller asked him a "few innocent questions, with emphasis on the family rela-tionship, requested identification—including his name and address, and whether he had ever been arrested in New York City . . . Before he left, I had a team of Narcotics Squad detectives, who were present on another case, take a good look at the visitor."

> The big conspiracy that was broken up months later as a result of fol-lowing this man fully justified keeping this information from the media and renewed my faith in that particular reporter who so readily picked up my cue at that interview (Klein, 1968:158-161).

In this example, the deception appears mild, even innocent. This inci-dent shows how deception is a loosely coupling theme. Police main-tained an illusion of truthfulness in their media responsibilities in order to further their ability to do their work. Deception was linked to concrete police activity and performed the function of obscuring real police prac-tices from a powerful institutional actor, the media.

Warrant Lies

The Fifth Amendment requires the police to obtain a warrant prior to a search of a residence. The warrant must be grounded in particularity, stating the area to be searched. A police officer must swear to its truth-fulness under oath. However, many officers really do not know what they are going to find, and their information is highly questionable. They have to rely on the truthfulness of informants. Cops have to swear to a judge that they are absolutely confident in the truthfulness of a snitch. More likely, they swear that they have uncovered the information themselves that they actually received from a snitch. This is perjury.

Perjury is particularly likely with regard to drug crimes. To obtain a warrant, a police officer is obligated to swear to a judge that the infor-mation has been thoroughly investigated and that the search is justified on reasonable grounds. In practice, such investigation is rare; investiga-tion requires an officer's presence at the place to be searched, and a police officer's presence there will alert suspects of the police's interest.

Hence, officers tended to rely heavily on informants' testimony. Cops do not have to inform the court who the informant is or how the informant received the information. Police officers frequently rely on the testimony of those who would tell him anything to get out of his grasp. The result is that "Everybody involved—the policeman, his sergeant and lieutenant, the captain who approves the warrant application, the assistant district attorney who approves it, and the judge who grants him the warrant—knows that the policeman is perjuring himself" (Rubinstein, 1973:385).

Perjury of the warrant process, Rubinstein argued (1973), is commonplace. It allows the police to obtain information about vice activity, albeit of questionable value and in all likelihood somewhat fictitious in its story line. Vice information is obtained by people involved in criminal activity. The motivation of a snitch is always questionable—petty revenges, deals to hold criminal process in abeyance, money for a fix. To use a military metaphor, if detectives are the foot soldiers of the war on drugs, then snitches are the point men. It is not a comforting metaphor.

Perjury is a web of distortion that can come unraveled in the courtroom. Rubinstein described a gambling (numbers) case in which an officer's warrant perjury was uncovered by counsel for defense. Through piercing cross-examination, it was revealed that the officer's warrant stating that the residence had been surveilled and that he had established a working relationship with the snitch were both perjured. The case was subsequently dismissed by the judge. To minimize problems associated with the discovery of perjury, sergeants will rely on particular officers comfortable during examination who are unlikely to expose a perjured warrant on the stand (Rubinstein, 1973).

Officers also job-shop to find a judge sympathetic to cops and flexible in their warrant demands. Warrants require that the place to be searched be specified, and that the object of the search be stated. By requiring a judge's signature on a warrant, the law ensures that an independent and impartial observer, the judge, believes that probable cause exists; that the crime occurred, that the person probably did it, and that the place searched is being searched on real evidence.[3] Officers know that they can judge-shop to find judges willing to sign questionable warrants. Consider one judge's admonition to an officer carrying a weak warrant: "This is an illegal warrant, so don't shoot nobody; don't kill nobody; just get the . . . [drugs] of the street!" (Sutton, 1991:439).

Testimonial Lies

More troubling are cases of police perjury of testimony on the witness stand. Unlike judge-shopping and administrative searches that play the truth game fast and loose in order to uncover criminal culpability, perjury is the intentional subversion of the intent of the law for the purposes of gaining a guilty verdict. The intent of perjured testimony is clear—obtain a guilty verdict when guilt is legally questionable. How frequent is perjury? Barker (1978), in his research on a police department in a small southern city, suggested that it was widespread. When officers were asked about the percentage of officers that had lied in court, officers reported that about 23 percent had done so. Moreover, only 28 percent reported that they would always report another officer for perjury. This pervasiveness suggests that support for perjury is a cultural phenomenon.

Skolnick: Mapp and the Truth Game

In a revealing piece, Skolnick (1982) discusses testimonial deception by the police. A study conducted by Columbia law students attempted to assess the effects of the 1961 *Mapp* decision[4] regarding the exclusionary rule on police behavior and the discovery of evidence in New York. The exclusionary rule prohibits the disclosure of evidence in violation of the Fourth Amendment. Prior to *Mapp*, evidence from unlawful or illegal searches was still admissible in court. After *Mapp*, it was not. New York was among the last of the states to adopt the exclusionary rule into state law. The findings of the research suggested that *Mapp* had little impact on police reform, but instead led to the fabrication of evidence in order to get around the exclusionary requirements. The data particularly illustrate the loose coupling process and how it changes to adapt to changes in due process law. The following table is reproduced from Skolnick's research.

How Evidence Found	Before *Mapp*		After *Mapp*	
	Number	%	Number	%
Narcotics Bureau				
Hidden on Person	35	(92)	3	(08)
Dropped/thrown on ground	17	(28)	43	(72)
Uniform				
Hidden on Person	31	(77)	9	(23)
Dropped/thrown on ground	14	(40)	21	(60)
Plainclothes				
Hidden on Person	24	(86)	4	(14)
Dropped/thrown on ground	11	(39)	17	(61)

Source: Skolnick, 1994:122.

The table (page 295) reveals changing patterns in the collection of evidence before and after *Mapp*. To gauge proportional differences, I calculated percentages and added them to the table. Pre- and post-*Mapp* differences are striking. Before *Mapp*, only 28 percent of the Narcotic Bureau arrests were based on drugs found on the ground. After *Mapp*, it was 72 percent, nearly three times the rate. For uniform and plainclothes officers, the ratio is lower, but still show an approximate 50 percent increase in the ratio of drugs found on the ground. If, as some argue, criminals rationally adapt their behavior in order to take advantage of the criminal law, why then would criminals, as suggested by these numbers, modify their behavior in such a way to dramatically increase their likelihood of arrest?

Skolnick concluded that officers were fabricating evidence in order to circumvent the rule of law under *Mapp*. This type of evidentiary fabrication is now appropriately called "dropsy," suggesting that individuals caught for the possession of drugs did not have it on their person, but were simply throwing it away. Moreover, they were throwing it away next to their bodies and in plain sight of the police. Perhaps the greatest culpability does not lie with the police, but with the courts, that they could sanction this silly fiction as a legally honest retelling of an arrest, that the courts would believe that drug users would cast their accursed contraband at the last moment away from their bodies, as if it were a scourge and they could be freed of its damning implications by putting it on the ground beside them for all to see, as if a police officer just might not see.

Police Proactivity and the Problem of Truth

Drug-related crimes place particular hardships on the process of gathering evidence. The absence of complainants and voluntary witnesses means that the police cannot operate in their traditional reactive role, waiting for citizens to call and report a crime. Reactive means that criminal investigation is prompted by a call from a citizen who needs assistance or wants to report a crime. Reactive policing facilitates the evidence gathering process. If it is a violent crime, the person that called frequently is both witness and victim. The presence of witnesses, a victim that will testify, and the ability to prove that a crime has occurred dramatically increase the likelihood that an arrest results in a conviction. Moreover, patrol is designed for reactive policing. Officers drive around in assigned geographic areas officially going nowhere in particular, a patrol style called "random preventive patrol" and they respond rapidly to high priority calls for assistance after a dispatcher has relayed the citizen's call to them.

Police proactivity is sharply different. Proactivity means that police, acting on their own initiative, develop information about crime and strategies for its suppression. Victimless crimes—victimless because there is no victim calling a dispatcher, who in turn sends out a patrol car to respond to a crime—require the police to develop their own intelligence about crime. Victimless crimes focus on the enforcement of drug laws, gambling, prostitution, and other areas of morality. Police must act proactively to enforce these laws—that is, they must develop their own sources of information to discover crime. This is very hard to do—who is going to tell a police officer that they are breaking the law?

That due process is more complicated for proactive crimes concerned with public morals than in reactive situations is revealed in analyses of prosecutorial decisions to drop cases (Walker, 1994). Examining legally serious crimes, Walker found that prosecutors tended to drop cases prior to trial for relatively straightforward reasons, the lack of witnesses and victims. For these crimes, problems associated with due process are so slight as to be statistically immeasurable, falling below one percent.

How about victimless crimes—morals crimes where there is no victim to act as complainant? When Walker examined prosecutorial discretion in drug cases he found that about 30 percent of the abandoned cases were rejected for due process reasons. The implications were clear: enforcement of morals violations was difficult within the sanctions of due process. Police find that they have little choice but to violate constitutionally afforded protections in order to enforce drug crimes (see also Skolnick, 1994:269-295).

Manning's Paradox

Police are under considerable public pressure to do something about criminal activity. Currently, this pressure is particularly intense with regard to drug crimes. Yet their ability to actually accomplish something is limited, and creates a tension between enforcement dreams and realistic capability. Manning (1977) characterized this dilemma as a conflict between the desired and the improbable, and put it in the following proposition:

> To the degree that formally constituted control agencies are faced with a paradox between what is formally expected of them in the community and what is possible, they will tend to retreat from a collective definition of morality, the law, and social order (Manning, 1977:5).

Of particular interest here is his use of the word retreat. Retreat to where, and why? The paradox is that public support for police anti-drug activity is a link in the production of police solidarity, the same solidarity that protects the police from public scrutiny. That is, public support for the police has the unexpected consequence of intensifying police efforts to hide their anti-drug activity.

I will discuss this complex paradox in terms of police proactive anti-drug activity. The police are bombarded with public messages to "clean up our cities" or "make the streets safe for our kids," messages to which they contribute to no small degree. These high-minded sentiments[5] drive the public perception that the police must act harshly against drug activity in all its forms. The public use and distribution of illicit drugs have been political lightning rods for decades now, and reveal an amazing longevity in byte-oriented campaign strategy at all levels.

Unfortunately, the police cannot do much about drugs. They can generate large numbers of arrests in inner cities where drugs are nearly as common as lead paint, but that is about it. The police can do little to actually stem the use and sale of drugs, and what little they do often places them squarely on the other side of the law (Marx, 1988; Skolnick, 1994; Miller, 1987). Without a complainant, their legal options are limited. Nobody's going to complain to the police that their crack was too weak or that their weed was cut with oregano.

If police want to do something about drugs, they have to know the merchandise. They cannot just buy small quantities from small-time dealers. They have to become a link in the distribution of drugs. They have to work their way up. They have to be able to recognize good shit, and to do so they have to know how it smells and how it tastes. They have to be prepared to introduce new users to dealers, and they have to buy and sell (Caldero, p.c.).

This, of course, is not an image of drug enforcement that most citizens would find commendatory. It is illegal. Cops must consequently avoid the harsh glare of external observation that would reveal (1) that they were frequently in violation of the law, and (2) that they were doing exactly what the public wanted to do, generating arrests for drugs, the only way they can—fabricating evidence, dropsy, lying on the witness stand, entrapment, in a word, by being more criminally sophisticated than the criminals. Simply put, the police are doing exactly what we want them to do. And they are doing their best to avoid being punished for it in the process.

Proactive drug intervention, consequently, is one of the contemporary drivers of loosely coupling elements in the culture of the police. Only by protecting themselves from exterior observation from management brass and from the public and its media representatives can the police do what is expected of them. They have to, as Manning put it, retreat from a collective definition of morality, the law, and social order. Every time the police make a drug arrest and disguise their illegal activity, we sustain comfortable illusions: we publicly bitch about how the constitution coddles criminals, without having to acknowledge that our bitching has real effects on police behavior. Nor do we have to look at the implications for democracy in America, as due process becomes increasing irrelevant except as an afterthought, when the time comes for a cop to cover his or her butt. And the police are driven further underground, into their culture that, with strong barriers erected against us the public, they can protect themselves from us, the public, for doing what we the people want them to do.

Manning and Redlinger:
The Ethics of Narcotics Interdiction

The pressures on the police to violate the criminal law in order to do narcotics enforcement should not be underestimated; they strongly influence enforcement activity and cannot be separated from it. Manning and Redlinger (1977) provide a chilling account of the pressures on officers to break the law, and how those pressures correspond to real instances of law-breaking and the obstruction of justice. Pressures to violate the law that are internal to the organization accumulate at the lowest level of enforcement, the line-officer or detective. Internal pressures stem from desires of officers for salary and promotion, implicit and explicit quotas (all units, they observe, have implicit quotas), administrative directives, desires of officers to maintain self-esteem in their work performance (read drug arrests), and unreasonable ideas of what they are able to accomplish.[6] Pressures to obstruct justice stem from efforts to protect informants, to create information through threat of prosecution, and to suppress information on cases pursued by other officers in order to promote one's own arrests.

Pressures to obstruct justice are strong. High-minded political platitudes to do something about drugs are translated through the chain of command as tacit acceptance to violate the law in order to make arrests. Media and prosecutorial pressures can also push officers to generate arrests. Community associations can place ideology ahead of the law. Grand juries encourage high-profile busts to show the public that something is being done about crime. These pressures coalesce in an "ambience" that "underscores the virtues of avoidance of the more obvious requirements of law enforcement" (Manning & Redlinger, 1977:157).

Patterns of agent corruption are as varied as are the pressures for obstruction and illegal behavior. Officers can take bribes, or protect informants by "making the case badly."

> A police officer who is skillful or experienced enough can write an affidavit that appears to be very strong, but is still open-ended enough to work in favor of a defendant when coupled with appropriate testimony from the arresting officer . . . The (Knapp) commission learned that it was not uncommon to pay policemen for such favors as lying under the oath and procuring confidential police records . . . (Manning & Redlinger, 1977:157-158).

Police drug involvement may take a variety of forms. Officers work in an environment where drugs are readily available, and they may use drugs. The notion is not farfetched: after all, obtaining drugs is their work. In some cases, Manning and Redlinger observed cops trafficking in drugs. Conspiracy to deal, as Manning and Redlinger note, is quite illegal, yet it is a requirement of work for undercover operatives.

Illegal searches and seizures are a constitutionally unwholesome side effect of contemporary drug intervention efforts. Officers may "see" drugs in plain sight and use that as a basis for a subsequent search of the property. Smelling drugs is also admissible for probable cause, even though there is no way to substantiate in subsequent court appearances that there was in fact an odor. Officers "flake" (add drugs) or "pad" (increase the quantity of drugs found) to accelerate the legal severity of the charge. The authors interviewed one police officer in Washington, D.C. who claimed that he had never made an arrest without flaking a suspect. Finally, the use of confidential informants has a number of consequences for agencies. Informants reverse the normal flow of criminal sanctions—informants are allowed to work off their charges through negotiations with prosecutors and thus obtain their freedom.

How are we to think about Manning and Redlinger's (1977) damning indictment of narcotics enforcement? One might retreat to high-mindedness, arguing that the police have to be turned loose to keep drugs out of the candy store, or like-minded rubbish. Such high-mindedness, of course, overlooks all of the important issues. For example, if the police are supposed to stop law-breaking, then they should not be breaking the law themselves, and by becoming a link in the production of drug crime, they are the ones putting drugs in the candy store.

Finally, one might suggest that violating officers are so-called "rotten apples" that should be fired from the force. Yet, the pressures associated with narcotics interdiction emerge from the process of supervision and the translation of political pressures through the chain-of-command.

Implicit pressures on the police to violate the law in the name of the law have a powerful mobilizing effect on the police subculture. Officers have to protect themselves from too close scrutiny, to develop barriers from external oversight. Thus, high-minded political philosophy drives the police further underground, retrenching the police culture. And the drug market is expanded by drug operatives who depend on the paradoxical illusion of its suppression for their market stability.

Langworthy: Deception and the Construction of Crime

Beyond proactivity, the police occasionally construct crime in order to uncover wrongdoing. Setting aside the question of whether we would all be better off without the police encouraging criminal activity, the police make strategic use of their skills and knowledge of crime to construct situations that invite the commission of crime. Through strategies called sting operations, the police invite individuals to commit crimes in a recordable way, to increase the likelihood of conviction for crimes otherwise difficult to identify and prosecute.

Theft is a crime for which police may set up sting operations. Uniform Crime Reports and victimization studies routinely report that theft is infrequently reported to the police, and even when it is reported, arrest is uncommon. The ratio of arrests for reported burglaries is about 1 to 10. Allowing for actual burglaries, the ratio is about 1 to 20; some estimate that the ratio between convictions and actual burglaries may approach 1 in 100. In other words, traditional reactive policing methods are ineffective in preventing burglary.

Many agencies are exploring proactive alternatives for theft enforcement. Police anti-fencing operations, commonly called stings, are used by an increasing number of departments. In these operations, police are presented as fences. Through covert use of tapes and other identifying techniques, stolen merchandise is identified. At the close of the sting operation, burglars are arrested, and with good fortune substantial quantities of stolen goods are returned to their rightful owners.

The Birmingham, Alabama, Police Department initiated a sting operation in 1985. A storefront operation was set up to catch stolen automobiles. The operation resulted in the recovery of 90 stolen cars and 66 offenders. At its conclusion in February 1986, the operation was celebrated as a success.

Langworthy (Langworthy, 1989) decided to assess the program. Of particular concern to Langworthy was the impact of the sting operation on existing levels of auto theft. His analysis resulted in findings less enthusiastic than those of the police department. The daily number of auto thefts increased by 4.46 autos per day during the sting and decreased to their previous level after the sting ended. Though he acknowledged that the finding was marginally significant, the conclusion was clear—the sting operation appeared to result in an increase in auto thefts. From a public relations standpoint, the project was a success, but when one considers the goal of lowering incidence of auto theft, the project was a failure. One is reminded of the medical witticism "The operation was a success but . . ."

In a follow-up paper, Langworthy and LeBeau (1992) assessed the spacial dispersion of auto thefts before and during the sting. Troubling was their finding that crime had changed its traditional geography. In his analysis of crime patterns, the authors found that the sting caused crime to displace, that is, criminals changed their criminal habitat to the area around the storefront operation. They noted that "the theft sites tended to be clustered around the sting operation rather than dispersed," and that the "density of the thefts clearly and abruptly decayed within short distances of the storefront" (Langworthy & LeBeau, 1992:547). Simply put, the sting operation had created a new class of unsuspecting victim.

One might think that the courts would not look favorably on the participation of the police in ongoing crime activity. However, this is generally not the case. Due process of law is violated only if the government acts on a wholly innocent individual and causes him to commit a crime that he never would have contemplated in the absence of government intervention (Silver, 1988). The law permits the police to tempt individuals into crime, and if the sting is successful, the trickery has paid off.[7] The police are encouraged to be deceptive, to lie, and to trick in order to achieve success (Marx, 1988). Even chiefs will lie in a wide variety of circumstances when they think deception is appropriate, such as taps and undercover investigations (Bouza, 1990).

Klockars: On Being Bad and Good

A paradox characterizes sting operations. Klockars captured the paradox and its loosely coupling consequence: "The more successful police are in appearing really bad, the more successful they must be in appearing good." By this he meant that:

> The core of the police role in sting operations is packed with behaviors which go against conventional norms of respectable behavior: lies, deceptions, concealments, and betrayals. At the conclusion of the sting operation these behaviors require a public accounting (Klockars, 1991b:258).

The public accounting to which he referred is a high-minded community relations effort that emphasized police effectiveness and efficiency, that their solution brought much gain to the communities, and that their work helped stem some community crime scourge. This end of the operation was marked by a dramaturgy of enforcement, a display put on for public consumption (Manning, 1977).

Klockars recognized the need to conclude the operation in a publicly palatable way. The end of the sting was the moment when "the police reconcile their behavior with public norms of respectability and create impressions of efficiency" (Klockars, 1991b:258). That this is a dramaturgical process is revealed in Klockars sharp critique of two federal documents summarizing 62 sting operations in 39 American cities since 1974, titled "Taking the Offensive and What Happened." High-minded claims that the stings had suppressed crime, he observed, could not be sustained on thoughtful examination of the data. He identified six flaws in the positive spin put on the sting operations by the documents: (1) the claim that "very high conviction rate" was no higher than ordinary conviction rates, (2) the official claim that subjects were considerably older and thus more likely to be career criminals was a mask to avoid arresting juveniles and alienating local community support, (3) the claim that one in five were fences was an exaggeration of the data, (4) the data itself was subjectively interpreted. Finally, (5) there was little evidence that stolen property was returned to the people from which it was initially stolen, in spite of claims to the contrary.

There is another issue not covered in Klockars' analysis. Police officers who carry out stings are openly deceptive in their interactions with the public, in the hopes that they will uncover criminal wrongdoing. It is a leap of faith to think that the police can be encouraged to engage in trickery and deception in police-citizen encounters, especially those sting-type encounters where there is a clear attempt to create recordable criminal behavior, and then to think that they will be choirboys in the courtroom where the stakes—their job, the case, and possibly their employment—are much higher. Yet judges make such leaps of faith daily.

When cops are rewarded for creating crime, what kind of message are we sending them? What officers are learning is how to play the truth game—first with criminals, next with the courts. With criminals, the truth game lies in convincing them that they—the police, too—are thievish crooks. With the courts, the truth game lies in convincing them that they—the police, too—are honest, God-fearing truth-seekers. If they fail at either, the game is over. The truth game, encapsulated by the nature of their work, is an invitation to ethical chaos. It is no wonder that the police retreat to their own, that they distrust the courts, the criminals, and the public. Their secrecy allows us not to have to recognize that they are doing exactly what we want them to do, for which we would have to punish them.

Endnotes

[1] "Practically speaking, it is impossible to enforce consensual crime statutes—bribery, drug-dealing, prostitution—without employing deception." (Skolnick, 1982:53).

[2] Cover Your Ass.

[3] Many observers of the courts confusedly believe that officers have to get a warrant even when they know that evidence will disappear during the warrant-obtaining process. This is simply untrue: Officers, fearing that evidence will be destroyed; flushed, or whatever, may secure a residence while they await the receipt of the warrant. Moreover, if they witness illegal behavior while legally involved in the securing of a residence, the warrant requirement, they may make a legal arrest.

[4] 367 U.S. 643 (1961).

[5] What exactly does the phrase "make the streets safe for our kids" say? What streets are meant? The single largest danger on our streets are automobiles, not drugs which are rarely present on the streets of middle-class America. Moreover, our kids are more than likely the problem—they are the group most implicated in DUI, in traffic accidents, and in crime.

[6] To the extent that the court has a standard to which they hold the police, it is called the "shock the conscience" test. This test emerged from a case, *Rochin v. California*, in which the police engaged in a warrantless search, choked the defendant to induce vomiting for suspected drugs, and finally has his stomach involuntarily pumped. The shock the conscience test, however, is a moral test, and does not guide the behavior of the courts in specific cases. For this reason, it has been of little use in recent years.

22

Cop Deterrence and the Soft Legal System

The 1979 film *Alien* told the story of a crew of space voyagers that encountered an abandoned spaceship in some deep emptiness in space. On the ship, a powerful alien was discovered; it was a creature of incredible ferocity. Its saliva dissolved metal, and its elongated skull-contoured visage harbored two sets of jaws, an inner set that extended an additional foot beyond the outer set to lash out and lacerate its prey. Reptilian in appearance, it moved with astonishing speed. Clever, it attacked in coordinated field maneuvers, and would strike suddenly with cold, deadly deliberation. It had an astonishing capacity to kill.

It was intelligent. The aliens had been the crew of a derelict ship designed in their fierce image, that through some accident had been severely damaged. In spite of astonishing odds, the aliens had survived. They did not strike against the humans until after they had been safely transported away from the ship.

I have meditated on the alien. Would such a creature have a philosophy? Would it imagine that its own life was a matrix of available opportunities, goals, bright futures? That it weighed its options and sought that which, for it, was best? That it, too, entered into a social contract, working with its own kind to further its self-interest? That it selected options based on some reasoned calculus of pain and pleasure? Would it believe itself free to select its destiny, unfettered by the obvious ontology of its destructive physiology? Would it find its identity in its amazing capacity to kill, or in some hope tethered to a dream of future tranquility? Could it encircle itself with philosophies about its essential goodness? Could it truly delude itself into believing that it was peaceful?

This is the knowledge that cops have. Their cynicism is driven by too keen an awareness of us. They recognize us for what we are; dangerous, unpredictable, violent, savagely cunning, a thin veneer of self-deluding civilization over an ontology that created a genuinely vicious top dog in a world of capable and talented reptilian, mammalian, and pescian predators. They know that there is only one way to control the alien. Only direct coercion can control it. That, alone, it understands. The alien is deterred, not by reason or foresight, but by force. Superior firepower deters the alien. Deterrence is through power, by immediate implementation of overwhelming counter force before the alien has a chance to respond.

This is the police idea of deterrence. Deterrence does not come from threatening or reasoning; neither are effective, both expose weakness, an inability to bring sufficient force to end a wrong *now*. Deterrence is the opposite; one deters by the use of force, and thus we are deterred. For all our high-minded philosophies, our belief in our innate goodness, in the end we understand the use of force. Deterrence is immediate, slamming, final. It is the only way to deal with the predatory top dog of the evolutionary ladder. Deterrence does not threaten to bring about punishment, deterrence ends the threat. Nothing else will work; all else is weakness.

Consider the comments of an officer interviewed for the book *Cops*.

> What people don't understand is that there are street criminals out there now who are irretrievable predators that just get off—it's a sexual experience—on peoples' pain and on peoples' crying and begging and pleading. They get off on it. They love it.
>
> You're not going to scare them. There's nothing you can do to them. You've got to defeat them somehow. To talk to them about any sense of morality, they don't have any sense of morality, they don't have any sense of right and wrong (Baker, 1985:298).

Muir captures the spirit of deterrence in his description of Officer John Russo. Note in the description that the alien "they" in Russo's description is not all the public, only bad guys. Russo saw the world as:

> divided into two camps, the builders, who "like to see progress, and the "night people," the predators, the destroyers. On the "good side" were the "family men," who "hustled," were ambitious, had "pride," got the job done, could handle ruffians, kept their defenses up and their powder dry. On the other side was the enemy . . . (Muir, 1977:22).

The legal system does not deter. It is soft and full of bluster; it threatens and reasons. This is the cop's view. Few irritations are greater to line officers than the inability of the legal system to put bad guys away. Klein relates the following story.

In less than two days the assistant district attorney presented the people's airtight case. But then, for the next two weeks, the defense turned the court into a carnival, the like of which even the old-timers had never witnessed. Though at no time did defense counsel contest the primary facts of the crime as presented by "the people," the presiding judge, over the objections of the assistant district attorney, permitted introduction of every irrelevant and immaterial bit of evidence imaginable to justify the acts of the defendant . . . Defense counsel managed to make out the defendant as a martyr in the eyes of the jury, and with the judge's charge consistent with his attitude throughout the trial, the finding of "not guilty"—justifiable homicide—was no shock.

When, shortly thereafter, the judge retired from the bench to become a law partner of the defense counsel, some unkind persons drew some nasty inferences (Klein, 1968:124).

The perceived weakness of the courts has two corollaries, noted by Van Maanen (1978) below.

Corollary 1: The Legal System is Untrustworthy

This theme has been around for far longer than have due process protections, and may be a truly international theme shared by all police officers (Chevigny, 1995). Consider the following quote:

In this city, criminals, as a rule, are quickly detected, but it does not follow that their punishment is equally prompt and salutary. Had criminals the same dread of the judiciary as they have of the Detective, they would give New York a very wide berth. But as matters now stand, a "crook" finds comfort in the reflection that the vigilance of the Detective department will, in all probability, be counteracted by the lack of promptness and the absence of severity in the subsequent stages of his experiences with the officers of the law; at all events he feels certain that expiation is not swift or certain (Costello, 1972:411).

This quote is a description of a New York City detective, originally published in 1885. The argument is strikingly similar to contemporary grouses about due process: lack of support from the courts, lack of swift punishment, bad guys are walking the streets. This element of police culture was in place fully 75 years before due process issues came under the scrutiny of the Warren court in the 1960s.

Today, distrust of courts is solidly entrenched in police culture. Manning (1978b:12) notes the following principle of police culture: "The legal system is untrustworthy; policemen make the best decisions about guilt or innocence." This principle says many things. To say that the legal system is untrustworthy means that it will not back up a police officer. The legal system, vis-à-vis prosecutorial discretion, does what it does pretty well—it evaluates the viability of cases based on criteria of evidence and witnesses. That, however, is not a police cultural standard. The standard cops use comes from within the culture.

> His most meaningful standards of performance are the ideals of his occupational culture. The policeman judges himself against the ideal policeman as described in the occupational lore and imagery. What a "good policeman" does is an omnipresent standard (Manning, 1978b:11).

What is the standard? To get bad guys off the street. To use the law if it will work for them, and to use whatever tools cops have if the law will not. The ideal cop is trickier than the law. Cops know who is bad. When the courts disagree, it is a sorry day for the courts, a sad day for the public. That is the standard.

Corollary 2: Stronger Punishment Will Deter

A corollary theme, also cited by Manning in the same (1978b) research is that "stronger punishment will deter criminals from repeating their errors." It is not simply that the courts provide penalties, it is that police view deterrence in a fundamentally different way than the courts. For the courts, deterrence lies in the lawful delivery of severe penalties in accordance with state statute. Court deterrence is a fantasy of disinterested and predictable application of the law. For the police, deterrence is quite personal, and is embodied in immediate, concrete exercise of coercion to control out-of-kilter situations. Consider another of Muir's (1977) observations of Officer Russo:

> Russo had a sophisticated understanding of deterrence theory, earned in the two "toughest" high schools in town and at his father's knee: "Don't ever let anyone bully you, or they will keep right on bullying you." He understood the value of a harsh example: "a show of force is a deterrent" (Muir, 1977:25).

Courts do not need to react to an immediate show of force by a violent suspect, nor do they have to worry about maintaining control of unpredictable situations. Courtroom workgroups, the term for the long-term administrative affiliations between judges, prosecutors, and defense counsels, have smoothed most of the unpredictability out of their decisionmaking through plea bargaining, and once a suspect is in the courtroom they pose little danger. Deterrence for the workgroup is a theory of the effects of the application of the criminal code to a specific criminal and to those that take heed. Deterrence is acted out in plea bargaining, a tool that guarantees that virtually every charged person receives some sort of punishment without all the trouble of a trial. Because of plea bargaining, 95 percent of prosecuted cases end up with guilty pleas. The law is consistent.

For police, deterrence is not a theory. It is the concrete way problems are resolved. It is acted out as toughness on the street. Dangerous or troublesome offenders are isolated, harassed or arrested (Van Maanen, 1978). Deterrence is achieved by being tougher and smarter than criminals. Deterrence is the concrete ability to discourage behavior through sheer toughness and aggression. If the courts would adopt principles of cop deterrence, they could actually do something about crime.

Distributive vs. Legal Justice

Wilson (1968) observed that there were fundamental conflicts between the police and the courts, and he conceptualized the conflict as a difference in models of justice. The courts, Wilson argued, operate by legal justice. Decisions to carry a case forward are based on the prosecutor's estimation of the likelihood of conviction, based on the viability of the evidence and presence of witnesses. When conditions are not favorable for a conviction, prosecutors drop charges.

Police, in situations involving the public order, tend to make arrest decisions on principles of distributive and retributive justice. Particularly in misdemeanor encounters, officers make arrests when no other strategy resolves the problem a citizen is causing for them. An arrest is a decision of last recourse, Wilson argues, when some person simply will not accept the police officer's efforts to resolve some problem. Arrestees in such encounters are frequently not criminals, who often try to get along with the police because they already know they are in trouble and wish to minimize their danger. On the contrary, arrestees are "those shitheads out to prove that they can push everybody around" (Van Maanen, 1978:221).

In these encounters, an arrest occurs because someone is perceived to deserve it. Legal considerations are secondary and sometimes irrelevant. Precisely those individuals that most "need justice" from a distributive point of view are cases that will not be carried forward by prosecutors who are more interested in evidentiary considerations. Prosecutors thus ignore those cases that frequently have the most moral meaning to the police, those dealing with "assholes" (Van Maanen, 1978).

The Supreme Court is frequently blamed for the inability of arrests to result in convictions. This argument is astonishing given the extremely low percentage of cases that are successfully challenged because of due process considerations, less than one percent of all violent and property crimes (Walker, 1994; Maguire & Pastore, 1995). If police culture is founded on concrete assessments of their working habitat, then how can they believe so strongly that they are handcuffed by the law?

Police perceptions about the court do not stem from the negative impact of the court on actual cases, though that argument is frequently used by police advocates. Perceptions stem from the court's clear efforts to reign in police behavior in a wide range of efforts during the Warren era in the 1960s. The police viewed that court's decisions as a betrayal of trust. It is a sense of betrayal relived every time they read a suspect his or her rights. A sense of treachery is still felt strongly by many police officers today.

It would be hard to overestimate the distress caused by the Warren court and its invocation of the Fourteenth Amendment to provide due process protections for states individually. The following story underscores the sense of betrayal police have felt about these decisions. This story begins with a 14-year-old boy who is murdered after making a weapon and then demanding too much for it. Detectives bring in two boys, aged 11 and 13, and a .22 caliber rifle.

> I attempted to question the eleven-year-old first. My first few questions, as to name, address, age, school attended, with whom he lived, were answered grudgingly. From then on, his replies to any question were: "I didn't do nuttin," "I don't know nuttin" and "I don't gotta tell nobody nuttin, and ya can't make me. I'm a juvenile, and ya can't lay a hand on me."

The story continues with the questioning of the 13-year-old, from whom poured the entire story.

> As is required when juveniles are apprehended, the boy's parents were notified and were present when all the facts had been ascertained. The mother of the eleven-year-old, highly indignant that her little darling was accused of shooting out another boy's eye, clasped him to her ample bosom. The father stood dumbfounded for a few moments in honest disbelief, but as the enormity of the crime penetrated his first shock, and with me urging him to get the truth from the boy himself, he pushed his wife aside and gave the kid a clout across the side of the head that sent him flying in a crumpled heap to the far corner of the squad room. Then he went over, picked him up and, raising his hand again threateningly, said, "Talk!" In no time at all, through trembling lips, the whole story came tumbling forth.

> The Supreme Court has made little Willie's statement, "I don't gotta tell nobody nuttin," the law of the land (Klein, 1968:61).

23

The Petty Injustice and Everlasting Grudges[1]

Theme: Bullshit

Many observers of the police have noted the profound distrust line officers hold for administrators in their own organization. Never completely obsequious in the presence of managers, when street cops are in the locker room before or after a shift (and they do not think that back-stabbing management kiss asses are present) they let out their true feelings. And their most heartfelt feelings toward managers are seldom friendly or kind.

Picture this. Two officers enter the locker room. Disdain and cynicism crowd their language. Looking over their shoulders when someone walks in, they complain about the newest policy directive, the lack of support from the lieutenant, favoritism in an assignment, or the dismal story of some sad sack that joined the wrong clique and has spent the past three months eating the shit end of the sergeant's stick. The locker room can be a moody, cheerless place.

This sentiment is rarely seen by outsiders. Observers have described this sentiment in terms of cultural precepts like "Do not trust bosses to look out for your interests," or "Always cover your ass" (Reuss-Ianni, 1983:16). Even these precepts, strongly worded as they are, do not fully capture the depth of the sentiments officers hold toward administrators or to the rules that govern their behavior. Consider the following way in which an officer describes rules listed in the department's General Orders.

> 140 years of fuck-ups. Every time something goes wrong, they make a rule about it. All the directions in the force flow from someone's mistake. You can't go eight hours on the job without breaking the disciplinary code. . . . no one cares until something goes wrong. The job goes wild on trivialities (Manning, 1978c:79).

The aphorism "bosses don't look out for my interests" does not capture the dark tenor of Manning's quote. The mood describes the disposition of someone who has repeatedly confronted and been frustrated by triviality. The tone is almost sad, certainly tired, and suggests a job crowded by minutiae passing for consequence. It is a person enduring an endless river of bullshit.

If a term could be identified that captured the corrosive sentiment line officers have towards management's use of authority and invocation of rules, the word would be bullshit. There is simply no other term that cuts to the essence of the mixture of scorn and fear officers have for this ubiquitous characteristic of their work environment. Day in and day out, in roll call, responding to dispatchers, filling out paperwork, doing activity for the sergeant, and conforming to new policy directives, line officers deal with an interminable stream of bullshit.

The use of vulgarity as an ethnomethodological device to describe police work has an artfully conceived precedent. Van Maanen (1978) gave currency to the term "asshole" for describing a key element of officers' occupational outlooks toward particular types of citizens. The use of the term "asshole" as an analytic device, he argued, was essential: the term held a great deal of common-sensical meaning for officers, and any other analytic term substituted for it to satisfy academic sensibilities was a deceit.

Van Maanen observed that, from an ethnographic point of view, the use of the term suspicion was a betrayal. It lacked the clarity of meaning captured by the term "asshole," at once poignant and vile, brimming with scatological meaning. Officers described some citizens as assholes, because to officers that is what they were. To use another term captured neither the spirit, the intent, nor the stigmatizing power of the word "asshole."

Of similar scatological salience for describing line officer attitudes toward management brass is the term "bullshit." No term better reflects officers' perceptions of the use of authority and regulations by administrators. The term "bullshit" carries an essence perhaps a bit ripe for gentler readership, but satisfactorily pungent as a fair-minded description of the way officers view their rule-laden administrative environment. Bullshit, conceived as the capricious invocation of authority, is an inevitable and ubiquitous cultural feature of the rank structure of American police organizations. It inheres in the militaristic chain of command—indeed, its strength lies precisely in the inability of lower-ranking officers to gain respite from it. It works.

Militaristic Chain-of-Command and the Production of Bullshit

The analytical value of the scatological term "bullshit" has not, to my knowledge, been explored in research on the police. A closely related term "chickenshit" has received acclaim as a literary device for describing the relations between soldiers and officers in World War I. In his brilliant book titled *Wartime*, Paul Fussell (1989) captures the essence of bullshit, and its link to chain-of-command structures. His description of attitudes of enlistees to the British service during World War I fits well the experience of many new recruits to police work. Fussell quotes a young recruit in the Royal Air Force:

> I was ready for death
> Ready to give it all in one expansive gesture
> For a cause that was worthy of death.
> What I never saw
> Were the weary hours of waiting while the sun rose and set.

But even worse than "the boredom and the inefficiency" were what really distressed him, "The petty injustice and the everlasting grudges." It is these more than anything that persuade him that the sacrifice he is making is "Greater than I ever expected" (Fussell, 1989:79-80).

Fussell's term for this is "chickenshit," that is:

> Behavior that makes military life worse than it need be. Petty harassment of the weak by the strong; open scrimmage for power and authority and prestige; sadism disguised as necessary discipline; a constant "paying off" of old scores; and insistence on the letter rather than the spirit of ordinances . . . Chickenshit can be recognized instantly because it never has anything to do with winning the war (Fussell, 1989:80).

Fussell's exposition of "chickenshit" captures the spirit of bullshit that characterizes relations between brass and line officers in police work. Ragonese (1991), in his memoirs as a New York City police officer, captures the flavor of bullshit that marked his early learning experiences in the police department. The following experience is of one of his first arrests, and in the aftermath of the arrest he begins to learn the unfairness of the status hierarchy in the police organization and in the courts. After making what he perceived to be a good pinch, Officer Ragonese learns lessons of status through a series of bullshit degradations from the courts, the detectives, and the desk sergeant.

In his story, the phone company had been hit by a strike, and he was posted at one of the offices. A woman approached him, telling him that a man around the corner was selling marijuana. He recognized that he was not supposed to leave the post, but also considered that this would be a good arrest. He made the arrest, then took the arrestee to lock-up. There he encountered his desk sergeant.

> "What in the fuck were you doin' in the library when you're supposed to be on god-damn strike post?"

> "Sarge, I was told . . ."

> "You were told to man a strike post, and when you man a fuckin' strike post in the 2-3 you never leave it until you're relieved." He paused and added sarcastically, "Whaddya wanna be, a supercop? I'll give you a supercop."

Officer Ragonese took the accused to the detective squad, where the paperwork on felons was done. The felon was fingerprinted, interviewed, and the detective filled out the arrest report. Officer Ragonese then took the prisoner downtown to try to get him into night court. Ragonese continues:

> Until then, while Rodriguez (the detainee) was kept in the court holding pen, I had to hang around the crowded complaint room where cops from all over Manhattan waited for prisoners to be processed.

> I hung around the complaint room for nine hours on Friday. I hung around again all day Saturday and Sunday. Jose Rodriguez wasn't arraigned until after eleven o'clock on Monday morning.

At this point Officer Ragonese is exposed to the informal status system in the courtroom.

> I arrived at court early, saw the front row was marked Police Officers, and sat down in it. A court officer immediately came up behind me and tapped my shoulder. "You can't sit there," he said.

> "The sign says Police Officers and I'm a police officer," I said.

> "The first row's for detectives."

> I shrugged and moved to the second row.

> "Can't sit there either. That row's for plainclothesmen."

> "Well, could you please tell me where I can sit?" I asked.

> "Rows three and four are for lawyers. You can sit in row five."

> The day's arraignments began and I soon heard the name of a detective from the 2-3 squad, along with a case number for Jose Rodriguez. "Hey, that's my prisoner," I said.

I was devastated. I went back to the 2-3 and told the desk sergeant, Vin McCann, "The detectives stole my collar." . . . I soon learned that uniforms got an arrest only when there was no way the detective squad could steal it from them.

Not only did I get no credit for arresting Jose Rodriguez, I got punished for it by the desk sergeant who'd reamed me . . . For weeks after I'd left the strike post, Lynch nailed me to every awful post he could come up with. His opening line was always the same. "You wanna be a super-cop?" Then he'd say something like: "Guard the burned-out building on Ninetieth and Lex" (Ragonese, 1991:23-25).

One might wonder what there is about a militaristic chain-of-command that lends itself to the proliferation of bullshit. My suspicion is that it does not lie with some dark tendency of an autocratic mind-set to seek picayune order for underlings, nor with the natural tendencies of narrow, tyrannical personalities that occasionally rise through the ranks of military and police service. Such leadership has been as widely cited in civilian life, and tends to haunt the upper levels of bureaucracies in all areas of contemporary society. No, it is not the leadership. Among police organizations, it is the nature of the rank-structure itself that is responsible for the profusion of bullshit.

Police organizations are quasi-military organizations. Like military organizations, a sworn officer's authority lies not in his or her assignment, as it does with civilian workforces, but in the rank. The ranks of the police range from line officers at the lowermost rungs to the chief on top, with normal intermediate ranks of sergeant, lieutenant, captain, and deputy chief. Under a rank-structure like this, all line officers are technically below all sergeants, who are themselves below lieutenants, and so forth.

Both military and police organizations share another characteristic—the person on the bottom, the dog-face in the army and the street cop in the police, actually does the work that the organization is supposedly about. Generals do not physically fight wars, and chiefs do not make arrests. Of course, a publicity-minded chief may occasionally show up at the arrest of a celebrated criminal, and a general advancing his or her political career may occasionally visit the front-line troops. But there is no question about who does the work that the organization seeks to accomplish, and where the blood-and-bone sacrifices are made. What, then, is it that chiefs and generals actually do?

I suppose that if you were to ask them, managers would say that they were holding strategy meetings, developing and maintaining the organizational plan, selecting tactical procedures, doing total quality management, holding "open door" sessions, meeting with important guests, and other important aspects of administration. But to what extent do top managers actually run the police organization? The astonishing history of police corruption in the United States stands as mute testimony that chiefs, in fact, have very little control over the behavior of line officers, or even know what line officers are doing. Indeed, chiefs tend to find out about problems like the rest of us—from an unwanted phone call, or over the local news (or if they are very unlucky, over CNN). How then is the illusion of organizational control, that is, that the administrative head of the dog can in fact wag the tail, maintained?

The illusion of control is sustained by changing the organizational focus from goal-oriented measures of effectiveness, such as community levels of crime, to a detailed, ritualistic concern for intra-organizational images of orderliness. Chiefs have extremely limited control over crime. Nor can they control street-cop behavior when they are on patrol. Images of orderliness are something over which chief administrators and higher-ranking officers have control. They have control over internal departmental processes, while their outcomes control is severely limited.

It is nearly impossible, for example, for a chief to find out if an officer is making arrests when conditions are suitable for an arrest. However, any ranking officer anywhere can, during roll call, end of shift, or during an inspection, harangue an officer if that officer's shoes are not shined to the appropriate level of luster. Similar process controls can regulate an officer's presence at meetings, their ability to do paperwork, and the orderliness of their uniforms. Bullshit thus emerges as the inevitable by-product of efforts to control system processes in the absence of verifiable or meaningful measures of organizational outcomes. Control of internal system processes occurs through rigid adherence to policies and rules, extreme attention to paperwork, and efforts to exert occasional control over personnel promotion, reward, and punishment.

The intensity of bullshit in militaristic chain-of-command organizations stems from the "rank-in-position" characteristic of their personnel systems. In chain-of-command systems, authority is associated with the rank an individual holds. Compare that to a bureaucracy, where authority is a property belonging to the person that holds a particular position (Guyot, 1979). The vertical structure of authority of militaristic structures provides for the central organizing principle of bullshit in such personnel systems. The principle is that expectations of orderliness expand downward through the chain of command. The principle is facilitated by the asymmetrical nature of knowledge in police organizations—higher-ranking officers all have previous experience as line officers and know how things work (Manning, 1978c). Put most simply and in the common vernacular, "shit flows downhill." The following story, taken from research on police in New York City, describes the preoccupation of executive officers with bullshit:

> They are always hassling us about keeping our hats on and shirts buttoned and then they send us out to muck our way through garbage, broken bottles, and piss . . . and I'm not even talking about alleyways, I'm talking about inside buildings . . . and duck bricks and bottles heaved

from those buildings [The officer pointed them out as we drove by]. All they care about is that someone might take a picture of one of us with our hats off and our collars open and it would look bad for them (Reuss-Ianni, 1983:37-38).

Bureaucracy and the Production of Bullshit

That quasi-military organizations produce bullshit as a fetid by-product of efforts to control the behavior of personnel is an annoyance. That they are also bureaucracies compounds the problem. The capacity of bureaucracy for capricious authority has been observed by Manning (1978).[2]

> The preoccupation with the symptoms of a problem rather than with the problem itself is typical of all bureaucracies. For one characteristic of a bureaucracy is goal-displacement. Bureaucratic organizations tend to lose track of their goals and engage in ritual behavior, substituting means for ends. As a whole, bureaucracies become so engrossed in pursuing, defending, reacting to, and, even, in creating immediate problems that their objective is forgotten. The tendency to displace goals is accelerated by the one value dear to all bureaucracies—efficiency. Efficiency is the be-all and end-all of bureaucratic organizations. Thus, they can expend great effort without any genuine accomplishment (Manning, 1978:21).

The result of this system of goal-displacement is the arbitrary disbursement of discipline for officers who work in a highly unpredictable and discretionary environment that cannot be brought into line with managerial ideas of efficiency. The organization punishes its members for violating procedures but offers no specifications for what they should do and how they should do it (Manning, 1978). This is, of course, bullshit in a very pure form.

There is a historical linkage between bureaucracy, chain-of-command, and bullshit. In what can only be described as a paroxysm of Orwellian newspeak, police executives founded what they called the police professionalization movement in 1893, so that they could better control the behavior of line officers (Fogelson, 1977; Walker, 1977). Turn-of-the-century reformists advocated both the development of chain-of-command accountability and bureaucratic efficiency to reduce political influence over line personnel. It was hoped that these developments would deter line officers from a rich and rewarding tradition of graft, and to convince them, vis-à-vis threat of punishment, of the moral value of the more austere crime control mission.

Ideas of organizational design advocated by police professionals were wildly inconsistent with commonplace ideas of the professions as embodied in law and medicine (see Hall, 1968). The process of police professionalization was more similar to mind-numbing bureaucratization than to ideas of creative decentralized decisionmaking associated with the professions (Brown, 1981). However, police reformers in the 1930s and the 1960s, finding themselves in a hole, dug deeper. Successive waves of the police professionalization movement were marked by accountability procedures increasingly rigid, as administrators sought to bring line officer discretion under control. This, Manning (1978c) observed, was an impossible mandate. The idea that the events in which police found themselves could be controlled and that managers could make police-citizen outcomes predictable was nonsense. The real consequence has been and continues to be the increasing rift between line personnel and management brass (Reuss-Ianni, 1983). Management seeks to use new technologies to expand bureaucratic controls, and line personnel carp, grouse, and seek petty revenges. The bullshit is never-ending.

The Measurement of Bullshit

In 1991, Mike Caldero and I wrote a paper that we described as an assessment of police stress. What we actually captured was the pervasive presence of bullshit. Findings in this paper suggest that bullshit is as thick in medium-sized departments as it is in large ones.

The research was conducted in five medium-sized departments in the Midwest in order to assess sources of police stress. Traditionally, stress has been attributed to the dangers of everyday police work, with other sources thought to be less consequential. Our findings were in sharp contrast to this common perception: when queried on perceived sources of stress, line officers consistently identified their own administration, top brass, middle management, and rules. Of 167 written responses to the simple and straightforward open-ended query "What is your principal source of stress," 114 officers identified the organization. Responses were particularly directed at top brass.

> If you need one element—it's the superiors who run this department . . . the chief and his kiss-asses who stab you in the back and don't really care about you as a human being. Well, you wanted to know, didn't you? In our department, it's that way (Crank & Caldero, 1991:347).

Management frequently were seen as out-of-touch with line personnel.

> One officer wrote that "The police department's entire top management is STAGNANT!' and another stated that "we need to retire some of the dinosaurs, and let the new supervisors with education and ability move up (Crank & Caldero, 1991:343).

Chiefs were occasionally singled out for criticism. One officer noted:

The greatest source of stress is the bullshit we get from the chief's office and city administration. By bullshit I mean the petty rules and restrictions they come up with to keep you from doing your job. Also the way they fuck some people over, but kiss other people's ass[3] (Crank & Caldero, 1991:344).

Middle-management and Sergeants were not overlooked. One respondent noted:

Over supervision by Sergeants. They arrive at a minor scene and quickly make a mountain out of a mole-hill, issue various orders to make themselves sound important, and then vanish into thin air leaving the beat officer to straighten out the mess they made (Crank & Caldero, 1991:344).

Another stated simply that "Chicken-shit staff will back-stab you, causing stress and low department morale."
Rules and regulations out of touch with the basic needs of officers were frequently cited by officers.

Rules and regulations . . . are detrimental when they do not allow you the freedom to do your job according to each situation that arises. Officers who become afraid to do their job effectively because of overstepping the bounds of the rules and the regulations are of no use to the public that depends on them (Crank & Caldero, 1991:345).

This frustration was noted pointedly by one officer:

I just wish we could forget about where we smoke, and how we park our cars and get back to police work. What the people with the gold badge in the main office seem to forget is that the man in the street is doing all the work (Crank & Caldero, 1991:345).

Bullshit often took the form of favoritism shown to particular officers. The following quotes revealed a style of bullshit very similar to Fussell's description of chickenshit, that is, a preoccupation with authority independent of the police crime control mission.

. . . favoritism, in that it is already well known in advance by supervisors which of their buddies they want promoted, and who will be held back, regardless of ability. Awards and evaluations are doled out to build or destroy careers. Supervisors do not know how officers are performing because they do not supervise them. They only count tickets and read reports at the end of the day. Tickets and popularity become the sole criteria for evaluation.

The absolute proof of this is in the records of the promoted [officers] themselves. The only other outstanding trait of these placehunting supervisors is their subservience toward their own "supervisors" matched by their own superciliousness toward their so-called "inferiors" and former comrades. These heroic knights of the coffee cup are so lacking in any real creative intelligence as to be truly amusing were it not for their indolence and inconsistency (Crank & Caldero, 1991:344).

Another protested:

Our administration likes to Monday morning quarterback and second-guess the officers. Our general orders, policies, and procedures are not used fairly and equally with all employees, and several read as if the chief is trying to write himself out of any liability, and in fact internal investigations are more like witch hunts (Crank & Caldero, 1991:347).

In our efforts to identify police stress, we had inadvertently unmasked a phenomenon far more important to understanding street cops culture: the pervasive presence of bullshit.

Training and Bullshit

For bullshit to achieve its maximum psychological effect, recipients have to learn to dread its inevitable appearance, to be always "looking over their shoulders" as it were, to despair over how something utterly trivial and harmless that they did could result in massive, unrelenting retaliation. They have to learn that no good deed goes unpunished and they have to cover their collective ass. They have to be sensitized to the faintest scent of bullshit, so that when the real thing occurs they will feel its fullest effect. This is why bullshit begins in academy training.

The introduction to bullshit in the Academy is well documented.

A recruit soon learns that to be one minute late to a class, to utter a careless word in formation, and to be caught walking when he should be running may result in a "gig" or demerit costing a man an extra day of work or the time it may take to write a long essay on, say, "the importance of keeping a neat appearance" (Van Maanen, 1978:297).

It is not surprising that pre-service training is modeled after military basic training, with its emphasis on deathly tedious lectures, stress training, combat focus, and the like. In this context, the idea of military "chickenshit" described by Fussell and police "bullshit" are more than metaphorically related; they stem from the same ontology—the adoption of a military training model.

Harris (1973) captures some of the nuances of the bullshit encountered by trainees. Bullshit took the form of maintaining a neat, polished image.

> Shoes not only had to be polished, they had to be spit-shined. Haircuts could not only be neat, they had to be cut almost weekly. Uniforms not only had to be tidy, they had to be ironed after each day's use (Harris, 1973:282).

The following is about a recruit that was given an unfavorable report for not attending to the professional "bullshit."

> Only one recruit in the class had been given a decidedly unfavorable report during his precandidacy interview. His report read something like this: need a shave, haircut, hair hanging over his ears and collar [he had a "mod" haircut]; he lacked any kind of military bearing, slouching down in chair during interview; he lacked enthusiasm shown by other candidates (Harris, 1973:282).

Academy personnel justified the attention to minutiae by what they referred to as a need to develop a highly polished, professional image. Harris can be forgiven for failing to recognize that staff was hiding their bullshit sensitivity training under the umbrella term "professionalism." One staff member told him that "The minute harassment was only designed to make the new man, who would be wearing the uniform for the first time, more conscious of his appearance." However, any cop who has experienced military service recognizes the gloss of professionalism for what it is, preparing recruits for their position in a quasi-military rank structure and the inevitable and insurmountable bullshit that goes with such a rank structure.

Bullshit Survival

The ubiquitous presence of bullshit fosters various responses among line-officers. Modes of adjustment enable officers to survive in an environment dense with rules and procedures. Four modes of adaptation are presented below: these are CYA, humor, clique formation, and cynicism. However, some do not adapt and bitterly separate from the occupation. Voluntary resignation, discussed last, is a catastrophic strategy for the deflection of bullshit.

CYA

CYA means, simply, cover your ass. By the time rookies have finished training, most know how to CYA. It is a lesson not forgotten. In other forms, it is called "watch your back," "watch your topnotch," or "lay low." The pervasiveness of the CYA adaptation to departmental bullshit has been widely noted. Van Maanen observed that:

> This "cover-your-ass" perspective pervades all of patrol work. In a sense, it represents a sort of bureaucratic paranoia which is all but rampant in police circles (Van Maanen, 1978:127).

CYA is a behavioral response that is least likely to result in disciplinary action. It carries with it cultural predispositions to pace your work and avoid the harsh glare of management interest. One of Van Maanen's interviewees gave the following recommendation to a new officer:

> You gotta learn to take it easy. The department don't care about you and the public sure as hell ain't gonna cry over the fact that the patrolman always gets the shit end of the stick. The only people who care about you are your brother officers. So just lay back and take it easy here. Makes things a lot smoother for us as well as yourself (Van Maanen, 1978:122).

This theme is also evident in Reuss-Ianni's (1983) distinction between management and cop culture, where the relationship between managers and line personnel was characterized as adversarial. Conflict between line personnel and managers was noted by Wilson (1968) in his discussion of the problems managers encounter in attempts to professionally transform traditional police organizations.

Humor and Bullshit

Officers are not mindless recipients of bullshit. They develop strategies to protect themselves against its more corrosive effects. One of these devices is humor (Pogrebin & Poole, 1988). The strategic use of "jocular aggression," Pogrebin and Poole argued, allowed lower-level personnel in a department to collectively and acceptably counter disagreeable policies and regulations. Humor aimed at supervisors deflected bullshit, promoted social solidarity among line officers, and resolved tensions that emerged in chain-of-command relations. In the following case, a sergeant was chided by one of his officers:

> The new sergeant was obviously fatigued from attempting to be with his patrol officers at every call. He was seen as constantly invading officers' territory and interfering with the tactics each officer had developed for

handling interactions with suspects and citizens. Jocular aggression was abundant that night, as evidenced in the remarks of one officer during debriefing:

> Hey, Sarge! Where were you when I got that call on those biker's loud music complaint over on the east side? I figure you could have made it there if you used your lights and siren. It was only about five miles from where you were. Hell, if you ran hot at 90 miles an hour, you could have been there to help me (Pogrebin & Poole, 1988:193).

Another example, again aimed at the same sergeant, was a subtle attack on his over-supervision of shift calls. The use of this corrosive form of humor was used by officers to corral some of the sergeant's more irritating behavior.

> Now we all see that the city wants us to cut down on our driving time to save on gas expenses. Sarge, you must have put on over a thousand miles tonight. You better be careful or the city manager is going to get on your ass. You know you've got to help the city save money in these times of cutback management (Pogrebin & Poole, 1988:194).

The presence of these humorous forms were a feint to the bullshit inherent in militaristic chain-of-command structures. They revealed the structural limits of authority in municipal police departments. Unlike military personnel, line officers are not wholly vulnerable to the whimsy of their administrators. Protected by labor representation, police officers' bills of rights, and strong personnel systems, officers have the capability, though limited, to respond to and re-direct upwards the bullshit flowing down the chain of command to them.

Clique Formation

Officers sometimes form cliques to deflect administrative bullshit. Manning (1978c) described the formation of two types of protective cliques: vertical and horizontal. Vertical cliques, formed between lower- and higher-ranking officers, allowed for the simplification of department procedures. These cliques dealt with situations that were "presented repeatedly, and that, if they were solved by the book, would be time consuming, potentially embarrassing, and explosive for all concerned" (Van Maanen, 1978c:84).

Vertical cliques involved collusions between officers and sergeants, who sought to avoid logging (making a permanent record of) particular types of calls to area cars or the police handling of particular property. By handling property and calls informally, senior officers were prevented from monitoring performance through written records.

Horizontal cliques were formed to protect line officers from superiors and from sergeants. These cliques included partners in the patrol car, crews in the reserve room, teams of plain-clothes officers, and spontaneous groupings of officers thrown together by a common problem. The purpose of such groups was to aid in the mutual resolution of problems and protection from arbitrary rules, and almost always involves the manipulation of the written record. The formation of horizontal cliques has also been described by Wilson in the following quote:

> One reason for the oft-noted tendency of patrolmen to form cliques, factions, and fraternal associations, is . . . to defend officers against what is to them arbitrary authority and "outside influence." The power of the administrator is to be checked because the administrator, if he is a strong man, is "out to get us," and if he is a weak one, is "giving way before outside pressure" (Wilson, 1968:73; also cited in Manning, 1978c, footnote 11).

The distribution of bullshit within and across organizational layers is poorly understood though widely experienced. Manning (1978b) developed a tri-polar notion of police culture, in which the cultural prerogatives of middle-management focused on administration issues. The administrative adroitness of middle managers is consistent with the notion that bullshit tends not to lie at rest in the organization. One suspects that adroitness included the capacity to deflect bullshit down the rank structure. A study of bullshit as experienced by middle-management and by administrative personnel might help to extend our knowledge of this concept.

Cynicism

In 1967, Arthur Niederhoffer wrote about a pervasive cynicism he had observed during his career in the New York City police department. He believed that cynicism was at the root of many problems associated with the police. Left unchecked, a brooding cynicism and its accompanying loss of faith in police work contributed to alienation, job dissatisfaction, and corruption. Cynicism began early in a police officer's career, reached full strength in the fourth and fifth year, at which point an officer was most vulnerable to corruptive influences. If officers could survive this period, sometimes they regained their moral commitment to police work.

Niederhoffer developed a 40-item index of cynicism that was subsequently refined by other researchers. A large literature, particularly the research of Regoli and his colleagues, re-examined Niederhoffer's scale, and has done so in a wide variety of circumstances (e.g., Regoli, 1976, 1977, 1979; Regoli et al., 1987; Poole & Regoli, 1979, 1980). This literature used the technique of factor analysis to see if Niederhoffer's cumbersome 40-item scale could be better broken down into smaller scales with more precise meaning. The question for Regoli was one of identifying the various aspects of cynicism obscured by Niederhoffer's bulky measure.

Regoli consistently identified a dimension he referred to variously as "cynicism toward the ideals of police work" (Regoli & Poole, 1979:39), "cynicism toward organizational functions" (Regoli, 1976:233), and "cynicism toward the organization" (Poole & Regoli, 1979:203). The consistent replication of this domain of content suggested that Regoli was tapping a cultural sentiment common among police organizations (see also Langworthy, 1987). What he called departmental cynicism was what I consider to be a brooding cynicism toward department bullshit.

That cynicism might be a cultural phenomenon was also explored by Wilt and Bannon (1976). They argued that measures of police cynicism tapped the argot of police officer culture, a language nuanced with frustration toward administrators. Cynicism emerged early on from language and attitude modeling in academy training. What appeared to be cynicism was in fact socialization through mimicry. They observed that "Such influence on the part of academy staff may well be enhanced by the recruit's desire to emulate experienced officers in an effort to shed their status as novices" (Wilt & Bannon, 1976:40). It may also have been motivated by a desire to quickly learn how to cover their butts, like more experienced officers. The contribution of Wilt and Bannon's analysis was the recognition that learning how to deal with departmental bullshit (what he referred to as cynicism) was a culturally transmitted product that occurs early in the career of an officer.

Voluntary Resignation

The force is not for everyone. Even those who are committed to the service, who are morally invested in their work, may one day abandon their positions as sworn police officers. The loss is great and unfortunate; not only has the department lost a substantial financial investment in an officer, but the public has frequently lost a faithful servant. Unfortunately, resignation may have little to do with occupational dangers, and a great deal to do with bullshit.

Traditionally, it had been thought that turnover among police officers was associated with differences between the expectations of patrol work and the reality of day-to-day police work. It had been suggested that the stresses and dangers of police work accounted for a police officer's decision to resign (Singleton & Tehan, 1978; Reiser, 1974). Resignation, however, may stem from pressures associated with the organization. Some officers, rather than put up with the administrative and rule-laden bullshit associated with chain-of-command authority, may abandon the occupation of policing.

That bullshit is not an uncommon reason for leaving policing is suggested in a paper by Sparger and Giacopassi (1983). In a study of the Memphis (Tennessee) Police Department, they assessed officers' reasons for voluntary resignations. They used an open-ended questionnaire to assess causes of resignation. And their findings sharply contrasted with the more conventional idea that occupational dangers accounted for resignations.

They found that virtually all resignations stemmed from departmental problems. The four reasons most frequently cited, in the order of selection, were (1) a perceived lack of opportunities for promotion, (2) departmental politics, (3) their efforts were not appreciated, and (4) pay and fringe benefit issues. The comment of one veteran revealed a deep sense of frustration:

> Unfortunately, you are not promoted for your wisdom, tact, ability, or leadership. You are generally promoted because you play their games and know the right people. No matter how well you accomplish your duties and how dedicated you were to the department, the person beside you could goof off and transact personal business all day and get paid the same amount (Sparger & Giacopassi, 1983:116).

Another officer, a 13-year-veteran, cited departmental politics for his resignation:

> Politics. Even though I was number 1 in nearly every category (apprehensions, recovery of stolen property, etc.) in my unit, I was made aware of the fact that I backed the wrong candidate for a political office. Hard work and dedication does not get you ahead. It's what team you are on (Sparger & Giacopassi, 1983:116).

The comments from this research are hauntingly similar to the findings of Crank and Caldero. It appears that when cops are asked to respond in their own words about problems they confront, sources of stress and reasons for resignation, the overwhelming source is the department. Bullshit appears to be a pervasive feature of the occupational landscape.

Whither Bullshit?

Police are at a watershed. Increasingly, departments are adopting a new philosophy, strategies and tactics under the rubric of community policing. However, the practical implications of the movement for line officer accountability (and by implication for the production of bullshit) have been generally unaddressed (although, see Klockars, 1991; Mastrofski, 1991; Crank & Langworthy, 1996). I will take advantage of this concluding section to hypothesize about the relationship between community policing and bullshit.

Contemporary advocates of community policing articulate a mission that re-asserts the authority and responsibility of the patrol officer on the beat. The needs of the local community, reformers contend, provide the justification for broad police intervention into the affairs of the citizenry. To accomplish community protection, the police department should have a way to geographically decentralize the delivery of some of its services, citizen involvement should be encouraged and sustained, and individual officers should be granted wide latitude in the conduct of their daily activities. By turning the police loose (to satisfy conservatives) but making them sensitive to the needs of citizens (to satisfy liberals) community policing sounds like a marvelous new idea, one that promises to finally, really do something about crime. Not everyone is sold.

In a forceful challenge to the community policing movement, Carl Klockars (1991) argued that community policing rhetoric was a sham for the use of force. He began by reconsidering Bittner's (1970) assertion that force was at the core of the police role, but that this truth was inherently offensive to society.

Community policing, Klockars argued, was simply the latest in a long tradition of police mystifications whose purpose was to conceal, mystify, and legitimate the police use of coercive force. Klockars' wisdom was in recognizing that the strength of community policing was in its ability to wrap police work, the "unrestricted right to use violent and, when necessary, lethal means . . ." "in aspirations and values that are extremely powerful and unquestionably good" (Klockars, 1991:531). Mastrofski (1991) added that the community policing movement carried significant, yet unrecognized, problems. Conflicts in purpose were disguised behind bold crime-control proposals. Particularly troubling were the implications of community policing for the control of the behavior of line officers. Even contemporary bureaucratic mechanisms, he noted, were ineffective in the control of police abuse, overwhelmed by the experience of socialization into police culture and the discretionary nature of day-to-day police activity. Is it responsible to expect that an expansion of what line officers do will not also be matched with a corollary expansion in rules and regulations? A possible outcome of community policing might well be an increase in the quantity of departmental bullshit.

In a recent paper, Bob Langworthy and I (1996) argued that the community policing movement would not lead to an abandonment of bureaucratic controls, but instead might lead to a sharp expansion of them. At a practical level, the police are likely to end up using a standard operating procedure expanded to deal with a community order mandate. And what if, as suspected, communities have different standards of acceptable conduct? Will officers have to enforce these different standards? The potential policy problems are nightmarish.

Contemporary mechanisms of accountability—chain of command and standard operating procedure—are highly institutionalized, and it is unlikely that they will simply disappear as organizational ways of doing business. To the contrary, any expansion of the police role is likely to be met with a parallel expansion of these accountability structures. A reasonable outcome for community policing, at least for line-officers, might be a sharp increase in bureaucratic bullshit and rigidity in paperwork accountability.

The police culture, in order to protect officers from administrative oversight, may expand to protect officers from the bullshit associated with expanded efforts to hold them accountable for ill-defined work. In other words, the expansion of accountability stemming from community-based policing efforts—in a word, "more bullshit,"—may have the undesired effect of strengthening secretive aspects of the police culture associated with bullshit survival.

Endnotes

[1] Fussell, 1989:80.

[2] Manning (1978:87) notes that "The quasi-military structure of police organizations creates the potential for capricious authority to be employed to define proper and adequate work . . . Rules legitimate punishment and provide rationalizations for administrative action."

[3] The italicized quotes or portions of quotes in this section are original quotes from Crank and Caldero's respondents that were not published.

Death and
Police Culture

**Section
V**

What does it mean to be a police officer? It means a great deal more than holding a 9-to-5 job, and the receipt of a paycheck. It is a celebration of a way of life, a way of thinking about the world, understanding and giving value to what one sees, reaffirming traditions. Yet, culture is more than a collection of themes linking meanings to occupational activities. Rites and ceremonies are invoked in particularly meaningful moments in the life of a culture (Trice & Beyer, 1984).[1]

Important rituals display symbols in concert and evoke great emotion for the police. Rituals may contain symbolic elements, yet they are more than symbolic displays. Rituals express the most fundamental reality underlying culture. They are emotional, they convey meanings, but most importantly, they live out a heightened sense of culture itself. Often vibrant with important symbols, they are meaning itself.

In this concluding section I am particularly interested in funeral rituals. Rituals surrounding the death of an officer are among the most emotionally potent events that can occur to a police organization. They are culture affirming, pulling together members of a culture after a profoundly shattering event. This section, focusing on funeral ceremonies among the police, seeks to convey this powerful emotional context. I look at police rituals from a traditional sociological perspective, assessing the meanings they have for outsiders. I also think about them as interior dramas, for the powerful feelings they evoke in participants.

I begin the section with a discussion of what ritual is. The anthropological literature has provided a great deal of literature on this topic, writing that unfortunately has been neglected in criminal justice studies. This literature conveys insight into the enormous power of funeral rituals. The discussion is at the outset a bit abstract, for which I beg forgiveness of the reader. I have borrowed extensively from the excellent discussion of ritual and authority provided by Katherine Bell (1992), to whom I am most grateful. It is hoped that the discussion of ritual provides insight into the forces that affect cop culture, and how culture survives its moment of greatest tragedy.

Endnote

[1] A badge, for example, does not need to conjure up the memory of a fallen officer—the badge says it all. Its power is not only in what it represents, but what it is. In linguistic terms, a badge is a metonymy—a type of metaphor in which a specific part embodies the meaning of a whole.

24

Thinking About Ritual

> The world as lived and the world as imagined turn out to be the same world (Geertz, 1973:91-92).

This comment, a testament to the power of the imagination to remake day-to-day reality in its desired image, captures the essence of a ritual. Ritual ceremonies are more than affirmations of the world given; they are tools for its construction as well. Rituals may identify group members and boundaries, label outgroups, provide a sense of status hierarchies, celebrate the sacred and stigmatize the profane. If culture is the way in which group members in concert live and give meaning to their world, rituals are the world imagined, evoked in powerful symbols and organized in ceremony. Rituals are powerful things in themselves, establishing and celebrating workaday meanings, investing tired symbols with renewed vigor and identifying important patterns of group authority.

That rituals are important cultural products has been widely noted (Geertz, 1973; Durkheim, 1965; Turner, 1974). A ritual is an action, though of a special type. A ritual is a bright fuse: it is an action that links cultural beliefs and morality with a group's behavior. Durkheim (1965:463) captured this idea when he characterized ritual as the "means by which collective beliefs and ideals are generated, experienced and affirmed as real by the community" (Bell, 1992:20). Put another way, a ritual acts out both group unity and diversity in displays of moral and religious significance.

There is a vast literature on rituals, its vastness that much more astonishing for its striking absence in criminal justice, where ceremony and ritual activity are commonplace. A brief review of theory of ritual activity provides insight into the breadth of perspective on this topic. This review is not exhaustive; the field is too broad and the task would easily put us outside the scope of this book. I extract from the literature those elements I think are the most fruitful for interpreting police rituals.

Rituals Act Out Existing Patterns of Social Relations

The idea that rituals promote social solidarity has been a central tenet of much research on ritual since the writings of Durkheim (1965). Rituals provide a "collective confidence in the well-being of society" as well as an "individual sense of participation on a redemptive activity" (Bell, 1992:213). This is particularly the case in a relatively homogeneous group like the police, who have a clear sense of their own symbols (Bell, 1992:213). Through behaviors that symbolically act out important group values and processes, rituals promotes consensus and solidarity among group members.

But how can this "solidarity-building" function of rituals be understood in a society as complex as the United States, with its many and varied status configurations? American society and its various subgroups are enmeshed in broad and complex patterns of authority. Municipal police are embedded in a complex institutional environment composed of many powerful actors—the courts, the mayor, labor organizations, and city councils, to name a few, and much of what the police do is about their relations with these groups. In complex social settings, solidarity rituals also become authority rituals, acting out and affirming patterns of in-group and out-group influence and antagonisms. Rituals direct participants' and observers' visions to existing patterns of authority (Lukes, 1975), praising some groups and damning others. Rituals consequently imbue patterns of authority in the culture with moral proscription and emotional content. The existing order of things is reaffirmed at a heightened moral intensity through ritual activity.

Consider the motorist who seeks to evade the police by speeding away after being instructed to pull over. This circumstance occasionally results in highly publicized high-speed chases. It is also poorly received by the police. It is routine in many departments for patrol officers to physically punish motorists who engage in this behavior, and is a phenomenon far more prevalent than most departments would like to admit. Such beatings have powerful ritualistic components. They act out of the authority of the state on the body of a wayward motorist. Such beatings are not carried out on "whim," but are deliberate and intentional. They clearly establish the authority of the police at a heightened moral level—the righteousness of police to exercise their authority to pull over motorists. These beatings are also a solidarity ritual—one which pulls together officers in a common moral sentiment of their authority.

Rituals Construct Meaning

Rituals not only reflect existing meanings, they construct new meaning. A ritual pulls together the beliefs a group has about itself, sometimes called its world-view, and acts out those beliefs in ways that are self-affirming. Rituals are thus events in which a culture both finds and celebrates its identity (Trice & Beyer, 1984). Rituals have a text-building quality; working with the basic stuff of symbols, cultural identity is constructed and acted out in a process of emergent meaning. Much like cultural themes, rituals reproduce the social world of its participants in a process of ongoing construction of meaning.

One cannot simply construct a theory of ritual. A ritual is a quality, a "sense," to use Bourdieu's (1977) term, of the socially informed body. A sense of ritual is a socially acquired sense, and reveals in its activity the micro-relations of society itself. To understand a ritual, one should not construct theory, but deconstruct the ritual itself, that is, look at its constituent parts to understand how they reveal the play of social relations. Only when one examines closely the various aspects of a ritual and considers them in terms of the broader cultural life in which they occur can one comprehend the meanings that they carry and the power relationships that they exhibit.

Consider funeral rituals among the police, for example. To understand the powerful and evocative elements of a funeral, observers have to note the symbols used, the organization of different police departments represented, the makeup and insignia of the color-guard, the words used and sentiments expressed in the elegy, and the actual activities of police officers before, during, and after the funeral. From activities both concretely carried out and symbolically meaningful, a theory of a police funeral can be constructed. By linking the elements of a funeral with the powerful themes of police work we begin to understand the significance a funeral of a slain officer holds for cops.

Rituals sometimes give energy to tired group values. Meanings that symbols hold for participants are stimulated by the ritual process. Symbols emerge quickened, reinvigorated with meanings and saturated with emotions. Group relations are acted out and fortified with meaning. Enemies are recognized and profaned during ritual activities. Funeral elegies and corresponding press write-ups will always talk about how "cop-killers" will be hunted down. The ceremonial display of elements of the slain officer's clothing are powerful statements of the rightness of codes of dress and insignia. Moreover, when a variety of departments are in attendance at a funeral, special attention is taken to ensure that representatives of different agencies are sharply dressed, that insignia are polished, that the agency standard is on display. Thus agency symbols are both highlighted for their universality (we are all cops here) and for their unique identifiers (we are members of this agency).

Ritual acts carry their meaning back to normal, daily activity. In many ways, the ritual process does not simply mirror but also precedes normal social life. Ritual activity has a vigor and energy that sustains group members through the hum-drum of daily life. In ritual, culture dreams of itself, and in daily life, members act out the dreams. In a circular, complimentary process, ordinary activity and ritual fulfill and create each other across the real and the imaginary.

Van Maanen's (1978) article "The Asshole" captures the sentiment of the way in which ritual activity and ordinary activity fulfill and create each other. The article has already been discussed previously in this book and I will not repeat that discussion here. The asshole was a type of individual, who, Van Maanen observed, did not conform to officers' definitions of circumstances, and challenged the right of the police to interact with them, with comments like "Why are you hassling me?" or similar rebukes to police authority. Van Maanen described a labeling process that I believe is more appropriately a ritual process of getting the asshole to admit that he or she is an asshole. It is common in rituals for a ritual participant, in the case of the police, the "bad guy," to admit their inferior status (or their wrongdoing). For the police, the taking into custody is a way in which the asshole tacitly admits to their wrongdoing. The ritual often cannot be concluded until such an admission of inferiority takes place. The beating or other form of "street justice" concludes the ritual activity. The ritual thus confirms the importance of ordinary police activity— keeping the world safe from assholes, and gives meaning to everyday police activity.

Ritual behavior intensifies the emotions associated with group symbols. The role of symbols in ritual should not be underestimated. Rituals are not so much conveyors of beliefs as they are carriers and potent invigorators of cultural symbols. Ritual activities do not promote belief so much as act out powerful symbols and identify important taboos. By repetitively employing a pool of symbols, rituals endow them with emotional content (Kertzer, 1988). Indeed, one of the most powerful aspects of a ritual is its capacity to invigorate symbols with emotional sentiment. According to this conception of ritual, rituals take on a meaning quite different from the lay conception of "ritual" as a repeated, structured activity without concrete meaning. Symbolic elements in ritual activity can give rise to new meanings and concepts about group identity (Turner, 1974). Ritual is activity in which groups, in a period of social structural "free fall," affirm their worldview and seek new meanings and symbols for their work-a-day activity.

In the play of ritual activity, values and norms become "saturated with emotion" (Turner, 1967:30). Obligatory status relationships in the work-a-day world are transformed into desirable emotional states during rituals. The ties that bind group members become elements of ritual celebration. The petty conflicts and grievances that characterize ongoing relationships between individuals are set aside, as relationships between individuals are celebrated, ennobling the purposes of the group. In this way, ritual does not simply affirm group cohesion, it creates it as well.[1]

Ritual activities can also level statuses, set aside customary differences in social standing in order to celebrate the group as a whole.[2] Turner, for example, distinguished between the work-a-day world, in which existing patterns of social structure characterize relationships among members of a group, and a condition he called communitas, in which group activities ritualistically leveled social distinctions in an affirmation of community togetherness. He referred to this period as a sort of social anti-structure, that is, when normal roles and obligations are set aside in order to celebrate the unifying elements of a group. During this period, individuals set aside their social differences and joined in a celebration of common symbolic and metaphorical elements of the culture. For Turner, this period of anti-structure was a particularly creative period. It was not only a celebration of existing group meanings, but a particularly fertile time for sharing and creating myth and culture.

This type of ritual activity is described in Wambaugh's (1975) description of choir practice. Choir practice, Wambaugh noted, was a time after work when officers got together and, frequently in a drunken revelry, celebrated their manhood. McNulty (1994) observed that choir practice had a ritualistic component. She focused on the opportunities afforded by choir practice to construct and exchange commonsense meanings. There are other ritual meanings associated with choir practice. Statuses are leveled, and roles and obligations are set aside during the festive gatherings. The rituals are about togetherness, the sharing of a common identity of "copness" different from distinguishing statuses during the regular course of the work-a-day world.

Ritual is the "thing itself." In 1980, Geertz made a fascinating observation about the nature of rituals. He stated that "Ritual is the thing itself." This interesting thought suggests that rituals do not simply serve the purpose of conveying messages. His thought is that a ritual is more basic: a ritual is not politics and power, acted out. A ritual is not simply a cultural carrier for shared beliefs, though it can do that. It operates at a more fundamental level, to identify that which is profane, and then to act on it. A creative process of belief construction may emerge during ritual activity, but the ritual is not itself about systematic beliefs or comprehensive world-views.

What is the "thing itself?" It is, simply, power (Geertz, 1980:135). A ritual is the action of social power and statement of existing patterns of authority. As Bell notes, it does not "disguise the exercise of power, nor does it refer, express, or symbolize anything outside itself" (Geertz, 1980:195). Power is not external to its workings. Ritual is power.[3]

The idea that ritual is power is carried by Bell in her recent work (1992). Focusing on the ritualization process, Bell argued that ritualization was a way of acting that demonstrated and reinforced certain types of power arrangements in society. It is strategic, in that it reveals both patterns of domination and subordination.

Patterns of domination and subordination are carried by ritual members simply by participating. Moreover, these ritual enactments are not different from the pattern of authority that exists in society, they are the pattern of authority in society. This serves several purposes. By concretizing existing relationships ritual fortifies social solidarity. It promotes the well-being and survival of that social group. And the members that participate in the ritual have affirmed both the strength of society and their own personal strength as well. As Bell notes:

> The person who has prayed to his or her god, appropriating the schemes of the hegemonic order in terms of an individual redemption, may be stronger because these acts are the very definitions of power, personhood, and the capacity to act (Bell, 1992:218).

In sum, rituals are an important part of culture: they highlight and act on symbols of threats and resistance, they invigorate emotional bonds among members, they profane out-members, they reinforce existing patterns of authority, they are solidarity-affirming, and they demonstrate power.

Rituals, powerful "things-in-themselves," are acted out by cops for cops, and thus are "cop things." It is in the context of funerals, as well as in the powerful themes that mark police culture, that we begin to understand the officer's T-shirt noted on the first page of the book—"it's a cop thing: you wouldn't understand." This means, simply, that themes and ritual activities are primarily aimed at the police themselves—though they may carry important symbolisms that carry meanings to outsiders, the primary audience for those meanings is cops. And cop funerals are the most important, most emotive of these rituals.

In ritual activities such as funerals, the symbols enacted are not simply reflections of the underlying power and authority in the organization. As suggested by Geertz' work, they are the power acted out in ritual behavior. They do not simply give meaning to activity, they are meaningful in themselves. That which is sacred is exalted, while that which is blasphemous is degraded.[4] They are things in themselves, and when done by cops, they are the "cop thing."

The following two chapters explore various elements of funeral ritual activities. This section looks at impact of line-of-duty deaths on local police cultures and how agencies respond to these events. The first chapter, called the culture eater, looks at the way in which the killing of an officer undermines the cultural bases for police action and thought. The period following the death of an officer is a profoundly disturbing experience across the department, and darkly reveals the importance of culture for social relations among cops. The death of a cop is also the death of culture, in microcosm—yet real nonetheless. Its impact on a local agency simply cannot be underestimated.

The final chapter looks at cop funerals. Culture, I argue, is reinvigorated through funeral rituals. The ritual process itself brings culture to life again. The funeral is about death, but it cannot be understood only in those terms. It is a revitalization of the life of the group. Symbols are prominently displayed that celebrate members essential "copness." A black band over the shield is a symbol of the ultimate sacrifice, but also is a powerful leveler of status—all officers are equally at threat of harm and danger. It thus unifies as well. The vast presence of police, often representing many different departments, in full dress blues, is a statement of "the thing itself." We are together, it says, unified, powerful. The death of one pulls us all together. The showing is a powerful statement of solidarity, a statement of the power in the culture itself. It is for cops. When it is over, culture is reaffirmed, a force to be reckoned with.

Endnotes

[1] Turner (1974:50) notes, ". . . it might be well to see structure as a limit rather than as a theoretical point of departure. The components of what I have called anti-structure, such as communitas and liminality, are the conditions for the production of root metaphors, conceptual archetypes, paradigms, models for, and the rest."

[2] See Bell (1992:37), for a critique of this notion of ritual activity. She notes, for example, that "The notion that ritual resolves a fundamental social contradiction can be seen as a type of myth legitimating the whole apparatus of ritual studies."

[3] Bell extends this idea as follows:
> . . . ritual activity is not the 'instrument' of more basic purposes, such as power, politics, and social control, which are usually seen as existing before or outside the activities of the rite. It puts interpretive analysis on a new footing to suggest that ritual practices are themselves the very production and negotiation of power relations (Bell, 1992:37).

[4] The image of ritual described in this book is in sharp distinction to the concept of ritual widely used in organizational theory today. Theorists, seeking to explain the way in which highly institutionalized organizations adapt to their environments, note the ceremonial importance of structures. Particular organizational structures reflect, by virtue of their function, broader values in the institutional environment. By adopting such structures, organizations thus gain legitimacy and enhance (or preserve) their access to resources. Such structures have sometimes been characterized as rituals of organizational activity. These differ importantly from rituals as I am examining them here. Instead of focusing on an organization, I am looking at a culture carried by its members, and moreover, one that has emerged in response to the structures' efforts to gain legitimacy in its institutional environment. For example, ceremonies of structure, for example, an affirmative action unit, may be used to gain organizational legitimacy in a city with a large African American population and with a long history of police problems. However, within the police culture, individuals thus hired may confront rituals of racial degradation from organizational members.

25

The Culture Eater

by Ronald Evans and John Crank

Death is always waiting, always hungry.

Culture is an enigma, a mysterious condensation of unity that prevails in all law enforcement agencies. You cannot see it, you cannot touch it, but you can feel it. No other occupation in the American workforce is so shielded and enlivened by culture as is law enforcement. In a nation that celebrates its capitalistic spirit, police officers stand out as an occupation whose loyalty and solidarity is not measured by the balance sheet. Cops, the most feared workforce in America, seem to have found what the rest of us seek—a feeling of community, a sense of shared identity.

Cop unity stems from the unique nature of their work. The uncertain and dangerous nature of the job, combined with the authority to arrest and to use force, knits close bonds among officers. Loyalty and safety are inseparable issues, and officers are resolutely focused on survival and backup in all street encounters and citizen calls for aid. Cops believe that they, acting alone and using their special skills and ironic common sense, can avoid the encroachment of infinite darkness. The integument of cop culture requires that they believe this. They are wrong.

Death is always there, hungry, waiting. In a metaphorical sense, the impact of death on the culture parallels an officer's killing. In perhaps the cruelest paradox of police culture, precisely those beliefs that unite line officers fail them utterly when an officer is killed in the line-of-duty. The death of an officer is a dis-affirmation of the most central elements of police culture—that a police officer, acting on the basis of his or her training, wit and skills, can control unpredictable situations. The ironic conversion of the work-a-day world to danger is complete, in a horrific way that yields no cultural safe haven. The occupational landscape of the working officer is wholly demonic, without sanctuary. The land discovered through their special sense of irony is not ruled by the police, but by death.

The killing of an officer gives the lie to culture. The clan is faced with the barren truth that they cannot control the edge, that they do not have a sufficient ability to see danger in the ordinary, that they are really not much tougher than the bad guys, that virtue is worth little in the cosmic scheme of things. A death reaffirms a simple truth transcendent and colder than culture could ever be: That soft flesh in a blue shirt is no match for hard steel. In the end, culture comes up short. Unpredictability means more than riding the wild, raw currents at the edge of the social order. It sometimes also means death, gritty and violent.

The death of a member has far-reaching effects in the tightly knit culture of cops. The death of an officer is a malevolence that nullifies the culture, at least temporarily. Officers retreat into themselves, to their families if they are blessed, to the bottle if they are not. Every encounter with the public generates fear. The unknown is dark, the unpredictable to be avoided. For some, there is no solace, only fearbite and suicide; death is out there and they seek it. Too many chances are taken. When an officer is killed the center cannot hold.

After a while, culture will return as a powerful force in the lives of cops. Collective grieving rituals play out deference and respect for the police and reaffirm culture in the play. Funerals among the police evoke unity and reassert the moral life of the whole; they signify the respect and need that we the outsiders have for them.

The funeral, a powerful reaffirmation of police solidarity, will bring together the police as nothing else can. Powerful symbols of clan and of country will begin the healing process. With the funeral the culture will again come to life in a powerful display of solidarity; a delusional phoenix, flowering drunken and celebratory from its ashes, believing against hope that through loyalty, virtue, training, and skill the unpredictable edge can be controlled. But for now, death reigns. The culture is vanquished, defeated by the values that nourished it. There is no peace, only solitude . . . and danger everywhere.

Violent death is not common. Violent death is not common among police officers. Because the number of officers in the United States has increased, their rate of felonious death has dropped in recent years. When one examines the number of officers killed per 10,000 police, the rate has fallen from approximately 3.4 in 1973 to its current level of 1.1 per 10,000 in 1993 (Fridell & Pate, 1997:581). The odds that an officer will be feloniously killed, only slightly greater than one in 10,000, seem to be slight, almost trivial—unless, of course, you are a cop.

The circumstances of officer killings are well known in the law enforcement community. Consider the period from January to November 1995. Sixty-three officers were feloniously killed. The most dangerous time, during an arrest, accounted for the death of 22 officers: Seven while attempting to apprehend robbery suspects, nine while attempting other arrests, three while attempting to apprehend burglary suspects, and three in drug-related matters. The other circumstances are as follows. Fifteen were killed while investigating suspicious persons, five while responding to disturbance calls, 10 in ambush situations, eight in traffic stops, and three while handling a prisoner. Handguns pose the greatest danger and account for 40 killings. Twelve resulted from rifles, three from shotguns, and one officer died after being stabbed with a knife. Six were killed in the Oklahoma City Bombing and one died after being run over by a motor vehicle.

The infrequency of cop killing is cold comfort. A spare statistic masks the jolting emotional impact that the death of an officer has on his or her colleagues. The shock of a killing erodes the comforting bindings of culture and initiates a psychological journey for those closest to the slain officer. The journey they take will seek the meaning of the death, and what little meaning they find reaffirms culture. The meanings are played out in collective grieving rituals and are about what it is to be a cop.

Police culture intensifies the effects of death on survivors. To understand the impact of death in the police culture, one needs to recognize the powerful unifying forces that underlie cop culture. Those who enter the policing occupation and fail to understand its cultural nuances are quickly singled out, labeled, and emancipated. These individuals are often passed over for promotions and removed from the social sphere of police life. For those who carry on, policing becomes a way of living and thinking, organized around core values—survival, beat responsibility, common-sense, not backing down, dealing with the brass, and an existential conservatism that seeks out the normal in everyday routines and distrusts all else.

The most powerful unifying force is their perspective on the world, their characteristic outlook. Police knowledge is a cultural phenomena, grounded in ironic common sense, developed in ordinary day-to-day routines and reinforced by fellow officers. This knowledge is a language both practical and value laden. It contains stories, rituals, metaphors and ironies that convey all that is valuable to the culture. It cannot be taught at the police academy and it cannot be learned from books or criminal justice courses. The symbolic term for the development of cultural knowledge is street experience, a term with a rich and multivocal set of significations. It is the ability to look at a seemingly normal situation and to know instinctively that something is wrong.

From apprentice training and from contact with precinct colleagues, "street experience" becomes a cultural tool kit, a store of lessons, stories, and aphorisms about the doing of police work (McNulty, 1994). Local cultural knowledge is constantly expanded through "war stories," the experiences of other officers, and daily activities. The collective body of traditions is constantly expanding and shifting (Crank, 1996).

As new officers are exposed to police work, the traditions and common-sense meanings of work become more important to their cop identity than the rules, regulations, bureaucracy, and due process laws that seek to control their behavior. Rules and laws are constrictive, having as their goal the control of cop behavior. Cultural knowledge is expansive, indirect in meaning, clear with its reservoir of practical sense and brimming with human emotion (Shearing & Ericson, 1991). Over time, cultural knowledge breathes life into daily routines. Officers bond emotionally from their shared experiences, through the collective symbols of solidarity. It is a closeness built into the word-view, central to and indivisible from the culture.

Death eats culture. The killing of a cop is a rupture of the collective. Solidarity is literally shattered—a culture carrier, storyteller, colleague, son-of-a-bitch, partner, troublemaker, prankster, backbiter, bullshitter is gone. Nor do killings allow for a reaffirmation of culture through the heroism of the officer. Death itself is usually more brutish than heroic. Consider the story (Baker, 1985) of a cop killing:

> Approximately two hours later (after the search had begun) they found her in the tall weeds of a vacant lot . . . Lozada's shield was under her body, her handcuffs were out and a necklace was laying on the ground nearby. Her .38-caliber service revolver was missing. She had been shot in the head, twice.

> It wasn't the kind of heroic death most cops picture for themselves, not exactly a blaze of glory. But Officer Lozada's death was a sadly typical police death. She was doing her job. Something inadvertent or unexpected had happened. She lost control of the situation and was murdered. There's nothing glorious or glamorous about dying all alone in a vacant lot full of rubble and garbage, but it happens much more often than those romantic gunfights at the O.K. Corral which many cops envision when they daydream the endings of their personal movies (Baker, 1985:338-339).

There is nothing in this killing that somehow reinforces cultural values. The death was bleak, a harsh moment in a desolate lot covered with rubble and trash. Whatever skills the officer had learned had not been enough. Her sense of suspicion had not been enough. Her knowledge had not been enough. Her firepower had not been enough, and, in fact, had been used to kill her.

Among members of the local organizational culture, the killing of a cop marks the onset of a period of anger and confusion. Revenge becomes an immediate and powerful sentiment. Someone will be blamed, and a search for the killer is relentless. Sometimes administration receives a piece of the blame, and the person who was killed is always scrutinized closely—what did they do wrong? Even in the event of a cop-killing, there is difficulty acknowledging that some situations are uncontrollable, that death will sometimes win, even when the best effort is forthcoming. A small element of blame, rarely spoken, sticks to the victim (Brooks, 1975).

The impact of a killing is more far-reaching than can be captured in simple ideas of police revenge on a suspect. Whether or not the death was heroic, a hero has died and the rules of the order—the defining cultural themes that make cops—are discredited. Police officers seek out the meaning in the death. This period can last for days, and prevails until the funeral ritual, the time-honored ceremonial procession to the place of interment. During this time, officers may relinquish their traditional rank and status differences and come together in solidarity. Members of the management culture are received by the rank and file but the reception is cool, shaded by skepticism and apprehension. This unity is shattered if the line officers attribute responsibility for the death to management errors. The mask of unity is maintained until internment and occasionally for brief periods beyond.

The emotional impact of an officer's death is immediate. For those close to the officer a renunciation takes hold, particularly in smaller departments where alliances are formed from impregnable solidarism. Close associates sometimes suffer from post-stress disorder and other psychological dysfunctions. Most will revisit the fatality many times seeking explanations, and many will endure feelings of self-imposed guilt. In what has been called a process of transition resignation, officers seek answers to the unanswerable: "What could I have done to change the outcome" and "Why was I selected to survive?" Officers who were an active participant in the fatal activity may be traumatized, and the families and careers of closest associates may experience a harsh and long-term impact.

A police officer killing catalyzes the sense of alienation cops feel toward the public. Police officers will project their emotional outrage on to the accused, the community, and anyone perceived to be an outsider. Never is the sense of "us vs. them" so strong. Cops display resentment at the media and are appalled at any publicity unfavorable to the slain officer, the department, or their profession. Any comment less than high-minded about the deceased is taken as betrayal. There is no room for shades of gray in any media presentation of an officer killing, nor tolerance for others who do not share their sentiment.

Death Links Institutions

Police and Families

A dichotomy frequently employed in analyses of social control processes is that between formal control, or the law and legal process, and informal control, usually described in terms of softer or more indirect means of behavior control, and carried by institutions such as the family, and the church (see, for example Cumming, Cumming & Edell, 1985). The dichotomy, focusing analytically on the differences in institutions as agents of control, leads us away from areas of institutional overlap. One such area is between the police and the family, a bond powerfully forged during the period after the death and at the funeral.

The Collection

When an officer is killed, a series of events link police agencies and the family of the deceased. These activities, though focused on families of the killed officer, sometimes encompass frightened families of the surviving officers. In ceremonies of institutional bridge-building, police departments affirm, in a practical way, how cops and families share a similar sense of values and of morality. The umbrella of police support is extended to the family of the killed officer in a variety of ways.

In both England and the United States, voluntary collections are made for the widows and children of policemen, both immediately at the time of death, and after, and ensure some degree of security for the officer's kin. For those participating in the funeral, the thought "this is how I'll be remembered" extends to an appreciation for the idea that their families will be remembered as well (Manning, 1977). As one observer wrote concerning a police funeral he observed in the United States, "in light of the various collections passed around the Department and the attention provided the widow and family in this case, one's attendance at the affair was thought by some to be something of a premium payment on a grand group insurance plan" (Van Maanen, 1976:9).

The collection is a powerful ritual linking the family of a slain officer to the police. The collection carries an implicit promise to do the same for all officers who contribute. In a paradoxical way, this bargain with death forges police solidarity. Honor is less problematic, and financial and other rights due the policeman are resolved communally. Through sharing, the eroded myth of police invulnerability, lost in the individual case, is re-established in the collective. The sacrament of sharing acknowledges death, but at the same time brings officers together. It is thus a powerful tradition for the reinvigoration of culture.

Concerns of Police Survivors (COPS)

In 58 communities across America, citizens have formed associations to provide financial security for survivors of officers killed in the line-of-duty. These groups, initially called Hundred Clubs, were organized in 1952 following the murder of a Detroit City Police officer (Chapman,

1986). In 1984, 110 survivors of law enforcement killings formed an alliance called "Concerns of Police Survivors" (COPS) in order to offer support to police families.[1] This was the first effort to form a national networking organization to aid survivors in the healing process and to provide guidance to agencies concerning line-of-duty death policies (Haddix, 1996).

COPS was founded in response to the feelings of many families of victims that they had been "totally abandoned by the department" (Sawyer, 1993:1). Feelings of abandonment, they argued, stemmed from two sources: fear and confusion on the part of the agency itself, and insensitivity on the part of officers and administration dealing with the event. These feelings were bolstered by the absence of formal policies to deal with line-of-duty death: at the time COPS was formed, fully 67 percent of law enforcement departments in the U.S. lacked formal policies for an officer's line-of-duty death. Whether intentional or not, agency insensitivity was a frequently cited concern for the families of slain officers. Consider the following example.

> I had to threaten suit against the department before they would sit down and tell me how it happened. I was able to see, and feel comforted, by the fact there was nothing he could have done to save himself. Through all this, the department had me thinking there was something to hide (Sawyer, 1993:8).

This story is not unique. In a related story told at a panel of Criminal Justice Professionals in Idaho (Rainer, 1996; also mentioned in Sawyer, 1993), the wife of an officer was made to wait for two hours to see her husband. He had been mortally wounded and the chief wanted her to wait until the chaplain arrived. When at last the chaplain made his appearance, the officer had died. The woman could have spent that time with her husband, and instead passed the last two hours of her husband's life alone.

The majority of police agencies in the United States lack sufficient resources to provide post-traumatic relief. Yet here the problems may be the most severe: in a small department, the loss of one officer can have a shattering effect on the well-being of its members. In a small community, the death of an officer will unsettle the entire citizenry.

Survivors have also noted the callousness of the media.

> I had just finished grocery shopping when I heard the chilling report of a police shoot-out on the car radio. The reporter was the one who informed me that it was my husband that had been killed. My neighbors found me, crying hysterically, parked in the middle of the road several blocks from home . . . (Sawyer, 1993:4).

The following incident shows how mismanaged deaths can have bitter consequences:

> A prisoner secreted a key, took a weapon from a deputy, and killed another deputy that had three months on the job. The media picked up the response on scanners. They tried to cover the body, but left the shoes exposed. The officer's wife saw the shoes on the news, ran to the closet, and discovered that her husband had worn those shoes that day. That was how she discovered her husband had been killed (Sawyer, 1993:6).

A notification of an officer's death is emotionally taut, and the notification may be painful for the deliverer. In an effort to assuage the grief, some officers may make promises that cannot be kept. Rainer (1996) described a notification in which an officer, giving a notification of a death, promised to take the officer's son fishing. The child went to the door every Saturday, waiting for an officer that never showed.

COPS provides a comprehensive set of support services for agencies and families that experience line-of-duty deaths. An emergency response team assists in the notification, provides support during the transition period, and helps arrange the funeral. They regularly meet with police managers to discuss preparedness for line-of-duty death. They assist agencies in the development of a family support team to provide a structured response to survivors. This team contains specific roles: Command liaison, benefits coordination, financial coordination, chaplain or minister notification and family liaison. Each of these will contribute to the healing process, both for departmental colleagues and for families. To further aid families, COPS provides a scholarship program for dependent children, adult children, and spouses of officers killed in the line of duty.

Death creates red tape. Wills, insurance policies, funeral schedules and plans for the distribution of possessions contribute to the mass of detail that overwhelm the grieving process in red tape. Both the department and the families cope with the mind-numbing bureaucratic superstructure of death in contemporary American society. Departments must deal with confidential emergency notification forms, family member notification, and information on parents and grown children. Officers are recommended to put together a "death benefit package" that includes information about life insurance, survivor death benefits or annuities paid by a retirement plan, state and/or federal benefits, social security and/or labor group benefit plans.

A latent, nonbureaucratic function is also served in the accomplishment of this enormous mass of detail: families are reminded of the liability of police work. In this way, bureaucratic anticipation of death accomplishes two things: (1) it replicates at an administrative level central themes of police culture: that the future is unpredictable, that police work is dangerous, and that the world really is a perilous place, and (2) it reproduces these cultural themes in the family of the victim, as well as in the families of other members of the local organizational culture.

Death is symbolic. The death of a police officer carries a symbolic component dramatically enacted by the police throughout the period prior to and including the funeral—that society itself is vulnerable. This observation has been noted by Manning (1977), and much of this section draws directly from his work. The killing of a police officer is an evocative symbol, played out by brass, media, and politicians, of a vicious onslaught on society by criminals. If the protectors are themselves vulnerable, if even such sacred symbols as the flag and secular symbols of power such as guns and handcuffs cannot protect the protectors, then how can the police protect the public? The "thin blue line" is a phrase that evokes the symbolic moral guardianship of the police. The killing of one is the purest of evils—an assault on society itself. Unconditional support from outsiders, particularly press and public officials, serves as a forceful affirmation of the moral righteousness of the police and the vulnerability of the society policed. Consider the following remarks rendered by Rev. R. Joseph Dooley, Chaplain of the Police and Firemen Society, at the funeral of an officer. Gail A. Cobb was the first American policewoman killed in the line of duty.

> Law Enforcement is not just a job. It is a whole way of life, a total commitment. If anything brings a police family or group of officers together it is an occasion such as this . . . police families know that this moment can come at any time. An attack on any of you becomes an attack against the country and all it stands for . . . in police work there is no sanctuary from a criminal's gun (*Washington Post*, September 25, 1974:1, cited in Manning, 1977).

His rhetoric captured the emotional power of police symbols. He asserted passionately that a war was being waged by criminals against the color of your uniform and the silver or gold of your badge. When Father Dooley pointed out that an attack on the police was an attack against the country, he was acknowledging the vulnerability of the police and to the moral order they sustain.

This rhetoric also reveals themes of isolation from the public, of being different and special. The police frequently confront the public as an adversary, and officers feel isolated when performing dangerous work. Cultural supports, acted out as friendship, support, and physical protection in crisis, are an internal phenomenon. The dramaturgy of an officer killing is aimed as much at cops as at the public. This does not mean that it is not manipulated by those seeking political or newsworthy gain.

High-mindedness at funerals is appropriate—no one wants to speak harshly of the dead when their words might cause pain to those close to the deceased, and when such talk would be regarded as petty or mean-spirited. And no politician would dare alienate the police and their supporters at such a moment. Consider the following use of evocative police symbols by an elected official:

> On 7 March 1995, in an emotion-charged ceremony in the New York State capital of Albany, Governor George Pataki signed into law the death penalty; for the first time in eighteen years New York has the power to inflict capital punishment. Realizing the significance of a ceremony introducing to the books a law that would allow the execution of cop killers, Governor Pataki signed his first name with the gold cross pen which Officer Sean McDonald had carried in his gun belt, and his last name with a black ballpoint carried in the memo book of Officer Raymond Cannon on the night that he was killed. Laura Cannon wept as she clutched her husband's black leather memo book to her chest; Sean McDonald's widow Janet stared toward the heavens for strength, but in the end she too could not hold back the tears (Katz, 1995:98-99).

Death links the police with broader elements in society. The ceremonious marshalling evokes religious observance, outpourings of condolence, and support from all segments of society. Through all the high-minded newspaper and media rhetoric, the public carries a large reservoir of genuine support for the police and sympathy for the families of those who die in the name of the public safety. Death and funerals are cop things, but they are things widely and sadly felt.

Police Death and the Government

The relationship between the police and the government is ambiguous. For most citizens, the police are its most visible representatives. The relationship between the municipal police and the government, however, has been tenuous (Walker, 1977). Cops tend to dispense their version of street-based justice more according to local community needs than to state law and municipal codes (Wilson, 1968). Some citizens even perceive American municipal police as the first line of local resistance in the somewhat unlikely event of a federalist military takeover. However, the federal government has built a variety of symbolic bridges that show their support for local police when a cop is killed.

An important symbolic contribution is the National Law Enforcement Officers Memorial in Washington, D.C. The names of nearly 14,000 slain officers appear on the walls of the memorial. During the four years since the memorial was dedicated, nearly 1,300 new names of fallen officers have been added to the monument's walls (National Law Enforcement Officers Memorial Fund, 1996). For the wall's witnesses, strangers curious and heartfelt in their interest, and families and cops that make pilgrimages, the ascetic etchings on the wall evoked profound emotions.

This evocative symbol of death conjures haunting images: were they tortured, did they suffer, did they feel terror; did they, at the last moment, reflect on some fatal error, or have the briefest moment to say good-bye to their family? Did they know that they were dying and could they let go? The symbol is intensely heroic—these must have been very courageous men and women who put their personal safety and lives on the line for total strangers, the same strangers that would not socialize privately with them, that feared them. The Memorial walls provide a rare public glimpse into the emotional territory of police culture.

The memorial is associated with a week of ceremonies, carried out annually in the Spring. During the month of May, National Police Week is observed in Washington D.C. A large number of fraternal organizations such as the Fraternal Order of Police, police unions, and families of police survivors participate in this event. Events include uniformed motorcycle rides from the Pentagon to the National Law Enforcement Officers Memorial, Candlelight Vigils, Survivor Seminars, Police Parades, a Police Officers Memorial Day Service, and the placement of Honor Guards at the Memorial. Individually and collectively, this is a time of bittersweet celebration—sadness for the death of the officer, celebration in the unity of police nationally.

The government also provides benefits to officers through the Public Safety Officers' Benefits Act. In 1976, Congress authorized a one-time financial benefit to the eligible survivors of public safety officers whose deaths are the direct and proximate result of a traumatic injury sustained in the line of duty (Bureau of Justice Assistance Fact Sheet, 1995). A police officer is thus armed with the knowledge and psychological comfort of financial stability for his/her family in the event of death in the line of duty. This support nourishes the culture of police work by offering the benevolence of federal economic support to the surviving family members.

Death and Brass

Reuss-Ianni (1983) described street and management cultures in antagonistic terms, characterized by frequent hostilities between the two cultures. The death of an officer does not change this fundamental antagonism but for a time sets it aside. Death draws together all officers, regardless of rank. Yet, those that have experienced the death of a colleague remark on the persistence of problems between management and street culture.[2]

McMurray (1990) captures this sense of street-management hostility. His research focused on assaults, and allows for a consideration of the way in which violence against police officers affects line-management relations. In a study of attitudes of assaulted police officers, McMurray observed that attitudes about organizational responsiveness to assaults on cops depended on whether they were street cops or managers. Police administrators believed that they were sensitive to assault issues, but line officers held a sharply different view, expressing concerns over administrative insensitivity. Assaulted officers frequently experienced what McMurray called a "second injury"—the perceived insensitivity and lack of responsiveness from those within the criminal justice system and from the community at large. When asked to rank events that disturbed them most following their being assaulted, "Nonsupport from management" was cited by 22 percent of the officers.

The following comments were made by McMurray's respondents:

Respondent 1: "Supervisors need to be trained in post-traumatic events, crisis intervention and, most importantly, how to listen."

Respondent 2: "The department is fairly good about your time off and doing the paperwork. However, they don't really concern themselves with the psychological aspect."

Respondent 3: "Seems like everyone abandons you. You're criticized more about what mistakes you made or your involvement. Any help you get seems like just a formality."

Respondent 4: "Department doesn't give a damn about the officers" (McMurray, 1990:46).

Respondents indicated that supportive services, particularly psychological counseling and time off, were inadequate. Many did not feel comfortable in using the services for fear of being labelled and feared a breach in the confidentiality by clinic staff. Perceived management insensitivity appeared to be limited to upper levels. Eighty-two percent indicated that their immediate supervising official, typically the sergeant, supported them after the assault.

Peer Support: Catharsis or Wound-Opening?

Many larger law enforcement agencies have developed a peer support group concept of counseling for their officers following line-of-duty deaths. Peer support groups are comprised of volunteer officers from all ranks who receive specialized training. They are available to respond to critical situations that require post-traumatic assistance and intermediate counseling. And they offer short-term post-traumatic relief, though typically they lack the formal training for more intensive or long-term psychological attention. However, peer groups are also feared: Communications with a team member may not be legally privileged and, as feared by officers in the previous example, may be introduced as court testimony. And officers may fear that their innermost fears of death may become a matter of public record, subject to analytical dissection in courtroom litigation.

Coping with death is hard on colleagues of the deceased. Survivors of a law enforcement line-of-duty death usually do not know whom to turn or how to seek help. They may not recognize that they need professional assistance or that such assistance is affordable or attainable. They fear stigmatization. The policeman, steeped in a cultural ethic of maleness, individual responsibility, physical strength, and control over the unpredictable, is particularly inept in absorbing the psychological consequences of the death.

Cops fear, often reasonably, that any display of mourning or grief will be taken as weakness, and recognize that they will appear unsuitable as a colleague or untrustworthy to back up another officer should they seek professional assistance. The possibility of court and management access to their records verifies to them that others will view any special assistance or consulting as weakness. Consequently, even in the event of a death, neither the courts nor department management are trusted.

Consider the following example. Five federal officers confronted eight armed tax protesters in an incident in North Dakota. After a firefight lasting less than 10 minutes, two of the officers were killed and two more received incapacitating injuries (Corcoran, 1990). A supervisor subsequently helped one survivor receive individual professional assistance. The arrangement was conducted covertly because personnel policy limited agency assistance to "adequate time off," 30 days of administrative leave at most. The fees for professional counseling were subsequently charged to the officer's private insurance carrier.

Following the officer's return to duty, management officials learned through rumor that the officer had sought professional assistance during his period of official recuperation. He was subsequently tarnished and labelled as "weak," a label that even his first level supervisor, who acknowledged his complicity in the counseling, could not dispel. Those close to the traumatic event provided support for the officer through traditional law enforcement support mechanisms, to no avail: a label of weakness dies hard in a police organization, and may be the most crippling of all labels. This stigmatization haunted the officer until his retirement some four years later. Management's exposure of the officer's counseling obstructed the psychological recovery of the officer and contributed directly to his early retirement.

Much of this chapter has been less than friendly to police administration, and deservedly so: support in line-of-duty death incidents has often been lacking and insensitive, planning is inadequate, and policies are often non-existent. Bureaucratic forms of management have been popular because they seem to hold the promise of rational solutions to organizational problems. They are, however, singularly ill-equipped to deal with more profound emotional, human problems routinely encountered by beat cops. Moreover, the administration must look toward the future, and cold as it seems, the department must carry on. The world must stop when an officer is killed, but only for a moment.

Much of the literature we have covered in this chapter, dealing with COPS and CISM are presented in the spirit of furthering administrative sensitivity and preparation. We will close this chapter with a story that celebrates this spirit.

> Vivian Lee's husband had been killed in the line of duty. She had always wanted to go to the Police Officers' Memorial in Washington, D.C., to see her husband's name on the wall. Finally, she found the opportunity and went. At the wall, Vivian found her husband's name, with a note taped by it. It was a long note from his daughter, about how she missed him, and how she wished he could be present at her high school graduation. It was then 10 years after his death. When she returned, she called the department, and the department sent six uniformed officers to sit in the front row at the daughter's graduation. At the end of the ceremony they handed her a bouquet of flowers (Rainer, 1996).

Endnotes

[1] The formal goal of Concerns of Police Survivors (COPS) is:

> To minister to the needs of families who have suffered the loss of a law enforcement officer in the line-of-duty. To extend a helping hand to stabilize the family's emotional, financial, and legal well being. To let the families know that others who have suffered the same loss can be of service to them during the periods of helplessness. To focus on the problems of the law enforcement profession which directly or indirectly lead to the loss of an officer's life.

[2] An average of 143 law enforcement officers are killed in the line of duty annually in the United States. Whether it is the result of an adversarial action or an accident, the trauma caused by each death is felt by family survivors and department personnel for many months, or even years, after the event. Still, most law enforcement agencies have not experienced a line-of-duty death. Perhaps for this reason, less than one-third have any policy dealing with this sensitive issue. It is little wonder, then, that agencies dealing with a line-of-duty death for the first time often respond inadequately to the needs of survivors (Haddix, 1996).

26

Good-bye in a Sea of Blue[1]

by Stephenie Lord, John Crank,
and Ronald Evans

Theme: Police Funerals

The day the new recruit steps through the doors of
a police academy, he leaves society to enter a "profession" that does more than give him a job: it
defines who he is. For all the years that he remains,
closed to the sphere of its rituals and its absurdities
in the town where he began, until he takes the ran-
som money of his pension and retires, he will be a
cop (Ahern, 1972:3).

In this frequently cited quote, James Ahern captures the spirit of
police work. In a sense more fundamental than symbols, more basic than
beliefs, cops share an identity. Their sense of self merges into a collective
identity, a sea of blue, in which only minor personality variations are tolerated. From the moment they join the force they see themselves as cops.
They face the world with a cop's face, they learn to wear it off work, and
they wear the face long after they leave the force. They collectively
dream retirement dreams of a farm or small ranch in the Pacific North-
west or in the Blue Ridge mountains, of a fishing boat off the Atlantic
intercoastal waterway. They fear a heart attack more than in-service
death—cops firmly believe that they will not live long after retirement.

Being a cop is solidarity personified. Superficially, it is a simple recognition of similarity, the sharing of common problems, dealing with troublemakers, handling and redirecting bullshit during roll call, talking to
others who understand what you are talking about. At a deeper level, it
is a sharing of identity. The similarity among all cops is that they are, after
all is said and done, cops. Finer distinctions of personality disappear in
the collective: cops recognize themselves in each other. Take an officer
from the high deserts of Idaho and put him on the mean streets of Savannah, and it will not take long for them to work out their differences. Their
common identity overrides fine points of geography. It is layered in symbols of copness, the badge and the shield, fraternal traditions, and in an
intensity of loyalty not diminished by subtleties of reason or logic.

Derived from occupational demands that bind officers together for safety, the fraternity is closed. Only cops understand cops. A man or a woman puts on the uniform in the morning, looks in the mirror, and sees a cop looking back.

Solidarity is a sentiment, though sentiment seems too weak a word for it. It is not a symbol, though it is sustained by powerful symbols and vocabularies of "cop" and "other." Solidarity, as Douglas (1986) observed, is about individuals being willing to suffer for the larger group and about expectations that other group members would do the same for them. The social bond that made solidarity is "taken to be something above question" (Douglas, 1986:1)

The puissance of police solidarity, though frequently noted, is not well understood. Its astonishing strength stems from the broad societal morality that provides the foundation for their values. Police work is a distillation and fermentation of those values, acted out on patrol. Institutional values may be the most compelling in the area of justice. It is here that our ideas of what is sacred are the strongest, that our focus is so resolutely fixed on what is morally right (Douglas, 1986).

Certainly it is the police that are the gatekeepers of public morality. Police embody justice morally defended; they perceive themselves to be sentinels of the American way of life.[2] Anyone who has accepted trust, demanded sacrifice, or has willingly given either knows the power of the social bond (Douglas, 1986). There is little psychological space for police officers to raise broad questions about their work, when to challenge means to question the morality of the institution of crime control itself. Absolute loyalty goes with the territory: to question justice is to doubt the work that cops do. To question public morality is perilous in society; one opens oneself to the most abusive sorts of criticisms. For cops, it is pernicious, unconscionable.

Cops are profoundly moral. Within the culture, the morality borders on absolute. Cherokee Paul McDonald captures this spirit in the cover page to his book *Blue Truth* (1991):

> Apologize?
> Me . . . apologize?
> Let me give you a little hint:
> > Never.
> Even when I did the wrong thing,
> I did it for the right reason.

It is a morality that is unquestioned—one does not think against the grain here. And there is no greater affront to this sense of morality than the killing of another cop.

A cop killing rolls through the sea of blue like a tidal wave. No offense is greater, none more vile. The cultural damage is large, it is an immediate blow. In a brief moment a battle has been lost. When the bad guys win, the fundamental legitimacy of police as society's guardians is brought into question.

The funeral ceremony is a ritual that re-establishes police authority and power. It does so at a personal level, conveying powerful sentiments of righteousness about being a police officer to officers in attendance. It also establishes authority symbolically, showing its nonpolice audience that it is the front-line bearer of society's morals. The funeral ritual here is truly a fuse. The collective ideas and beliefs are acted out in a variety of processions and displays of solidarity. At the cultural level, the funeral is about the re-invigoration of cops' symbols. All important symbols are on display, and all are celebrated by the sea of blue. Each aspect of the funeral—the march to the grave, the salute to the fallen officer, the color guard—each element is an invocation of powerful symbols of copness. In a tragic way, the funeral ritual is how the police culture celebrates its identity.

No ceremony is more potent for cop loyalty than is a funeral of a police officer killed in the line of duty. This symbolic event, rich in tradition, binds officers unlike anything else. The funeral of an officer strengthens the bond of those individuals who are sworn to protect society, the same society that took their beloved member away. It is solidarity itself that is on display in police funerals. As Geertz observed, the funeral ritual is the "thing itself," power, established at a moral level within the police culture and legitimization of purpose for society.

The solidarity displayed in a funeral ritual is more than some academic concept—it is a physical, tangible entity. A sea of blue is an apt metaphor that captures its turbulent energy. To experience the sea of blue is to understand all over again, and for some cops to comprehend for the first time, what it means to be a cop. Some officers never experience it. All are moved by it. It is unmistakable, emotionally moving, bringing cops together in a profound way, in full dress. It haphazardly mixes moments of tedium, of standing-around-doing-nothing-wishing-you-could-get-a-smoke-and-a-beer with the feeling that "now I understand what it's all about." Consider Baker's (1985) words on this topic:

> At this point Officer Lozada's coffin reappeared and we stood in silence with our hands over our hearts. As the trumpeter hit the first three notes of taps, the ex-lieutenant whispered "Jeeze, I hate it when they play that shit." The crowd broke up like kids getting out of school. Those officers who didn't have to return to duty went looking for a bar. The cops from other jurisdictions and other states were looking for a good time (Baker, 1985:342).

A similar sentiment was expressed by a colleague who served as a pallbearer for military funerals. He commented on its tedious formality and the overwhelming desire to get it over with quickly. Yet, when the flag was folded and passed to the family, he felt a profound sense of why he was there, and of what it meant to be a member of the cop fraternity.

The inevitable status differences that characterize cop relationships are present at funerals but are on a grander scale, as cops from different departments check each other out. Showing off different jurisdictions' patrol cars and their latest gadgetry is a main event at funerals. Baker captures the blend of the ordinary and the sacred: "you go out of respect, but as soon as the funeral is over the cops begin to mingle and talk about the bad guy they just shot or the one they kicked the shit out of. Ten minutes later, every one of them is checking out the police cars from the other states" (Baker, 1995:342).

Goings-on such as these are no less an expression of solidarity than the formal procedures of the burial. In funerals, there is a mix and blend of ideas, stories, and traditions that intermingle organizational cultures. Departments learn about what others are doing. The sea of blue is a vast intermingling of different organizational cultures, and they are mutually reaffirming in the ways of ordinary life that are meaningful to cops.

To cops, the funeral of an officer has an occupationally derived meaning. The imagery of the ceremony, the collective acting out of the occupation's mission, and the display of sacred symbols provide a focus for the end of the psychological journey that started with the death of a colleague. When officers come together for the funeral, the ritual of solidarity and the large array of symbols carry personal meaning. Through symbols like the black-banded badge, the flag, the elegy, and the military salute, officers sense their identity as a part of the collective—they are cops, and that is good.

The message, though collective, is also intensely personal. Assurance flows from the ceremony to all officers and their families. To honor a single policeman, all share in the honor. Each thinks, "This is the way I'll be remembered by those that care for me the most." To die in the line of duty means that the officer will live on, as a collectivity, into eternity. The death of a hero breathes new life into the culture.

Funerals are a drama acted out for the public. Surprisingly few writers have discussed police funerals. Among them, Manning (1977) has focused on their symbolic elements. Though recognizing the culturally reinvigorating qualities of funerals,[3] Manning particularly focused on the cultural symbolism of funerals. A funeral and the messages portrayed therein, he suggested, are aimed at the public audience and served symbolic purposes of image construction. Funerals are a dramaturgy: they act out powerful themes that convey messages to a public audience. The powerful symbols inherent in police funerals reinforce the public images of the police, their occupation, and their role in society.

Manning identified five aspects of funerals that carried symbolic meaning for the public. The first was the righteousness of the police presence in everyday society. The police represented the concern the state has for the welfare of its citizens and the state's authority to intervene in the affairs of the citizenry. Traditional values of duty, honor, patriotism, and dedication were acted out for the public inspection.

Second, the presence of officers in large numbers reminds us that social control is ubiquitous. Not only are the police gathered in large numbers, but they are in full dress, each department distinctly marked. The funeral color-guard is made up of members of diverse departments. The orderly gathering, coordinated actions, seemingly calculated movement, and uniformed appearance contribute to this public perception. The display of agency diversity, together with large numbers of officers in attendance, transmits the message that the local police department is part of a larger purpose.

Third, the police represent an absolute morality, and the funeral conveys their readiness to enforce this morality. Police work is timeless and unchanging: the police are prepared to act at anytime and under any circumstance. The power involved in such a responsibility creates an image of sacredness. This responsibility was endowed to the police by the state. With the state at the root of police power, police actions and occupational operations can be readily justified. The killing of a cop chisels away at the state's authority. The funeral displays officers in full gear, committed absolutely to good ends. Lest anyone doubt why cops exist, look across the sea of blue.

Fourth, the killing of a police officer undermines the fundamental principle that police coercion can fix problems. When a police officer is killed, symbolically it is the police (and the public) that lose and the criminals that win. Police are shown to be as vulnerable as are the rest of us. Such an idea is unacceptable not only to police culture, but to a society that believes in the police as protectors of citizens. A killing is a chink in the protective armor. With the funeral, the system of power is re-established—the authority of the police is reclaimed symbolically. To outside observers, the police unite in body and spirit behind their fallen comrade, as if to say *"You will have to kill us all to stop us."*

Fifth, the killing of an officer undercuts the legitimacy of society itself. When an officer is killed, doubts extend to all of the symbols—the flag, for example, and the city seal—that link the occupation of policing with broader patterns of authority in society. And the equipment and technology that the police use, are they for nothing? Equipment, such as guns, nightsticks, badges, police cruisers, the 911 system, are supposed to aid and protect the police. How can the police protect the public if their equipment cannot help them?

In a funeral, these items are on conspicuous display. How can one question weaponry when it is so clearly and forcefully displayed on so many officers? Police cruisers are awesome in parade, and their power in the service of good is unquestionable. The funeral thus reveals a primal truth of social control: the officer who was killed lives on in spirit, and it is a vengeful one. One officer might be killed, but a sea of blue cannot be stopped. There will be no rest for a cop killer.

Funerals are for cops. Funeral rites are not only symbolic. Officers look across a sea of blue and see their future among the living. Culture is an immediate and powerful presence. The funeral contains powerful, solidifying symbols of copness.

Funeral rites are powerful symbol carriers. They are what they seem to be, solidarity acted out on a solemn occasion. Officers are brought together, and their display of solidarity, en masse, is solidarity, the thing itself. The presence of 20,000 officers at a funeral in New York City need send no message. Officers share the grief of the loss, and reaffirm their bond as officers. There is not so much a shared message as a shared feeling. A sea of blue united in loss and reaffirmation. Solidarity, acted out in the powerful traditions, of police funerals, are affirmed and strengthened among the members of the police culture.

Funerals are about collective grief. Of all things that trouble us, among the most difficult are the death of friends. Humans do not deal well with death. Cops, at funerals, seek out solidarity to dispel their sense of loss. Consider the following statements. "When one dies, we all die a little inside" (Greene, 1991). "When a police officer dies in the line of duty, some of life's breath in all of us is taken away" (Schmitt, 1989). "Anytime a cop dies, a piece of every other cop dies—it's horrible" (Schmitt, 1989). "We're all in the same boat. They are shooting at all of us. We have to stick together" (Jennings, 1990).

These statements are about the killing of an officer, but each conveys more than the death itself. The death of one is in its way a death experienced by all. A funeral is also a tangible "thing in itself," though it may serve symbolic ends. Like the death itself, it can be hard-edged, emotionally intense. It is a death not sensed symbolically, but bitterly experienced, deeply troubling, personal. Funerals can be tough.

The aura of solidarity, unity, and fellowship permeate the atmosphere of a funeral. Personal friendship is not a prerequisite for emotional intensity; the emotions caused by a funeral are culturally pervasive. Consider the following comment: "I don't think it matters if you know him or not. I know I feel a part of it today, it's a camaraderie" (Priest & Jenkins, 1989). New York's Mayor Rudolph Guiliani understood this solidarity when he "promised the family of [a] slain N.Y.P.D. officer that the sea of blue surrounding them . . . would never evaporate" (Martin, 1994). The widow of another officer was told "as you walk out of the church today, I want you to look at the sea of blue. They are all here because they love you and your children . . . I want to make you a promise: that even though he has left us we will never forget him" (Hevesi, 1994). One officer attending the funeral of another officer with whom she had graduated from a police academy summed up the sentiments of this moment of grief: "I've lost a good friend. I'm just so sad" (Reed & Miller, 1995).

Dynamics of Solidarity:
Agency Participation, Symbols, and Rites

The display of solidarity extends beyond the jurisdictional lines of the agency to which the slain officer was assigned, sometimes beyond the department, the city, the state, and even the country. Members of police agencies from far and wide travel to honor a fallen comrade, and sometimes funerals attract thousands of attendees. There was the green and gray of New Hampshire; the cardinal of the Royal Canadian Mounted Police; the Grays of Connecticut, Alabama and Pennsylvania, and the blues of New Jersey, Massachusetts, Michigan and Indiana" (Schmitt, 1989).

The sheer numbers in attendance reinforce the solidarity of cops. Note the following descriptions of funeral attendees: "Thousands Mourn FBI Agent Slain During Stakeout" (Smith, 1994), "Nearly 4,000 Officers Pay Tribute to Slain Deputy" (Katz, 1994), "2,500 Fellow Officers at Funeral for Ganz" (Lozano, 1994), and "4,000 Attend Rites Honoring Policeman as 'Fallen Hero'" (Wilgoren, 1993). With such a vast presence of copness, the outpouring of support, of concern, of solidarity is overwhelming.

Funeral solidarity does not dissolve all boundaries: beyond the family of the deceased officer, the public is not invited to the funeral itself. The funeral of an officer, although a publicized event, imparts a sense of foreignness to outsiders. A cop's sense of isolation from the public carries into the honoring of a fallen police officer. This sentiment is revealed in the account of the procession of mourners en route from a funeral home to a cemetery in the Washington D.C. area (Meyer, 1994). Along the route, roads and portions of a major highway were closed down to allow for the mile-long procession to pass. The image of the public being held at bay, separate, silent observers to the procession, underscored the distance between cops and the general population.

Rites rich in tradition and symbolism are evident in a police funeral. Black bands worn over the badge, or on the arm of a mourning officer depict a display of honor for the fallen comrade. Bagpipes performing "Amazing Grace" during the parade or "Taps" at the interment, helicopters flying in formation, and a 21-gun salute are significant police funeral traditions (Meyer, 1994). One will see a wreath bearing the badge number of a fallen officer, white-gloved hands snapping a salute, and a motorcycle cortege (Hevesi, 1994). The meaning of these symbols is copness, not to be understood but felt, to know what it is to be a cop. The solidarity of the funeral, through the sheer physical presence of officers and the diverse symbols of copness, breathes life into police culture.

The following is a compilation of various accounts of funerals. I assembled this account to provide the cultural sensibility of solidarity, evoked by symbols rich in police tradition. This is the final offering from the culture of the police: to feel this is to begin to understand.

Yesterday the Emerald Society band's snare drummers, clad in blue and gold kilts, stretched a black cloth across the heads of their drums to give their instruments a uniquely mournful tone, like the roll of distant thunder (Sack, 1989).

To the muffled drums and the pipers' wail of 'Amazing Grace,' . . . 4,000 officers . . . stood stock still and saluted when the hearse glided to the curb before the Romanesque-style basilica. A limousine preceding the hearse was laden with bouquets and wreaths, one bearing the fallen officer's badge number.

With practiced precision, six members of a police honor guard bore the coffin into the church on their shoulders, their white-gloved hands folded before them (Hevesi, 1994).

Flanking them was a police honor guard in dress uniform colors as varied as their origins. There was the green and gray of New Hampshire; the cardinal of the Royal Canadian Mounted Police; the grays of Connecticut, Alabama, and Pennsylvania, and the blues of New Jersey, Massachusetts, Michigan, and Indiana (Hanley, 1990).

Surrounding the church, the officers were several acres of solid dress blue in numberless somber ranks, punctuated by white gloves snapping a salute. Black bands covered the badges of the officers in attendance while back at the police station, black wreaths and arm bands marked the passing of an officer (Firestone, 1994).

Inside the church, uniformed police lined the perimeter beneath the stained glass windows as the officer was eulogized as a fair and dedicated man who made the ultimate sacrifice. The strengths and numerous commendations were noted of the officer's service of duty (Morgan, 1989).

Afterward, a rumbling cortege of hundreds of police cruisers and motorcycles escorted the hearse to the cemetery. Names of far-flung police agencies crawled past at 5 mph in the red-and-blue flicker of cruiser strobes (Reed & Miller, 1995).

To allow for the procession to pass, portions of the Capital Beltway and other roads along the route were temporarily closed (Meyer, 1994).

Once at the cemetery, the grieving widow was presented the flag that had draped her husband's coffin. She was surrounded by a sea of solemn blue whose gold badges shimmered in the sunlight. This sea of blue she was told, would never evaporate. As a 21-gun salute was made to honor the deceased, a formation of law enforcement helicopters flew overhead. Finally, a lone bugler sounded the 24 notes of "Taps" as the fallen officer's coffin was slowly lowered into the ground (Martin, 1994).

This compilation is a montage of symbols and rites: officers in formation, bagpipes playing "Amazing Grace," muffled snare-drums, the snapping salute, black bands covering the officers badges, black arm bands, and wreaths on the police station wagon, a sea of uniformed officers, the cortege of police cruisers and motorcycles, the red-and-blue flicker of cruiser strobes, the American flag, the elegy of the ultimate sacrifice, the 21-gun salute, the dirge of bagpipes, and the bugler sounding the mournful sounds of "Taps." These symbols may convey powerful meanings to outsiders, but the public is not their primary object. They are aimed at and felt most strongly by cops.

The symbols in the funeral descriptions above are all about cops and fallen cops. They emphasize the oneness that the occupation embodies, the copness that is shared among the members. En masse, they are an affirmation of power, the solidarity of police culture reinvigorated and focused. All of the meaning, the traditions, the themes that bring meaning to the occupation are intensified at the funeral. The symbols that mourn the individual celebrate the collective. This, they impart, is what it means to be a cop. The death becomes a sacrament: in its rich symbolism and complex rites, all officers share the blood of the slain officer. The individual identity of the officer is lost, but a hero lives forever. His death was a powerful blow to police culture, but the funeral, its rites and proud traditions, bring culture to life again. As an individual he is mourned, but as a cop he is celebrated in dense symbols of copness, of the rightness of being a cop. All of the meanings in the ceremony are collective: the culture vibrates as a visible, tangible entity steeped in symbolic imagery. It is alive and vital. It's a cop thing.

An Ordinary Death

On June 21, 2002, Chief Alan Creech of Nampa, Idaho was killed in a plane accident. As accidents go, it was quite ordinary, almost typical for the treacherous high mountains, deep valleys, and sudden changes in wind and temperatures of the high Sawtooths. It might seem odd to talk about an ordinary police death. It is a dry phrase, absent the passion that marks the life of an officer, a very human sort of life, the life of a culture carrier. Yet death, for police as for other citizens, tends to come in all shapes and forms, sometimes sooner and sometimes later, sometimes expected and sometimes surprising.

Culture is located in the everyday, and death finds us in the everyday as well. The measure of culture is not captured in the death of an officer only because it is a felonious killing. Most officers will die in ways having little to do with violent strangers. Yet the life course they choose—police officer, community member, culture worker—provide the settings for their death. It is in the flow from cultural life to physical death that we begin to understand the ordinariness of being a cop—and the extraordinariness of culture.

On June 21, 2002, Nampa, Idaho Chief Alan Creech and Reserve Officer Mark Hupe were scouting a location for Creech's church camp in the high forest near the Sawtooth Mountains. Witnesses said that the Beechcraft attempted to land, then tried to regain altitude. The engine backfired, the plane clipped a couple of trees, and a section of the tail broke off. The plane went down and burst into flames. Both officers were killed instantly.

Creech started life hard. He was raised in foster care, and early on developed a theme central to his life: a sympathy for the hardships of the poor and victimized. Creech had worked through the ranks locally. In his youth, he was known as "Crash Creech" for his tendency to wreck patrol cars. One officer observed that the frequency of his crashes hastened his rise to detective—the department could not afford to keep him in a patrol car.

A memorial service was held for both officers on June 21. Preceding the ceremony, a procession of patrol cars from departments across the region followed the funeral car. The ceremony itself was traditional for a fallen officer, with bagpipes, drums, and flags. In the front of the Idaho center, where the ceremony was carried out, were placed many bouquets of flowers and large photographs of both men. Honor guards were provided from surrounding agencies.

In the speakers, Creech could witness what it meant to be a culture maker and carrier—an active participant in the life of a community, and recognized for one's work across the political and ethnic spectrum. He had worked with the Boys and Girls Club of Nampa, First Congregational Church basketball team coach, co-director of the Pilgrims Cove Camp board, Nampa Lions Club, and many other local activities that embedded him in the moral life of the community.

He was remembered as "husband, father and grandfather, camp director, lawman, deacon, camp director [sic], counselor, jokester, and avid camper" (Forester, 2002). He was recognized as an advocate for the Latino population, and his loss, one participant said, would be a blow to the local Latino community. At the time of his death, Chief Creech had returned to Boise State University where he was undertaking work for a Master's Degree in criminal justice. In the sum of the words of the speakers one could understand how police culture blends seamlessly with local municipal culture, and that one is in many ways a mirror of the other.

The ceremony concluded with a final call-out over police radio, enhanced so that the 3,000 in attendance could hear:

> *300 and 382 at 10-42 (officer ending tour duty). 300 and 382 are final 1-42.*

Endnotes

[1] The title of this section was taken from Martin, "Good-bye in a Sea of Blue: Slain Officer Laid to Rest" in *The New York Metro Times* 20 March 1994, sec. 35.

[2] Douglas notes that ". . . the idea of justice still remains to this day obstinately mystified and recalcitrant to analysis. If we are ever to think against the pressure of our institutions, this is the hardest place to try, where the resistance is the strongest." This is, as she notes, Durkheim's doctrine of the sacred.

[3] The funeral serves, he states, to "recoat moral bonds, to elucidate the norms of society, to symbolize deference and respect for the police as a moral unit."

Postscript

The officer glanced out the front window panels. Then, Gatorade in hand, he turned away from the cooler. He walked through the aisle closest to the window, moving toward the front of the store. I glanced briefly at his eyes. He did not make eye contact or acknowledge my glance. But he knew I was safe. I was "other," but not dangerous. He did not miss details like that. Of course, he knew that the moment I entered the store. This was Las Vegas after all, and we were in an area dangerous even for this reckless city. I paid for my juice and walked out into the bright Vegas evening, hoping that events would never conspire to bring our paths together.

John P. Crank

References

Adams, Ronald J. (1980). *Street Survival: Tactics for Armed Encounters*. Northbrook, IL: Calibre Press.

Ahern, James (1972). *Police in Trouble: Our Frightening Crisis in Law Enforcement*. New York, NY: Hawthorn Books.

Allen, David N. and Michael G. Maxfield (1983). "Judging Police Performance: Views and Behavior of Patrol Officers." In Richard R. Bennett (ed.) *Police at Work: Policy Issues and Analysis,* pp. 65-86. Perspectives in Criminal Justice 5. Beverly Hills, CA: Sage.

Alpert, Geoffrey and John MacDonald (2001). "Police Use of Force: An Analysis of Organizational Characteristics." *Police Quarterly*, 18(2):393-410.

Angell, John (1971). "Toward an Alternative to the Classic Police Organizational Arrangements: A Democratic Model." *Criminology*, 9:185-206.

Appadurai, A. (1988). "Putting Hierarchy in its Place." *Cultural Anthropology*, 3-1.

Arrigo, Bruce and Karyn Garsky (1997). "Police Suicide: A Glimpse Behind the Badge." In R. Dunham and G. Alpert (eds.) *Critical Issues in Policing: Contemporary Readings*, Third Edition, pp. 609-925.

Auten, James H. (1985). "The Paramilitary Model of Police and Police Professionalism." In A. Blumberg and E. Niederhoffer (eds.) *The Ambivalent Force,* Third Edition, pp. 122-132. New York, NY: Holt, Rinehart and Winston.

Bahn, C. (1984). "Police Socialization in the Eighties: Strains in the Forging of an Occupational Identity." *Journal of Police Science and Administration*, 12(4):390-394.

Baker, Mark (1985). *Cops: Their Lives in Their Own Words*. New York, NY: Pocket Books.

Balch, Robert (1977). "The Police Personality: Fact or Fiction?" In D. Kennedy (ed.) *The Dysfunctional Alliance: Emotion and Reason in Justice Administration*, pp. 26-46. Cincinnati, OH: Anderson Publishing Co.

Barker, Joan (1999). *Danger, Duty, and Disillusion: The Worldview of the Los Angeles Police Officers*. Prospect Heights, IL: Waveland Press.

Barker, Thomas (1978). "An Empirical Study of Police Deviance Other Than Corruption." *Journal of Police Science and Administration*, 6-3:264-272.

Barker, Thomas and David Carter (1994). "Police Lies and Perjury: A Motivation-Based Taxonomy." In T. Barker and D. Carter (eds.) *Police Deviance*, Third Edition, pp. 139-153. Cincinnati, OH: Anderson Publishing Co.

Barker, Thomas, Rodney N. Friery, and David L. Carter (1994). "After L.A., Would Your Local Police Lie?" In T. Barker and D. Carter (eds.) *Police Deviance*, Third Edition, pp. 155-168. Cincinnati, OH: Anderson Publishing Co.

Barlow, David and Melissa Barlow (2000). *Police in a Multicultural Society: An American Story*. Prospect Heights, IL: Waveland Press.

Bayley, David (1969). *The Police and Political Development in India*. Princeton, NJ: Princeton University Press.

Bayley, D. and Egon Bittner (1989). "Learning the Skills of Policing." *Law and Contemporary Problems*, 47:35-59.

Bell, Katherine, (1992). *Ritual Theory, Ritual Practice*. New York, NY: Oxford University Press.

Bellah, Robert N., Richard Madsen, William M. Sullivan, Ann Swidler, and Steven M. Tipton (1985). *Habits of the Heart*. Berkeley, CA: University of California Press.

Berger, Peter and Thomas Luckmann (1966). *The Social Construction of Reality*. Garden City, NY: Doubleday.

Berman, Jay S. (1987). *Police Administration and Progressive Reform: Theodore Roosevelt as Police Commissioner of New York City*. New York, NY: Greenwood Press.

Betz, Joseph (1988). "Police Violence." In F.A. Elliston and M. Feldberg (eds.) *Moral Issues in Police Work*, pp. 177-196. Totowa, NJ: Rowman and Allanheld.

Bittner, Egon (1990). *Aspects of Police Work*. Boston, MA: Northeastern University Press.

Bittner, Egon (1970). *The Functions of Police in Modern Society*. Washington, DC: National Institute of Mental Health.

Black, Donald (1980). *The Manners and Customs of the Police*. New York, NY: Academic Press.

Black, Donald (1973). "The Mobilization of Law." *Journal of Legal Studies*, The University of Chicago Law School, Volume II:125-144.

Blumberg, Mark (1989). "Controlling Police Use of Deadly Force: Two Decades of Progress." In R.G. Dunham and G. Alpert (eds.) *Critical Issues in Policing: Contemporary Readings*. Prospect Heights, IL: Waveland Press.

Bonifacio, Philip (1991). *The Psychological Effects of Police Work: A Psychodynamic Approach*. New York, NY: Plenum Press.

Bordua, David J. and Albert J. Reiss (1986). "Command, Control, and Charisma: Reflections on Police Bureaucracy." In M. Pogrebin and R. Regoli (eds.) *Police Administrative Issues: Techniques and Functions*. Millwod, NY: Associated Faculty Press.

Bourdieu, Pierre (1977). *Outline of a Theory of Practice*. London: Cambridge University Press.

Bourdieu, P. and L. Wacquant (1992). *An Invitation to Reflexive Sociology*. Cambridge: Polity Press.

Bouza, Anthony (1990). *The Police Mystique: An Insider's Look at Cops, Crime, and the Criminal Justice System*. New York, NY: Plenum Press.

Bracey, Dorothy (1976). *A Functional Approach to Police Corruption*. New York, NY: Criminal Justice Center, John Jay.

Brewer, J. (1990). *Inside the URC*. Oxford: Clarendon.

Brooks, Pierce (1975). ". . . Officer Down, Code Three." Schiller Park, IL: Motorola Teleprograms.

Brown, Michael K. (1981). *Working the Street: Police Discretion and the Dilemmas of Reform*. New York, NY: Russell Sage Foundation.

Bureau of Justice Fact Sheet (1995). "Public Safety Officers' Benefits Program." *National Criminal Justice Reference Services*. Washington, DC: U.S. Department of Justice.

Burke, Kenneth (1969). *A Grammar of Motives*. Berkeley, CA: University of California Press.

Caldero, Michael (1997). "Value Consistency Within the Police: The Lack of a Gap." Paper presented at the Annual Meeting of the Academy of Criminal Justice Sciences, Louisville, Kentucky.

Caldero, Michael (1995). "Community Oriented Policing Reform: An Evaluation and Theoretical Analysis." Doctoral Dissertation.

Calson, Daniel (2002). *When Cultures Clash: The Divisive Nature of Police-Community Relations and Suggestions for Improvement*. Upper Sadde River, NJ: Prentice-Hall.

Carter, David (1994). "A Taxonomy of Prejudice and Discrimination by Police Officers." In T. Barker and D. Carter (eds.) *Police Deviance*, Third Edition, pp. 247-264. Cincinnati, OH: Anderson Publishing Co.

Chambliss, W. and R. Siedman (1971). *Law, Order and Power*. Reading, MA: Addison-Wesley.

Chapman, Samuel G. (1986). *Cops, Killers and Staying Alive*. Springfield, IL: Charles C Thomas.

Chan, Janet (1996). "Changing Police Culture." *British Journal of Sociology*, 36(1):109-134.

Chan, Janet (1997). *Changing Police Culture: Police in a Multicultural Society*. Melbourne: Cambridge University Press.

Chan, Janet (2001). "Negotiating the Field: New Observations on the Making of Police Officers." *The Australian and New Zealand Journal of Criminology*, 34(2):114-133.

Chevigny, Paul (1995). *Edge of the Knife: Police Violence in the Americas*. New York, NY: The New Press.

Chevigny, Paul (1969). *Police Power*. New York, NY: Pantheon Books.

Christensen, Wendy and John Crank (2001). "Police Work and Culture in Non-Urban Setting: An Ethnographic Analysis." *Police Quarterly*, 4(1):69-98.

Christie, N. (1994). *Crime Control as Industry: Toward Gulags, Western Style*. New York, NY: Routledge.

Christopher, Warren and the Independent Commission on the Los Angeles Police Department (1991). *Report of the Independent Commission on the Los Angeles Police Department.*

CNN (2000). "Report faults LAPD Culture for Corruption." September 11. www.cnn.copm/2000/US/09/11/lapd.report/

Corcoran, James (1990). *Bitter Harvest.* New York, NY: Viking Books.

Coser, Lewis (1956). *The Functions of Social Conflict.* New York, NY: The Free Press.

Costello, Augustine E. (1972). *Our Police Protectors*, Third Edition. Montclair, NJ: Patterson Smith.

Cox, Terry C. and Mervin F. White (1987). "Traffic Citations and Student Attitudes Toward the Police: An Examination of the Interaction Dynamics." *Journal of Criminal Justice.*

Crank, John (2003). *Imagining Justice.* Cincinnati, OH: Anderson Publishing Co.

Crank, John P. (1997). "Celebrating Agency Culture: Engaging a Traditional Cop's Heart in Organizational Change." In Q. Thurman and E. McGarrell (eds.) *Community Policing in a Rural Setting*, pp. 49-57. Cincinnati, OH: Anderson Publishing Co.

Crank, John P. (1996). "The Construction of Meaning During Training for Parole and Probation." *Justice Quarterly*, 31(2):401-426.

Crank, John (1995). "The Community Policing Movement of the 21st Century: What We Learned." In J. Klofas and S. Stojovic (eds.) *Crime and Justice in the Year 2010*, pp. 107-126. Albany, NY: Wadsworth Publishing.

Crank, John P. (1994). "Watchman and Community: A Study of Myth and Institutionalization in Policing." *Law and Society Review*, 28:2.

Crank, John P. (1992). "Police Style and Legally Serious Crime: A Contextual Analysis of Eight Municipal Police Departments." *Journal of Criminal Justice*, 20-5:401-412.

Crank, John and Michael Caldero (2000). *Police Ethics: The Corruption of Noble Cause.* Cincinnati, OH: Anderson Publishing Co.

Crank, John P. and Michael Caldero (1991). "The Production of Occupational Stress Among Police Officers: A Survey of Eight Municipal Police Organizations in Illinois." *Journal of Criminal Justice*, 19-4:339-350.

Crank, John P. and Robert Langworthy (1996). "Fragmented Centralization and the Organization of the Police." *Policing and Society*, 6:213-229.

Crank, John P. and Robert Langworthy (1992). "An Institutional Perspective of Policing." *The Journal of Criminal Law and Criminology*, 83:338-363.

Crank, John P., Betsy Payne, and Stanley Jackson (1993). "Police Belief-Systems and Attitudes Regarding Persistent Police Problems." *Criminal Justice and Behavior*, 20-2:199-221.

Crank, John P. and Lee Rehm (1994). "Reciprocity Between Organizations and Institutional Environments: A Study of Operation Valkyrie." *Journal of Criminal Justice*, 22-5:393-406.

Crime Commission (see Presidents Commission on Law Enforcement and the Administration of Justice).

Cullen, Francis, Bruce Link, Lawrence T. Travis, and Terrence Lemming (1983). "Paradox in Policing: A Note on Perceptions of Danger." *Journal of Police Science and Administration*, 11:457-462.

Cumming, Elaine, Ian Cumming, and Laura Edell (1985). "Policeman as Philosopher, Guide, and Friend." In A. Blumberg and E. Niederhoffer (eds.) *The Ambivalent Force*, Third Edition, pp. 212-220. New York, NY: Holt, Rinehart and Winston.

David, Deborah and Robert Brannon (1976). *The Forty-Nine Percent Majority: The Male Sex Role*. Reading, MA: Addison-Wesley.

Davies, Robertson (1994). *The Cunning Man*. New York, NY: Penguin Books.

Davies, Robertson (1975). *World of Wonders*. New York, NY: Penguin Books.

DeMichele, Matthew (2001). "Community Policing in Battle Garb: A Paradox or Coherent Strategy?" In P. Kraska (ed.) *Militarizing the American Criminal Justice System,* pp. 82-101. Boston, MA: Northeastern University Press.

DiCristina, Bruce (1995). *Method in Criminology: A Philosophical Primer*. New York, NY: Harrow and Weston Publishers.

DiMaggio, Paul (1991). "Interest and Agency in Institutional Theory." In W. Powell and P. DiMaggio (eds.) *The New Institutionalism in Organizational Analysis*, pp. 3-19. Chicago, IL: University of Chicago Press.

Dobash, R.E. and R.P. Dobash (1992). *Violence, Women, and Social Change*. New York, NY: Routledge.

Doerner, William G. (1985). "I'm Not the Man I Used to Be: Reflections on the Transition From Prof To Cop." In A.S. Blumberg and E. Niederhoffer (eds.) *The Ambivalent Force: Reflections on the Police*, Third Edition, pp. 394-399. New York, NY: Holt, Rinehart and Winston.

Domanick, Joe (1994). *To Protect and Serve: The LAPD's Century of War in the City of Angels*. New York, NY: Pocket Books.

Douglas, Mary (1986). *How Institutions Think*. Syracuse, NY: Syracuse University Press.

Dunlap, Charles (2001). "The Thick Green Line: The Growing Involvement of Military Forces in Domestic Law Enforcement" In P. Kraska (ed.) *Militarizing the American Criminal Justice System,* pp. 29-42. Boston, MA: Northeastern University Press.

Durkheim, Emile (1966). *The Division of Labor in Society*. Translated by George Simpson. New York, NY: The Free Press.

Durkheim, Emile (1965). *The Elementary Forms of the Religious Life*. New York, NY: The Free Press. Originally published in 1915.

Eck, J.E. and W. Spelman (1987). *Problem Solving: Problem-Oriented Policing In Newport News*. Washington, DC: National Institute of Justice.

Eco, U. (1984). *Semiotics and the Philosophy of Language*. Bloomington, IN: Indiana University Press.

Edwards, S. (1990). "Violence Against Women: Feminism and the Law." In A. Morris and L. Gelsthorpe (eds.) *Feminism Perspectives in Criminology*, pp. 71-101. Philadelphia, PA: Open University Press.

Eller, Jack (1999). *From Culture to Ethnicity to Conflict: An Anthropological Perspective on International Ethnic Conflict*. Ann Arbor, MI: University of Michigan Press.

Ericson, Richard V. (1991). "Mass Media, Crime, Law, and Justice." *The British Journal of Sociology*, 40:205-226.

Ericson, Richard V. (1989). "Patrolling the Facts: Secrecy and Publicity in Police Work." *The British Journal of Sociology, 40:205-226.*

Ericson, Richard V. (1982). *Reproducing Order: A Study of Police Patrol Work*. Toronto, CN: University of Toronto Press.

Feldberg, Michael (1988). "Gratuities, Corruption, and the Democratic Ethos of Policing: The Case of the Free Cup of Coffee." In F. Ellison and M. Feldberg (eds.) *Moral Issues in Police Work*, pp. 267-276. Totowa, NJ: Rowman and Littlefield Publishers, Inc.

Felson, Marcus (1994). *Crime and Everyday Life*. Thousand Oaks, CA: Pine Forge Press.

Fielden, Scott (1995). *Music City Blues*. Johnson City, TN: Overmountain Press.

Fine, Gary and Sherryl Kleinman (1979). "Rethinking Subculture: An Interactionist Analysis." *American Journal of Sociology*, 85:1-20.

Firestone, David (1994, December 7). "Saying a Painful Farewell to a 'Hero for Our Times.'" *The New York Times*, B:3.

Fletcher, Connie (1991). *Pure Cop*. New York, NY: Pocket Books.

Fletcher, Connie (1990). *What Cops Know*. New York, NY: Pocket Books.

Fogelson, Robert M. (1977). *Big-City Police*. Cambridge, MA: Harvard University Press.

Forester, Sandra (2002). "Chief, Reservist Eulogized with Humor, Tears." *Idaho Statesman*, June 28:1, 5.

Foucault, Michel (1995). *Discipline and Punish: The Birth of the Prison*, Second Edition. Translated by Alan Sheridan. New York, NY: Vintage Books.

Fridell, Lorie and Antony Pate (1997). "Death on Patrol: Killings of American Police Officers." In R. Dunham and G. Alpert (eds.) *Critical Issues in Policing*, Third Edition, pp. 580-608. Prospect Heights, IL: Waveland Press.

Fussell, Paul (1989). *Wartime: Understanding and Behavior in the Second World War*. New York, NY: Oxford University Press.

Fussell, Paul (1975). *The Great War and Modern Memory*. London: Oxford University Press.

Fyfe, James J. (1978). "Shots Fired: A Typological Examination of New York City Police Firearms Discharges, 1971-1975." Unpublished Ph.D. Dissertation, School of Criminal Justice, SUNY Albany, New York.

Garfinkle, Harold (1967). *Studies in Sociology*. Englewood Cliffs, NJ: Prentice-Hall.

Geertz, Clifford (1983). *Local Knowledge*. New York, NY: Basic Books.

Geertz, Clifford (1980). *Negara: The Theatre State in Nineteenth Century Bali*. Princeton, NJ: Princeton University Press.

Geertz, Clifford (1973). "Thick Description: Toward an Interpretive Theory of Culture." In *The Interpretation of Cultures*, pp. 4-30. New York, NY: Basic Books.

Geller, William A. and Kevin J. Karales (1981). "Split-Second Decisions: Shootings of and by Chicago Police." Chicago Law Enforcement Study Group.

Geller, William A., Kevin J. Karales, and Michael S. Scott (1991). "Deadly Force: What We Know." In C. Klockars and S. Mastrofski (eds.) *Thinking About Police*, Second Edition, pp. 446-476. New York, NY: McGraw-Hill.

Gibson, J.W. (1994). *Warrior Dreams: Manhood in Post-Vietnam America*. New York, NY: Hill and Wang.

Goffman, Irving (1962). *Behavior in Everyday Places*. Garden City, NY: Anchor Books.

Goffman, Irving (1959). *The Presentation of Self in Everyday Life*. Garden City, NY: Anchor Books.

Goldstein, Herman (1987). "Toward Community Oriented Policing: Potential, Basic Requirements, and Threshold Questions." *Crime & Delinquency*, 33(1):6-30.

Goldstein, Herman (1979). "Improving Policing: A Problem-Oriented Approach." *Crime & Delinquency*, 25:236-258.

Goolkasian, G.A., R.W. Geddes, and W. DeJong (1989). "Coping with Police Stress." In R. Dunham and G. Alpert (eds.) *Critical Issues in Policing*, pp. 498-507. Prospect Heights, IL: Waveland Press.

Gould, Stephen Jay (1989). *Wonderful Life: The Burgess Shale and the Nature of History*. New York, NY: W.W. Norton and Company.

Greene, Jack R. and Carl Klockars (1991). "What Police Do." In C. Klockars and S. Mastrofski (eds.) *Thinking About Police: Contemporary Readings*, pp. 273-284. New York, NY: McGraw-Hill, Inc.

Greene, Marcia Slacum (1991, October 16). "For Slain Police, 2 Walls of Honor." *The Washington Post*, D:5.

Greenfeld, Lawrence, Patrick Langan, and Steven Smith (1997). *Police Use of Force: Collection of Statistical Data*. Washington, DC: Bureau of Justice Statistics.

Gregory, Kathleen L. (1983). "Native-View Paradigms: Multiple Cultures and Culture Conflicts in Organizations." *Administrative Science Quarterly*, 28-3:359-376.

Guyot, Dorothy (1979). "Bending Granite: Attempts to Change the Rank Structure of American Police Departments." *Journal of Police Science and Administration*, 7:235-284.

Haddix, Roger C. (1996). "Responding to Line-of-Duty Deaths." *FBI Law Enforcement Bulletin*.

Hall, John (1999). *Cultures of Inquiry: From Epistemology to Discourse in Sociocultural Research*. Cambridge, UK: Cambridge University Press.

Hall, John and Mary Jo Neitz (1993). *Culture: Sociological Perspectives*. Englewood Cliffs, NJ: Prentice-Hall.

Hall, Richard (1968). "Professionalization and Bureaucratization." *American Sociological Review*, 33:92-104.

Hanley, Robert (1990, March 10). "Police Mourn Death of One of Their Own." *The New York Times,* 29.

Harmon, Michael M. (1995). *Responsibility as Paradox: A Critique of Rational Discourse of Government*. Thousand Oaks, CA: Sage.

Harris, Richard (1973). *The Police Academy: An Inside View*. New York, NY: Wiley.

Hartmann, Francis X. (1988). "Debating the Evolution of American Policing." *Perspectives of Policing #5*. Washington, DC: National Institute of Justice.

Heidensohn, F. (1992). *Women in Control? The Role of Women in Policing*. New York, NY: Oxford University Press.

Herbert, Steve (1997). *Policing Space: Territoriality and the Los Angeles Police Department*. Minneapolis, MN: University of Minnesota Press.

Herrington, Nancy (1997). "Female Cops—1992." In R. Dunham and G. Alpert (eds.) *Critical Issues in Policing*, Third Edition, pp. 385-390. Prospect Heights, IL: Waveland Press.

Hevesi, Dennis (1994, May 1). "Thousands in Brooklyn Mourn Fellow Officers Killed in Chase." *The New York Times*, 35.

Hill, K. and M. Clawson (1988). "The Health Hazards of 'Street Level' Bureaucracy: Mortality Among the Police." *Journal of Police Science and Administration*, 16:243-248.

Hunt, J. (1990). "The Logic of Sexism Among Police." *Women and Criminal Justice*, 1:3-30.

Hunt, Raymond G. and John M. Magenau (1993). *Power and the Police Chief: An Institutional and Organizational Analysis*. Newbury Park, CA: Sage.

Jennings, Veronica (1990, April 3). "3,000 Salute Trooper." *The Washington Post*, E:1

Johnson, Patricia (2000). *On Gadamer*. Wadsworth Philosophical Series. New York: Wadsworth.

Kaplan, Robert (1998). "Travels into America's Future." *Atlantic Monthly*. August.

Kappeler, Victor. E. (1993). *Critical Issues in Police Civil Liability*. Prospect Heights, IL: Waveland Press.

Kappeler, Victor. E., M. Blumberg, and G.W. Potter (1993). *The Mythology of Crime and Criminal Justice*, Second Edition. Prospect Heights, IL: Waveland Press.

Kappeler, Victor. E., S.F. Kappeler, and R.V. del Carmen (1993). "A Content Analysis of Police Liability Cases: Decisions of the Federal District Courts, 1978-1990." *Journal of Criminal Justice*, 21:325-337.

Kappeler, Victor. E., Richard D. Sluder, and Geoffrey P. Alpert (1994). *Forces of Deviance: The Dark Side of Policing*. Prospect Heights, IL: Waveland Press.

Katz, Jack (1988). *The Seductions of Crime: Moral and Sensual Attractions in Doing Evil*. New York, NY: Basic Books.

Katz, Jesse (1994, November 29). "Nearly 4,000 Officers Pay Tribute to Slain Deputy " *The Washington Post*, B:3.

Katz, Samuel M. (1995). *NYPD*. Osceola, WI: Motorola International Wholesalers and Retailers.

Katz, Samuel M. and Mark H. Moore (1988). *The Evolving Strategy of Policing*. National Institute of Justice, Perspectives on Policing 4. Washington, DC: U.S. Government Printing Service.

Kerner, Otto and the National Advisory Commission on Civil Disorders (1968). *Report of the National Advisory Commission on Civil Disorders*. Washington, DC: U.S. Government Printing Office.

Kertzer, David I. (1988). *Ritual, Politics, and Power*. New Haven, CT: Yale University Press.

Klein, Herbert T. (1968). *The Police: Damned If They Do, Damned If They Don't*. New York, NY: Crown Publishers, Inc.

Klockars, Carl B. (1991a). "The Rhetoric of Community Policing." In C. Klockars and S. Mastrofski (eds.) *Thinking about Policing*, Second Edition, pp. 530-542. New York, NY: McGraw-Hill.

Klockars, Carl B. (1991b). "The Modern Sting." In C. Klockars and S. Mastrofski (eds.) *Thinking about Policing*, Second Edition, pp. 258-267. New York, NY: McGraw-Hill.

Klockars, Carl B. (1986). "Street Justice: Some Micro-Moral Reservations." *Justice Quarterly*, 3(4):513-516.

Klockars, Carl B. (1985). "The Idea of Police." *Law and Criminal Justice Studies*, vol. 3. Beverly Hills, CA: Sage.

Klockars, Carl B. (1980). "The Dirty Harry Problem." *The Annals*, 452:33-47.

Knapp Commission (1986). "An Example of Police Corruption: Knapp Commission Report on Police Corruption in New York City." In T. Barker and D. Carter (eds.) *Police Deviance*, pp. 22-39. Cincinnati, OH: Anderson Publishing Co.

Knowles, Jeffrey J. (1996). "The Ohio Police Behavior Study." Columbus, OH: Office of Criminal Justice Services.

Kraska, Peter B. (2001). "Crime Control as Warfare: Language Matters" In P. Kraska (ed.) *Militarizing the American Criminal Justice System*, pp. 14-28. Boston, MA: Northeastern University Press.

Kraska, Peter B. (1996). "Enjoying Militarism: Political/Personal Dilemmas in Studying U.S. Paramilitary Units." *Justice Quarterly*, 13-3:405-429.

Kraska, Peter B. (1994, January). "The Police and Military in the Post-Cold War Era: Streamlining the State's Use of Force Entities in the Drug War." *Police Forum*, 1-8.

Kraska, Peter B. (1993). "Militarizing the Drug War: A Sign of the Times." In P. Kraska (ed.) *Altered States of Mind: Critical Observations of the Drug War*, pp. 159-204. New York, NY: Garland Publishing.

Kraska, Peter B. and Victor E. Kappeler (1997). "Militarizing American Police: The Rise and Normalization of Paramilitary Units." *Social Problems*, 44-1:101-117.

Kraska, Peter B. and Victor E. Kappeler (1995). "To Serve and Pursue: Exploring Police Sexual Violence Against Women." *Justice Quarterly*, 12-1:85-112.

Kraska, Peter B. and D. Paulsen (1996). "Forging the Iron Fist Inside the Velvet Glove: A Case Study of the Rise of U.S. Military Units." Paper presented at the Annual Meeting of the Academy of Criminal Justice Sciences, Las Vegas, Nevada.

Lakoff, George and Mark Johnson (1999). *Philosophy in the Flesh: The Embodied Mind and its Challenge to Western Thought*. New York: Basic Books.

Lakoff, George and Mark Johnson (1980). *Metaphors We Live By*. Chicago, IL: University of Chicago Press.

Lane, Roger (1992). "Urban Police and Crime in Nineteenth-Century America." In Michael Tonry and Norval Morris (eds.) *Modern Policing*, pp. 1-50. Chicago, IL: University of Chicago Press.

Langer, E. (1975). "The Illusion of Control." *Journal of Personality and Social Psychology*, 32:311-328.

Langworthy, Robert (1989). "Do Stings Control Crime? An Evaluation of a Police Fencing Operation." *Justice Quarterly*, 6:27-45.

Langworthy, Robert (1987). "Police Cynicism: What We Know from the Niederhoffer Scale." *Journal of Criminal Justice*, 15:17-35.

Langworthy, Robert and James L. LeBeau (1992). "The Spacial Distribution of Sting Targets." *Journal of Criminal Justice*, 20:541-551.

Levi-Strauss, Claude (1966). *The Savage Mind*. Chicago, IL: University of Chicago Press.

Los Angeles Times (2002). "Our Gangs, Our Terrorists." January 5. www.latimes.com/news/opinion/la-editorial-gangs010502.story.

Lozano, Carlos (1994, January 4). "2,500 Fellow Officers at Funeral for Ganz." *Los Angeles Times*, B:1.

Lukes, Steven (1975). "Political Ritual and Social Integration." *Sociology: Journal of the British Sociological Association,* 9-2:289-308.

Lyng, Stephen (1990). "Edgework: A Social Psychological Analysis of Voluntary Risk Taking." *American Journal of Sociology*, 95-4:851-886.

Lyng, Stephen and David Snow (1986). "Vocabularies of Motive and High Risk Behavior: The Case of Skydiving." In E.J. Lawler (ed.) *Advances in Group Processes*, vol. 3, pp. 157-179. Greenwich, CT: JAI.

MacIntyre, A. (1984). *After Virtue: A Study in Moral Theory*, Second Edition. Notre Dame, IN: Notre Dame University Press.

Maguire, Kathleen and Ann L. Pastore (1995). *Sourcebook of Criminal Justice Statistics, 1994*. Washington, DC: National Institute of Justice.

Mannheim, Karl (1936). *Ideology and Utopia*. New York, NY: Harcourt, Brace and World.

Manning, Peter (1997). *Police Work: The Social Organization of Policing*, Second Edition. Prospect Heights, IL: Waveland Press.

Manning, Peter K. (1995). "Economic Rhetoric and Policing Reform." In V. Kappeler (ed.) *Police and Society: Touchstone Readings*, pp. 375-391. Prospect Heights, IL: Waveland Press.

Manning, Peter K. (1993). "Violence and Symbolic Violence." *Police Forum*, 3(1):1-6.

Manning, Peter K. (1989). "The Police Occupational Culture in Anglo-American Societies." In L. Hoover and J. Dowling (eds.) *Encyclopedia of Police Science*. New York, NY: Garland.

Manning, Peter K. (1979). "Metaphors of the Field: Varieties of Organizational Discourse." *Administrative Science Quarterly*, 24:660-671.

Manning, Peter K. (1978a). "Lying, Secrecy, and Social Control." In P.K. Manning and J. Van Maanen (eds.) *Policing: A View from the Street*, pp. 238-254. Santa Monica, CA: Goodyear Publishing.

Manning, Peter K. (1978b). "The Police: Mandate, Strategies, and Appearances." In P.K. Manning and J. Van Maanen (eds.) *Policing: A View From the Street*, pp. 7-31. Santa Monica, CA: Goodyear Publishing.

Manning, Peter K. (1978c). "Rules, Colleagues, and Situationally Justified Actions," In P.K. Manning and J. Van Maanen (eds.) *Policing: A View From the Street*, pp. 71-89. Santa Monica, CA: Goodyear Publishing. Reprinted from R. Blankenship (ed.) (1976). *Colleagues in Organizations*, 263-289. New York, NY: Wiley.

Manning, Peter K. (1976). "Rules, Colleagues, and Situationally Justified Actions." In R. Blankenship (ed.) *Colleagues in Organizations*, pp. 263-289. New York, NY: Wiley.

Manning, Peter K. and Lawrence Redlinger (1977). "Invitational Edges of Corruption: Some Consequences of Narcotic Law Enforcement." In Paul Rock (ed.) *Drugs and Politics*, pp. 279-310. Rutgers, NJ: Society/Transaction Books.

Manning, Peter K. and Lawrence Redlinger (1970). *Police Work*. Cambridge, MA: The MIT Press.

Martin, Christine (1994). "Illinois Municipal Officer's Perceptions of Police Ethics." Chicago, IL: Statistical Analysis Center, Illinois Criminal Justice Information Authority.

Martin, Douglas (1994, March 20). "Good-bye in a Sea of Blue: Slain Officer Laid to Rest." *The New York Metro Times*, 35.

Martin, Susan E. (1997). "Women Officers on the Move: An Update of Women in Policing." In R. Dunham and G. Alpert (eds.) *Critical Issues in Policing*, Third Edition, pp. 363-384. Prospect Heights, IL: Waveland Press.

Martin, Susan E. (1990). *On the Move: The Status of Women in Policing*. Washington, DC: Police Foundation.

Martin, Susan E. (1980). *Breaking and Entering: Policewomen on Patrol*. Berkeley, CA: University of California Press.

Marx, Gary T. (1988). "Who Really Gets Stung? Some Issues Raised by the New Police Undercover Work." In F. Ellison and M. Feldberg (eds.) *Moral Issues in Police Work*, pp. 99-128. Totowa, NJ: Rowman and Allanheld.

Mastrofski, Stephen D. and Robert Worden (1994). "Community Policing and Police Organizational Structure." Paper presented at the Annual Meeting of the Law and Society Association.

Mastrofski, Stephen D. and Robert Worden (1991). "Community Policing as Reform: A Cautionary Tale." In C. Klockars and S. Mastrofski (eds.) *Thinking About Police: Contemporary Readings*, Second Edition, pp. 515-529. New York, NY: McGraw-Hill, Inc.

McDonald, Brian (2002). *My Fathers Gun*. Docudrama. Arts and Entertainment: 43505.

McDonald, Cherokee Paul (1991). *Blue Truth*. New York, NY: St. Martin's Paperbacks.

McKeon (1957). "The Development and Significance of the Concept of Responsibility." *Revue Internationale de Philosophie*, 11:3-32.

McMurray, Harvey L. (1990). "Attitudes of Assaulted Police Officers and Their Police Implications." *Journal of Police Science and Administration*, 17-1:44-48.

McNulty, Elizabeth W. (1994). "Generating Common-Sense Knowledge Among Police Officers." *Symbolic Interaction*, 17:281-294.

Mead, G.H. (1950). *Mind, Self, and Society*. Edited by C.W. Morris. Chicago, IL: University of Chicago Press.

Meyer, Eugene (1994). "Brutality Decried as Officer is Buried." *The Washington Post*, B:1.

Meyer, John W. (1983). "Institutionalization and the Rationality of Formal Organizational Structure." In J. Meyer and R. Scott (eds.) *Organizational Environments: Ritual and Rationality*, pp. 261-282. Newbury Park, CA: Sage.

Meyer, John W. and Brian Rowan (1977). "Institutionalized Organizations: Formal Structure as Myth and Ceremony." *American Journal of Sociology*, 83:430-463.

Meyer, John W. and W. Richard Scott (1983). "Centralization and the Legitimacy Problems of Local Government." In J. Meyer and R. Scott (eds.) *Organizational Environments: Ritual and Rationality*, pp. 199-216. Newbury Park, CA: Sage.

Miller, George I. (1987). "Observations on Police Undercover Work." *Criminology*, 25:27-46.

Miller, Mark R. (1995). *Police Patrol Operations*. Placerville, CA: Copperhouse Publishing Co.

Monkkonen, Eric H. (1981). *Police in Urban America, 1860-1920*. New York, NY: Cambridge University Press.

Moore, M., R. Trojanowicz, and G. Kelling (1988). *Crime and Policing*. Series title: Perspectives on Policing. Washington, DC: U.S. Department of Justice.

Morgan, Thomas (1989, March 8). "Police Mourn Officer Slain in Brooklyn." *The New York Times*, C:1.

Muir, William K. (1977). *Police: Streetcorner Politicians*. Chicago, IL: University of Chicago Press.

National Institute of Justice (1995). "Technology Transfer From Defense: Concealed Weapon Detection." *National Institute of Justice Journal*, 229:1-6.

New York Times (2002). "Bronx Street Named for Diallo." Associated Press. July 11.

Niederhoffer, Arthur (1967). *Behind the Shield*. Garden City, NY: Doubleday.

Nussbaum, Martha (2001). *Upheavals of Thought: The Intelligence of Emotions*. Cambridge, UK: Cambridge University Press.

O'Conner, C. (1993, March). "Explosive Charges of Kids Who Rape." *Glamour*, 231:274-278.

Office of International Criminal Justice (1996). "National Law Enforcement Officers Memorial Fund," Chicago, IL: CJ the Americas, On-Line. Dec.–Jan.

Oliver, Melvin L. and Thomas M. Shapiro (1995), *Black Wealth, White Wealth: A New Perspective on Racial Inequality*. New York, NY: Routledge.

Paoline, Eugene (2001). *Rethinking Police Culture: Officers Occupational Attitudes*. New York: LFB Scholarly Publishing LLC.

Paoline, Eugene, Stephanie Myers, and Robert Worden (2000). "Police Culture, Individualism, and Community Policing: Evidence from Two Police Departments." *Justice Quarterly*, 17(3):575-606.

Pepper, Steven C. (1942). *World Hypotheses*. Berkeley, CA: University of California Press.

Perez, Douglas W. (1994). *Common Sense about Police Review*. Philadelphia, PA: Temple University Press.

Pogrebin, Mark R. and Eric D. Poole (1993). "Vice Isn't Nice: A Look at the Effects of Working Undercover." *Journal of Criminal Justice*, 21-4:383-394.

Pogrebin, Mark R. and Eric D. Poole (1991). "Police and Tragic Events: The Management of Emotions." *Journal of Criminal Justice*, 19:395-403.

Pogrebin, Mark R. and Eric D. Poole (1988). "Humor in the Briefing Room." *Journal of Contemporary Ethnography*, 17-2:183-210.

Poole, Eric D. and Robert M. Regoli (1980). "Examining the Impact of Professionalism on Cynicism, Role Conflict, and Work Alienation among Prison Guards." *Criminal Justice Review*, 5:57-65.

Poole, Eric D. and Robert M. Regoli (1979). "Police Professionalism and Cynicism: An Empirical Assessment." *Criminal Justice and Behavior*, 6-2:201-216.

Powers, Mary D. (1995). "Civilian Oversight is Necessary to Prevent Police Brutality." In P.A. Winters (ed.) *Policing the Police*, pp. 56-60. San Diego, CA: Greenhaven Press.

President's Commission on Law Enforcement and the Administration of Justice (1968). *The Challenge of Crime in a Free Society*. New York, NY: E.P. Dutton and Company.

Priest, Dana and Kent Jenkins (1989, March 28). "Thousands Honor Officers Whose 'Cause was Good.'" *The Washington Post*, C:1.

Punch, Maurice (1999). *Policing the Inner City*. London: MacMillan.

Ragonese, Paul (1991). *The Soul of a Cop*. New York, NY: St. Martin's Paperbacks.

Rainer, Trish (1996). "Critical Incident Stress Management." Presentation at the Annual Meeting of the Criminal Justice Professionals, Boise, Idaho.

Redfield, Robert (1940). "The Folk Society and Culture." *The American Journal of Sociology* 45:731-742.

Reed, Mack and Joanna Miller (1995, August 10). "2,000 Mourners Bid Farewell to Slain Simi Valley Officer." *Los Angeles Times*, A:1.

Regoli, Robert (1979). "The Measurement of Police Cynicism: A Factor Scaling Approach." *Journal of Criminal Justice*, 7:37-51.

Regoli, Robert (1977). *Police in America*. Washington, DC: University Press of America.

Regoli, Robert (1976). "An Empirical Assessment of Niederhoffer's Cynicism Scale." *Journal of Criminal Justice*, 4:231-241.

Regoli, Robert, John P. Crank, Robert G. Culbertson, and Eric D. Poole (1987). "Police Cynicism and Professionalism Reconsidered: An Assessment of Measurement Issues." *Justice Quarterly*, 4-2:281-286.

Regoli, Robert and Eric Poole (1979). "Measurement of Cynicism: A Factor Scaling Approach." *Journal of Criminal Justice*, 7:37-51.

Reiner, R. (1985). *Politics of the Police*. London: Wheatsheaf.

Reiser, M. (1974). "Some Organizational Stresses on Policemen." *Journal of Police Science and Administration*, 2:156-169.

Reiss, Albert J. (1971). *The Police and the Public*. New Haven, CT: Yale University Press.

Reuss-Ianni, Elizabeth (1983). *Two Cultures of Policing: Street Cops and Management Cops*. New Brunswick, NJ: Transaction Books.

Richardson, J.F. (1974). *Urban Police in the United States*. Port Washington, NY: National University Publications.

Ritti, R. Richard and Stephen Mastrofski (2002). "The Institutionalization of Community Policing: A Study of the Presentation of the Concept in Two Law Enforcement Journals. Paper presented for National Institute of Justice Final Report. Grant # 2000-IJ-CX-0021. April.

Ritti, R. Richard and Jonathan H. Silver (1986). "Early Processes of Institutionalization: The Dramaturgy of Exchange in Interorganizational Relationships." *Administrative Science Quarterly*, 31:25-42.

Roberg, Roy, John Crank, and Jack Kuykendall (2000). *Police and Society*, Second Edition. Los Angeles, CA: Roxbury Publishing Company.

Rothwell, J.D. (1971). "Verbal Obscenity: Time for Second Thoughts." *Journal of Western Speech*, 35:231-242.

Rubinstein, Jonathan (1973). *City Police*. New York, NY: Farrar, Strauss, and Girox.

Sack, Kevin (1989, November 15). "Perils for Police Stressed at First of 3 Funerals." *The New York Times*, B:4.

Sackmann, Sonja (1992). "Culture and Subcultures: An Analysis of Organizational Knowledge." *Administrative Science Quarterly*, 37:140-161.

Sacks, Harvey (1972). "Notes on Police Assessment of Moral Character." In David Sudnow (ed.) *Studies in Social Interaction*. New York, NY: The Free Press.

Sapp, Allen D. (1994). "Sexual Misconduct by Police Officers." In T. Barker and D. Carter (eds.) *Police Deviance*, Third Edition, pp. 187-200. Cincinnati, OH: Anderson Publishing Co.

Sawyer, Suzanne F. (1993). *Support Services to Surviving Families of Line-of-Duty Deaths*. Camdenton, MO: Concerns of Police Survivors, Inc.

Scharf, Peter and Arnold Binder (1983). *The Badge and the Bullet: Police Use of Deadly Force*. New York, NY: Praeger.

Schmitt, Eric (1989, November 17). "6,000 Officers Mourn Death of a Detective." *The New York Times*, B:1.

Scott, Richard (1991). "Unpacking Institutional Arguments." In W. Powell and P. DiMaggio (eds.) *The New Institutionalism in Organizational Analysis*, pp. 164-182. Chicago, IL: University of Chicago Press.

Scott, W. Richard and John Meyer (1992). "The Organizational of Societal Sectors." In J. Meyer and W.R. Scott (eds.) *Organizational Environments: Ritual and Rationality*, pp. 129-140. Newbury Park, CA: Sage Publications.

Searle, John (1998). *Mind, Language, and Society: Philosophy in the Real World*. New York, NY: Basic Books.

Shanahan, Peter (2000). "Police Culture and the Learning Organization: A Relationship?" Paper presented at the annual meetings of the Australian Vocational Education and Training Research Association.

Shearing, Clifford and Richard V. Ericson (1991). "Culture as Figurative Action." *British Journal of Sociology*, 42:481-506.

Sherman, Lawrence (1988). "Becoming Bent: Moral Careers of Corrupt Policemen." In F. Elliston and M. Feldberg (eds.) *Moral Issues in Police Work*, pp. 253-265. Totowa, NJ: Rowman and Littlefield Publishers, Inc.

Sherman, Lawrence (1982). "Learning Police Ethics." *Criminal Justice Ethics*, 1:10-19.

Shusta, Robert M., Deena R. Levine, Philip R. Harris, and Herbert Z. Long (1995). *Multicultural Law Enforcement: Strategies for Peacekeeping in a Diverse Society*. Englewood Cliffs, NJ: Prentice-Hall.

Silver, Isidore (1988). "Ethics, Police Practices, and American Constitutional Law." In F. Elliston and M. Feldberg (eds.) *Moral Issues in Police Work*, pp. 163-172. Totowa, NJ: Rowman and Allanheld.

Simmel, Georg (1919). *Conflict*. Translated by Kurt W. Wolf. Glencoe, IL: The Free Press.

Singleton, G. and J. Tehan (1978). "Effects of Job-Related Stress on the Physical and Psychological Adjustment of Police Officers." *Journal of Police Science and Administration*, 6:355-361.

Skolnick, Jerome (1994). "A Sketch of the Policeman's Working Personality." In *Justice Without Trial: Law Enforcement in Democratic Society*, Third Edition, pp. 41-68. New York, NY: Wiley.

Skolnick, Jerome (1982). "Deception by the Police." *Criminal Justice Ethics*, 1:40-54.

Skolnick, Jerome and James Fyfe (1993). *Above the Law: Police and the Excessive Use of Force*. New York, NY: The Free Press.

Smith, Leef (1994). "Thousands Mourn FBI Agent Slain During Stakeout." *The Washington Post*.

Sparger, Jerry R. and David J. Giacopassi (1983). "Copping Out: Why Police Leave the Force." In R. Bennett (ed.) *Police at Work: Policy Issues and Analysis*, pp. 107-124. Perspectives in Criminal Justice 5. Beverly Hills, CA: Sage.

Spradley, James P. and David W. McCurdy (1975). *Anthropology: The Cultural Perspective*. New York, NY: Wiley.

Stoddard, Ellwyn (1968). "The Informal 'Code'of Police Deviancy." *Journal of Criminal Law, Criminology and Police Science*, 59:201-213.

Storms, Lowell H., Nolan F. Penn, and James H. Tenzell (1990). "Policemen's Perception of Real and Ideal Policemen." *Journal of Police Science and Administration*, 17:40-43.

Strecher, Victor (1995). "People Who Don't Even Know You." In Victor Kappeler (ed.) *The Police and Society: Touchstone Readings*, pp. 207-224. Prospect Heights, IL: Waveland Press.

Sutton, L. Paul (1986). "The Fourth Amendment in Action: An Empirical Review of the Search Warrant Process." *Criminal Law Bulletin*, 22-5:405-429.

Swanton, B. (1981). "Social Isolation of the Police: Structural Determinants and Remedies." *Police Studies*, 3:14-21.

Swidler, Ann (1986). "Culture in Action: Symbols and Strategies." *American Sociological Review*, 51:273-286.

Sykes, Gary W. (1996). "Police Misconduct: A Different Day and Different Challenges." *Subject to Debate: A Newsletter of the Police Executive Research Forum*, (March, April):10-3:1,4-5.

Sykes, Gary W. (1989). "The Functional Nature of Police Reform: The Myth of Controlling the Police." In R. Dunham and G. Alpert (eds.) *Critical Issues in Policing: Contemporary Readings*, pp. 286-297. Prospect Heights, IL: Waveland Press.

Sykes, Gary W. (1986). "Street Justice: A Moral Defense of Order Maintenance Policing." *Justice Quarterly*, 3:497-512.

Terrill, William and Stephen Mastrofski (2002). "Situational and Officer-Based Determinants of Police Coercion." *Justice Quarterly*, 19(2):215-248.

Thompson, Hunter (1971). *Fear and Loathing in Las Vegas:A Savage Journey to the Heart of the American Dream*. New York, NY: Warner.

Trice, Harrison M. and Janice M. Beyer (1984). "Studying Organizational Cultures Through Rites and Ceremonials." *Academy of Management Review*, 9-4:653-669.

Trojanowicz, R.C. (1980). *The Environment of the First-Line Supervisor.* Englewood Cliffs, NJ: Prentice-Hall.

Turner, Victor (1974). *Dramas, Fields, and Metaphors: Symbolic Action Human Society*. Ithaca, NY: Cornell University Press.

Turner, Victor (1969). *The Ritual Process: Structure and Anti-Structure*. Chicago, IL: Aldine.

Turner, Victor (1967). *Forest of Symbols: Aspects of Ndembu Ritual*. Ithaca, NY: Cornell University Press.

Uchida, Craig D. (1989). "The Development of the American Police: An Historical Overview." In R. Dunham and G. Alpert (eds.) *Critical Issues in Policing: Contemporary Readings*, pp. 14-30. Prospect Heights, IL: Waveland Press.

Van Maanen, John (1978). "The Asshole." In P.K. Manning and J. Van Maanen (eds.) *Policing: A View From the Street*, pp. 221-238. Santa Monica, CA: Goodyear Publishing.

Van Maanen, John (1974). "Working the Street: A Developmental View of Police Behavior." In H. Jacob (ed.) *The Potential for Reform in Criminal Justice*, vol. 3, pp. 83-84, 87, 100-110. Beverly Hills, CA: Sage.

Van Maanen, John (1973). "Observations on the Making of Policemen." *Human Organization*, 32:407-418.

Van Maanen, John and Stephen Barley (1985). "Cultural Organization: Fragments of A Theory." In P. Frost, L. Moore, M. Louis, C. Lundberg, and J. Martin (eds.) *Organizational Culture*. Beverly Hills, CA: Sage.

Van Maanen, John and Stephen R. Barley (1982). *Occupational Communities: Culture and Control in Organization*. TR-10: Technical Report. Cambridge, MA: Sloan School of Management.

Violanti, J. (1995). "The Mystery Within Understanding Police Suicide." *Law Enforcement Bulletin*, 64:19-23.

Waddington, P. (1999). "Police (Canteen) Culture: An Appreciation." *British Journal of Criminology*, 39(2):287-309.

Walker, Samuel (1994). *Sense and Nonsense About Crime and Drugs: A Policy Guide*, Third Edition. New York, NY: McGraw-Hill.

Walker, Samuel (1990). *The Police in America*, Second Edition. New York, NY: McGraw-Hill.

Walker, Samuel (1984). "Broken Windows and Fractured History: The Use and Misuse of History in Recent Police Patrol Analysis." *Justice Quarterly*, 1(1):57-90.

Walker, Samuel (1977). *A Critical History of Police Reform*. Lexington, MA: Lexington Books.

Wambaugh, Joseph (1987). *The Choirboys*. New York, NY: Dell.

Wambaugh, Joseph (1973). *The Blue Night*. Boston, MA: Little, Brown, and Co.

Warnke, Georgia (1993). *Justice and Interpretation*. Cambridge, MA: The MIT Press.

Weber, Max (1946). "Politics as a Vocation." In H. Gerth and C. Wright Mills (eds. and translators) *From Max Weber: Essays in Sociology*, pp. 77-128. New York, NY: Oxford University Press.

Wesley, W. (1970). *Violence and the Police*. Cambridge, MA: The MIT Press.

White, Mervin, Terry C. Cox, and Jack Basehart (1994). "Theoretical Considerations of Officer Profanity and Obscenity in Formal Contacts with Citizens." In T. Barker and D. Carter (eds.) *Police Deviance*, Third Edition, pp. 223-245. Cincinnati, OH: Anderson Publishing Co.

White, Mervin, Terry C. Cox, and Jack Basehart (1988). "Perceptions of Police Verbal Abuse as an Influence on Respondent Attitudes Toward the Police." Paper presented at the Annual Meeting of the Academy of Criminal Justice Sciences, San Francisco, California.

White, R. and C. Alder (eds.) (1994). *The Police and Young People in Australia*. Cambridge: Cambridge University Press.

White, Susan O. (1986). "A Perspective on Police Professionalism." In R. Regoli and E. Poole (eds.) *Police Administrative Issues*, pp. 221-232. New York, NY: Associated Faculty Press.

Whitehead, Alfred North (1925). *Science in the Modern World*. New York, NY: Macmillan.

Wilbanks, William (1987). *The Myth of the Racist Criminal Justice System*. Monterey, CA: Brooks/Cole Publishing Co.

Williams, Hubert and Patrick V. Murphy (1990). "The Evolving Strategy of the Police: A Minority View." *Perspectives on Policing*, 13. Washington, DC: National Institute of Justice.

Willis, Paul (1990). *Common Culture: Symbolic Work at Play in the Everyday Cultures of the Young*. Boulder, CO: Westview Press.

Wilgoren (1993, March 16). "4,000 Attend Rites Honoring Policeman as 'Fallen Hero.'" *Los Angeles Times*, B:1.

Wilson, James Q. (1993). *The Moral Sense*. New York, NY: The Free Press.

Wilson, James Q. (1968). *Varieties of Police Behavior: The Management of Law and Order in Eight Communities*. Cambridge, MA: Harvard University Press.

Wilson, James Q. and George Kelling (1982, March). "Broken Windows: The Police and Neighborhood Safety." *Atlantic Monthly*, 127:29-38.

Wilt, M.G. and J.D. Bannon (1976). "Cynicism or Realism: A Critique of Niederhoffer's Research into Police Attitudes." *Journal of Police Science and Administration*, 4:38-46.

Wood, B. (1984). *Slavery in Colonial Georgia*. Athens, GA: University of Georgia Press.

Wolfe, Eric (1982). *Europe and the People Without History*. Berkeley, CA: University of California Press.

Wuthnow, Robert, James Davidson Hunter, Albert Bergesen, and Edith Kurzweil (1984). *Cultural Analysis*. London: Routledge & Kegan Paul.

Zhao, Jihong, Ni He, and Nicholas Lovrich (1998). "Individual Value Preferences among American Police Officers: The Rokeach Theory of Human Values Revisited." *Policing: An International Journal of Police Strategies and Management*, 21:22-36.

Znaniecki, Florian (1936). *The Method of Sociology*. New York, NY: Farrar and Rinehart.

Zucker, Lynne G. (1991). "The Role of Institutionalization in Cultural Persistence." In W. Powell and P. DiMaggio (eds.) *The New Institutionalism in Organizational Analysis*, pp. 83-107. Chicago, IL: University of Chicago Press.

Index

Aborigines (Australian), community policing interventions and, 47-49
Absolute authority, right to intervene as, 87-88
Absolute morality, police funerals and, 357
Abuses, of force, 105
Academic studies. *See also* Cultural studies force in, 101-107
Accepted lies, 291
Accidental police shootings and killings, 138
Accountability
    alienation of street officers and, 94
    community policing and, 94
    contemporary mechanisms of, 327-328
    factors preventing, 278
    games theory and paradox of, 286-288
    individualism and, 281-282
    individual-level, development and sustenance of police culture and, 288
    mechanisms of, 94, 281
    outsiders theme and, 274
Accreditation, 41
Action, common sense and, 166, 221
Adams, Ronald J., 134, 136
Administration. *See* Management; Police organizations
Administrative "bullshit," 68
Administrative control, individualistic approach of line officers and, 283-286
Administrative environment, 68-69
Administrative images, of patrol, 95n
Administrative oversight
    loosely coupling and, 270
    secrecy and, 277
Administrative policy, control of police behavior and absence of social self in police-citizen encounters, 179
Administrative review
    solidarity vulnerability to, 251-252
    use of force violations and, 110
Administrators. *See also* Brass; Chiefs; Management; Police executive
    line officers' distrust of, 311-312
    preoccupation with bullshit, 316-317
Adventure, perception of in police work, 168
Adversity, solidarity, loose coupling themes, and, 6-7

Aesthetics, of local culture, 35-36
African-Americans
    acceptable force against, 100
    institutionalized economic discrimination, wealth, and, 267n
    negative attitudes toward, 260
    political power of and racial bias against, 260-261
    racism in American policing and, 258-259
Aggressiveness, individualism and, 282
Aggressive order maintenance, 34
Ahern, James, 250-251, 276, 353
Alder, C., 52n
Alienation, after officer killings, 343
Allen, David N., 68
Alpert, Geoffrey P., 53, 55, 68, 78, 104, 105, 157, 160, 197, 205, 226, 230, 257, 273, 275, 286
Andersen, Hans Christian, 170
Anecdotal stories. *See* Stories
Angell, John, 113
Anticipation, of danger, 5, 142
Anti-drug activity, common sense begetting common sense and, 218-220
Anti-structure, 337n
Appadurai, A., 19
Armamentarium, suspicion in, 146
Arrests
    back-stage and front-stage dramaturgy in, 250
    as basis for in misdemeanor encounters, 309
    coercive authority in, 249
    cover charges and, 292
    officer killings during, 341
    officer safety and, 250
    potential for turbulence in, 174
Arrest warrants, seduction and, 187-188
Arrigo, Bruce, 139
Articulable suspicion, automobile stops and, 150
Articulation
    in courts, 70-71
    in media, 71-72
    organizational, of police-citizen interactions, 67

Art of exceptionality, suspicion as, 148

Assailant geographies, danger and, 161

Assaults
on officers as measure of danger, 159
perceptions of management after, 349-350

Asshole(s)
labeling of, 209-211, 334
morality, coercion, and, 207
mythos in interactions with, 105
police behavior towards, 88
recognition and, 146
rough justice and, 108
as shared cultural theme, 54, 60
term as analytic device, 312
violence and perceived slights to police authority by, 191

"Asshole, The" (Van Maanen), 209
ritual activity in, 334

Attitudes. *See also* Boys-will-be-boys attitude
gender abuse and change in, 232
individuals drawn to police work and pre-dispositional, 241
police behavior and, 16-17
police socialization and, 241-242
toward rules, individualistic perceptions of police work and, 284
variations in police organizations, 30

Audiences
and boundaries for police culture, 63-72
for line officers, 54, 65

Auten, James H., 116, 117, 125

Authoritarianism, personalities drawn to policing and, 241

Authority
guns and, 132-134
moral (*See* Police morality)
rituals and, 332
rituals and societal patterns of, 336
solidarity and challenges to, 198
vertical structure of, in militaristic chain-of-command organizations, 316
violence and perceived slights to, 191

Authority of the state
excessive force and, 107-109
patrol intervention and, 275

Authorization, of organizational structure and behavior, 41

Automobile stops. *See also* Traffic stops
articulable suspicion and, 150
probable cause and, 150, 153n
suspicion and, 149

Autonomy, of patrolmen, individualism and, 283

Axiomatic knowledge, 46, 47

Back-up support, solidarity and, 246

Bacon, Francis, 143

Badge, as metonymy, 330n

Baker, Mark, 139, 241, 252, 276, 342, 355, 356

Balch, Robert, 241

Bannon, J.D., 325

Barker, Joan, 25, 137-138

Barker, Thomas, 110, 193, 291, 295

Barley, Stephen R., 37, 45, 54

Basehart, Jack, 182

Bayley, 191, 286

Bayley, David, 52n, 54, 94, 124, 128, 129, 132, 165, 179-180, 183, 215

"Be aggressive when you have to, but don't be too eager" trait, edge control and, 181-182

Beat, 82-83
as moral responsibility, 205

Behavior
acquisition of, 41
authorization of, 41
cultural themes, sentiment, and, 53
imposition of, 40
imprinting of, 41
incorporation of, 41-42
inducement of, 41
knowledge of, 86-87
precipitating suspicion, 147

Behavioral component, of culture, 16-17, 53

Behavioral cues, suspicion in pedestrian stops and, 149

Bell, Katherine, 330, 331, 332, 335-336, 337n

Bellah, Robert N., 266

Berger, Peter, 32, 222, 228n

Berman, Jay S., 115

Betz, Joseph, 118-119, 120

Beyer, Janice M., 329, 333

Binder, Arnold, 127, 131-132

Bittner, Egon, 54, 55, 85, 101, 102-103, 115, 117, 165, 167, 179, 183, 215, 249, 277, 283, 327

Black, Donald, 7, 16, 66, 67, 95n, 142, 249, 256

Black Americans. *See* African-Americans

Blading (police stance), 151

"Blue curtain" secrecies, 94

Blue Truth (McDonald), 354

Blumberg, Mark, 37, 71, 134, 156, 157

Body searches, common sense about, 215-216

Bonifacio, Philip, 240

Bordua, David J., 206

Boundaries, of police culture, 54

Bourdieu, Pierre, 48, 333

Bouza, Anthony, 107, 201, 209, 233, 237, 265, 266n, 283, 302

Boys-will-be-boys attitude
police sexual misconduct and, 230
police sexual violence and, 194

Bracey, Dorothy, 281

Brass. *See also* Administrators; Chiefs; Management; Police executive
  officer deaths and, 349-350
  secrecy from, 277-278
  as shared cultural theme, 54, 62
Bravery
  displays of, 233
  fear and excitement in, 235
  as special case of masculinity, 232-235
  unpredictability and, 234-235
  in war, 233-234
Brewer, J., 52n
Bribery, vs. gratuities, 196n
"Broken Windows" (Wilson and Kelling), 92, 124
"Broken windows" analogy, 92-93
Brooks, Pierce, 248, 343
Brotherhood in blue, 237
Brown, Michael K., 145, 237, 239, 282-283, 318
Brute facts, material component of culture and, 17
Bullshit, 311-328
  clique formation and, 323-324
  community policing and, 326-328
  CYA (cover your ass) and, 322
  cynicism and, 324-325
  humor and, 322-323
  line officers' responses to, 321-326
  measurement of, 318-320
  militaristic chain-of-command and, 313-317
  rank-in-position personnel systems and, 316-317
  term as analytic device, 312
  training and, 320-321
  voluntary resignation and, 325-326
Bureaucracy(ies), 269
  authority in, 316
  production of bullshit and, 317-318
Burke, Kenneth, 218
Bypassing, organizational structure, 42-43

Caldero, Michael, 26, 42, 59, 62, 62n, 94, 100, 141, 152, 184n, 205, 298, 318-320, 326, 328n
Cannon, Raymond, 348
Canteen culture, 16-17
Carlson, Daniel, 151
Car stops. *See* Automobile stops
Carter, David L., 110, 291
Chain-of-command
  accountability and, 94, 327-328
  bureaucracy, bullshit, and, 317-318
  production of bullshit and militaristic, 313-317
Chambliss, W., 276
Chan, Janet, 4, 13-14, 18, 24-25, 38, 47-49, 52n
Change
  culture and, 3-4

local police cultures studies and, 34
Chapman, Samuel G., 344
Charismatic chief, 278
Chevigny, Paul, 132, 262-263, 264, 274, 292, 307
Chickenshit, term as analytic device, 313
Chiefs. *See also* Administrators
  bullshit, stress, and, 319
  charismatic, 278
  officer behavior, corruption, and, 315-316
  police solidarity and, 206
Choir practice, ritual activity and, 335
Christensen, Wendy, 30, 60
Christie, N., 117
Christopher, Warren, 6, 197
Christopher Commission, on minority group harassment in LAPD, 257, 263
Citizen-invoked interactions, 66-67
Citizens' review boards, accountability paradox and, 287
Clawson, M., 139
"Clear time," 85
Clique formation
  bullshit and, 323-324
  as loosely coupling mechanism, 284
Cluster analysis, in police culture study, 49
Cobb, Gail A., 347
Code of secrecy. *See* Secrecy
Code of silence, racism and, 256
Coercion, 5
  in arrests, 249
  at core of police role, 103
  force and, 107
  legal vs. illegal, 109-110
  as mechanism for distribution of justice, 108
  paradoxes of (Muir), 207-209
  in sexual seductions, 192-193
Coercive territorial control, 5
  in context of felony/misdemeanor encounters, 67
  defined, 77-78
  dominion and, 78
  force and, 78
  guns and, 78
  irony and, 223
  morality and, 205
  suspicion and, 225-226
Cognitions, structuring of, 46-47
Collection, as ritual linking family of slain officer to police, 344
Collective identity, of police, 353-354
Collective sense-making, culture as, 46
Commitment, police territories and, 82
Common knowledge, shared typifications as, 33
Common sense, 32, 213-227
  action and, 221
  communication of, 218

conversion of ordinary environment into ironic environment and, 225-226

deconstructed from the obvious, 222-223

identifications of danger, 227

irony trope and, 223

organizational culture and, 214-216

police work and, 61, 213-216

relativity of, 222

as story-telling, 216-223

subjectivity and, 220-221

tactics, 270

tautology of, 221-222

vs. technical knowledge, 216

transmission of through police stories, 180

uncertainty of police work and, 164, 165-167

Common-sense knowledge, interactive process as, 32

Communitas, rituals and, 335

Community policing
accountability and, 94

"blue curtain" secrecies and, 94

bullshit and, 326-328

cultural knowledge and, 47-49

emergence of institutional facts and, 34

entrenchment of police culture and, 93-94

first era of, 43

individualism and, 286

management-line hostilities and, 93

non-masculine skills emphasized in, 231-232

police racism and, 259

problems in, 327

second era of, 43

territorial responsibility and, 92-94

transmission of elements of, 43-44

use of force and, 102-103

velvet glove vs. paramilitary component in, 124-125

COMSTAT, 41

Concerns of Police Survivors (COPS), 344-346
formal goal of, 352n

Conflict
emergence of cultural elements and, 18-19

group cultures and intergroup, 21

police culture, intergroup interactions, and, 25-26

police solidarity and group, 197-198

solidarity and conflict with outside groups, 61

solidarity and social, 6

Confluence, of themes of occupational activity, 56

Consciousness of difference, in subcultures, 45

Consensual crime statutes, 303n

Consent
decrees, 40

strategies for circumventing legal considerations and, 290

Containment, of minorities, 264

Control. *See also* Edge control
illusion of in police organization, 315-316

individualism and limits on occupational, 280

principle of, 174

Co-optive strategies, toward media, 71-72

Cop killings. *See* Death; Officer killings

Cops (book), 306

"Cop things," rituals as, 336

Corcoran, James, 351

Corruption
chiefs' control of officer behavior and, 315-316

as contributor to social context of policing, 281

in drug enforcement, 299-300

"rotten apple" theory and, 281

slippery-slope materialism and, 189-190

of solidarity, 250-251

Coser, Lewis, 6, 61, 197-198, 232

Costello, Augustine E., 203-204, 307

Court(s)
articulation in court environment, 70-71

conflicts with police, 309-310

cops' interaction with, 65

deterrence view of, 308-309

police perceptions about, 310

shock the conscience test and, 304n

untrustworthiness of, 307-308

Courtroom workgroups, deterrence and, 308-309

Cover charges, 292

Cover your ass. *See* CYA (cover your ass)

Coward, use of word, 233

Cox, Terry C., 182

Crank, John P., 4, 18, 26, 30, 41, 42, 43, 44, 59, 60, 62, 62n, 93-94, 100, 102-103, 109, 117, 142, 151, 152, 161, 176, 184n, 197, 214, 215, 218, 226, 227, 247, 248, 270, 279, 281, 318-320, 326, 328n, 339, 341, 353

Creech, Alan, 361-362

Crime. *See also* specific types
compared to police work, 189-190

deception and construction of, 301-302

dramatization of, 239

felony and misdemeanor encounters, 67

property, 66

seductions of, 189-190, 190-191

slippery-slope materialism and police involvement in, 189-190

violent, 66

Crime control
institutionalized forms of, 40

loosely coupling themes and, 270-271

Crime deterrence. *See* Deterrence

Crime is war metaphor, 113-114. *See also* Militarism; War on crime

Crime reports, as working context of suspicion, 148-149
Criminal code, suspicion and, 143-144
Criminal justice programs, transmission of culture of policing in, 244-246
Criminology, Katz' mythology of, 111n
Cues, suspicion and, 148-149
Cultural adaptations, to unknown, 141-142
Cultural autonomy, 20-21
Cultural celebration, unpredictability and, 166-167
Cultural competencies, police discretion and, 36
Cultural differentiation
    within police departments, 45-46
    and structuring of cognitions, 46-47
Cultural elements
    institutionalization of, 39
    similarities in, 38-43
Cultural identity, 19, 199
    conflict and, 18, 26
    empirical measures to generate, 50
    group interactions and, 25-26
    solidarity and, 198
Cultural knowledge. *See also* Knowledge; Police knowledge
    cognitive devices of, 46
    community policing and, 47-48
    cultural participation and, 47
Cultural participation, cultural knowledge and, 47
Cultural similarity, elements of, 38-43
Cultural solidarity. *See* Solidarity
Cultural structures, police occupational practices as, 17-18
Cultural studies
    cultural autonomy and, 20-21
    location of culture and, 24-25
    objectivity, observer dependency, and, 21-24
    of police culture, 25-27
    thought experiment and issues in, 20-25
Cultural themes, 53-62. *See also* specific themes
    danger as, 160-161
    emotions and, 57-58
    identification of, 46-47
    inclusiveness of, 55
    loosely coupling, 62, 269-271
    and mixing of cultural elements, 53-54
    observer and, 58-59
    and occupational activity, 56
    onion metaphor and police, 59-62
    overly emphasized themes, 55
    selection of, 54-55
    shared, 54
    similarities and differences in, 30
    solidarity, 197-199

squads and, 65
thematic overlap and, 56-57
of the unknown, 60-61, 141-142
use of force linked with, 105-107
Cultural tool kit, 5
    community policing and, 44
    interactive process as, 32, 33
    lies in, 291
    street experience as, 341
    in training, 226
Culture. *See also* Culture of policing; Police culture
    anecdotal stories and history of, 55
    behavioral component of, 16-17
    distinction between subculture and, 29-32
    embedded nature of, 31-32
    emergent component of, 18-19
    humans as carriers of, 24-25
    ideational component of, 16
    material component of, 17
    nature of knowledge and, 19-20
    police work through lens of, 2-4
    social structural component of, 17-18
    as thematic topography, 55
    working definition of, 15-19
Culture analysis, 4
Culture-as-eyes, 2-3
Culture construction, as creative activity, 18
Culture in action perspective, of community policing, 44
Culture of policing
    separation from formal organizational processes, 271n
    transmitters of, 242-246
Culture transmission
    community policing and, 43-44
    institutional to local view of, 42-43
Cumming, Elaine, 344
Cumming, Ian, 344
CYA (cover your ass), bullshit and, 322
Cynicism
    bullshit and, 324-325
    departmental, 325

Danger. *See also* Occupational danger
    anticipation of, 5, 142, 155-161
    assailant geographies and, 161
    assessing, 156-157
    common-sense identifications of, 227
    as cultural theme, 160-161
    functional and dysfunctional fear of, 158
    and officer safety, 160
    and paradox of policing, 157-158
    police cultural focus on, 162n
    realistic measures of, 158-160
    siege mentality and, 161
    solidarity and, 198

squad system, organizational structure, and, 159

symbolic assailant and, 160-161

threat and unpredictably of, 61

vs. unpredictability, 163-164

viewed through lens of culture, 155-156

Dark side, of solidarity, 250-252

Davies, Robertson, 107, 213

Deadly force encounters, edgeworker and, 179

Deal, 42, 62

Death, 339-352. *See also* Funerals

brass and, 349-350

collections after, 344

cop culture and, 339-340, 342-343

COPS and, 344-346

failure to control the edge and, 176-177

government and, 348-349

impact of, 336-337

infrequency of violent, 340-341

linkage of police agencies and families after, 343-344

as measure of danger, 158-159

mourning or grief displays after, 351

nature of cop killing, 342-343

of partner, stress and, 248-249

peer support groups and, 350-351

in police culture, 7, 58

red tape created by, 346-347

stigmatization and need for professional assistance after, 351

symbolic component of, 347-348

unifying forces in police culture and, 341-342

"Death benefit package," 346

Deception, 196n, 289-304

in arrests, 292

construction of crime and, 301-302

as culturally supported norm, 291

ethics of narcotics interdiction and, 299-300

Manning's paradox and, 297-299

Mapp decision and collection of evidence, 295-296

toward media, 292-293

in obtaining warrants, 293-294

police lies and, 291

in proactive drug intervention, 298-299

proactivity, victimless crimes, and, 296-297

sting operations and, 301-303

truth game and, 289-291

Deconstruction

in police work, 225

training and, 226-227

DeJong, W., 248

Del Carmen, R.V., 193

Departmental cynicism, 325

Departmental organization

local police culture and, 63

squads, 63-65

Department review. *See* Administrative review

Detachment, paradox of, 207

Deterrence, 39, 305-310

courtroom workgroups and, 308-309

geographical, 83

institutionalized forms of crime control and, 40

perceived weakness of legal system and, 306-307

police, 309

random preventive patrol and, 22

stronger punishment and, 308-309

untrustworthiness of legal system and, 307-308

Deviant lies, 291

Diallo, Amadou, 61

DiCristina, Bruce, 25

Dictionary knowledge, 46

police, 47

Differentiation

of platoons, 64

of squads, 64

DiMaggio, 40

Directory knowledge, 46

police, 47

Discovery of evidence, *Mapp* decision, 295-296

Discretion. *See also* Prosecutorial discretion

community policing and, 93

cultural competencies and, 36

felony crime and, 142

felony/misdemeanor encounters and, 67

intervention and, 67

order maintenance situations and, 141-142

professionalization and control of, 93

in random preventive patrol, 85

tolerated lies and, 291

Dispossession, paradox of, 207

Dissemination, of common culture, squad personnel transfers and, 64-65

Distributive justice, vs. legal justice, 309-310

Doctrine of the sacred (Durkheim), 363n

Doerner, William, 134

Domanick, Joe, 104, 206, 229

Dominion, vs. territory, 78, 82

Dooley, R. Joseph, 347

Douglas, Mary, 18, 354, 363n

Dramaturgy

in arrests, 250

of officer killing, 347

police morality as high-minded, 203-206

in social interaction, 238

of solidarity, 238-239

in sting operations, 303

Drug courier profiles, suspicion, intervention, and, 150-151

Drug crimes

gathering evidence in, 296

prosecutorial discretion in, 297

Drug enforcement. *See also* Narcotics case
    management; Proactive drug intervention
    illegal searches and seizures in, 300
    police organizational power and authority
        for, 282
    pressures in, 299, 300
    use of common sense by agents, 223-224
Due process
    arrests, convictions, and, 309-310
    arrests and, 249, 250
    police beliefs and, 71
    proactive crimes and, 297
    sting operations and, 302
Dukakis, Michael, 266n
Dunlap, Charles, 114
Durkheim, Emile, 197, 331, 332, 363n
Dynamic affirmation, 53
Dysfunctional fear, of danger, 158

Eck, J.E., 85
Eco, Umberto, 218, 228n
Edell, Laura, 344
Edge control, 61
    and edgework, 176-179
    interaction turbulence and, 142, 173-184
    vs. maintaining the edge, 174-176
    moral component of, 181
    prevention of excesses of unpredictability
        and, 175, 184
    profanity and, 182
    traits relevant to, 181-182
Edgework (Lyng)
    absence of social self in, 179
    and context of ordinary police work, 183-
        184
    death and, 176, 177
    illusion of control and, 177
    irony and, 177
    self-actualization and, 177-178
Eller, Jack, 18, 19, 21
Emergency response team, of COPS, 346
Emergent properties. *See also* Interactionist
    perspective
    of culture, 32
    of local police culture, 60
Emotional dynamics, of solidarity, 239-241
Emotional polarity, of police work, 185
Emotions
    in cultural study, 57-58
    in police-citizen encounters, 104
E.N.D. (Eradicate Narcotics Dealers), 304n
End-of-shift interactions, 64
Enforcement-related activity, patrol time spent
    on, 95n
Entrapment, undercover work and, 188
Environmental structure, incorporation of, 41-
    42

Environments. *See also* Institutional
    environment
    administrative, 68-69
    court, 70-71
    cultural themes, interactions, and, 65
    expectations of police in, 65
    media, 71-72
    street, 66-67
Ericson, Richard V., 32, 33, 52n, 53, 54, 71-72,
    173, 180, 184n, 205, 214, 215, 216, 217,
    218, 221, 223, 226, 228n, 342
ESCORT, 139n
Ethical prescriptions, in ideational element of
    culture, 16
Ethics, 281-282
    statements of, 41
Ethnic identity, 19, 21
Ethnicity. *See also* Minority groups; Racism
    asshole identification and, 60
    as common sense base for investigation,
        257-258
Evans, Ronald, 339, 353
Evidence
    in drug-related crimes, 296
    Mapp decision and, 295-296
Excessive force, 107-109
    corrupt and deviant associations and, 111n
Excitement, anticipation of unpredictability
    and, 167-169
Exclusionary rule, *Mapp* decision and, 295-296
Executive officers. *See* Administrators; Brass;
    Chiefs; Management
Expectations, of police in different environ-
    ments, 65
External-group conflict, solidarity and, 6
External influence, police cultures and, 269
Extortionate transaction, use of force as, 207

Face, paradox of, 208
Families. *See* Families of killed officers; Police
    families
Families of killed officers
    COPS and, 344-346
    linkage to police agencies, 343-344
    media experiences of, 345-346
    red tape created by death and, 346-347
F.A.T.S. (firearm training instruction) video,
    137
Favoritism, bullshit and, 319-320
Fear(s), 174
    of danger, 158
    of unknown, 141
    use of force and, 105
Feldberg, Michael, 189
Feldmen, Martin, 196n
Felony crimes, 67, 142
Felson, Marcus, 66, 117
Female officers, percentage of, 229

Field
> failure of reforms and, 48
> socialization process and, 49
Fielden, Scott, 106
Field interrogation, reasonable suspicion and, 145
Field training
> loyalty reinforced in, 238
> secrecy from brass in, 277
Field Training Officers
> solidarity and recruits' assignment to, 246-248
> training protocols and, 270
Figurative action, interactive process as, 32
Final frame perspective, 185
Fine, Gary, 17, 18, 26, 30, 37
Firestone, David, 360
Fletcher, Connie, 87-88, 147, 161, 168, 169, 171, 171n, 175, 187, 188, 201, 211, 214, 219, 255, 258, 276-277
Fogelson, Robert M., 243, 317
Force
> abuses of, 105
> academic studies of, 101-107
> Bittner, Klockars, and, 102-103
> coercion and, 107
> community policing and concealment of, 327
> conflict and, 62
> within cultural environment, 100
> cultural solidarity and, 105-106
> effectiveness in use of, 79
> emergence of culture around, 106-107
> as extortionate transaction, 207
> fear and, 105
> legal vs. illegal coercion and, 109-110
> linkage with police culture themes, 105-107
> media portrayals of, 98
> organizational "bullshit" and, 106
> overview of police use of, 98-101
> perspectives on excessive, 107-109
> public's view of, 98
> seductive quality of, 105
> standards for use of, 99
> street sense and, 78
> training and, 78
> triggers of, 101
> Wesley and, 101-102
Formal control vs. informal control, in social control processes analyses, 343-344
Foucault, Michel, 108
Fourteenth Amendment, due process decisions and, 310
Fourth Amendment
> territorial dominion of police and, 270
> truth game and, 290
Framing (frames)

of police culture, 14, 29
selection of for police culture, 50-51
Fridell, Lorie, 340
Friery, Rodney N., 110, 291
Functional fear, of danger, 158
Funerals, 7, 248-249, 353-362
> accounts of, 360
> agency participation, symbols, rites, and dynamics of solidarity in, 359-361
> collective grief in, 358
> of Creech, Alan, 361-362
> elements in, 333
> formality and tedium of, 355-356
> group values and, 333
> high-mindedness at, 347-348
> loyalty and, 355
> power of, 329-330
> and re-establishment of authority and power, 355
> as revitalization of life of group, 337
> shared grief and reaffirmation of bonds in, 358
> solidarity and symbols at, 340, 356
> status differences at, 356
> symbolic meaning for public provided by, 356-358
Furman, Mark, 266n
Fussell, Paul, 117, 204, 212n, 233, 234, 320, 328n
Fyfe, James J., 55, 99, 104, 105, 107, 116, 131, 138-139, 197, 278

Gadamer, 59
Gambits
> in traffic stops, 183-184
> turbulence, control, and, 174
Games theory, accountability problem and, 286-288
Garfinkle, Harold, 32, 36
Garsky, Karyn, 139
Gatekeepers, police as, 354
Gates, Daryl, 206, 229, 263
Geddes, R.W., 248
Geertz, Clifford, 3, 7, 19, 31, 32, 33, 213, 215, 331, 335, 336, 355
Geller, William A., 134, 138, 139, 140n
Gender. *See also* Masculinity; Sexual harassment
> department policies and, 232
Generational transmission, of policing culture, 242
Geographical crime deterrence philosophy, 83
Geographical knowledge
> human geography linked with physical geography, 87-88
> of territory, 85-87
Geographic differentiation, of platoons, 64
Giacopassi, David J., 326

Gibson, James, 121, 122
Goal-displacement, in bureaucracies, disbursement of discipline and, 317
Goffman, Irving, 131, 152, 238
Goldstein, Herman, 85, 88
Goolkasian, G.A., 248
Government, police death and, 348-349
Gratuities, vs. bribery, 196n
Greene, Jack R., 85, 95n
Greene, Marcia Slacum, 358
Greenfield, Lawrence, 98
Gregory, Kathleen L., 54
Grief, 58
    after cop deaths, 351
Gritty unpredictability, 169-171
Grounded aesthetics, 35-36
Group(s)
    conflict, solidarity, and, 61, 197-198
    police culture and interactions with, 4-5
    values and rituals of, 333
Group cultures, conflict between groups and, 21
Group socialization. See Police socialization
Guiliani, Rudolph, 358
Guns
    authority and, 132-134
    as brute fact practicality, 17
    controlling power of, 133-134
    culture of policing and, 129-130
    frequency of usage, 134
    occupational identity and, 130-132
    point shooting and, 135
    police shootings and, 138-139
    police suicides by, 138-139
    and police work as heroic occupation, 128
    socialization and police thinking about, 127
    training and, 135-138
Guyot, Dorothy, 18, 41, 316

Haddix, Roger C., 345, 352n
Hall, 19
Hall, John, 15, 17, 23
Hall, Richard, 317
Hanley, Robert, 360
Hansen, Dick, 263
Harassment, of minority groups, measurement of, 261-262
Harmon, Michael M., 280, 286-287
Harris, Richard, 230, 321
Hartmann, Francis X., 92, 261
He, Ni, 59
Head shots, in gun training, 137-138
"Heart," of police officers, 59
Heidensohn, F., 230
Herbert, Steve, 89, 104
Hermeneutic conversation, frames for thinking about culture and, 51
Herrington, Nancy, 232

Hevesi, Dennis, 358, 359, 360
High-mindedness
    at funerals, 347-348
    police morality and, 203-206
Hill, K., 139
Hiring, of minorities, 264
History of racism, in American policing, 258-259
Horizontal cliques, formation of, 324
Horse and blinders analogy, 2
Horton, Willie, 266n
Human body, cops' view of, 169-171
Human geography, physical geography and, 87-88
Human nature, institutionalized forms of crime control and, 40
Humor
    bullshit and, 322-323
    grit in, 171
Hundred Clubs. See Concerns of Police Survivors (COPS)
Hunt, J., 232
Hunt, Raymond G., 168, 201, 283
Hupe, Mark, 362
Hyper-danger, PPUs and, 124
Hyperreality, edgework and, 178

Idaho State Academy, training program of, 253n
Ideal officer, perceptions of, 235n
Ideational components
    of culture, 16
    in municipal police organizations, 30
Identity. See also Cultural identity; Ethnic identity
    collective, 353-354
Identity kit. See also Cultural tool kit
    for police, 131
Illegal searches and seizures, in drug enforcement, 300
Illicit sexual behavior, by police, 193
Illusion of control
    edgework and, 177
    in police work, 178
Imposition, of organizational structure and behavior, 40
Imprinting, of organizational structure, behavior, and knowledge, 41
Incorporation, of environmental structure, behavior, and knowledge, 41-42
Individualism, 279-288
    accountability and, 281-282
    entrepreneurship vs. administrative control, 283-286
    games theory and paradox of accountability, 286-288
    inner-direction, aggressiveness, and, 282
    and loyalty, partners and, 283

occupational control limits and, 279

organizational models vs. individual models and, 285-286

personal responsibility and, 279- 280

police corruption and, 281

as root metaphor, 280-281

self-sufficiency and, 283

Individual models, vs. organizational models, 285-286

Individual responsibility. *See* Personal responsibility

Inducement, 196n

of organizational structure and behavior, 41

Informal control. *See* Formal control vs. informal control

Informants

in drug enforcement, 299, 300

obtaining warrants and, 294

Information

release of friendly, 72

shift work and exchange of, 68

Information withheld, 292-293

Inner circle, of reporters, 72

Innocent people, maintenance of control and, 183

Institutional environment, 4

institutionalized occupational environment of policing, 279

police as subculture in, 38-44

principal actors in cop's, 274

Institutional facts, 21-22

community policing and, 34

language as, 22-23

observer-dependent element of, 22

Institutional inspection, 271n

Institutionalization, community policing movement and, 43-44

Institutionalized economic discrimination, 267n

Institutionalized organizations

individual police departments as, 279

loose coupling in, 269-270

research on, 269

Institutionalized sexist ideology, linkage with occupational sexual harassment, 196n

Institutional perspective, 4

subcultural elements and, 29

Insularity, 278

Interactionist perspective, 4, 29

police as local culture, 32-37

Interaction turbulence, and edge control, 5-6, 142, 173-184

Interactive training

guns and, 137

scenario introducing recruits to uncertainty, 166

Intergroup interactions, police culture and, 25-26

Internal affairs. *See also* Administrative review

accountability paradox and, 287

Internal review, 68. *See also* Administrative review

street officers' response to, 6

Internal security, in post-9/11 era, 114

International Association of Chiefs of Police (IACP), 115, 243

Inter-organizational sector, elements of police culture in, 38

Interpretation of text, language and, 27n

Intervention

drug courier profiles and, 150-151

expansion of scope of, 92-93

right to, as absolute authority, 87-88

Invisibility

of police, 274-275

postulates of, 275-276

Irony(ies), 228n

deconstruction in training and, 226-227

edgework and, 177

of organizational structure, 223-227

in routine traffic stop, 227

of suspicion, danger and, 161

suspicion and, 225-226

trope, 218, 223

Irrationality, paradox of, 208

Isolation, 64, 347

Jackson, Stanley, 109, 214

Jenkins, Kent, 358

Jennings, Veronica, 358

Job-shopping (judge-shopping), in warrant process, 294

Jocular aggression, 322-323

Johnson, Lyndon, 113, 261

Johnson, Mark, 23, 216, 288n

Johnson, Patricia, 27n

Justice, models of, 309-310

Justice Without Trial, 261, 266n

Kappeler, S.F., 193

Kappeler, Victor E., 37, 53, 55, 67, 68, 71, 78, 104, 105, 111n, 118, 122, 123, 156, 157, 160, 161, 162n, 193-194, 194, 195, 196n, 197, 205, 226, 228n, 230, 243, 257, 271, 273, 275, 276, 286

Karales, Kevin J., 138, 139

Katz, Jesse, 190-191

Katz, Samuel M., 111n, 348, 359

Kelling, G., 83, 258

Kelling, George, 92, 124

Kerner, Otto, 256

Kertzer, David I., 334

King, Rodney, 206, 263

Klein, Herbert T., 91, 132, 201-202, 203, 293, 307, 310

Kleinman, Sherryl, 17, 18, 26, 30, 37

Klockars, Carl B., 55, 78, 85, 87, 94, 95n, 102-103, 111n, 249, 270, 302-303, 326, 327
Kluckhohn, 19
Knapp Commission, 288
    corruption investigation of, 251, 252
Knowledge. *See also* Cultural knowledge; Police knowledge
    acquisition of, 41
    culture and nature of, 19-20
    geographical, 85-87
    imprinting of, 41
    incorporation of, 41-42
    from real-world experiences, 32
    and social setting, 222
Knowles, Jeffrey J., 193, 261
Kohn, 134
Kraska, Peter B., 27, 67, 78, 113, 118, 119, 121, 122, 123, 124, 125, 127, 130, 193, 194, 195, 196n, 243
Kuykendall, Jack, 30

Lakoff, George, 23, 216, 288n
Lane, Roger, 114, 115, 117
Langan, Patrick, 98
Langer, E., 177
Language
    and common cultural identity, 31
    to control situations, 182
    ethnographic investigation and, 23-24
    as fundamental institutional fact, 22-23, 27n
    in police culture study, 25
Langworthy, Robert, 4, 18, 30, 41, 93-94, 270, 279, 281, 301-302, 325, 326, 327
Law enforcement
    dramatury of occupational solidarity and, 239
    vs. order maintenance, 141-142
    solidarity and, 249-250
Law Enforcement Assistance Administration, 261
"Law Enforcement Officers Killed in Action," 219
LeBeau, James L., 302
Legal basis, of suspicion, 144-145
Legal coercion, vs. illegal coercion, 109-110
Legal justice, vs. distributive and retributive justice, 309-310
Legal system. *See also* Court(s)
    perceived weakness of, 306-307
Lens of culture
    day-to-day activities viewed through, 32-33
    police attitudes toward minority groups through, 261
    police work through, 2-4
Levi-Strauss, Claude, 19
Liberal court system, as shared cultural theme, 54

Lies
    accepted, 291
    arrest, 292
    deviant, 291
    media (information withheld), 292-293
    placebo, 291
    tolerated, 291
    as verbal strategies, 291
Line-of-duty deaths, 336-337. *See also* Death; Officer killings
Line officers. *See also* Squads; Street cops
    accountability and, 281-282, 326
    administrative control and individualistic approach of, 283-286
    administrative distrust of, 311-312
    administrative environment and, 68-69
    audiences for, 54, 65
    autonomy of, 283
    chiefs' control of behavior of, 315-316
    common sense and, 214
    courts and, 70-71
    craft-oriented worldview of, 109
    as cultural-carrying group, 63
    deadly encounters and, 132-133
    external prying and protection strategies, 288
    guns and background of, 129-130
    gun usage by, 134
    inner-directed, 282
    loosely coupling themes and, 62, 270
    management relationships and, 277-278
    media and, 71-72
    patrol vs. courtroom behavior of, 70-71
    professional view of, 109
    street environment and, 66-67
    traditional cultural orientation of, 52n
    "war on crime" mentality of, 116-117
    warrior persona and, 118-119, 121, 128-129
Literature, on police culture, 14
Local culture
    aesthetics of, 35-36
    change and, 34
    emergent properties of, 60
    police as, 29, 32-37
    as product of modern society, 21
    racism in local police cultures, 257
    squad as basic unit of local cop culture, 65
    transmission of, 36-37
Location of culture, in cultural studies, 24-25
Loosely coupling
    clique formation as mechanism of, 284
    occurrence of, 271n
    task ambiguity and, 67
    themes, 6-7, 62
Loosely coupling cultural themes, 269-271. *See also* specific themes

Lord, Stephenie, 353
Los Angeles Police Department
    Christopher Commission and, 257, 263
    racism and, 262-263
Lovrich, Nicholas, 59
Loyalty
    corruption and, 250-251
    dramatization of, 240
    funerals and, 355
    and individualism issues, partners and, 283
    partner-style, 246
    solidarity and, 237-238
Lozano, Carlos, 359
Luckmann, Thomas, 32, 222, 228n
Lying, by police, 291
Lyng, Stephen, 176-179

Machismo. *See also* Masculinity
    in police-citizen interactions, 104
Magenau, John M., 168, 201, 283
Maguire, Kathleen, 310
Maintaining the edge. *See* Edge
    control
Management. *See also* Administrators; Brass;
    Chiefs; Police executive; Sergeants
    assaulted officers perceptions of, 349-350
    line-of-duty deaths and bureaucratic forms
        of, 351-352
    line officer accountability, game metaphor,
        and, 287
    line officers distrust of, 311-312
    relationships with line officers, 277-278
Management brass. *See* Brass
Management culture
    perspective of territory, 82
    as police subculture, 45
    rules and procedures vs. domain of local
        territorial responsibility, 90
    street culture, officer death, and, 349-350
Management-line hostilities, community polic-
    ing and, 93
Mannheim, Karl, 222
Manning, Peter K., 1, 16, 38-39, 45-46, 47, 50,
    52n, 53, 54, 60, 61, 63, 65, 73n, 78, 107,
    161, 164, 167, 181, 189, 197, 205, 214,
    215, 217, 218, 223-224, 228n, 238-239,
    249, 252n, 274, 276, 277, 281, 282, 283-
    286, 291, 297, 299-300, 302, 307-308,
    311, 312, 317, 318, 323, 324, 328n, 344,
    347, 356
"Man" role, themes in, 231
Mapp decision, collection of evidence, decep-
    tion, and, 295-296
Martin, Christine, 193, 261
Martin, Douglas, 358, 360, 363n
Martin, Susan E., 133-134, 229, 230-232, 235n,
    248, 257, 264, 276
Martinez Vidales, Jesus, 263

Marx, Gary T., 188, 224-225, 298, 302
Masculinity, 229-235
    bravery as special case of, 232-235
    community policing and, 231-232
    as cultural theme, 229-230
    Martin's study of, 230-232
    negative police behavior and, 230
    as subcultural trait, 232-233
"Master detective" metaphor, 284-285
Mastrofski, Stephen D., 43, 44, 100, 270, 326,
    327
Material component, of culture, 17
Maxfield, Michael G., 68, 69
McDonald, Cherokee Paul, 354
McDonald, Sean, 348
McKeon, 280
McLuhan, Marshall, 17
McMurray, Harvey L., 349-350
McNulty, Elizabeth W., 54, 163, 165-167, 214,
    217, 218, 221, 223, 225, 226, 227, 335,
    341
Mead, G.H., 179
Meanings, in interactionist perspective, 32
Measurement
    of bullshit, 318-320
    of police racism, 261-262
Media
    danger to police depicted in, 156
    environment, 71-72
    high-mindedness of police morality in, 205
    lies to, 292-293
    police mythology and guns in, 131-132
    police organization cultural similarity and,
        65
    resentment toward after cop killing, 343
    responsibility and territory fusion and rela-
        tions with, 91-92
    social dynamics of police work and, 17
    survivors of killed officers and, 345-346
    transmission of local police culture
        through, 37
    use of force in, 98
Metaphor(s). *See also* Root metaphor
    in dramatization of crime, 239
    "master detective," 284-285
    as master trope, 218, 228n
    of war, militarism and, 117-121
Metaphorical imagery, police behavior and,
    217-218
Meta-theme, police and public's expectations,
    7
Metonymy, 228n
    badge as, 330n
    as special trope, 218, 228n
Mexico State v. Cohen, 150
Meyer, Eugene, 359, 360
Meyer, John W., 6, 38, 42, 62, 269, 270, 271n,
    279

Michaels, Tom, 151
Middle-management, bullshit, stress, and, 319
Militarism, iv
    defined, 114
    dimensions of militarization and, 119
    and metaphors of war, 117-121
    new warrior ideology and police, 121
    police identity and, 118-119
    in police organizational structure, 115-116
    police paramilitary units (PPUs) and, 122-124
    professionalism, reform, and, 114-116
    symbolic purposes of, 117
    we-them attitude and, 119
Militaristic command structure, 41, 313-317
Militarization, of police, 102
Military personnel, as transmitters of culture of
    policing, 243
Miller, George I., 298
Miller, Joanna, 358, 360
Mills, 218
Minority groups
    community policing in Australia and, 47-49
    hiring in police organizations, 264
    internal agency conflicts with racist over-
        tones and, 264-265
    police attitudes toward, 261
Misdemeanors, 67
    basis for arrest decisions in, 309
    discretion and, 95n
Monkkonen, Eric H., 114
Moore, M., 83, 258
Moral agents, police as, 201
Morality. *See also* Police morality
    dominion over turf and, 81-82
    funerals and, 357
    of police, 354
    public, 354
Moral responsibility, edge control and, 181
Morals crimes. *See* Victimless crimes
Morgan, Thomas, 360
Morris, 138
Mourning, after cop deaths, 351
Muir, William K., 18, 175, 207-209, 212n, 249,
    306, 308
Multiple cultures
    frame, 29
    in police organizations, 4
Multiple group membership, transmission of
    local police culture and, 37
Multiple subcultures, of police within organiza-
    tional setting, 45-50
Municipal police organizations
    cultural themes in, 30
    ideational components of, 30
Murphy, Patrick V., 256, 258-259
Myers, Stephanie, 4
Mythology of policing

diffusion of potentially dangerous situations
    and, 180
guns and, 131

Narcotics case management, 285-286. *See also*
    Drug enforcement
Narcotics interdiction. *See* Drug enforcement
Narrative, in ethnography, 23-24
National Law Enforcement Officers Memorial,
    348-349
National Police Week (May), 349
Neitz, Mary Jo, 15, 17
Newman, Kenneth, 261
New Mexico v. Mann, 150
New South Wales Police Department, culture
    and reform in, 47-49
Newspaper reporters, 71-72
New warrior ideology, 121, 128-129
Niederhoffer, Arthur, 1, 54, 66, 324-325
911 rapid response to citizen calls, 40
Noble cause, 42-43
Normal, suspicion and, 148
Normative orders (Herbert), 89
Norms
    deception as, 291
    informal racist, 265
"Not in progress" crimes, 95n
Nussbaum, Martha, 57-58

Objectivity, and observer dependency in cul-
    tural observation, 21-24
Obscenity, to control situations, 182
Observer(s)
    police cultural themes and, 58-59
    predispositions of and views of police cul-
        ture, 31
Observer dependency
    and objectivity in cultural observation, 21-
        24
    police culture and, 25
Obstruction of justice, in drug enforcement,
    299
Occupational activity, cultural themes and, 56
Occupational control limits, individualism and,
    280
Occupational danger. *See also* Danger
    aggressive seeking of, 178
    police cultural focus on, 162n
Occupational environment, institutionalized, of
    policing, 279
Occupational identity, guns and, 130-132
Occupational niches, subsubcultures and, 45
Occupational segmentation, of police culture,
    46
Occupational sexual harassment, institutional-
    ized sexist ideology of police and, 196n
O'Conner, C., 67

Officer(s). *See also* Line officers; Squads; Street cops
    "heart" of, 59
    media portrayals of, 98
    ordinary lives of, 98
    perceptions of ideal, 235n
    typical, 245-246
Officer killings. *See also* Death
    anger, confusion, and revenge after, 342-343
    brutish nature of, 342
    circumstances of, 340-341
    dramaturgy of, 347
    as measure of danger, 158-159
Officer safety
    arrests and, 250
    automobile stops and, 153n
    danger and, symbolic weight of, 160
    drug interdiction training, suspicion, and, 151
    focus in POST training, 176, 247-248
    right and wrong categoric codes and, 207
    training and, 62
Oliver, Melvin L., 267n
Onion metaphor, for police culture, 59-62
On-the-job sexual activity. *See* Police sexual violence (PSV); Seduction
Operational perspective, of territory, 82
Operation Hammer (LAPD), 262-263
Operation Valkyrie, 151
Order maintenance
    dealing with, 103-104
    vs. law enforcement, 141-142
    patrol time spent on, 95n
    personal authority in, 104
Organizational administration. *See* Administrative environment
Organizational articulation, of police-citizen interactions, 67
Organizational culture, common sense and, 214-216
Organizational models, vs. individual models, 285-286
Organizational pressures, ethical/legal violations and, 281-282
Organizational structure
    acquisition of, 41
    authorization of, 41
    bypassing of, 42-43
    cultural themes and, 53-54
    impact of danger and, 159
    imposition of, 40
    imprinting of, 41
    inducement of, 41
    ironies of, 223-227
    militarism in, 115-116
    police culture and, 63

Organizational theory, concept of ritual in, 337n
Organizational traditions, 3
Outer circle, scandal and, 72
Outsiders
    avoiding trouble and, 274, 277
    invisibility of, 274-276
    lying low and, 274, 277
    as occupational disposition, 273-276
    secrecy and, 276-278
Overclass, alienation of police from, 265

Pain compliance, 78
Paoline, Eugene, 4, 46, 47, 49-50, 52n
Paradoxes of coercion (Muir), 207-209
    detachment, 207
    dispossession, 207
    of face, 208
    irrationality, 208
Paradox of policing (Cullen), 157-158
Paramilitarism. *See also* Militarism; Police paramilitary units (PPUs)
    characteristics of police, 125n
    professionalism, reform, and, 114-116
Parrish v. Lukie, 193
Partners
    death of, 248-249
    individualism and loyalty issues and, 283
    solidarity of, 248-249
Partner-style loyalties, 246
Pastore, Ann L., 310
Pataki, George, 348
Pate, Antony, 340
Patrol. *See also* Random preventive patrol
    invisibility in, 275
Patrolman. *See* Line officers; Officers; Squads; Street cops
Paulsen, D., 122, 123, 124, 125
Payne, Betsy, 109, 214
Peace, use of force and, 101-102
Peace Officer Standards and Training (POST). *See* POST training
Pedestrian stops, suspicion, behavioral cues, and, 149
Peer groups
    pressure, corruption and, 251
    support from following line-of-duty assaults and deaths, 350-351
Penn, Nolan F., 235n
Perez, Douglas W., 68
Perjury
    of testimony, 294-295
    in warrant process, 293-294
Personal authority, in order maintenance situations, 104
Personal injury, concerns of police, 179-180
Personal responsibility
    acted out in police organization, 39

individualism and, 279-280
line officer accountability and, 281-282
Personal settings, suspicion in, 151-153
Perspectives, on police culture, 4
Physical geography, of police work. *See* Coercive territorial control
Physical structure, social structural component of culture and, 17
Placebo lies, 291
Platoons, 64
Plea bargaining, deterrence and, 308, 309
Plessy v. Ferguson, 258-259
Pogrebin, Mark R., 64, 68, 225, 233, 322-323
Point of view. *See* Standpoint
Point shooting, 135
Police abuse, acknowledgment of, 212n
Police agencies. *See* Police organizations
Police authority. *See* Authority
Police axiomatic knowledge, 47
Police behavior, masculinity as aspect of, 230
Police-citizen contacts
    citizen-invoked interactions, 66-67
    organizational articulation of, 67
    profanity and obscenity in, 182
    traffic stops, 67
    use of police force in, 98-101
Police-citizen encounters and interactions
    absence of reflective, social self in, 179
    dramaturgy of solidarity in, 238
    emotions in, 104-105
    high-mindedness and, 206
    potential for turbulence in, 174
    power differentials and sexual activity in, 194, 195
    respect and machismo in, 104
    unpredictably of, 104-105
Police culture
    audiences for, 63-72
    boundaries of, 54, 63-72
    death and, 339-340
    death in, 7, 58
    descriptions of, 13-14
    distrust of courts in, 307-308
    emotions in, 57-58
    engaging police on own terms and, 27
    in individuals, 26
    intergroup interactions, conflict, and, 25-26
    issues in studies of, 25-27
    language and, 25
    observer-dependency and, 25
    onion metaphor for, 59-62
    organizational structure and, 63
    perspectives on, 4
    reproduction of, 26
    research, 1
Police dictionary knowledge, 47
Police directory knowledge, 47
Police executive. *See also* Management

high-mindedness, police morality, and, 206
    police solidarity and, 206
Police families, as transmitters of culture of policing, 242
Police funerals. *See* Funerals
Police knowledge
    coercive territorial control as, 5
    daily routines and, 342
    as practical and value-laden language, 341
Police morality, 201-211. *See also* Morality
    assholes and, 209-211
    coercion and, 205
    as high-minded dramaturgy, 203-206
    media's vision and, 205
    paradoxes of coercion and, 207-209
Police occupational worldview. *See also* Worldviews
    suspicion in, 152-153
Police officers. *See* Line officers; Officer(s); Squads; Street cops
Police organizations
    front and back stage in, 238
    as institutionalized organizations, 279
    linkage of families of killed officers, 343-344
    militarism in structure of, 115-116
    minorities in, 264-265
    multiple cultures in, 4
    personal responsibility and, 39
    as quasi-military organizations, 315
    sources and prevalence of racism in, 257
    value-laden, 279
Police paramilitary units (PPUs), 122-124
    hyper-danger and, 124
    proliferation of, 124
Police personality, suspicion as characteristic of, 143
Police presentational strategies, 73n
Police professionalism movement, black officers and, 259
Police-Public Contact Survey, on police use of force, 98
Police recipe knowledge, 48
Police role
    coercion at core of, 103
    traditional reactive, 296
Police sexual violence (PSV), 193-194
    boys-will-be-boys genre and, 194, 230
Police shootings, of police, 138-139
Police socialization
    attitudinal dispositions and, 241-242
    personal injury concerns and, 179-180
Police studies, concept of culture in, 4
Police subcultures, iii
    within organizational setting, 45-50
Police territories. *See* Territory(ies)
Police training. *See* Training
Police types, cluster analysis and, 49-50

Police violence. *See also* Excessive force; Force
as overreaction to potential/real danger, 108
Police work, 4-5. *See also* Working environment
braveness and situations in, 234
community policing and mystification of, 103
compared to criminal activity, 189-190
daily, 4-5
game metaphor applied to street-level, 287
human action in production of culture in, 24-25
through lens of culture, 2-4
machine model of, 115
maintenance of public order vs. law enforcement in, 95n
normative orders and, 89
physical geography of, 78
professional model of, 115
self-perception and perceptions of, 284
subjective notion of, 221-222
unpredictability and, 167-169
Policing. *See* Police work
Policy(ies)
administrative, control of police behavior and absence of social self in police-citizen encounters, 179
dealing with line-of-duty deaths, 345, 352n
gender and department, 232
Political factors, suspicion and, 144
Political machines, progressive reform and, 115
Political power, of African-Americans, racial bias and, 260-261
Poole, Eric D., 64, 68, 225, 233, 322-323, 324, 325
Positive contacts transmission, of culture of policing, 243
Post-9/11 era, police/military interaction in, 114
Post-stress disorder, after officer killings, 343
POST training, 99-100
aspects of, 247
guns, occupational identity, and, 130
guns in, 135-138
loosely coupling from everyday police work and, 270
loyalty reinforced in, 238
officer safety as focus in, 176, 247-248
perceptions of danger underscored in, 157
secrecy from brass in, 277
solidarity and, 246-248
Potter, G.W., 37, 71, 156, 157
Powell, 40
Power
re-established in police funerals, 357
rituals as, 335-336

Power differentials, between women and police officers in sexual abuse cases, 194, 195
Powers, Mary D., 256
Predispositions of observers, view of police culture and, 30
Preliminary hearing, articulation through, 70
Pretrial phase, articulation through, 70
Priest, Dana, 358
Print media, social dynamics of police work and, 17
Private knowledge, geographical knowledge as, 86
Private (covert) performances, of police, 73n
Private space, creating in public places, 86
Proactive drug intervention, 298-299
Proactive policing, 83-84, 95n
random patrol as, 83-84
Proactivity
due process and, 297
victimless crimes and, 296-297
Probable cause, 153n
automobile stops and, 150, 153n
reasonable suspicion and, 145
Problem-oriented policing, 88
Problem solving
common sense and, 215
interactive perspective and, 33
reproduction of culture and, 33
Production pressures, ethical/legal violations and, 281-282
Profanity, to maintain control, 182
Professional assistance, after cop death, 351
Professionalism
functions of, 252n
line officers' "world views" and, 109
militarism, reform, and, 114-116
occupational ideas of, 111n
occupational solidarity and, 238-239
Professionalism movement, 102
Professionalization
control of line discretion and, 93
police, bureaucratization and, 318
Professional political model (Weber), 208
Profile stops, 150-151
Progressives, police reform and, 115
Project on Policing Neighborhoods (POPN) study, 100-101
Property crimes, citizen-invoked interactions and, 66
Prosecutorial discretion
in drug cases, 297
function of, 308
Psychological dysfunctions, after officer killings, 343
Public. *See also* Police-citizen contacts; Police-citizen encounters and interactions
cops' interaction with, 65
expectations of police, 7

officer killings and, 348
police funerals providing symbolic meaning for, 356-358
police view of, 274
secrecy of police and, 276-277
Public morality, police as gatekeepers of, 354
Public (open/accessible) police performances, 73n
Public Safety Officers' Benefits Act, 349
Punch, Maurice, 38, 52n
Punishment, deterrence and, 308-309

Race
asshole identification and, 60
and structure of wealth in United States, 267n
symbolic assailants and characteristics of, 161
Racism, 255-266
containment and, 264
cultural conceptualization of self-fulfilling practice and, 256-257
future of police, 264-266
historical context of, 258-259
in local police cultures, 257
Los Angeles Police Department and, 262-263
measuring police, 261-262
police-minority interventions and, 260-261
reinforcement of informal racist norms, 265
research on police, 256
Skolnick on, 260-261
sources and prevalence of in police organizations, 257
term usage as misleading, 266n
Ragonese, Paul, 136, 137, 155-156, 159, 160, 234, 313-315
Rainer, Trish, 345, 346, 352
Random preventive patrol, 296
"clear time" in, 85
geographical crime deterrence philosophy of, 83
as institutional fact, 22
as institutionalized crime control, 40
officers' use of time during, 85-88
as proactive police work, 83-84
vs. traditional, reactive styles of policing, 95n
value choices in, 85
Random reactive patrol, vs. problem-oriented policing, 88
Rank, as boundary to police culture, 54
Rank-in-position personnel systems, bullshit production and, 316-317
Rational-technical knowledge, vs. common sense, 216
Reactive policing, 83-84, 95n
Reasonable suspicion, 144-145

Recipe knowledge, 46
police, 48
Recruits. *See also* Training
bullshit and, 321
drawn from culture of policing, 244
introduction to uncertainty, 166
secrecy from brass and, 277
socialization process and, 48-49
views of, 26
Redfield, Robert, 19
Redlinger, Lawrence, 249, 281, 282, 299-300, 304n
Red tape, created by officer's death, 346-347
Reed, Mack, 358, 360
Reforms
and culture in New South Wales police organization, 47-49
and distinction between culture and sub-culture, 30
militarism, professionalism, and, 114-116
police cultural influence and, 6
police response to, 47-48
research on police culture and, 14
Regoli, Robert, 324-325
Rehm, Lee, 151
Reiner, R., 14
Reiser, M., 325
Reiss, Albert J., 104, 206
Relativity
of common sense, 222
of values, 22-23
Remedy phase, in labeling assholes, 209
Reno, Janet, 123
Reporters. *See* Newspaper reporters
Reproduction, of culture, 1, 26
Resignation, bullshit and, 325-326
Resistance, training in use of force and, 100
Respect, in police-citizen interactions, 104
Responsibility, 90-91. *See also* Personal responsibility
community policing and territorial, 92-94
police territories and, 82
territory fusion, media relations, and, 91-92
Ressentiment, 198
Retributive justice. *See* Distributive justice
Reuss-Ianni, Elizabeth, 1, 45, 46, 47, 54, 63, 68, 89-90, 95n, 168, 181-182, 248, 275, 311, 318, 322, 349
Revolvers. *See* Guns
Rhetorical strategy, profanity usage as, 182
Richardson, J.F., 258
Righteousness, funerals and, 356-357
Risk-taking
edgeworkers and, 177-178
recruits and, 227
Ritti, R. Richard, 43, 44
Ritual(s), 7, 331-337. *See also* Funerals

concept in organizational theory, 337n
as "cop things," 336
emotional states during, 334-335
emotions, group symbols, and, 334-335
essence of, 331
group values and, 333
importance of, 329
"is the thing itself" perspective, 335-337
leveling of statuses in, 335
meaning constructed by, 333-337
myth about, 337n
pattern of authority in society and, 336
as power, 335-336
social solidarity and, 332
symbols in, 334
Rizzo, Frank, 278
Roberg, Roy, 30
Rochin v. California, 304n
Roll call, 68
Root metaphor, individualism as, 280-281
Rothwell, J.D., 182
"Rotten apple" theory, of police corruption, 281
Rough justice, suspects and, 108
Rowan, Brian, 6, 269, 270, 279
Rubinstein, Jonathan, 63, 64-65, 68, 73n, 85-87, 97, 104, 105, 109, 130, 135, 139-140n, 143, 146-148, 149, 150, 294
Rule of law, police accountability for, 143
Rules and regulations
bullshit, stress, and, 319
manipulation of, 284
Russo, John, 306

Sack, Kevin, 360
Sackmann, Sonja, 15, 46-47, 50
Sacks, Harvey, 214
Sapp, Allen D., 191-192, 194, 230, 235n
Sawyer, Suzanne F., 345, 346
Scandal, impact of, 72
Scharf, Peter, 127, 131-132
Schmitt, Eric, 358, 359
Scott, Michael S., 134, 139, 140n
Scott, W. Richard, 38, 40, 42, 62
Searches and seizures, in drug enforcement, 300
Search process, administrative process and, 290
Searing, Clifford, 228n
Searle, John, 21, 22, 27n
"Second injury," 350
Secrecy, 274
brass and, 277-278
of outsiders, 276-278
public and, 276-277
Sector assignments, 86
Sectors, 82
Seduction, 142, 185-195
bright edge of, 185-186
of crime, 189-190, 190-191

perceived slights to police authority, violence, and, 191
sexual, 191-193, 193-195
undercover work and, 188
use of force and, 105, 111n
Segmentation
within organizations, 46
within police departments, 45-46
Seidman, R., 276
Self-actualization, in edgework, 177-178
Self-perception, perceptions of real police work and, 284
Self-sufficiency, in police work, 283
Sentiment, 53. *See also* Emotional dynamics; Emotions
September 11, 2001 terrorist attacks, internal security and, 114
Sergeants
bullshit, stress, and, 319
limitations of supervision by, 68-69
Severeid, Eric, 212n
Sexual abuse cases, power differentials and, 194
Sexual harassment. *See also* Police sexual violence (PSV)
boys-will-be-boys attitude and, 230
institutionalized sexist ideology of police and, 196n
by police officers, 193
Sexual misconduct. *See* Police sexual violence (PSV); Sexual harassment
Sexual seductions and sexual activity, 191-193
coercion in, 192-193
cultural bases for, 195
research on, 193-194
Shanahan, Peter, 13
Shapiro, Thomas M., 267n
Shared cultural themes, 54
Shared typifications, interactive process as, 32, 33
Shearing, Clifford, 32, 33, 53, 54, 173, 180, 184n, 214, 215, 216, 217, 218, 221, 223, 226, 342
Sherman, 134
Sherman, Lawrence, 189, 273
Shift differentiation, of squads, 64
Shifts
end of, 68
end-of-shift interactions, 64
internal review, 69
roll call, 68
rotating, 73n
sergeant supervision, 68-69
standard operating procedure and, 69
working schedules for, 63-64
Shock the conscience test, 304n
"Show balls" trait, edge control and, 181
Siege mentality, 60, 161
Silver, Isidore, 302
Simmel, Georg, 197

Simpson, O.J., 266n
Singleton, G., 325
Situationally justified force, 102
Situational uncertainty, 61
    unpredictability and, 5, 142, 163-171
Sixth sense suspicion, 145
Skin-color, as common sense base for investiga-
    tion, 257-258
Skolnick, 168, 191, 286
Skolnick, Jerome, 1, 54, 55, 94, 99, 104, 105,
    107, 116, 124, 128, 129, 131, 143, 144,
    148, 151, 152, 153n, 160, 161, 197, 237,
    241, 260-261, 278, 291, 295-296, 298
Slave patrols, 258, 266-267n
Slaves, evolution of policing and, 258
Slippery-slope materialism, police involvement
    in crime and, 189-190
Sluder, Richard D., 53, 55, 68, 78, 104, 105,
    157, 160, 197, 205, 226, 230, 257, 273,
    275, 286
Small-town traditions, as transmitters of culture
    of policing, 243
Smith, Leef, 359
Smith, Steven, 98
Snow, David, 176
Social action, products of, 18
Social conflict, solidarity and, 6
Social control
    funerals and, 357
    as institution, 39
    newspaper reporters as agents of, 71-72
Social groups, emergence as product of new
    relations among, 18
Social identity, of police, 5
Socialization, as heterogeneous process, 48-49
Social mobility, of police recruits, 245-246
Social solidarity. *See* Solidarity
Social standing, leveling in rituals, 335
Social structural component, of culture, 17-18
Social structure, cultural themes and, 53-54
Solidarity, 237-252, 354
    administrative review and, 251-252
    challenges to police authority and, 198
    cultural themes of, 6-7, 197-199
    cultural transmission of, 237
    dangers of police work and, 198
    dark side of, 250-252
    dimensions of, 248-252
    dramaturgical aspect of, 238-239
    emergence within culture of policing, 241-
        246
    emotional dynamics of, 239-241
    enforcement mandate and, 249-250
    in funerals, 340, 355, 356, 358, 359-361
    group conflict and, 197-198
    killing of cop and, 342
    as layer in onion metaphor, 61-62
    loyalty and, 237-238

outsiders theme and, 273
of partners, 248-249
POST training, field training, and, 246-248
presentational strategies and, 238-239
profanity usage and, 182
public support for police and, 297
rituals and, 332
task ambiguity and, 67
and transmission of culture of policing,
    242-246
use of force and, 105-106
Soul of a Cop, The (Ragonese), 156
Sour grapes antagonism, 198
South, American modern-style of policing
    developed in, 258-259
Sparger, Jerry R., 326
Spelman, W., 85
Squads
    cultural themes and, 65
    division of, 64
    end-of-shift discussion/interaction in, 64
    impact of danger and, 159
    personnel transfers and, 64-65
    working schedule for, 63-64
Standard operating procedure (SOP), 68
    accountability and, 94
    as accountability mechanism, 327-328
Standard Operating Procedure (SOP) manuals,
    68, 287
Standards
    of performance in police occupational cul-
        ture, 308
    for use of force, 99
Standpoint
    narratives and, 24
    popular vernacular and, 22
    values as, 23
Statistical procedures, in police culture study,
    49-50
Stigmatization
    and need for professional assistance after
        cop death, 351
    process in labeling assholes, 208-209
Sting operations
    and creation of crime, 301, 302, 303
    paradox in, 302-303
    for theft enforcement, 301-302
Stoddard, Ellwyn, 197, 256
Stopping power, 130, 139-140n. *See also* Guns
Stories
    anecdotal, as carriers of cultural history, 55
    common sense and, 216-223
    as metaphors with other types of tropes,
        228n
    power in training, 220
    as synecdoche, 218
Storms, Lowell H., 235n
Strecher, Victor, 174

Street cops. *See also* Line officers
  common cultural elements shared by, 57
  cultural elements of, 90
  police culture and, 3
  professional/military model and, 116-117
Street culture, management culture, officer
    death, and, 349-350
Street environment
  citizen-invoked interactions in, 66-67
  as layer in onion metaphor, 60
  traffic stops in, 67
Street experience, as cultural tool kit, 341
Street justice, 107-108
Street-management hostility. *See* Management;
    Management culture; Street culture
Street sense, force and, 78
Stress
  bullshit and, 318-320
  death of partner and, 248-249
Structural roles, transmission of local police
    culture and, 37
Subcultural differentiation, and clusters of
    police types, 49
Subcultures. *See also* Multiple subcultures
  distinction between culture and, 29-32
  overlapping, 37
  police organizations viewed in terms of, 29
  subpopulations' analytic separation from,
    49
Subjective vision, of police, 221-222
Suicides, among police, 138-139
Survivors. *See* Death; Families of killed officers
Suspects, rough justice and, 108
Suspicion, 5, 142, 143-153
  as art of exceptionality, 148
  behavioral clues for, 147
  car stops and, 149
  craft of, 145-148
  crime reports and, 148-149
  danger and irony of, 161
  danger of unknown and, 61
  drug courier profile and, 150-151
  honing of, 147
  irony and, 225-226
  legal and political factors and, 143-144
  as mobilization for police behavior, 150
  officer safety and, 151
  in officers' social and personal settings,
    151-153
  pedestrian stops and, 149
  in police occupational worldview, 152-153
  reasonable suspicion, 144-145
  sixth sense suspicion, 145
Suspicious odors, 171n
Suspicious stare, as display of power, 146-147
Sutton, L. Paul, 70, 290, 294
Swanton, B., 143
Swidler, Ann, 5, 32, 33, 35, 44

Sykes, Gary W., 93, 115, 117, 193, 201
Symbolic assailant
  danger and, 160-161
  racial characteristics of, 161
Symbolic interactionist view, of
    culture, 18
Symbolic meaning, for public, police funerals
    providing, 356-358
Symbols
  in funerals, 337, 340, 356, 357-358, 359-
    361
  in killing of police officer, 347-348
  National Law Enforcement Officers Memor-
    ial as, 348-349
  rituals and, 334-335, 336
Synecdoche
  as special trope, 218, 228n
  stories as, 218

"Taking the Offensive and What Happened,"
    303
"Tales of the ridiculous," uncertainty of polic-
    ing in, 167
Task ambiguity
  coercive territorial control and, 67
  solidarity, loose coupling, and, 67
Technical knowledge, vs. common sense, 216
Tehan, J., 325
Television, transmission of local police culture
    through, 37
Tension, unpredictability and, 167
Tenzell, James H., 235n
Terrill, William, 100
Territorial control, coercive, 77-78
Territorial responsibility, community policing
    and, 92-94
Territory(ies), 60
  dominion and, 82
  geographical knowledge and, 85-87
  Herbert's normative orders and, 89
  linkage to responsibility, 89-90
  media relations and fusion with responsibil-
    ity, 91-92
  moral transformation of, 81-94
  officers' efforts to limit management intru-
    sion into, 90-91
  operational/management culture perspec-
    tive of, 82
  organization of, 82-83
  of people and territories of geography, 87-
    88
  private space in public places in, 86
  random preventive patrol and control of,
    83-84
Terrorist and terrorism, as metaphorical orga-
    nizing power, 119-120
Terry v. Ohio, 145
Testimony, perjury of, 294-295

Text, interpretation and language of, 27n
Theft, proactive alternatives for theft enforcement, 301
Thematic overlap, 56-57
Themes of the unknown, 60-61. *See also* Unknown
Thompson, Hunter, 184n
Thought experiment, themes in cultural studies and, 20-25
Tolerated lies, 291
Traditional culture, as police subculture, 45
Traditional policing styles, street violence and, 108
Traffic stops, 67. *See also* Automobile stops
    complexity and contingent nature of, 183-184
    contingencies for action in, 165
    training on unpredictability and danger in, 227
    use of force in, 99
Training. *See also* Field training; POST training
    bravery and, 233
    bullshit and, 320-321
    deconstruction learned in, 226-227
    focus on officer safety in, 176, 247-248
    force and, 78
    heuristic trope in, 227
    importance of guns in, 135-138
    interactive, 137, 166
    invisibility learned in, 274-275
    ironic, 226-227
    loyalty reinforced in, 238
    masculinity emphasized in, 230
    power of stories in, 220
    stories to reinforce existing worldview in, 228n
    in use of appropriate force, 99-100
Transition resignation process, after cop killing, 343
Transmission of culture of policing, 242-246
Transmission of local culture, 36-37
    media diffusion and, 37
    multiple group membership and, 37
    structural roles and, 37
    weak ties and, 37
Trice, Harrison M., 329, 333
Trojanowicz, R.C., 68, 83
Tropes, 217-218
    Eco's characterization of, 228n
    as stories, 218
True Masculine Role, The (Domanick), 229
Truth game, 289-290
    dimensions of, 291
    reasons for, 290
    variations to, 289-290
Turbulence. *See also* Interaction turbulence
    potential for in police-citizen interactions, 174

Turner, Victor, 7, 218, 331, 334, 335, 337n
Typifications
    as common knowledge, 33
    shared, 32, 33

Uchida, Craig D., 115
Uncertainty. *See also* Situational uncertainty; Unpredictability
    as layer in onion metaphor, 60-61
Undercover work
    ironic conversion in, 224-225
    seduction and, 188
Uniform Crime Reports, 239
Universities, as transmitters of culture of policing, 244-245
Unknown. *See also* Unpredictability
    cultural adaptations to, 141-142
    methods of dealing with, 5
    themes of, 5-6, 60-61
Unpredictability, 34. *See also* Edge control
    adventure in police work and, 168
    bravery and, 234-235
    common sense and, 164, 165-167
    cultural celebration and, 166-167
    of danger, 61
    vs. danger, 163-164
    excitement and, 167-169
    grittiness of, 169-171
    gun training and, 135-136
    humor and, 171
    kinesis of, 163
    as shared cultural theme, 54
    and situational uncertainty, 5, 142, 163-171
    tediousness of, 165
    tension and, 167
Upwardly mobile working-class type, of police recruits, 245-246
Urban riots (1960s), police and, 259
"Use-of-force" standards, 99
Us vs. them attitude. *See* We-them attitude

Value(s)
    choices in random preventive patrol, 85
    of normative orders, 89
    personal responsibility, 39
    as products of institutional environment of policing, 59-60
    relativity of, 22-23
    rituals and, 333
    as standpoint, 23
    traditional, 279
Van Maanen, John, 1, 16, 25, 26, 37, 45, 46, 54, 66, 70, 78, 87, 104, 105, 107, 146, 164, 167, 168, 173, 175, 181, 182, 183, 185, 191, 205, 207, 209-210, 220, 227, 238, 242, 244, 247, 273, 275, 277, 307, 309, 312, 320, 322, 323, 334, 344
Velvet glove, community policing as, 124

Vernon, Bob, 229
Vertical cliques, formation of, 323
Victimless crimes, police proactivity, deception, and, 296-297
Videos, in guns training, 137
Violanti, J., 139
Violence
    fantastic elements in production of, 190-191
    racial, of LAPD, 262-263
Violent crimes, citizen-invoked interactions and, 66
Violent death. *See* Death
Vollmer, August, 83
Voluntary resignation, bullshit and, 325-326
Voluntary risk-taking, edgework and, 178

Wacquant, L., 48
Waddington, P., 14, 16-17, 31, 38, 52n
Walker, Samuel, 71, 83, 93, 115, 116, 162n, 168, 241, 267n, 287, 297, 310, 317, 348
Walking patrol, 2
Wambaugh, Joseph, 230, 240, 289, 335
War metaphor. *See* Crime is war metaphor
Warnke, Georgia, 51, 52n
War on crime, 113
    racial violence and, 263, 264
War on terrorism, 120
Warrant(s), 304n
    articulation through process, 70
    deceptions about, 293-294
Warren court, due process decisions, police perceptions, and, 310
Warrior, line-officers and persona of, 118-119, 121, 128-129
Warrior Dreams (Gibson), 121
"War stories," 157
    danger in, 160
    expansion of local cultural knowledge through, 341
Wartime (Fussell), 312
Weak ties, transmission of local police culture and, 37
Wealth, race and structure of in United States, 267n

Weapons. *See also* Guns
    in officer's arsenal, 130
Weapons training, importance of, 135-138
Weber, Max, 31, 124, 208, 212n
Wesley, W., 101-102, 108, 276
Western worldview, 20
We-them attitude, 119, 120. *See also* Solidarity
    after cop killing, 343
    criminals, public, and, 273
White, Mervin, 182
White, R., 52n
White, Susan O., 116
Whitehead, Alfred North, 222
Wilbanks, William, 256
Wilgoren, 359
Williams, Hubert, 256, 258-259
Willis, Paul, 18, 33, 35, 36
Wilson, James Q., 1, 16, 23, 39, 67, 85, 92, 93, 95n, 103-105, 108, 124, 141, 233, 249, 282, 287, 309, 322, 324, 348
Wilt, M.G., 325
Wolfe, Eric, 19
Women. *See also* Police sexual violence (PSV); Sexual harassment
    boys-will-be-boys attitude and, 230
    as officers, 229
Wood, B., 267n
Woodworth, 168
Worden, Robert, 4
Working-class backgrounds, masculinity theme in, 231
Working environment
    encouragement of masculine behaviors in, 231
    individualism encouraged by, 280
Working personality, suspicion as characteristic of, 153n
Working schedule, for squads, 63-64
World views, of line officers, 109

Youth culture, grounded aesthetics of British, 35-36

Zhao, Jihong, 59
Znaniecki, Florian, 32